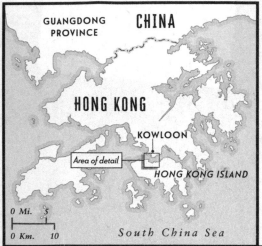

GUANGDONG
PROVINCE

CHINA

HONG KONG

KOWLOON

Area of detail

HONG KONG ISLAND

South China Sea

0 Mi. 5
0 Km. 10

HONG KONG

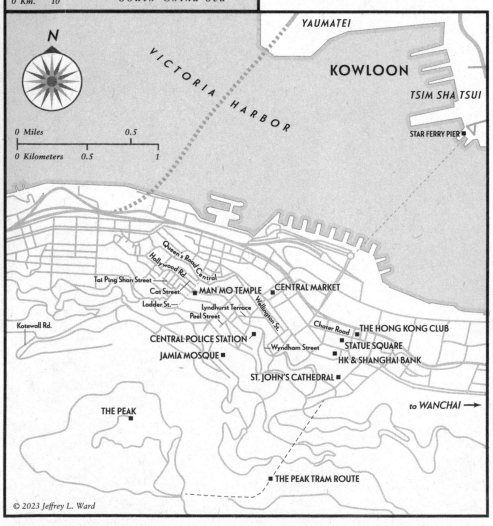

YAUMATEI

VICTORIA HARBOR

KOWLOON

TSIM SHA TSUI

STAR FERRY PIER ■

N

0 Miles   0.5
0 Kilometers   0.5   1

Queen's Road Central
Hollywood Rd.
Tai Ping Shan Street
Cat Street
Ladder St.
Lyndhurst Terrace
Peel Street
■ MAN MO TEMPLE   ■ CENTRAL MARKET

Wellington St.

Kotewall Rd.

Chater Road
THE HONG KONG CLUB
CENTRAL POLICE STATION ■
— Wyndham Street
■ STATUE SQUARE
JAMIA MOSQUE ■
HK & SHANGHAI BANK

ST. JOHN'S CATHEDRAL ■

to WANCHAI →

THE PEAK ■

■ THE PEAK TRAM ROUTE

© 2023 Jeffrey L. Ward

FORTUNE'S BAZAAR

THE MAKING OF
HONG KONG

VAUDINE ENGLAND

SCRIBNER

New York   London   Toronto   Sydney   New Delhi

Scribner
An Imprint of Simon & Schuster, Inc.
1230 Avenue of the Americas
New York, NY 10020

First Scribner hardcover edition May 2023

For information about special discounts for bulk purchases, please contact Simon & Schuster Special Sales at 1-866-506-1949 or business@simonandschuster.com.

The Simon & Schuster Speakers Bureau can bring authors to your live event. For more information or to book an event, contact the Simon & Schuster Speakers Bureau at 1-866-248-3049 or visit our website at www.simonspeakers.com.

Interior design by Davina Mock-Maniscalco
Interior map by Jeffrey L. Ward

Manufactured in the United States of America

10 9 8 7 6 5 4 3 2 1

Library of Congress Control Number: 2022051400

ISBN 978-1-9821-8451-3
ISBN 978-1-9821-8453-7 (ebook)

CONTENTS

THE DIFFERENT CITY

Defining Hong Kong has never been easy. Geographically, it comprises one main island and more than 260 others, plus the Kowloon Peninsula, whose hinterland, known as the New Territories, is contiguous with the mainland of the People's Republic of China. That land link has been its secret of success, or its ball and chain, depending on who is looking, and when. Beyond that border, however, are more important determinants. Hong Kong sits virtually bang central in eastern Asia, the midpoint between the northern states of East Asia—China, the Koreas, Japan—and the southern states loosely grouped as Southeast Asia. To the west of Hong Kong sits not only China but the land mass linking it to India, the Turkic lands, and Europe. To the east lies the western coast of the Americas, with yet another sea route of importance. There sits Hong Kong in the middle of it all.

End point or entry point, which one is it? Doorway to other lands, or destination in its own right? As a city, it has always been both. As those varied currents from all directions have brought people, ideas, technologies, and conflicts, spoor has been dropped. In Hong Kong, those influences have found traction and grown in their own way. The result is a place in between all others, but special in itself.

In total, Hong Kong covers 428 square miles, making it smaller than the five boroughs of New York City but bigger than Singapore.

Despite the dramatic high-rise architecture of its urban centers, three quarters of Hong Kong's land mass is not developed; 40 percent of it is designated as country park.

The key that opened Hong Kong to the world has always been the deep-sea harbor. Protected by the peaks of Hong Kong Island on one side and the Kowloon Peninsula on the other, it gave shelter to pirates and smugglers from tropical storms or random oversight. Here opium clippers and floating warehouses could moor, while sending their produce into China with or without official sanction. Here, deep-hulled ships packed in tens of thousands of eager migrants from impoverished China, eager to try their luck in the goldfields or trading zones of the West. Here, too, those stately passenger liners of a globalizing world would deliver new arrivals from Liverpool, Marseille, or beyond, through the Suez Canal and across Arabian, Indian, and Asian seas.

Also landing in this harbor would be generations of mobile labor, be they refugees from conflicts around Asia and within China, or what we now call economic migrants—people trying to better themselves and their bank balances by adapting to new markets and their needs. Here in Hong Kong, Philippine revolutionaries such as José Rizal (in Hong Kong 1891–92) and Emilio Aguinaldo (1897–98) plotted independence while Spain and the United States fought over their future. In this harbor, the revolutionary Ho Chi Minh found sanctuary in 1930–33 while forming the Vietnamese Communist Party, which he would ride to nationalist victory over French colonialism. Here would be proxy wars, too, between the many contenders for power in neighboring China, be they Nationalist and/or Communist, religiously inspired rebels and/or democratic.

Like Macao, the formerly Portuguese enclave just an hour away by fast boat, Hong Kong was precisely the handy kind of small but clever place always needed on the edge of huge empires—hideaway and refuge, petri dish or sewer, and always a service stop providing fuel of all kinds for next ventures. Tied to a great power on the other side of the world (in this case, imperial Britain), Hong Kong was yet dominated by the forces at work closer to hand in the swirling currents of nineteenth- and early-twentieth-century Asia. Indeed, when it didn't exist, Hong Kong had to be created.

Labeled a British Crown Colony, this port city had taken on a life of its own long before anyone in London had learned how to manage it. Deniability might have been in its DNA, for Hong Kong was made of, and dealt daily with, peoples, institutions, traders, and ideas from states that had no formal sway there (from Boston to Borneo, Burma to Beijing). At the same time, Hong Kong could generally ignore the bureaucrats nominally in charge back in London— they were a very long way away and the post was slow.

Unlike the tropics to the south, Hong Kong can boast of seasons, with a cool winter for a few months at the turn of each year; its summers suffer tropical cyclones and intense humidity—or what chroniclers of the nineteenth century used to call noxious vapors, miasmas, and rotting torpidity. Discovery of the connections between malaria and the mosquito, plague and rats, and even of variant coronaviruses, have put all that delicious vocabulary to waste.

In 1841, the main island of Hong Kong was home to fewer than five thousand scattered villagers, mainly fishing and farming folk. By 2019, it had 7.52 million people, 92 percent of whom were of Chinese ethnicity. Most (about 89 percent) speak Cantonese, and almost 5 percent claim English as their tongue. After twenty-two years of Chinese rule, Hong Kong still has two official languages—English and Chinese. Cantonese had achieved dominance over the many different Chinese dialects in use by the 1960s, with Mandarin or Putonghua, the official language from Beijing, very much a minority pursuit until recently. Significant other population groups include those from the Philippines and Indonesia (approximately 200,000 people from each, most of whom are domestic contract workers), and India.[1]

Under the rule of the Chinese Communist Party, it has become normal to call Hong Kong "a Chinese city." Still, the question of what Hong Kong *is* remains in dispute. Wayward child, spoiled brat, a festering sore on the bottom of China, a thriving financial center, a special home to millions—which is the real Hong Kong? Is the depiction of Hong Kong as focus of a century of humiliation, exploitation, and spiritual pollution believed any more than the glorious British imperial vision of the bringing of benevolent civilization to benighted heathens?

Despite its formal status as a colony under the British Crown, Hong Kong's identity has long been challenged, in some minds at least. Back in 1972, China's representative to the United Nations, Huang Hua, delivered a speech in which he said that Hong Kong and Macao were not, in fact, colonial territories at all, but merely domestic matters of China to which its rulers would attend when the time was ripe. This meant, to China at least, that Hong Kong would not be subject to the pattern of decolonization being followed elsewhere in which colonies were prepared for self-rule or even independence. The treaties by which China had signed away first the main island of Hong Kong and then the Kowloon Peninsula were not, China said, worth the paper they were written on. It was a telling moment, and one virtually overlooked in all the excitement of President Nixon's first trip to China and Britain's desire to attain ambassadorial status there before them. China's position never changed.[2]

The location that gave Hong Kong its reason for being leaves it prey to far larger forces at work. Being in the middle of it all, as in a game of piggy-in-the-middle, leaves Hong Kong jumping up and down trying to catch the ball that is repeatedly being tossed between protagonists on either side of it. At times, as when in 2020 the talk was all of a new Cold War between China and the United States, Hong Kong is the sadly battered football, used by each side to score goals against the other. While promised autonomy as a Special Administrative Region under Chinese sovereignty, Hong Kong's leaders are appointed by Beijing. A national security law imposed without reference to the local legislature punishes "collusion" with foreign powers, yet Hong Kong's trade bodies want the World Trade Organization to help them keep the "Made in Hong Kong" label in preference to "Made in China."

As ever, each formal ruling class sees itself as of supreme impor-tance, from the British colonials in their white suits promenading be-tween club, cathedral, and counting house, to the Chinese bureaucrats now running the security apparatus from behind darkened glass. Yet as ever, daily life has a definitional power of its own. More signifi-cant to generations of Hong Kong people is how they met, made love, made money, made homes—in short, how they constructed their daily lives. That process, call it evolution or attrition, reshaped the rocks on which Hong Kong was built, making it something much more than the mental constructs in Britain's or China's mind.

How and why is Hong Kong so different from China? Because it has lived a different history, it is made of different peoples, and their lives over generations have forged a different place. Hong Kong never had real democracy during its 156 years of British rule, but it clearly experienced life differently from the Chinese mainland and its neigh-bors across the southern seas. As a Crown Colony, like it or not, it also experienced life at variance with those "treaty ports" that European and Japanese empires set up within nineteenth-century China. For-eigners in those ports enjoyed an extraterritoriality that made them subject to their own laws, not China's, but lacked the full weight of Crown protection.

Clearly, Hong Kong was never "just another Chinese city." Had it been, forcing Hong Kong under mainland Chinese rule would have been a simple matter. Aware of but not living immediately through Chinese imperialism, revolution, and Communist rule, its young peo-ple now, born well after the end of British rule, insist they are Hong Kongers before they are Chinese. Only in its history can any explana-tion for Hong Kong's difference be revealed.

Yet if Hong Kong's current place in the world is confusing, its place in history is even more so. Both the official Chinese and British mythologies remain just that—legends created to justify a form of rule that seems to its rulers to be desirable at the time. Popular mytholo-gies, like all clichés, seem useful at first, based as they always are on a germ of truth. Yet they, too, have their limits: Hong Kong's fabled "melting pot," its role as meeting point between East and West, its "unique" blending of hardworking Chinese zeal with Western technologies. Anyone arriving in a new place, destitute and desperate to get ahead, is going to work hard; that is hardly a Chinese prerogative. The wealth and dominance of the West at the time that Hong Kong was coming into being would of course give that input a great monetary and political worth. More to the point is that as with any great port city, peoples from all over the world would arrive, create opportunities, forge relationships, and build new worlds.

Not enough histories of Hong Kong have focused closely on the mass of people who through their lives have accidentally created the place. Given Hong Kong's proximity to the vast Chinese mainland, the vast majority of its people are ethnically Chinese. But some explanation of that gap between the few thousand of 1841 and the 7.5 million of 2019 is necessary. At least up until the 1960s, virtually everyone in Hong Kong came from somewhere else. And what of that 8 percent who were not defined as "Chinese"? Who were they and where did they come from? If indeed there was some kind of melting pot, why do people speak of "the Chinese" as one unvariegated lump, distinct and different from "Europeans," another homogenous lot? Neither definition holds for either group, as every category includes its differences within.

Most important, one thing surely universal to all human activity is the likelihood of cross-fertilization—or sex, to give it another name. Is it not possible that this happened in Hong Kong, too, and that along with a whole lot of people coming from all over the world, there was also the creation of a new and distinct kind of Hong Kong people? This would at least constitute a different mindset if not the creation of new racial mixes, too. If so, that might go some way toward explaining why Hong Kong is different to this day.

————

This book quickly outgrew its origins as a history of those peoples created by what used to be pejoratively called miscegenation—the

Eurasians of Hong Kong. Problems of definition soon intruded. What is a Eurasian? Are we thinking of certain people as making up a racial group, a class in some kind of status hierarchy, or simply people who are interesting and have not yet had their due in Hong Kong history books?

The traditional idea of a Eurasian was as the product of a relationship between a Westerner and an Asian. But human beings never slip so simply into such clean categories. What do we mean by a Westerner, or indeed an Asian? All racial definitions are in trouble these days as a growing body of research shows that race, in terms of blood and DNA, does not actually exist. It would be more scientifically accurate to claim that we are all Eurasians now.

In a historical frame, however, it is pointless to deny that during the nineteenth and earlier twentieth centuries racial categories were casually applied automatically, with vast effect, on everyone. The generalization is of a Western man arriving in the mysterious Orient, easily seduced into a range of new delights including the beautiful women, with the inevitable result of one thing leading to another. As the nineteenth century progressed, and some Asian men went to the West for study or business, they brought back Western wives, creating a new version of the Eurasian.

A significant body of people often called "Eurasian" were in fact a product of other mixtures. Parsis are the tribal group tracing their roots back to Persia, bound by the Zoroastrian religion, and they intermarried with Indians through their many generations of life in India, based in Gujarat and particularly Bombay. As Parsis moved eastwards with their ship-owning and other trades, they met and married others, producing families such as the Kotewalls in Hong Kong, who were a mix of Parsi and Chinese blood and generally identified as Eurasian. Or what about unions that were not east-west or north-south, but between, say, Indian men and Burmese women? Again, the essence is in the mixing, never mind who is doing it.

The historian Anthony Sweeting began his (unfinished) history of Eurasians by noting that the Hong Kong definition was "always

flexible," including "the offspring of first and later generation Eurasians who intermarried within the Eurasian community or with European, Chinese or other Asian partners." Sweeting meant "all those
residents of Hong Kong prepared to accept a Eurasian designation,
as well as people of mixed Asian origin who identified themselves, at
least to some extent, with Eurasians."[3] The sole dissertation done on
the subject, back in 1975 by Stephen Fisher, similarly urged a "social,"
self-identifying definition, not a "biological" one.[4]

The original usage of *Eurasian* in India was often understood as
interchangeable with *Anglo-Indian*, which itself often included people who saw themselves as entirely "white" but who had been in India
so long that they had become so different from their British compatriots as to require a different label. As soon as one person meets
another, even more when one people meets another, hierarchies and
categorization begin. Of course, real life is so complex and mixed-
race intercourse so endemic that all such variations, be they labeled
sometimes as "mestizo," "mulatto," or today's "persons of color," are
bound to be haphazard. Charles Hirschman has argued that ethnicity, with its meaning of a social group with shared culture, faith, and
language, is a much better concept than race because "it is explicitly
subjective, it acknowledges multiple ancestries, and it recognizes that
ethnic groups are porous and heterogenous."[5]

The problem, however, with taking a self-identifying definition of
Eurasian is the fact that generations of mixed-race people in Hong
Kong denied they were ever Eurasian. According to a member of one
such leading family, Eric Peter Ho, this approach was passed on early
in life. On being beaten up by a schoolmate at St. Joseph's College in
Hong Kong in 1934 at the age of six, he understood neither the term
half-caste nor its accompanying expletives. "Furthermore, I found that
my parents were not very communicative on the subject. The clear
message I did get was that the word *Eurasian* was to be eschewed as
being somewhat shameful and offensive."[6]

We each have the right to describe ourselves as we please, but
a historian is surely allowed to look at larger trends. Why talk of

a Chinese elite in Hong Kong when most of the people involved in the late nineteenth and early twentieth centuries were at least half non-Chinese? On the one hand, the mixed-race child's upbringing by a Chinese mother in Chinese ways was taken to indicate his or her Chineseness, placing nurture above nature in the self-definitional stakes. Yet can one deny that a mixed hue to the face, a different "look" and varied traditions and daily habits, had an effect on the prospects for these various partly Chinese people? Even after Sir Paul Chater, that Armenian orphan of Calcutta, had become richer than anyone, more powerful in governance and business than most, and the man who created Hong Kong's business district, its first coal mines, churches, and much more, this knight of the realm was still labeled "a coloured magnate" by an aide-de-camp to the governor because of his Armenian roots and birth in Calcutta. Perhaps wealthier and at least as aspirational was Sir Robert Ho Tung, son of a Dutch father and Chinese woman; whenever he caviled at constantly funding whatever cause he was presented with, suddenly he was a "half-caste" instead of Britain's, or China's, dearest friend.

The neglect of Hong Kong's different peoples seems infected not only by racism but misogyny, too—as if the fact that most Western and other men in early Hong Kong had sex with Chinese and other women was of no importance, because women, especially non-white women, were of no importance. This, too, was false reasoning.

The role of women has long been overlooked. Families sold them or gave them into servitude and, given little choice in the matter, some women entered into relationships with foreigners. The smart or lucky ones transformed their vulnerability into positions of power, raising and educating mixed-race children, many of whom went on to conquer new worlds. It is the women's stories that, sadly, remain largely untold as records in their voices barely exist. These women deserve admiration, not the neglect still evident in lingering taboos in some families. Their survival has been conflated with shame at their commodification, yet, as we shall see, their achievements were both surprising and lasting.

Far from being a fact that could be brushed under the carpet, it was precisely the varied origins of many Hong Kong people, including the Eurasians, that defined their futures, be they marked by failure or success. Wrote Eric Peter Ho, who rose high in Britain's colonial government: "In the late nineteenth and into the twentieth century, there was considerable prejudice against Eurasians from both Europeans and Chinese. This prejudice made many of them the more determined to 'make good' . . . With wealth would come status . . . they would contribute generously to local charities and worthy causes. All of this, no doubt, helped to make some of them what they became: leaders in the Hong Kong community."[7]

Looking at Hong Kong's social history, it is clear that one should err on the side of ambiguity and multiple identities, avoiding binary simplicities. My definition of *Eurasian* became ever broader as this book developed. Along with people who were traditionally defined as Eurasian, Hong Kong's history has been shaped in important ways by people who were Armenian, Jewish, Portuguese, and Parsi. The definition of *Eurasian* here, then, draws on the generally overlooked geographical core of the term: Eurasia. This continent stretches from Asia to Europe and back; its scope allows us to include all the main peoples of early Hong Kong. That is no accident, of course: the earliest trading routes linking Asia and Europe, pre-dating the Silk Road, still rested on the fact of continental connection. Hong Kong has functioned variously as a key link in a chain or even as a terminus, an end point, in the nineteenth century's increasingly global exchange. Little wonder, then, that it collected peoples from all along this global highway.

One can have a lot of fun with different variations on the theme, as soon as real lives are allowed into random categories. In her study of the mestizo of the Dutch East Indies, Jean Gelman Taylor found that migrants were not only "white," and that "locals" included Indians, Japanese, diverse Indonesians, other Asians, and Portuguese.[8] Meanwhile, so-called sojourners often plan to go "home" but never get there, and settlers sometimes move on. State archives, such as the census, divide people by race, religion, occupation, and contracts, ignoring the reality that borders are permeable, ambiguous, and flexible.[9]

Tacking back in time to an earlier Asian port city—Makassar (in today's Indonesia)—Heather Sutherland describes a group of people who were defined to some extent by race and class, the translator/interpreters or "Gatekeepers, capable of shaping both perceptions and policy. Their ability to bridge cultural divides was crucial, but consequently their identities could appear ambiguous and their loyal ties uncertain . . ."[10] Similar were the *banian* of Calcutta, the *dubash* of Madras, or the *comprador* of the China coast. Such "interpreters" formed "an inter-connected complex of clans . . . [where] ties of marriage, descent, and friendship were not merely functional to their role . . . but also formed the very fabric of their personal lives and social world."[11] These families, as in Hong Kong, "were anything but neatly bounded and homogenous, they sprawled across the religious, cultural, political, and bureaucratic categories that shape our sources and theoretically organized society and government," wrote Sutherland.[12]

She has stressed that the categories we put people in are not what they are, but an ideological or political fiction. Far more revealing is the way people behave and interact. People also move between categories with varying degrees of social ingenuity. Looking for one word to describe such people is doomed to failure, she warned, adding that verbs work better than nouns when describing people who are busy making, navigating, forging, being, discovering, and becoming.[13]

Here are the chameleons of a dynamic port city, the people able to parlay their mixed heritages, multilingualism, or simply their open minds into positions of indispensable power. Some were pivots, or go-betweens, yet not all Eurasians had to be middlemen or -women; many simply lived their colorful and varied lives, eating Chinese noodles after Catholic mass, wearing Western fur coats while receiving their Chinese New Year *lai see* gift packets. Some of these mixed peoples achieved great wealth and a kind of power; others had it thrust upon them. Some actively sought it, others never quite made it; many others didn't care. Here are the "exotics," the outliers, the pioneers and progenitors of sometimes great ideas and achievements. Here are people who worked out, over a couple of generations, how to make a virtue of necessity, taking their hybrid state as a starting point for cross-cultural power. Many have simply stepped around taboos, learned new ways, met and loved different people. The result is a place defined not by clear categories of "white" or "yellow," West or East, Christian or heathen. Most of these boxes don't apply.

Indeed, the more one dives into the web of early peoples and their lives in Hong Kong, the more one begins to feel sorry for that tiny clutch of British men in their suits tottering between club and counting house, who thought they were running the place. These colonists, as the historian Christopher Munn writes, tried to "re-create a form of bourgeois English life in their bungalows, gardens, clubs and churches . . . Although composed of only a few hundred people, 'the community' was as hierarchical as that in any English town."[14]

Luckily, outside this world bustled a fascinating mix of Indians, Parsis, Goans, Macanese, Malays, Filipinos, Japanese, and West Indians, and Lascars, or seamen and -women of Indian, Malay, and Filipino origin. Those among the colonial elite who took a few steps to one side of their treasured central business district or up the hill behind it would find a far more exciting, throbbing world of commerce and intercourse. It is in these more mixed margins that this book seeks to dwell.

By choosing to focus on these in-between peoples I will largely ignore the obvious and well-known families such as the Jardines, Dents, and Swires, and many important Chinese clans. I make no apology for keeping my Chinese characters to a minority in this tale when clearly they have formed the majority of the population of Hong Kong before, during, and after its British period. Not until after World War Two was the majority actually born in Hong Kong. They had come when times were tough on the mainland (i.e., most of the time), escaping rebellion, war, famine, and insecurity, going home when peace returned. This book looks for the lesser-known but at least as vital people—Hong Kong's post-1841 firstborn.

———————

History is forever being rewritten. In British times, Hong Kong was a glory of imperial governance and its tale was told from the top down, detailing the governors and their friends. Chinese nationalist tales have focused on Hong Kong's Chineseness and on Western oppression. Not until the 1980s did Hong Kong people begin systematically to tell their own story. This was partly thanks to the obsessive curiosity of the theologian and genealogist-turned-historian Rev. Carl T. Smith. He was the first to find how diverse, rich, and interesting were the many lives lived beyond the small circle of the tight colonial elite. He showed how much of the making of Hong Kong took place in what the colonialists saw as the borderlands, those rough districts on what they thought were the edges of town, the unknown worlds of the Parsi opium warehouses or Chinese temples, the obscure sanctuaries of Christian mission work or good-time bars along the western end of the city's main artery (Queen's Road). The mixing of peoples in raucous brothels, and shadowy relationships across divides of race, gender, and class, were so incomprehensible to the British that they named these areas not suburbs or districts but "bazaars." The word seems to conjure a chaotic world of oriental mystery and mess, yet it's where Hong Kong's first indigenes were found.[15]

Enjoying the motley throng is only part of the untold story, however. More challenging is to find out how diverse people interacted—if they did—and how power played. As the leading historian John Darwin puts it: "Empire is still widely imagined as the intrusion of a more or less homogenous group of (European) settlers, businessmen or officials into zones inhabited by stable indigenous societies enjoying varying degrees of political and cultural unity. The more we learn about pre-colonial and colonial societies, the more unsatisfactory this conventional picture appears."

Traditional societies were often nothing of the sort, and, in Hong Kong, anyway, barely existed. *Indigenous* also means many things. Empire, says Darwin, was "often a jerry-built shack whose shape changed constantly with the shifting balance of collaboration and control" and: "Imperialism gained much of its impetus not from the energies of its nominal overlords, but from the vigour with which other subordinate groups took advantage of new political and economic conditions."[16]

Without its in-between people, Hong Kong simply could not have functioned, and would not have worked. Hong Kong's chameleons were crucial to its emergence as a thriving Asian port city. They help define Hong Kong's difference to this day.

1

THE WORLD TO HONG KONG

Until the first half of the nineteenth century, Hong Kong was a far-away and largely unknown place, a place where a few thousand farmers and fisherfolk lived on the spectacular island. This island was dramatic and staggeringly beautiful, marked by a steep, ancient mountain that arose out of deep seas and sheltered bays that gazed out over a random smattering of more islands and bays. Traders sailed past these islands and up the Pearl River to imperial China's most far-flung outpost of Canton (today's Guangzhou). On the southern coast of Hong Kong Island, today's residential and tourist spot of Stanley was then the largest village, called Chek-choo; next largest was the fishing village of Wong Chuk Hang, now Aberdeen. People lived in stone huts, grew rice, harvested grass, and quarried stone, all on a small, entirely local scale.

To say dramatic change was about to arrive is a vast understatement. But we must go back before going forward to understand why. A great many factors that would create its future were already in play, even though Hong Kong was simply nowhere on the world map before 1841. That earlier global map of trade was densely populated with all manner of peoples and commodities, stretching from East Asia, across the Indian Ocean through the Middle East and Mediterranean, into European markets and back. Southeast Asia—those islands and seas between Malaysia, Indonesia, the Philippines, and India—was the spaghetti junction through which this ever more complex trade threaded and would grow. Strategic river ports brought produce out of Southeast Asian uplands so it could be exchanged with Chinese, Indian, Arab, and Malay traders. Ideas moved, too, when Hindu, Buddhist, and Muslim teachers crisscrossed the southern oceans.

By the 800s if not earlier, trade had flowed across the Arabian Sea to Indian ports such as Quilon or Calicut, through the straits between India and Ceylon to Indonesia's Aceh, well before the Chinese thought of joining in. Once Canton became a destination, and if the pirates of Malacca and around Singapore could be managed, the route stretched northwards. Ships sailed up the coasts of Champa (now southern Vietnam), the Gulf of Tonkin, and Hainan to China. Or they took the more dangerous but bountiful route along the north coast of Borneo to southern Taiwan and Fujian. After Spain's conquest of southern America spurred the extraction of silver, that silver was exported to the Spanish Philippines, and so the route would take in Manila, too.

Imagine the riches being extracted and bartered, and the people of many hues and faiths making it happen—buying and selling the elephant tusks, rhino horns, aromatic woods, incense, cloves, nutmeg, gums, resins, birds' nests, bird of paradise feathers, and much more. China needed silver from Manila and Japan, Europe wanted Southeast Asian spices and Chinese silk and ceramics, and everyone needed India's cottons. Temporary populations of traders between monsoons sparked the growth of trading hubs across the region. Soon, these foreign private traders joined the region's long-established so-called country trade in goods across and within Asia.

Between Britain's occupations of the Malaysian island city of Penang in 1786 and Singapore in 1819, it also won the Napoleonic Wars. Victory not only secured Britain's position as the world's foremost naval and economic power; it also produced a lot of newly unemployed, adventurous young men, ready to explore the seven seas. The British enjoyed rich Asian experience through their brief tutelages of Manila (1762–64), Malacca and Padang (1765), Maluku (1796 and 1810), and Java (1811–16). They brought new ideas about "free trade" with them. The Portuguese, Dutch, and Spanish had each tried to gain sole control of a key commodity and enforce a monopoly, violently punishing any transgressors. The British, instead, sought preferential access through special relationships and speed, freer of state control. Singapore and Penang drew in producers who could exchange rice, sugar, tin, coffee, and pepper for manufactured items, Indian cottons, firearms, and opium.

The idea of Hong Kong surfaced in 1815 as "a convenient station on the eastern coast of China," a last resort where trade could be carried out from an "insular position."[1] Such an island or promontory was widely assumed to be Chusan, halfway up the Chinese coast; others suggested Ningpo or Formosa (Taiwan). In 1834, however, Lord Napier mooted the taking of Hong Kong.

Two years later, the *Canton Register* of April 25, 1836, felt no hesitation: "If the lion's paw is to be put down on any part of the south side of China, let it be Hongkong; let the lion declare it to be under his guarantee a free port, and in ten years it will be the most considerable mart east of the Cape . . . Hongkong, deep water, and a free port for ever!"

Hong Kong then grew into a global city because of the active trade routes through, and within, Southeast Asia going back hundreds of years. Those trade routes are often forgotten as the popular imagination fixates on a merely twentieth-century version of globalization, ignoring all those that have gone before. Exchange of peoples, goods, ideas, and technologies was well established long before the Europeans joined in.

Hong Kong joined this strong chain linking ancient trading routes and changing commodities by becoming home to the right kind of people—individuals who knew the trades, the shipping, the commodities and markets, and how to mediate among them all—those, it should be noted, who enjoyed a sense of adventure. These in-between people were agents to all, they made and recorded the trades, acted as interpreters, bookkeepers, secretaries, brokers, suppliers, and, most of all, as "Secret-Keepers."[2] Once Hong Kong was founded as the latest free trading port under British rule, it would become a magnet to precisely these kinds of people. They came from all over, drawn by the sweet sharp tang of opportunity.

The British first occupied Hong Kong—the harbor at least—in 1839 when British traders had to decamp from Canton via Macao. A search for food on the mainland caused the little-known Battle of Kowloon Bay (September 4, 1839); the entire occupation lasted just a couple of months.[3] Trading firms led by William Jardine, Alexander Matheson, and others had encouraged the British government to go to war with Canton in order to secure freer conditions of trade.

On January 25, 1841, Captain Sir Edward Belcher of the Royal Navy landed on Hong Kong Island's northern shore with a small body of men, naming it Possession Point.

The next day, a mainly military crowd assembled, showing firmly wherein British power lay. Two thousand seven hundred Indian soldiers stood by as Sir Gordon Bremer, naval commander of the British Expeditionary Force, took possession of the island in the name of the Crown. There to witness the moment were James Matheson of Jardine Matheson and Co., Albert Sassoon, scion of the Baghdadi Jewish house based at Bombay, and several Parsi traders—Cawasjee Pallanjee, representative of Cursetjee Bomanjee and Co., F. M. Talati, and Rustomjee Dhunjee Shaw of the leading P. F. Cama and Co. Writing to William Jardine on January 30, James Matheson reported his private circumnavigation of the island in cheerful terms. But a separate boatload carrying eight protestant missionaries was less sanguine: "They walked over the hills and visited the villages, but while expressing great hopes for the future of the place under British Rule, they concluded that it was far from being a favourable situation for missionary purposes. According to their estimate the island contained not more than 2,500 people, residing in three or four wretched villages."[4]

Exactly who raised the British flag on Hong Kong soil remains a significant mystery. One version keeps the story within British naval and military lines, identifying the flag-raiser as the midshipman who would become Admiral Sir William Dowell. Young Dowell would have been just fifteen in January 1841, so he might have been that man in that time and place. Just as feasible, however, is that, as his family claimed, the flag was hoisted by a young Mohammed Arab; his regiment's records are not complete so it's hard to confirm it either way. If Arab raised the flag, then Hong Kong's roots in a multiethnic community of peoples linked into ancient trading routes across the Indian and other oceans is clear.[5] Even without that, Arab's life tells us other stories, too—as we will see in this chapter. He later ran boarding-houses for seamen and owned houses in the streets stretching uphill from the European business district, helping to forge a neighborhood central to the community of in-between people.

This brief but decisive first Anglo-Chinese war, or Opium War, resulted in the Treaty of Nanking between Britain and China. As well as ceding Hong Kong Island in perpetuity, this agreement also opened the five mainland Chinese "Treaty" ports of Amoy, Canton, Shanghai, Foochow (Fuzhou), and Ningpo (Ningbo). The document was signed, sealed, and delivered in print in 1842, and when London and Peking (Beijing) heard of it, neither capital was happy. But by the time they saw the small print, there was little they could do to stop it. Boatloads of diverse characters were already assembling—Southeast Asian sailors, Portuguese clerks, Parsi investors, Jewish traders, Muslim entrepreneurs, and many more.

A victorious Britain had just triumphed over that slumbering, inconvenient giant, imperial China. But London's bureaucrats were divided over what to do with Hong Kong; ideas for how to set up and run the place were a mess. Finding the right people, deciding policy when letters to London took many months by sea, being ignorant about the different peoples arriving from all over, facing unforeseen hitches in world markets—this was all a wild west in the East. The locale had gained renown as a stunningly attractive trading center, linked locally to the opium trade at Canton and Macao, regionally to the vital "country trade" of forest and marine products around Southeast Asia, and internationally to world markets.

Hong Kong soon quickly became a base for British troops, colonial bureaucrats, a few exotic characters who "made it" by getting rich, and many Chinese who had nothing left to lose on the mainland. But who else arrived in Hong Kong and chose to stay, to make homes and a society there?

What of all the perfectly ordinary people who staffed the businesses, ran the taverns, stocked the ships' chandleries, and placed bets on the horses? What of all those multicolored peoples who lived, worked, loved, and died in the steep streets up from the central business district? A tiny minority of white men in stiff suits knew the central Queen's Road, but the energy and drive were with those striding up the hill to streets still named Gage, Peel, and Graham, or west down Wellington Street and into the heaving shop-fronts of Bonham Strand. Behind the grand facades of the first court building, church, and barracks, and the nouveau riche splendor of the *taipan*'s (big boss's) homes and office, was a busy catch-as-catch-can world of coolie laborers, moneylenders, shipowners, shopkeepers, commission brokers, bar owners, and workingwomen. The ships could not dock, the trades could be neither recorded nor paid for, the food and drink and laundry and more intimate needs of the traders could not be provided, without a rapidly growing society of people drawn from much more than a purely British or Chinese pool. The city was seeded by its Asian trades, and so needed its Asian traders.

———

Seeing the later results of events of almost two hundred years ago is bound to complicate a proper understanding of the events as they actually happened. Hong Kong's early years were chaotic and, for many, deadly; no one yet understood the role of mosquitoes in causing malaria, and thousands died from fevers and bad water. Rules were arbitrary and personal safety uncertain. Who knew how it would turn out or what could happen? But the deep-sea harbor and wide-open possibilities were enough to continue to draw people from far and wide. Those people would bump up against one another, fall in love, compete mercilessly, live on top of one another, create new industries, build families, and above all create a home. The relentless construction of the city drew on many ingredients—a wide variety of racial, religious, and cultural groups, a ready facility with the calculus and appetite for risk, and a drive to get ahead. Jews hailing from Baghdad or Venice would come, so, too, would Parsis, those trading gentlemen of Bombay with roots in Persia and a steady Zoroastrian faith. Armenians who had already left their Central Asian home generations ago, some to find new lives in India, would join the journey to Hong Kong. Muslim entrepreneurs would staff and stock the ships carrying people and trade to Hong Kong. Malays and Manila men came to build on their long experience with European maritime empires arriving on their shores.

With no stake in a hierarchical Chinese empire, members of the Tanka boat people minority or the migratory Hakka people of China had quickly made themselves indispensable to the foreign traders assaulting China's batteries up the Pearl River into Canton. By offering provisions and local knowledge to the victorious British forces, they earned themselves land grants and a future in Hong Kong. Overlooked, as usual, in all the bustle, were the low-slung sampans carrying women ready to swab decks, to supply vegetables and perhaps other treats. These women were making a dash for freedom, too.

Hong Kong's few streets would soon be ringing to the sounds of Farsi, Gujarati, English, China coast pidgin, German, French, Dutch, Spanish, Portuguese, Italian, and more. The most numerous people were Chinese sampan and bumboat crews, followed by *Lascars*, an umbrella term that sometimes referred specifically to Indians but usually to Asiatic seafarers in general. The ships could not sail without sailors who understood Western-style rigging—thus, these men were not initially Chinese but Malay, Filipino, and Indian. Hindu and Muslim merchants had been active in the Persian Gulf since at least the ninth century; those networks not only survived the rise of European companies but helped fuel them.[6]

Only by engaging with the various peoples who had arrived on the China coast before them would the British be able to get ahead.

The exchange between Hong Kong and its southern neighbors was not confined to goods. Its people moved, too. Many of them met, and mixed.

In earlier phases of world trade, led by the Portuguese, Dutch, and finally the British, it was entirely normal to cohabit with a local woman, through whom one gained access to the local society and particularly its market. Southeast Asian women had often been the moneymakers of the family, operating with some autonomy, under a system of accepted serial monogamies. They might "marry" a trader for the duration of that man's residence in port, parting amicably when that time was up and when he had paid or given whatever had been promised. This system enabled women to move on without shame.[7] It was a world in which everything was hybrid, and the word *foreign* covered not just "Westerners" but even those Southeast Asians operating outside their own home area.[8]

And here we may return briefly to the story of Mohammed Arab, the young sailor who perhaps raised the British flag of victory in 1841. He lived, loved, and prospered in an archetypal Hong Kong life. In his will, drawn up by his brother with the lawyer Henry Charles Caldwell, one of his properties was bought from a "Protected Woman" and transactions were witnessed by Portuguese clerks; his earliest property deals were with Chinese shopkeepers, a timber merchant, carpenters, contractors, single Chinese women (sometimes specifically "boatwomen"), and men from Malabar or Macao. He was on business terms with Douglas Lapraik, a future prominent figure in British society, as well as George Duddell. His Western interlocutors are described in documents as "gentlemen," and then, so is he. Subsequent generations moved on from boardinghouses into drapery, brokerage, architecture, accountancy, consular and government service. Mohammed Arab was also one of three trustees responsible for the founding of the Mohammedan Cemetery in May 1867.[9]

More telling, perhaps, for this man deemed respectable enough for an admiring obituary in the local press, is that he had a Malay wife, an Arab wife, and a Chinese mistress and, in his will, gave property, education, and respect to the offspring of each liaison as well as to his handful of adopted daughters. His son Hajee, from his Chinese mistress, Ahoy, was given a house and requested to be brought up in the Mohammedan religion; his Arab wife, Phoorja, was left well looked after and was to be guardian of Arab's "minor children" as well as her own. When she died in 1887 she left a third of her wealth in trust for Hajee, "commonly called Hajee Mahomed Arab and the child of Ahoy (otherwise called Cho Oi), who was formerly the mistress of my late husband, for maintenance and education."[10] Such daily lives may not be those normally portrayed of the citizens who built the empire, but were reality nonetheless.

The result when all these varied peoples and practices collided was bound to be rough and ready. Imagine a frontier town settled by such distinct and different cultures, combining ideas and practices from the Mediterranean to the Indian Ocean to Malay river ports, coming up against Chinese habits and a numerically insecure but militarily strong Britain. Such freedom must have been exciting, yet there was little time to think about it, as docks had to be built, warehouses filled, and ships dispatched. As Hong Kong was settled, some British would cling desperately to a notion of a white, ordered society. But Hong Kong's hybridity would prove irrepressible. This was perhaps no true melting pot, but rather a glorious mosaic.

2

FRESH OFF THE BOAT

From its early days Hong Kong was marked by the arrival of ambitious, hardworking newcomers who strove to find their place and make their fortune in the hustle of the new settlement. Such individuals make up some of the tiles forming the mosaic of this port city—tiles of great cultural and racial diversity. Some of those arriving on this new shore rose mightily to heights of wealth and worldly success, others simply lived rich lives as parts of a colorful, shifting whole. All were integral parts of a whirling new world of opportunity, little knowing at the time how their separate steps toward self-help and survival would create a new and special place.

Most of our people here arrived with little—perhaps a professional skill or a small amount of capital or trading goods. Almost all men without women, our first arrivals would find a bed or room to sleep in, and perhaps had a warehouse to go to. Meetings with fellow traders or new friends would happen at street-corner tea or noodle stalls. Once more established, they might rent their own apartment, from which they could walk to their new-built offices. The one suit they arrived in would be carefully laundered until a second one could be made to order. Sometimes this clerk or that middleman would sign a deal that would allow a firm step upward, into one's own company, or from simple trading into shipping, from construction work into property investment, from hawking to corner store to emporium.

At first, these lives were all focused on the servicing of trade—be it by government permit or forward finance, the staffing of ships or the housing of sailors onshore. As the settlement grew by a few hundreds and then by thousands, those servicing needs developed. Now tailors and carriage makers could make a living alongside the ship chandlers and opium peddlers. There were no banks yet, nor any form of stock exchange. Security rested only in who you knew, with money kept literally close to the chest, traded in quiet conversations or guarded by a trusted heavy, preferably bound by ties of blood or clan. Not yet did Hong Kong have schools or churches, formal "society" or consensual culture. Matsheds—those flimsy shacks made from straw matting—lined the shore, with only a few people able to afford the men needed to build a stone home. When the typhoons came, few were safe and the wealth that mattered—the ships and what they carried—was most vulnerable.

Our newcomers here, though, would gradually, steadily, change all that. Within one decade and beyond, they built homes then found wives and started families. They invested in their communities, helping to fund the church or mosque or temple, gathering to establish clubs and schools, finding time to attend horse or boat races. This burgeoning society of multiple strands would soon provide enough demand to sustain not just tailors and saddle makers but milliners, cake makers, and seamstresses of silk.

Who were these strivers? How did this process begin? A sampling of those among the first to literally step ashore in 1841 shows a shared drive to get ahead but also a vast diversity of origins, cultures, races, and fates.

Young Leonardo d'Almada no doubt dressed as carefully as usual that day in January 1841. Leaving behind his teens in the Portuguese island enclave of Macao on the southern Chinese coast, his pens and papers were packed with precision. He was a clerk, due to accompany his boss, Captain Charles Elliot, the superintendent for British trade in China, to the brand-new settlement of Hong Kong. When young Leonardo stepped onto Hong Kong Island's narrow northern shoreline, he was the first of many Portuguese "bridesmaids" to what a later Portuguese chronicler called the "marriage" of two nations keen on profit, Britain and China. This marriage relied on the Portuguese for literate witnessing, matchmaking, and consummation.[1]

Leonardo's father had been in colonial service to the Portuguese government; he died at Malacca on his way back to Portugal just as his two Goa-born sons moved to Hong Kong with the British government. Leonardo would become clerk to Hong Kong's Executive and Legislative Councils and acted briefly as colonial secretary (although even when he got British nationality he never gained parity of pay or position). In 1846, he gave this home and land to the Italian Canossian Order of Roman Catholic nuns, who arrived in Hong Kong in 1858; his daughter Anita joined the convent there, as did Governor Bowring's daughter Emily. His brother, José Maria d'Almada e Castro, rose to become private secretary to Governor John Pope-Hennessy in 1877. José had many children; they worked in banks or government, or as solicitors, starting a family tradition that continues to this day. Daughters married into the Remedios, Gutierrez, and Carvalho families, all to be lasting names of Hong Kong.

A compatriot of Leonardo would become one of the wealthiest men in early Hong Kong: João Joaquim dos Remedios. Entrepreneur and diplomat, his first success was in opium; after he settled in Hong Kong by 1848, he made a fortune in land. In 1868, he was made consul general for Portugal, but was also accused by the *China Mail* of keeping coolies against their will in horrendous conditions as part of the transport of indentured labor from Macao to Havana and Callao, for the guano trade (he successfully sued for libel). His son João Henrique dos Remedios married into the D'Almada e Castro family. Today's D'Almada Remedios clan, also to intermarry with the Barretto family, thus has one of the longest post-1841 lineages possible in Hong Kong. Their longevity highlights how vital the Portuguese community has been—and still is—to Hong Kong.

Fresh off the boat, too, in 1842 was Alexandre Grande-Pré, son of a former assistant to the governor of Macao. An early clue to the mixing that made Hong Kong was that he could translate Malayu, Bengalee, and Portuguese into English; he would need those languages when mediating between the police and sailors from around the world. As a later Hong Kong–born writer with Portuguese roots, Stuart Braga, put it, these were "tanned and bronzed sailors, rough men of many nations, [who] came ashore intent on pleasure and a gay time" in saloons and boardinghouses, "some of decidedly ugly reputation. Did a roaring business in Hongkong town," with frequent fights with pistols and knives drawn among "the veriest riff-raff of society."[2]

The Portuguese kept coming, such as João Hyndman, fourth clerk in the British Superintendency of Trade. His father was Captain Henry Hyndman, who had resigned his commission with the British East India Company in Singapore and settled at Macao; there he married a local woman and his sons acquired Portuguese citizenship. João's brother Henrique left Shanghai for Hong Kong to join the Noronha printing firm, another lasting Portuguese name of great significance for Hong Kong. It was thanks to the fathers at Macao's St. Joseph's College that young Delfino Noronha, fresh off the boat in 1844, had learned English, Chinese, Malay, and Portuguese— and the craft of printing. Once trained as compositors, typesetters, and printers, such men could work at firms, newspapers, and missions across the delta, and in Hong Kong.[3]

Delfino Noronha's family had reached Macao in the early 1700s, probably from Goa; Delfino was about sixteen when he married Umbelina Maria Basto, herself of mixed origins. Just twenty when he arrived in Hong Kong with a small press in hand, Noronha set up on the edge of the central business district, in Oswald's Terrace, Wellington Street. He printed the *Hongkong Almanack* for 1847; in 1849 he produced a strikingly intricate theater program on silk; his wife helped with the inking and working of the press. He became government printer, a lucrative and prestigious position.[4] Noronha and Co. would last until 1941, and Noronha's personal contributions to Hong Kong would include co-founding Club Lusitano, donating to the Catholic Cathedral, and pioneering the settlement of Kowloon.

––––––––

Framjee Jamsetjee was one of several Parsi merchants who put on their long gowns and distinctive tall white hats, curious to see what new landfall the British were making in January 1841. Maybe the new harbor would prove useful; after all, the Parsis already owned a third of the total shipping involved in the India-China trade. Hong Kong was declared a free port on June 7, 1841, a week before it would hold its first land auction, and Framjee was there. Captain Elliot had already been called home with a flea in his ear for getting above himself, taking an island no one in London knew they wanted. But his successor, Henry Pottinger, found most of Elliot's innovations too effective to demolish, including the contentious land auction (technically the sale was out of order as Britain did not get full legal possession of the territory until a year later).

Who, apart from the Jardines, the men who had already amassed wealth as opium traders through Canton, would choose to risk hard cash on land on this unknown island? The Parsis. Buying land involved not only the purchase price but a commitment, as buyers had to build within six months or lose the site. Few had yet gone so far as to close down their homes or offices in Macao but, without exception, all the first buyers of land were Parsi or Western, namely: Dhunjibhoy Ruttonjee Bisney, Dent and Co., Dirom and Co., Ferguson, Leighton and Co., James Fletcher and Co., Fox, Rawson and Co., Framjee Jamsetjee, W. and F. Gemmell and Co., Gribble, Hughes and Co., R. Gully, Charles Hart, Holliday and Co., Hooker and Lane, Jamieson and How, Jardine Matheson and Co., Captain Larkins, Lindsay and Co., MacVicar and Co., Captain Morgan, Pestonjee Cowasjee, P. F. Robertson, H. Rustomjee, Turner and Co., and Robert Webster. Three years later, a second sale was held with many of the same names

appearing, notably Framjee Jamsetjee, who this time bought a further
ten lots. The only individual to outspend him was the Jardines-linked
Robert Strachan.

Framjee Jamsetjee's story is fascinating because though undoubtedly a pioneer of early Hong Kong, he was neither happy nor wildly
successful, repeatedly advertising his property for rent or sale until the
day of his departure.[5] His early enthusiasm for property in Hong Kong
soon wore off, although he had built, as the *Friend of China* newspaper
of September 6, 1846, described, "that pleasant and healthy residence
known as Framjee's bungalow surrounded by well stocked garden and
commanding a fine view of the bay with a large sea frontage." He donated cash to causes such as the building of St. John's Cathedral, that
still-dominant pastel-hued Gothic structure on a knoll just up the hill
from town. But a "Final Notice" in the *Friend of China* on October
22, 1854, stated baldly: "Mr Framjee Jamsetjee, the oldest inhabitant
of Hong Kong, being tired of the colony and obliged to leave at last,
requests all accounts to be sent for liquidation."

Perhaps Framjee had made his move too soon. F. M. Talati visited in 1841 but chose to keep doing his business in precious stones
and oils, jewels, and silks from Macao for another year before moving to Hong Kong. The Talati firm is active in Hong Kong to this
day. Cowasjee Pallanjee and Co., in Canton since 1794, had bought
two valuable marine lots in the first land auction, and would become
dominant in its new home. "The local yarn market [in Hong Kong]
was opened every morning by this firm and it acquired such a reputation that it was said 'What Cawasjee Pallanjee says, goes in Hong
Kong.'"[6]

Heejebhoy Rustomjee was another buyer in the first land sale; his
father had gone to China in 1834, trading from Macao and Canton to
Shanghai, Singapore, Penang, Calcutta, and England. When Heejebhoy failed to find the $12,000 he had promised for Hong Kong's first
seamen's hospital, his friends at Jardine's stepped in. But Rustomjee's
philanthropic urges were strong; he backed the big donation by Parsis of rice to the starving poor in Canton in 1858, the Parsi gift of a

bandstand to the Botanical Gardens in 1864, and five Victoria Jubilee Fountains around Hong Kong in 1867.

Dadabhoy Rustomjee, buyer of two marine lots in the first land auction, came from an illustrious family in India; in Canton he had offered his servants to the English factory to look after the fatally ill Lord Napier, the latest emissary seeking easier terms for trade from the Chinese empire. Rustomjee was doyen of the Parsi merchants in Canton and his business equaled that of the once-dominant trading house Dent and Co. and Jardine Matheson.[7] He was one of the four Parsis among the sixteen foreigners banished for opium trading from Canton in 1839; while in Macao, Dadabhoy Rustomjee offered his Hong Kong house as lodging for Chinese Commissioner Keying on his visit in November 1845, so it was soon known as "Keying House." When in June that year the Oriental Bank was opened in Hong Kong, he was one of two Parsis among the seven directors. Sadly, before the end of 1848, Rustomjee was insolvent.[8]

More successful were two other Parsi early adopters of Hong Kong: Bisney and Buxey. Dhunjibhoy Ruttonjee Bisney, a poor man of Surat, had two sons, Eduljee and Ruttanjee, whose business expanded from Bombay to Calcutta, Burma, Malaya, and China. The younger brother, Ruttanjee, had two sons, one of whom, Dhunjibhai Ruttanjee Bisney, moved from Canton to Hong Kong, where he was a founding director of the Hongkong, Canton and Macao Steamboat Co., member of the Hong Kong Volunteer Corp., and donor of the Bisney Cup at the Jockey Club, whose birth he also attended.

Framjee Jamsetjee Buxey, buyer of Marine Lot 36, could trace his name back to Surat, too, where his forebears had served the British and received a gift of lands near Crawford Market in Bombay. A relative, Jehangirji Faramji Buxey, who had left for China in 1829, became a partner in Ruttanjee Hormusjee Camajee and Co. in Hong Kong. Many of his descendants married into Hong Kong's Parsi elite; the future Sir Hormusjee Nowrojee Mody was also related. These names retain their resonance in today's Hong Kong—in street names, in their philanthropies (Mody was the key financier of the founding of the University of Hong Kong), and in their cultural and religious practices.

————

Before Hong Kong was settled, foreign traders were confined to a row of thirteen "factories" in Canton, meaning a combined warehouse, office, dealing room, and residence. These were called simply the English Factory, the American, Danish, Spanish, French, Swedish, Dutch, and other factories. Members of each lived and worked on the same spot for the half-year they were allowed by Chinese rules to be there, taking in and selling on cargoes from South and Southeast Asia. They were allowed no family life and little freedom of movement but had the chance of making fortunes if they stuck it out. The other half-year they mostly retired to Macao, waiting for the monsoon winds to turn. The restrictions of factory life were part of the fuel that would provide tinder to the Opium Wars.

Living in the same factory there as the Parsis were members of another important diasporic trading community, the Armenians; indeed, it was an Armenian ship that brought the first Parsi to Canton, a Mr. Readymoney, in 1756. Armenia once stretched from the Mediterranean to the Caspian Sea before coming up against the Roman and Byzantine empires, the Seljuk Turks, then the Russian invasion of 1828, after which it was divided into Turkish, Persian, and Russian portions. At least a million Armenians died in the Turkish genocide of 1915; by the end of 1920 all that was left was Soviet Armenia, one tenth of the original. Throughout, Armenians kept alive their language and their two Christianities (Catholic Armenian and Armenian Orthodox). A global diaspora, formed over hundreds of years, has played key roles in global trading empires.

It was an Armenian who had eased the (English) East India Company into Bengal, northeast India, helping to lay the groundwork for British power at Calcutta. The negotiator Khojah Phanoos Kalandar, in London in 1688 with his nephew Khojah Israel Sarhad, signed the deal and was granted a monopoly in the garnet trade in return. For

Khojah Israel Sarhad, there would be a future role in the founding of Calcutta, where the Armenians had been for half a century before the English. Kalandar had no descendants in the male line but his daughter married Khojah Minas of a noble Julfa family. Their granddaughter Begroom married the famous Agah Catchick Arrakiel of Calcutta in 1771. Arrakiel was head of Calcutta's Armenian community in the late eighteenth century, renowned for his loyalty to the British Crown, though it brought him to ruin.[9] One of Arrakiel's daughters, Elizabeth, married Johanness Sarkies, of another illustrious Calcutta family, later generations of which founded the Raffles, Strand, and Eastern and Oriental Hotels across Southeast Asia. Another Arrakiel daughter married Gregory Apcar in 1827, younger brother of Arratoon Apcar, the founder of Apcar and Co., the shipping firm that brought many people to Hong Kong. One more descendant of Arrakiel was Catchick Paul Chater, who through vision and daring would drag Hong Kong into the twentieth century.

Like the Parsis, the Armenians were active money brokers, borrowing cheaply in Macao and lending expensively in Canton; most Canton merchants were in hock on a large scale. Trade was fraught with risk but the Armenians showed that small itinerant traders could make a profit; they were determined and independent, and readily accepted by both Protestants and Catholics. Their role in the China trade has been long ignored, yet they were at the center of it.[10] As with the Parsis, so, too, with the Armenians and the British. They needed one another; there was symbiosis and often genuine friendship. Just as often there was a racial contempt, grounded in hard and heavy commercial competition.

—————

As vital as the people ready to invest in land in Hong Kong's first year were the people able to provide the labor to run the harbor. Shaikh Moosdeen was one such man, his job title of *ghaut serang* originating in Malay and his business first based in Macao. He was the contractor for sailors to man the ships, which meant he and his deputies ran lodging houses for sailors, almost all of whom were practicing Muslims. It was part of his job to provide all-around care of the men being contracted out to ships and other work. Unsurprising, therefore, that the first mosque was built on the corner of Shelley and Mosque Streets, where Moosdeen lived, and under his supervision. From the start, the mosque included lodging for Muslims passing through the colony. Highlighting the early importance of the Muslim community to Hong Kong, it had its own cemetery from 1858.

Of course, racial prejudice has always been present in Hong Kong. Yet as in the story of Mohammed Arab, the possible flag-raiser, Shaikh Moosdeen, one of the most important figures for the early functioning of the port, also married a Chinese woman, Aleesah (or Lee Yun Tsoi). By the time he died in 1873, his two Indian-Chinese sons were already in government service. The *Hong Kong Times* of July 3, 1873, described him as Hong Kong's "oldest Mohammedan resident"; aged seventy-three, this Madras-born leader of men died highly respected. His sons had offspring who would marry Muslims and Chinese on through the generations. Other Muslim-Chinese dynasties were formed, such as that of Hatim Khan. He had been a kitchen hand on the ill-fated ship *Nerbudda*, wrecked off the coast of Formosa. Notoriously, the British officers and men sailed off in the only available lifeboats, leaving 240 Indian soldiers and others to their fate, many of whom faced terrible imprisonment there. Khan managed to escape his Chinese captors and reach Hong Kong by 1842. Here he married a Chinese woman, established a small restaurant, and lived happily ever after, as have his descendants in Hong Kong. The Rumjahn family (or Ramjahn) also traces its roots back to an Indian sailor who married a Chinese woman who then converted to Islam; her name is unknown, but their son also married a Chinese. Three of Khan's four sons married Chinese women, something that gradually became accepted if the Muslim man was wealthy; it was harder for richer Muslim daughters to marry "down" to a Chinese, suggesting it was wealth more than race and faith that divided.[11]

This was not a society that condemned its peoples on color or marital choice alone.

————

The first Jewish resident of Hong Kong was either Samuel H. Cohen, who arrived from Australia in January 1844, or Jacob Phillips, who arrived late in 1843 or early 1844 from Birmingham, England. Cohen was a wandering adventurer, who moved on to Shanghai after a couple of years; he tried to join his co-religionists at Kaifeng but by 1849 had joined the California gold rush instead. Phillips, by contrast, had a profitable business in China with branches in Manila and Australia. He had been an apprenticed jeweler before entering into partnership with Benjamin Phineas Moore in the East. Phillips's nephew joined him in Hong Kong, but Phillips went back to England in 1851. The *China Mail* thought he had been underappreciated for his "great qualities," his intelligence and hospitality.[12]

As with the Parsis and the Armenians, Jews were in Asia long before the western Europeans. Communities on India's Malabar Coast provided advance bases for Jews following sea routes to the China coast; the first known synagogue in China was built in the Sung dynasty capital of Kaifeng in 1163. As with the Parsis and Armenians, the Jews were always more than just traders. They were brokers, agents, and intermediaries, but also tycoons and unofficial politicians, too, needing to be on good terms with everybody. They suffered the disadvantages of exclusion and insecurity, at the same time as garnering the benefits of a tight-knit community with a common language and traditions, in which bonds of trust and custom reduced risks and costs.

Baghdad, terminus of the Silk Road, was home to some Jews for generations, until a rise in forced conversions and other persecutions in the early nineteenth century made British-ruled India look good, with its claimed freedom of religion and trade. Jewish families would soon begin trading there in opium, rice, teak, tobacco, jute, saltpeter, textiles, gems, ship supplies, groceries, liquor, and ice. Remarkably, this story, which moved on from Bombay to Canton, to Hong Kong and Shanghai, can be told through the span of just one family: the Sassoons.

The first David was born around 1749 to an affluent family, traceable back over five generations. Now "Sheikh Sassoon," he managed to retain the favor of the entire Ahmet Pasha reign in Baghdad, "an achievement no less delicate, but assuredly more hazardous, than that of his grandsons in retaining the affections of a King of England," as the author Cecil Roth tartly reminds us.[13] David was state treasurer for more than forty years, leading the Jewish community in Baghdad, active in its religious and administrative activities; he was also a poet.

Traders then moved freely from Mesopotamia to Damascus, Aleppo, and Basra; one early Sassoon traveled regularly from Baghdad to Kut, selling corals to Arabs. Baghdad was central: "Bales of bright silks were shipped hundreds of miles on rafts by the mercers of Bushire; India and far-off Kabul sent cotton goods, horses, gold and silver ornaments, while coffers of spices and trinkets of every kind arrived by sea, or more usually by camel caravan, from Java and Singapore," enthused another chronicler of the Sassoons, Stanley Jackson.[14] Yet even the pasha's treasurer was not immune to the periodic bouts of anti-Semitic rage, and by the 1770s David Sassoon had secret passages built into the walls of his home, ready for escape. After his patron, Suleiman Pasha, was deposed in an 1811 revolt, he retired in favor of his son, another David, aged thirty-six, who spoke Hebrew, Arabic, Turkish, and Persian.

The situation for Jews in Baghdad kept deteriorating, so, in the late 1820s, "accompanied by his octogenarian father, and probably assisted by disguise and judicious bribery, David Sassoon escaped from Baghdad by night."[15] They sailed downriver to the port of Basra, where more of their family joined them, before crossing to Bushire (Bushehr), the upstart port on the east side of the Persian Gulf where a British trade agent was based. Here, in 1829, David Sassoon senior died. And from here, in 1832, young David set sail for Bombay and "realized its beauty and its promise. He saw British rule, and . . .

appreciated its blessings."[16] David collected the family from Bushire and moved.

Bombay was a raw city of about 200,000 people at the time, home to Hindu, Jew, Armenian, Parsi, Arab, Portuguese, "half-castes," a few European and native troops, and a handful of Britons. David Sassoon began by exporting textiles to Persia, Baghdad, and the Gulf, importing goods that could be resold to Britain. He bought wharfs and offered dock and storage space in Bombay to merchants from Afghanistan and Russia in return for their exotic goods. Then he invested in real estate. Starting what would become a tradition of support—to clan, faith, information, and identity—David built synagogues and backed Judeo-Arabic newspapers and scholars. When the Sassoons reached Singapore, they built a synagogue; when they went to Rangoon for teak, they built a synagogue; vast philanthropies followed as they extended their network through Asia.

That network arose thanks to David's two successive wives, who produced fourteen children with thirty-five years between oldest and youngest. Helped by a reputation for "unswerving personal probity and uprightness,"[17] David sent the first of his sons, Abdullah, on trips back to Baghdad, soon making Sassoon the largest Indian firm in the Gulf trade. Then David heard about China and sent his second son, Elias, to open a China office at Canton, then Hong Kong, then Shanghai. Almost all the Sassoon sons served apprenticeships in the China offices. There were also agencies at Yokohama, Nagasaki, and back in Calcutta. By 1854, David Sassoon was a millionaire, but he was just getting started. Sassoon offices were staffed mainly by fellow Jews, usually sent out from Bombay, and united by common roots, training, and worship. Jewish traders usually brought their families, more so than did the early Parsi merchants. At this stage, the Parsis were as great if not greater than the Jews in the China trade. By the 1870s, the position would be reversed, with the Sassoons in control of the opium trade and expanding largely into property up and down the China coast. One generation later, they were wealthy enough to buy their way into the British aristocracy, replete with country estates, racing stables, and Mayfair mansions. Regardless which community was on top, the opium trade among India, Persia, and China became almost totally dominated by non-Europeans—Baghdadi Jews, Parsis, Gujarati Muslims, Persians.

This trade had become the central pillar of regional commerce, and the secret of Britain's imperial success in East Asia. For decades, it and other Western empires had struggled to find something the Chinese market was prepared to pay for, in exchange for the tea and silk and ceramics that the West was all too keen to buy from China. Opium existed already inside China, especially among elite circles, where lying on couches while servants heated nuggets for inhalation was framed as a sensual delight. Once the British worked out that their Indian subjects and collaborators knew how to grow it in bulk, a new trading world emerged—and new markets among China's lower classes lined up for addiction.

The British in India were soon overseeing the growing and auction of opium, which was then transported to markets all over Asia, but especially into China. Some missionaries and other moralists tut-tutted at the trade; yet this was also the time when opium was consumed widely in Britain (often as "tonic" or "laudanum salts") and elsewhere, too. Legislation to restrict it was a long time coming— and the Chinese imperial establishment hemmed and hawed about whether and how to ban it. Chinese traders liked the smell of profit, too, but by the 1830s had come to see the drug's role in the weakening of their people. The successful traders—first British adventurers and their Parsi colleagues, and then clans such as the Sassoons—were those most adept at riding the waves of acceptance and illegality with dexterity.

When Elias David Sassoon turned up in 1845 he was thus probably the third known Jew in Hong Kong; he was joined a year later by his brother Abdullah, later to be known as Sir Albert David Sassoon, and Dawood Moses. As subjects of the British Empire in India they were categorized as British in Canton and Hong Kong, too. They did not open an office in Hong Kong until 1857, when the outbreak of the

Second Opium War forced them out of Canton. Elias made Shanghai—a few days' sail up the China coast—his personal base from 1850, when he broke away from the family firm to set up E. D. Sassoon and Co. He was looking beyond opium toward importing metals, muslins, cottons, and Dutch East Indies spice. Elias's heir, Victor Sassoon, would also choose 1930s Shanghai over Hong Kong, where he risked and lost the most. With the Sassoons largely absent from Hong Kong from the start of the twentieth century, their place as leaders of the Jewish community would be taken by a former staff member, Eleazor "Elly" Kadoorie, who, when he flew the Sassoon nest to make his own conglomerate, would start a new dynasty of wealth-making and giving still in Hong Kong today.

Those fresh off the boat at the birth of Hong Kong included another key class of entrepreneurs, the Tanka and Hakka people of China. The British assumption, based on their experience in Canton, was that Hong Kong would be a small, predominantly foreign port town, with the only Chinese present being servants and staff of European trading houses. They were rapidly proved wrong. Chinese flocked to this freer society where chances seemed manifold.

Take Loo Aqui from Poon Yu district in Whampoa. For his well-timed "loyalty" to the British, he was granted land in what would become Hong Kong's Lower Bazaar. He soon grabbed more, and even before 1842 was running a gambling tent and brothel; in 1845, he built a theater. When Middle Bazaar inhabitants were moved farther uphill to Taipingshan, an area known as Hong Kong's "Chinatown," he built a market there; by 1850, he was collecting rent from more than a hundred houses and shops. Alongside the gambling and prostitution he also held the monopoly for the local sale of opium. Thanks to men such as Loo Aqui, the first markets of Hong Kong lacked for nothing.[18] Bishop George Smith, visiting in 1844, wrote that Loo Aqui lived "in a style much above the generality of Chinese settlers, who are commonly composed of the refuse of the neighbouring mainland . . . After the peace he was at first afraid to return to the mainland, lest he should be seized as a traitor by the Mandarins. In the end he settled at Hong Kong, where he is said to encourage disreputable characters by the loan of money, and in various ways to reap the proceeds of profligacy and crime."[19]

Loo Aqui was not alone. The arrival of the British fleet in Hong Kong Harbor attracted anyone able to make a living from it, supplying food or services of whatever kind. The Tanka people, whose presence in Hong Kong both pre-dated and followed the first British settlers, lived and died on their boats, not allowed by Chinese tradition to live onshore or go to school. No wonder some grabbed the chance offered by British rule to escape such limits. A powerful example is Kwok Acheong, whose wealth was rooted in his provisioning of the British Army and Navy during the First Opium War. When the Peninsula and Oriental Shipping Company opened in Hong Kong in 1845, he became their comprador, or key local manager; he later bought its engineering and shipbuilding department and developed a fleet of steamships, providing keen competition to the Hongkong, Canton and Macao Steamboat Co. He died in 1880, honored and respected, one of Hong Kong's wealthiest and most prominent men.

Another early leader was Tam Achoy, who arrived in 1841. He was granted rights to the easternmost lots of the Lower Bazaar and began buying up adjoining property until he had a long sea frontage. The roots of his fortune lay not in property but in contracting; he also became broker for thousands of laborers leaving China for work in the United States or beyond, chartering ships and building a jetty on his seafront to dock and fill them. As the recognized leader of the Chinese community, his name topped most of the subscription lists for worthy causes; he was a trustee for Chinese temples and was credited in 1857 by the editor of the *Friend of China* newspapers as the most creditable Chinese in the colony.[20]

Twelve-year-old Wei Akwong had been plucked, literally, off the streets of Macao, where he was a homeless beggar, and taken in by the good Christians of the Morrison Education Society in 1837. This sent him to Singapore for an education in Chinese and English, although he never became a convert. He, too, was in Hong Kong in 1842, first as clerk in a churchman's house then as comprador and landowner. Compradors were key figures in East Asian commerce, key intermediaries between foreign and local traders and financiers. They handled local staff, bill-paying, and commercial intelligence collection and traded on their own accounts, too. Men such as Wei Akwong could be interpreter one day and comprador to the Mercantile Bank of India, London and China the next, a job one of his sons inherited on his death in 1878.[21]

As the motley crew gathered, the pace of events picked up—the *Friend of China & Hongkong Gazette* moved its press to Hong Kong by March 24, 1842, in time to announce an organized currency, a post office, and the erection of barracks. The Central Market opened in June 1842, swiftly followed by a Roman Catholic church and a Baptist chapel. Yet apart from two floating opium warehouses in the harbor (for the Jardine and Dent companies), there seemed to be almost no trade. Competition from the other Treaty Ports compounded the treaty confusion, no doubt deliberate, over whether Chinese were allowed to trade freely at Hong Kong. Rampant piracy and the general lack of any effective legal system put all at risk.

Her Majesty's Deputy Superintendent of Trade A. H. Johnston decided in 1843 that Hong Kong was "precipitous and uninviting." Government Treasurer Montgomery Martin was even less inspired. The landscape had "a greenish hue, like a decayed Stilton cheese . . . uninviting . . . desolate . . . the granite is rotten and passing, like dead animal and vegetable substances, into a putrescent state . . ." With sunshine, "a noxious steam or vapour rises from the fetid soil, yielding a gas of a most sickly and deleterious nature . . . This morbific gas . . . slowly mingles with the surrounding atmosphere, and when not causing immediate illness, produces a depressing effect on mind and body which undermines and destroys the strongest constitutions . . .

There does not appear the slightest probability that, under any circumstances, Hong Kong will ever become a place of trade."

Worse still was the moral depravity. The Chinese authorities' block on the migration of respectable Chinese meant, said Martin, that Hong Kong was populated by "a continual shifting of a Bedouin sort of population, whose migratory, predatory, gambling and dissolute habits, utterly unfit them for continuous industry, and render them not only useless but highly injurious subjects in the attempt to form a new colony."

Yet what Hong Kong was to benefit from most was precisely this shifting, Bedouin sort of population who may well have been predatory but were also enterprising and industrious. Hong Kong promised novel freedoms—to worship freely, to go ye forth and multiply, to get ahead. The *Chinese Repository*, a magazine run by Americans in Canton, was so impressed that it felt "the time will soon come—we cannot doubt it—when religious toleration will become universal . . ." It noted with approval the arrival of the mosque and a Chinese temple even before a British chapel had been built.[22] While the majority of the early population of new Hong Kong focused on making a quick fortune and going home, wherever that was, a nucleus of stayers soon formed. They were contractors and builders, compradors, government servants, and the handful of Chinese Christians cut off by their families for their new faith. Each of these had the incentive to settle down for the long term.

Little thought was given to what this "British" colony would look like after this kaleidoscopic throng of peoples and desires was tossed together. Formal Britishness was asserted at once, through flag and free trade, through laws, land auctions, and stone buildings. Yet while these imperial statements were being made, ever more of Hong Kong's mingling mass assembled. White British sailors would soon be drinking and carousing in taverns where the sensual delights were indubitably local, be they Chinese or variations of Southeast Asian brought north with trade. Unsurprisingly, one thing led to another. Officials and moralists might fear or despise mixed unions—yet families would form, of whatever hue. Even apart from mutual desire, when states are weak, no structure other than family offers such trust and ways to make and move money around.

Here, more than in sexy Shanghai, grew schools, places of worship and clubs open specifically to mixed-race children, differing cultural obsessions, widely variant religious traditions. Perhaps because it was so normal to deal with Portuguese newspaperman, Parsi financier, Jewish philanthropist, Scottish trader, and English pub owner, all in the course of one day, people took the mosaic for granted. This is how a professional and middle class were born—here lay the roots of Hong Kong as a city trading the world.

3

HONEY

"HONEY At Mrs Randall's—a small quantity of good Honey in small jars,
also Gin, Brandy, Sherry, Port, Champagne, Claret, Bottled Beer,
Porter etc etc. Lyndhurst Terrace, Victoria, 12th June 1851."

For "honey," read sex. Madame Randall had been an actress in Australia before she came to Hong Kong. Her advertisement in the city's newspapers hinted at a rich, bittersweet world. She was advertising her brothel, which acquired fame for its impressive client list, and Mrs. Randall's highly effective means of bill collection. She would send messengers to the offices of this or that judge or merchant, where the mere mention of the name Mrs. Randall ensured instant compliance to quell the "gup." For "gup," read gossip.

Mrs. Randall's offerings of "honey," as well as those in other local houses of prostitution, were as diverse as the clients they served. Some brothels featured European women exclusively, while others were strictly staffed and frequented only by Chinese or other Asians. Hong Kong was rapidly absorbing people from all over the world and quickly learned how to satisfy all tastes.

In 1848, one of the colony's earliest visitors to leave a record, Benjamin Ball, enjoyed Hong Kong's colorful aspects, enumerating the passing throng as comprising "the English, American and Chinese, the Spanish, French, Portuguese, Persians, Bengalese, Javanese, and Manilla Indians, the German, Italian, Russian, Danish, Swiss, Dutch, Belgian, Pole, and the Arab, Turk, Armenian, Tartar, Siamese, African, and South American." He also rather liked the "small sailor taverns, every evening lively with the fiddle, drum, tambourine and dancing. Looking in at the door of the front room, if the screen is removed, can be discovered a party of sailors, of all nations—black and white—with a sprinkling of English and Ceylon soldiers from the garrison, enjoying themselves after their own fashion. Early in the evening they are in a state of high glee; later, their spirits begin to flag and they have to replenish them from a well-stored bar at the back part of the room; still later, some of them become so low-spirited that the interposition of their comrades is needed to induce them away, and occasionally the police have to render their assistance. In the long line of square windows, without glass, over the Chinese shops, sit a certain class of Chinese women, ogling and looking out on the passers-by."[1] It was in such bars and boardinghouses where much of this wide range of people came together.

For the arrivals who were averse to any hint of mingling with other races, or incapable of even imagining it, establishments such as the British Hotel, managed by Henry Winiberg, offered a respectable option, particularly if you were unable to afford or enter the members-only (and mostly British) Club House.[2] But the real life of Hong Kong was elsewhere. By 1847, edging westwards from the center of town along Queen's Road, there were more than a dozen taverns, from Giovanni Gachi's Britannia to George Jones's Fortune of War, Matthew da Costa's Rainbow Inn, the Phoenix, the London, and the Pilot Boat Inn. George Mills's Neptune Tavern had the advantage of two separate entrances, for anyone needing more flexibility in their social lives. George McQuin advertised his Beehive Tavern:

"Within this hive, we're all alive, and pleasant is our honey; If you are dry, step in and try, we sell/s for ready money."

A complex, variegated world emerged: Chinese-only brothels that catered to Chinese of different classes, Chinese brothels solely for Westerners, Western brothels that served only Westerners, as well as other kinds of arrangements in between, most notably the Protected Woman. Soon rampant venereal disease prompted regulation, at least to protect foreign men. But trafficking of women continued to flourish. The British administration cared only for the health of its own, particularly its sailors and soldiers whose patronage of brothels was understood as a necessary evil, whom regulation might as well attempt to keep healthy. The far larger Chinese world of prostitution remained obscure to them and was impossible to police anyway, not least because leading Chinese community leaders were active participants. This traditional system used poor girls as domestic workers called *mui tsai*, meaning "little sister," and women as salable commodities.

A high-class Chinese brothel was much more than just a place to have sex. Indeed, consummation seems almost to have been an afterthought. Far more important was the provision of a place to dine, drink, and converse with business colleagues, while the presence of beautiful and often intelligent women providing stimulating conversation at one's side conferred status. Such brothels were multi-floor pleasure palaces, with sophisticated entertainments including performances by singers and actors, elaborate banquets, and highly painted and fashionably dressed women. Some of these women acquired fame as courtesans, achieving ever-higher status the more they refused a rich and powerful man's advances.[3] Slipping down the hierarchy of Chinese brotheldom, however, sex, rather than face or status, became more obviously the currency.

Whereas in the West women often "fell" into prostitution by force or by having been caught in extramarital sex and thus banished from respectable life, the Chinese world was more direct. Chinese prostitutes were not fallen women, but objects subject to sale, mortgage, and investment. It was commonplace that girls would be bought from poor families to be trained in the seductive art.[4] Patriarchy meant that only sons were important to a family line, carrying the all-important name of the ancestors into future generations. Daughters, by contrast, were a liability unless they could be sold into domestic service or brothels, command a high price in the form of dowry, or enable commercially useful connections through marriage. Later attempts were made to

tackle the issue of voluntary work versus slavery, but the debate itself showed the chasm between Western notions of individual agency
(albeit still limited for women) and Asian societies in which choice
was an impossible dream. At this stage in the early to mid-nineteenth
century, it was a virtually meaningless debate when so few other options were available to women. But curiously, despite colonial oppression and humiliation, some of these women would find they had more
rights under British imperialism than they ever had under Chinese.

Among those brothels that catered to Westerners, the highest class
served military and ship's officers as well as middle-ranking merchants
(the most elite of Hong Kong's tycoons had no need to go out for
sex—it was brought in-house, as we shall see). One clue to the presence of these classy establishments would be the flower stalls nearby,
as the convention of taking flowers to one's lady love persisted even
when it was a commercial transaction, and perhaps even lent it an air
of respectability. At the bottom rung were those brothels serving itinerant sailors and laborers. There were also exclusively Japanese brothels, in a different part of town, serving a group all their own.[5] This
segregation occurred partly because the 1857 Contagious Diseases
Ordinance applied only to brothels serving Westerners, requiring the
working women to have weekly checkups and compulsory treatment
against venereal disease. But it was also because many Chinese men
were repelled by women who had been sullied by Westerners—and
vice versa.[6]

Even so, segregation was never complete. A clutch of brothels for
foreigners stood in the so-called Chinatown district of Taipingshan,
and the surrounding neighborhood was "marginal cosmopolitan,"
noted the scholar Philip Howell, in his study of the Contagious Diseases Ordinance. It was neither exclusively European nor Chinese,
being home to "a mixed and polyglot group composed of middle-class
or wealthy Chinese, Chinese prostitutes serving non-Chinese, European prostitutes, Indian, Parsee and Muslim merchants and shopkeepers, a few scattered Portuguese and Macanese, and protected
women . . . The mixed nature of this district alerts us to the fact that

racial segregation was more of an ideal than an achievable reality in Hong Kong."[7]

The ordinance was intrusive and brutally enforced. Unlike domestic British laws, it regulated the existence of brothels and made brothel keepers responsible for registering their workers; advocates argued that this helped ameliorate the aspects of slavery inherent in the trade. Also unlike domestic versions, Hong Kong's law allowed no possibility of "redemption" through retraining for other work.[8] All imperial contagious disease legislation made women solely liable for surveillance and detention, not men. Sexually active women were seen as the source of the problem, with the moral murkiness of prostitution justifying punitive measures. While these saved some women from dying of a truly dreadful disease, the testing or responsibility of men was never seriously considered.[9] In an example of the nuance of empire at work, debt bondage, a system akin to slavery whereby people were forced to work to pay off a debt that was often used against women in Chinese brothels, was illegal under British law. Yet this same law brought European and American women under the contagious disease ordinances only twenty years after the local women, and even then allowed them to be tested at home whereas Chinese and Japanese women suffered genital exams at government clinics.[10] Infected women were detained in the Lock Hospital, where segregation and then-prevalent methods of mercury solutions and carbolic acid were used.[11]

Imposition of much harsher inspection and punishment regimes in the 1867 Contagious Diseases Ordinance sat alongside the granting of legal recognition, bearing both rights and responsibilities, to brothel owners, all of whom were women. Some women might, through their menfolk, have found roles in businesses from boat-cleaning to food or other stalls in the public markets. But if a Chinese woman wanted to run her own enterprise, then brothel keeping was one of the few trades where she could conduct business, make a profit, and accumulate property—something women were unable to do in China.[12] Brothel keepers, though admittedly by exploiting other women, learned how to raise capital, manage personnel and customer relations, meet market demand, keep and monitor accounts, determine credit ratings, deal with the colonial administration, and more. And it was a highly profitable business.

It was not without its horror stories, though. In one early case, in 1846, a brothel keeper threw out an ill prostitute onto a waste pile where she subsequently died, yet when the case was taken to court the jury failed to classify this as murder.[13] The young woman had become diseased as a result of her work. After treatment by local doctors failed to help, the madam put her out to save her brothel from infection. The coroner guided the jury to conclude that the death was an act of God, prompting outrage in some legal circles. But his comments seem to imply that the habit of tossing out sick women with the rubbish was far from unusual.

A far better option than working in a brothel was to be a Protected Woman. The elite level of Western society in Hong Kong had few dealings with brothels, and a Protected Woman was a discreet alternative, these arrangements sometimes even evolving into genuinely caring relationships. Being a Protected Woman meant more than merely being "kept"; the term implied a formal status. The system was pervasive and—outside the usual hypocrisies of public society—both normal and expected. William Caine, the colony's first chief magistrate and later colonial secretary, had a daughter, Elizabeth, by his Chinese Protected Woman sometime in 1843. (Meanwhile his wife, Mary Ann, either tried and failed to live with this or just left anyway in 1845. We do also know, however, that she had a son, one of whose names was Fearon, which may or may not imply she'd had an affair with her husband's colleague Samuel Fearon, so the infidelity may have been reciprocated.)[14]

Protected Women existed in a class separate to the mere working women in the brothels. When the intellectual Wang Tao visited Hong Kong in the early 1860s, he found "gaudy houses sporting brightly painted doors and windows with fancy curtains. These are the brothels, which are literally packed with singsong girls. It is a pity that most of them have large natural feet . . . About half of the girls can be considered attractive." He then moves on to consider the "protected" class of girls sometimes called "salt water maids": "As many of them are kept by Europeans, they have become quite wealthy and own houses of their own. The finest among them are attractive in their own way with roundish faces and seductive eyes . . ."[15] Salt water maids were so called because they were often Tanka, or boat women, from the people living on boats along the coast. From this grew a Chinese prejudice that all Tanka women were prostitutes, when in fact they were also sailors, ship cleaners, and independent traders of vegetables, fowl, and pigs, as well as services such as washing and mending clothes.

Wang Tao's early account already hints at the possibility of upward social mobility for the Protected Woman. Of course, some women claimed they were "protected" only as a cover for active prostitution with several clients, and no doubt some unwitting foreign men inadvertently lent their names to such enterprises while choosing to believe the woman was there for them alone. But the extent of "protection" offered by their clients also varied greatly. Just like mistresses throughout history, these women needed to keep their wits about them to mitigate their vulnerabilities.

Looking through the archives of property transactions, we can see that some Protected Women managed to acquire substantial estates. These were the lucky ones.[16] While this was still a position of dependency, it was freer than being trapped in a brothel or an abusive Chinese family. The Protected Woman was at least only accountable to one man—and he was often absent. In the meantime, she could sponsor loan associations, lend money, take a financial interest in brothels, or train children who had been bought or adopted for concubinage. Once they were wealthy, these women often bought property together. At least two such sisterhood houses were formed, on Peel and Graham streets.[17] The first documented evidence of a land grant by a foreigner to a Protected Woman was in July 1845, when a merchant, F. J. Porter, conveyed a lot in Queen's Road West to

"Akew" for the nominal sum of five dollars. She sold it the next year for seven hundred dollars.

The social historian Carl T. Smith has found examples of women who established large households as the result of sometimes even fleeting relationships with foreign men. His study of land records revealed that between 1843 and 1852 there were eighteen women landowners designated as "females," four "spinsters," and one "boat woman." The records for 1856–62 gave no detail of gender or place of origin in land records; after 1863, the word *female* was not used, but *single woman*, *spinster*, and *unmarried woman* did appear. Thus, from 1863 to 1884, a total of 205 single women were listed as landowners, many of them probably Protected Women. This was still of course only a tiny proportion of overall commercial life (it amounted to less than 3 percent of the transacting population at the time), but it showed a route ahead for Chinese women who would not have had that opportunity in China. It was precisely thanks to intercultural mixing—and particularly thanks to sex with foreigners—that these women could rise above the limits of their own society and become the torchbearers for a new world in which mixed-race people would succeed.[18]

———

Having a mistress was quite normal for foreign men in Hong Kong, be they British, Parsi, Jew, European, or American—and there is no evidence to show this ever affected their careers or was disapproved of in any official way. Peter Vine, a partner in the Hong Kong law firm Deacons, found that in the 1850s there were just fifty expatriate wives and four hundred expatriate men. "This did not imply that the unaccompanied males were expected to lead celibate lives. On the contrary, perhaps the majority developed liaisons with Chinese or Portuguese ladies, but they were expected to behave discreetly, and not to embarrass the expatriate wives and their children by openly flouting these relationships."[19] The term *Portuguese* here meant someone not entirely European but with a mixture of Portuguese and Chinese roots, probably from Macao.

Osmund Cleverly, a merchant shipping captain and brother of Charles Cleverly, surveyor general in the colonial government, had two children baptized in 1845. No mother's name is listed in the records and the children's surname is their father's first name. The next month he married a British woman named Ellen Fagin and had at least one further child with her. He was clearly running two families.[20] The auctioneer George Duddell had a son baptized at St. John's Cathedral in early 1850, George Minza; the record specifies the child is illegitimate and no mother is named. Samuel Clifton, a police inspector, spawned legitimate and illegitimate children, again suggesting the existence of parallel families once he married Frances Augusta Clifton and moved to Shanghai, where they had children baptized as their own.

At this mid-century moment, the example of William Stewart, a partner in Jardine Matheson and Co., stands out. Stewart's will, of September 2, 1845, bequeathed to "Alloy . . . a Chinese female known to my executors in China" the sum of $7,700, about a third of which was earmarked for the purchase of a house in a location of her choice and the rest was to form a monthly payment (thus it was not under Alloy's personal control but administered on her behalf). Wrote Stewart: "My executors will invest the sum as to yield a pension for her future support, she having no one but me to look for the means of diverting starvation in her old age." He also bequeathed a portrait of Alloy to his colleague Andrew Jardine. William Stewart had been in China since October 1835, and would die in Hong Kong a short eleven years later. In these early, personality-forming years of Hong Kong, such public acknowledgment of a local relationship—revealing one's Chinese lover through a portrait gifted to a colleague—would raise few eyebrows. Later in the nineteenth century and certainly by the early twentieth, such frank avowal of "miscegenation" would be heavily frowned upon.[21]

At a different point on the class scale was John Stewart (sometimes rendered Steward) who first appeared in 1849 as an officer on a schooner off Amoy, modern-day Xiamen on China's southeast coast. By 1860, he was running a boardinghouse at 43 Hillier Street, where he remained until at least 1876. Registered with the London Missionary Society Chinese Congregation, he had a daughter baptized, and promised to marry her Chinese mother, in 1883. He was respectable enough to make it onto the colony's Jury List, a sure mark of recognition in a small society lacking professional men, and he was a business partner of our old friend Mohammed Arab.[22] His will also demonstrated his deep ties in the local community: Abdool Razak Madar was his executor, his estate went to someone named Ng Shee, and his burial was recorded at St. John's Cathedral under the appellation "John Steward of Lascar Row."[23]

Non-European men also had Protected Women. A deed of settlement drawn up by the merchant Mahomed Ebrahim Hajee Asgar when he was about to leave Hong Kong in 1883 provided for Hung Assoo and their five children. Asgar appointed another merchant to be trustee for Hung Assoo and to be responsible for overseeing the management of Inland Lot 125 on her behalf, as compensation for eleven years of cohabitation.[24] We already know of men such as Mohammed Arab with his Malay, Arab, and Chinese wives. Other extended families grew from these roots. When Leong A-peen, wife of Shaik Madar, died in 1863, she left one of her two properties to her daughter, who married the clothier Abdul Kurreem. Such was the genesis of the web of the prominent Arab, Madar, and Kurreem or Curreem families, whose descendants still live in Hong Kong.

These legal records only tell us about those with something at stake—a bequest in a will perhaps, or a property transaction marked down in the Land Registry. Church and cemetery records provide yet more examples.[25] The merchant Phineas Ryrie had a long-standing relationship with a Chinese woman; he left money to their daughters, Maggie and Eva. David Sliman, with Jardine's for many years, had a daughter, Lam Yu-shi. David Culloch, from an old Scottish family, worked for Turner and Co. for more than twenty-five years and took a leading part in the management of the Hongkong Hotel; on his death he left the income from a property to his Chinese woman, Young A-chun, for the rest of her life.

Among all these women's stories, one in particular has become well-known—that of Ng Akew, the brilliant survivor, entrepreneur, and archetypal salt water girl. Replete with drugs, sex, smuggling, and success, her story has been rediscovered thanks to Carl T. Smith. His background in genealogical research triumphed over his ecclesiastical training and his decades in Hong Kong became ever more focused on researching the lives of Hong Kongers as they were actually lived.[26]

Ng Akew's birth or arrival in Hong Kong goes unrecorded, but through reports of the Cumsingmoon Affair in the *Friend of China* starting October 13, 1849, we get a fascinating insight into the life of this feisty woman, who was also sometimes known as Hung Mow ("red haired") Kew. The newspaper editor, typically, given the hypocrisy of the times, felt obliged to apologize for even covering the subject: "Irregularities have grown out of the demoralized condition of the foreign residents in China, partly from the branches of their traffic [the smuggling of opium], partly from the long term during which society was nearly without the influence of educated and refined European families. The last few years have seen wonderful changes in the social conditions of the foreign residents, and we now speak more of what was than what is; but . . . its shameless immoralities are too open and too observable."

Ng Akew's protector was James Bridges Endicott, captain of the ship *Ruparell*. Its function was to receive stores of opium arriving from India and beyond, preparatory to the sale (and smuggling) of the drug into China. Endicott was from a prominent family traceable back through six generations to the longest-serving governor of the Massachusetts Bay Colony, John Endecott, and thus a founding family of New England.[27] Although he would later found Thomas Hunt and Co., which would move its main business to Hong Kong, he resided mainly in Macao. As with all our other leading businessmen who made local liaisons with their Chinese or Asian women, he had a high standing in the community. When he died in Hong Kong (on November 5,

1870), the *China Mail* of November 7, 1870, described him as "one of the few remaining pioneers of civilization in our Colony . . . He was very generally respected, and his sound and shrewd counsels will be missed by many who have profited largely by them." The numerous attendance at his funeral "indicated the respect in which the deceased gentleman was generally held." All this, despite his well-known relations with Ng Akew.

Back in 1849, the *Friend of China* recorded that Ng Akew was "a shrewd intelligent woman, without any of those feelings of degradation which Europeans attach to females in her condition."[28] On the contrary, her relationship with Endicott empowered her to enter business on her own account. First, she decided to take up trading opium in a small way, buying eight chests full of the drug that Endicott, as captain of a receiving ship, had legitimately recovered from a ship wrecked in the September 1848 typhoon. These she shipped to a west coast port where they were seized by pirates. Akew's response was to pay the pirates a visit, "being a woman of strong determination . . . and bully them into compensating her by threatening them with the vengeance of her foreign friends." The cowed pirates gave her betel nut in great quantity in exchange, but the profit from its sale didn't cover her loss. Ignoring her man's advice to let it go, Akew then took one of her own boats and chartered another and went to visit the pirates a second time. "Through intimidation or effective bargaining, she was able to return with her two ships and six other heavily armed junks laden with cotton, cotton cloth, sugar, pepper, rice, oil cakes, oil fish and dye stuffs," wrote the newspaper.

Unfortunately, Akew's six vessels full of goods attracted the attention of a British captain who notified the Hong Kong authorities, and of an American schooner, which aimed to seize the goods, assuming them to be the product of smuggling. But neither the British authorities, who gave protection to the opium trade in Hong Kong, nor the Americans, who were officially committed to suppressing it, could act against Ng Akew. If the Americans had seized the goods, it would be an admission that they knew the produce derived from an opium deal that had its roots in the activities of a respectable American, Endicott. So they handed the case over to the British, who then had to drop it, as it was outside their jurisdiction.

Ng Akew had left out any mention of pirates in her story, simply saying her cargo was given in lieu of opium that pirates had seized from her ship. It was all a marvelous tangle, as while the opium trade was illegal in China, British Hong Kong relied on it and many Americans also thrived from it. The upshot was that Ng Akew had managed, through sheer grit, wit, and determination, to score a significant profit by parlaying her unique position between Chinese and foreign powers, both in bed and in business.

When Endicott felt the need to marry a Miss Ann Russell in Macao on October 19, 1852, and to discard Akew, he nevertheless still wanted to provide for her. The day before his marriage, he executed a deed of trust that conferred on Ng Akew, "spinster, a Chinese female, residing in Macao, and mother and guardian of Achow, a Chinese infant of ten years or thereabouts," two well-placed pieces of land in Hong Kong. The trustees appointed were two merchants who were also protectors of Chinese women: Douglas Lapraik and William Scott. Endicott then took two of the sons and one of the daughters he'd had with Ng Akew with him back to America, leaving Akew with one of each.

Akew then moved officially to Hong Kong and entered an alliance with Fung Aching, a local businessman. Together they bought more land in 1855–56. A newspaper article about a fire that destroyed Fung's houses on one of Akew's lots referred to him as her husband and a man of means. When he left Hong Kong in 1856, Fung left at least three more properties to Akew.

Most of Akew's business dealings outside her property portfolio were loan schemes with women like her. In 1868, she was the principal of ten "single women" who bought a site on Graham Street between Hollywood and Staunton streets, in the heart of what is today called Soho, a central zone both then and now for multiracial business, residence, and pleasure-seeking. But after a decade of these schemes, it seems that Akew had finally overextended herself. A suit was brought against her to recover a debt, which prompted a rash of ten further cases brought by widows and single women to recover funds from schemes she had promoted. Akew petitioned for bankruptcy.

Thanks to her entrepreneurship, Ng Akew does not appear to have needed to seek more protectors during her career; her income from her various business deals and from the properties left to her by Endicott and Fung meant she could bring up her children and extend her commercial empire in relative comfort. She left no personal papers but no doubt she enjoyed friendships with fellow businessmen and -women, with the temple, mahjong table, and dining table of central importance. Little of this was at risk when bankruptcy forced her to sell her personal property at public auction, because her residence itself was held in trust. The auction, however, offers an insight into the lifestyle of this clever woman, who had moved from serving a foreign man to being her own boss. Her decor of choice included custom-made Blackwood marble-top tables, chairs, and stools, Blackwood carved sofas, chairs, and tables, chimney glasses, engravings, pictures, lamps, carpets, clocks, bookcases, a sideboard, crockery, glass and plated ware, vases, ornaments, teakwood wardrobes, a toilet table and glass, washstands, and one iron safe.[29]

Now stout and aged fifty-eight, Akew was left with enough to live on comfortably for years. She had managed to exploit to the full the opportunities inherent in having a relationship with a foreigner. Not for her the later hang-ups about what the Chinese state would call a "century of humiliation," or postcolonial chroniclers would call colonial oppression. Instead, the arrival of the global trading world on her doorstep had brought opportunity. Thanks to her early ties with an American ship captain, she could find her way through the muddle of hypocrisies and contradictory trading laws to make her own profit and build her own life. Only by exploiting that mixed-up world created by the differences between East and West—in trade as well as in personal relationships—could Ng Akew get ahead. Her story offers a template of why Hong Kong existed, and how it created a character all its own.[30]

An added quirk to the story comes from James Endicott's wife, Sarah Ann, who, according to Endicott's will, had given "unceasing care and devotion" to all of his children, including "those who stand in relationship of step-children as of her own, she having made no distinction in the treatment of them."[31] Perhaps inspired by her husband's acceptance of all his varied children, and her own understanding of the realities of Hong Kong life, Sarah seems to have taken on the panoply of responsibilities from that life with an open mind. This was not the society long popularized in colonial histories as a British elite centered around the merchants' dining tables and The Hong Kong Club. This was the real life of the majority of Hong Kongers, a few steps up the hill.

Where these diverse worlds met, Hong Kong's newest indigenes were born, a first generation of children who were, often, racially mixed. Until recently, however, many descendants of Hong Kong's first Eurasians have sought to downplay or deny their roots—often because acceptance meant admitting one's great-grandmother was a prostitute. Yet many of these women, who literally gave birth to multicultural Hong Kong, learned to manipulate a system that could hardly have been more brutally stacked against them. "From the Chinese point of view, women, whether they were wives, concubines, daughters or *mui tsai*, were always someone's property, never free agents, and therefore were never entitled to move about 'voluntarily.'"[32] In a world where every female had a price, the only route to success was to make sure that price was a high one. Some of these women did just that.

4

HOME

Life in this settlement, one day downstream through the delta of the Pearl River from the trading harbor of Canton, was fraught with insecurities. It was on that tortuous riverine route that opium was traded, and where wars fought for its control slaughtered thousands and redrew maps of colonial conquest. It was down that river that the tens of thousands of Chinese fleeing poverty and strife would travel to try their luck in Hong Kong. As that delta debouched into the deepwater harbor of Hong Kong Island's northern shore, shallow-bottomed Chinese skiffs navigated through the tea and opium clippers that had raced in from the other side of the world. New arrivals would find a first foothold in tenements where clans or contacts combined. But a new way of life had to be learned, and ways to make a living found—perhaps cleaning those clipper hulls, unloading heavily fragrant sacks, pandering to others' desires, building new docks and boardinghouses, and trading vegetables.

Many men, women, and children fell by the wayside, never surmounting a lifetime of deprivation. But fortunes were also being made, seemingly overnight.

The British overlords had originally envisaged merely a warehouse station, with opium hulks able to provision from the harbor. But now so many people were arriving that Hong Kong was becoming a bustling, quarrelsome, feverish but determined sort of place. Roads had to be built, a prison provided, and a rudimentary justice system devised. Throughout the early decades, robbery, often with violence, was commonplace. Yet still Hong Kong was safer for many than China, and people were on the move.

In 1853, leaving aside the British garrison, Hong Kong's total of 39,017 people comprised 37,536 Chinese (living onshore and in boats), of whom slightly more than 6,000 were female; 194 "temporary residents" (mainly sailors); 352 Indians, Malays, and Manila men (Filipinos) with just 38 of these being women; 459 Portuguese (of both Macao and Goa), 137 of them women; and 476 Europeans and Americans, 86 of them women.

Less than two decades later, the population had trebled. The 1871 census showed a "European" population of 2,736 people, 684 of them women. Among more categories was one described as "Goa, Manila, Indian and others of mixed blood," numbering 1,388; "Chinese in the employ of Europeans" (7,617), Chinese living in the city of Victoria (72,984), in villages (10,507), and on boats (23,709). A summary table listed "Whites," "Chinese," and "Coloureds" to reach a total of 84,147 men and 33,619 women, thus 117,766 people.

Helped along by the triumph of steam shipping over sail, Hong Kong was becoming a great port city in the mid-nineteenth century, just in time. It would pull in an intense variety of peoples to help create and fuel its growth.

––––––––

Robert Thom was a scholar and a gentleman. He was also made the British consul in Ningpo, China, when he already had a Chinese wife—not a mistress or passing fling, but a wife. This fact was simply recorded in the press of the time without comment. In all the effusive eulogies on his untimely death in 1847, not one mention was made of his private life; all focused on what an excellent chap he had been. When Thom went out of his way (and perhaps beyond his position) to protect his wife's brother from a mob, this was seen by the press of the time as an instance of loyal duty despite the trouble he then faced with "native," that is Chinese, not British, authorities.[1] The *Chinese Repository* journal, not known for writing with tongue in cheek, could only praise him as one "who zealously promoted every honest effort to extend our intercourse with this peculiar people."[2]

Thom had been a player in the highest circles of diplomacy in the East since he contributed to the drafting of the Treaty of Nanking, which brought Hong Kong as a Crown Colony into legal being. He had defied death when carrying a truce flag during the First Opium War at Amoy in 1840; his zeal and exertion during military engagements at Chusan, Canton, and Chinhai were also praised. Fluent in Chinese, he produced texts teaching not just language but also "How to meet and greet and eat" and "On the harmony which ought to exist between husbands and wives"; "Mr Thom made himself at home with the Chinese, caring little where or with whom he might chance to be. Whether with the high official or with the lowest coolies, he always had something to say, saw something to admire, and found something to learn."[3]

This is not a sorry tale of racial discrimination against a man for having married a Chinese woman. Clearly, his marriage did not hurt his career, as has long been asserted was always the case in the dark old colonial days. Marriage across races was far more common than generally assumed, although the state of the records does not help; the government did not appear to take marriage very seriously, as a registrar was not even appointed until 1852. Church records were more reliable—if, of course, the people marrying were members of any church.[4] The case of Thom, and others to follow, shows that marriage across racial boundaries may not have helped a man get ahead, but it was neither a necessary nor a sufficient condition to stop him in his tracks.

———

More ambiguous—in every way—are the life, career, marriage, and family of Daniel Richard Francis Caldwell. Thanks to the unpublished diary of John Evelyn Fortunatus Wright,[5] we learn that Caldwell, his good friend and godfather to one of his sons, was "slim but well built with peculiar largish blue eyes which the natives cannot at all understand." Wright says, "He is a most amusing, good-tempered person, sings a good song, tells capital yarns maintaining at the same time a most unassuming, gentlemanly bearing. His common name among the Celestials is 'Jam Quie' which literally means, 'Conjuring Devil.'" Caldwell could also enliven a dinner party with "some very clever juggling." Wright and Caldwell had been confirmed together in 1851 by the Anglican Bishop George Smith at St. John's Cathedral; apparently Caldwell admitted to a wild misspent youth in Singapore until he was thrown out by his family in 1834, fled to China, smuggled opium, womanized, got ill, returned to Singapore, and joined the British Expeditionary Force to return to China, ending up in Hong Kong.

Caldwell quickly became indispensable to a government that barely understood its environment, and faced continuing conflict with China and high rates of crime and piracy on the seas in and around Hong Kong. Gunboat diplomacy had broken down China's barriers against foreign trade but had not allowed much time for anyone in London to think about how to rule a place where most people spoke Chinese and other unknown tongues. Early administrators had not expected Hong Kong to be much more than a depot for foreign shipping but, simply because Hong Kong was not China, it became quickly, wildly popular. Chinese fled the Taiping Rebellion on the mainland, they fled poverty, women fled total control, and people left Macao, and South and Southeast Asia, in hopes of making their fortune in Hong Kong.

In short, Hong Kong needed people like Caldwell.

He was English, but not an insider, having been born in 1816 on St. Helena, where his father was a merchant and member of the St. Helena Volunteers. Rather than Eton and Oxbridge or a life in the lesser gentry of England, Caldwell grew up in Penang and Singapore and could soon communicate in several dialects of Chinese, Malay, Hindustani, and even Portuguese. He was a man of the tropics, washed up in Hong Kong, where he would find both disgrace and fortune. He had sailed in the same fleet with Major Caine (a future colonial secretary). Settling in Hong Kong in 1842, he became interpreter in the Magistrate's and Supreme Courts, then assistant superintendent in the police. After a life of huge ups and downs, he died on October 2, 1875. His lavish gravestone still stands in the Hong Kong Cemetery.

So, too, does that of his wife, Mary Ayow (or Ayou) Chan. Caldwell was one of the few early white men to go so far as to marry his Chinese love. Not only that—he first married her according to Chinese rites, and seven years later, in St. John's Cathedral in 1851, to the open approval of the bishop and his wife. This is the first recorded marriage between an Englishman and a Chinese. He proceeded to have every one of their numerous children baptized in the cathedral and educated (often in Western schools), launching what is probably Hong Kong's first legitimate Eurasian clan.[6]

Mary Ayow Chan's origins are obscure, but she was clearly a woman of character. She did not merely consent to her husband making her respectable in British colonial eyes: she was an enthusiastic Christian convert, active in charity and a member and benefactor of the Chinese congregation of the London Missionary Society. For several years, her household included a private chaplain from Foshan, China.

Subsequent crises in Caldwell's career have been blamed on his multihued home life, yet both the times, and his activities, were more than dramatic enough in themselves to provoke controversy. The debate has long been whether Caldwell's career was so tumultuous—he was investigated for variants of corruption twice, sacked once, and eviscerated by a segment of the press—due to racial prejudice fueled by his Chinese marriage. For the conservative critics, he was himself a "half-breed," corrupt by nature, further tarnished by spending too much time with the Chinese, and, anyway, his wife was a harlot. To those more sympathetic to this charismatic, clever man, the weight of accusations against him was both racist and fueled by the petty jealousies of a small, fretful, and fractious colonial administration struggling under an ineffective governor (John Bowring) in a time of general unease. After all, there were piracy, armed robberies, and fires, plus attacks on foreigners. One such was the poisoning of a batch of bread destined for foreign tables in 1857, during the Second Opium War, in a failed attempt to wipe out the colonial community.

Even his critics weren't sure how to judge this man who thwarted clichés and lived off nuance. Indicative of the conservative colonialist's view, G. B. Endacott's biographical sketch claimed Caldwell was "never quite trusted" and as "a man of mixed blood and married to a Chinese, he possibly was not completely accepted socially." To Endacott, "there was always something slightly shady about him"; "scandal and intrigue seemed to shadow him." And yet, and yet, one had to admit he was extraordinarily versatile. No matter what the colonialists thought of him, he always had a unique place in the Chinese community; leading local friends hired him as mediator with the West, intelligence gatherer, and trusted fixer.

Was Caldwell the victim of a vicious power struggle, or the architect of his own fall (and later resurrection)? The answer, as ever, lies in between. All of it was true, both for and against. The key is that Caldwell was necessary; indeed, early Hong Kong would have gone along much better if only there had been many more Caldwells. Here was a man used to Eastern ways, able to communicate and make genuine lasting ties with other peoples, capable of running informers to tell him of forthcoming pirate attacks, devious enough to exploit that knowledge to his own advantage, honest enough to gain the Royal Navy's deep respect, collegial enough to rise high in the Freemasons, and loving enough to give his wife, Mary, the high standing and family home accruing to a colonial official.

He trod a fine line between what was legal or not, and had myriad opportunities for self-aggrandizement through a level of local knowledge that no other contemporary of his in government could hope to achieve. Of course he had friends more than ready to save his life or perjure themselves on his behalf, and naturally he would do the same for them. This was a frontier town at a time of stress; these were not the corridors of Whitehall. Caldwell as a character was inevitable.

From the very few newspapers (written almost entirely by one man each) and the even fewer travel chronicles of the time, a picture has emerged of Hong Kong in the 1850s as "a snobbish, gossipy, rancorous, mostly male community—a village community—only held together by mutual fear of Chinese insurrection or disaffection. Everyone, including government servants, was out to feather his nest, to make a killing as speedily as possible so as to escape back to England, or rather to Scotland, before typhoid fever, malaria or cholera took him to an early grave at the Colonial cemetery, Happy Valley."[7] Perhaps Caldwell's crime was that he was not plotting escape. Like generations of Eurasians and others to come, he was committed to making his life in Hong Kong.

A contemporary insight into Caldwell comes from Albert Smith, a stage performer of London who traveled abroad for fresh material with which to enthrall audiences of the Victorian age. He'd already been to Constantinople and up Mont Blanc. He was in Hong Kong in August–September 1858 and met the government's great and good (from the governor down), dining frequently with the leading men of commerce. He found them dedicated only to the almighty dollar, noting he never saw a young clerk "with a book in his hand" (hardly a problem confined to nineteenth-century Hong Kong). Yet this was not the heart of Hong Kong, this was not where the drive and energy and innovation were to be found. For that, Smith had to delve into the life beyond the Brokers Gutter in front of The Hong Kong Club, and stride uphill, exploring the worlds of the Chinese around Taipingshan, the raucous sailors' bars to the west, the artisan and laboring workshops up the teeming side streets. For that, too, he needed to meet the Caldwell family with whom, on September 27, he spent "one of the most agreeable evenings with his family, that I had spent at Hong Kong. Mrs Caldwell is Chinese, and the little children speak in the language. At ten I went out with him, armed, for a prowl about the low quarters, and saw a wonderful deal."[8]

One moment Caldwell garnered praise for having recognized an escaped convict while passing a barber's shop; the next he was excoriated for his reliance upon his friend and informer Too Apo, who was soon exposed and convicted as an extortionist and one who traded in false confessions. Fulsome testimonials then followed from the Royal Navy, which he guided on numerous expeditions against pirates, where he "enabled the Commanders of Her Majesty's Ships to distinguish between the innocent and the guilty, a question of great difficulty without such assistance . . ."[9] When Caldwell went on sick leave in 1850, three people were needed to cover his post. Dogged by low pay and debt, Caldwell quit government work in 1855 and entered a business partnership with Ma-chow Wong. But the government couldn't function without him and lured him back a year later, now as registrar general and protector of Chinese inhabitants and, in 1857, licenser of brothels. This powerful concentration of power in Caldwell's hands over the vast majority of Hong Kong's people was because, wrote the hapless Governor John Bowring, only Caldwell could keep the Chinese quiet.[10] It was Caldwell, too, who solved the puzzle of how the Chinese in court would swear to tell the whole truth when the Bible was irrelevant to them; he suggested replacing the judicial oath with a (non-Christian) Declaration of Truth, which if not observed would amount to perjury; this was made law in 1856.

In 1858, Attorney General Thomas Anstey launched a vicious attack accusing Caldwell of consorting with pirates (his old friend Ma-chow Wong), keeping brothels, consorting with a prostitute (meaning his wife, Mary, presumably on the assumption that all Chinese women were prostitutes), and much more. Two government inquiries followed, revealing just about every insecurity about race, gender, and empire then felt in Hong Kong. Caldwell was never entirely innocent; however, no evidence was found of illicit money made by Caldwell, nor of him lying to the Executive Council; besides, the Chinese were deeply unwilling to give any evidence against him. The second inquiry, in 1860–61, was spurred by competing professional jealousies and a greater public awareness of rot within government, as well as, perhaps, the now-suspended Anstey's frantic angst. It must have been galling indeed for men who outranked Caldwell to have no riposte available when he noted that, unlike him, they couldn't tell one "Chinaman" from the next.

His good friend William Caine, with whom he had first sailed to China and who similarly straddled racial and ethical boundaries, managed to keep his career on track, rising to the heights of colonial secretary and even lieutenant-governor. Perhaps that's because although he had Chinese lovers, he did not go so far as to marry any of them. However, another officer, Clifton, had, like Caine, married a Western woman, thereby deflecting attention from his illegitimate half-Chinese offspring, yet Clifton was dismissed on charges of systematic fraud and extortion in supposedly more freewheeling Shanghai.

What perhaps makes more sense is to focus less on Caldwell's marriage and more on the fact of his closeness to the Chinese community, of which his marriage was merely one part. After all, Wong saved Caldwell's life at some point and adopted as goddaughter a woman called Awoon, who had been a mistress of Caldwell's. This was a far closer tie than mere business partner and virtually made Caldwell Wong's adopted son.[11] Wong knew the criminal underbelly of Hong Kong of which he was a part, and his role as informer to Caldwell was also well known—and happily exploited by the government when it suited. But when Caldwell showed loyalty to this kind of family, and when there were dyspeptic moralistic ranters such as Anstey around, and a few thwarted colonial civil servants feeling threatened by the whole time and place, Caldwell was a suitable whipping boy.

The Caldwell case was not a good look for Hong Kong back in the imperial capital of London. *The Times* thundered that Hong Kong was "always connected with some fatal pestilence, some doubtful war, or some discreditable internal squabble; so much so that, in popular language, the name of this noisy, bustling, quarrelsome, discontented, and insalubrious little island, may not inaptly be used as an euphemous synonym for a place not mentionable to ears polite . . ." As for the man himself, "there is a fault also in the position of Mr Caldwell who is allied by marriage to the Chinese population and who, therefore, never can disabuse the Chinese of the notion that he is as one of them, and can be acted upon as they are acted upon."[12]

Yet when deprived of a government career by the judgment against him in the second inquiry, Caldwell made himself even more indispensable, as a private detective. No one had better access to the Chinese world and, for the Chinese, no one could better express their fears and knowledge than he. Caldwell arbitrated disputes and was made head of a semiofficial secret police. By 1868, he'd been hired by the Chinese holders of the monopoly in legalized gambling. Before the end of the 1860s, the business establishment and even some senior government men were once more friends of Caldwell, singing his praises. Without him, they could, it seems, do nothing, at least with the locals, who so vastly outnumbered the colonial elite. Some chroniclers will argue that Caldwell's active Freemasonry throughout his ups and downs helps explain how he survived it all; however, there were Freemasons on both sides of the battle over Caldwell's career. The new attorney general, Julian Pauncefote, said: "I know there are different opinions on this matter. Some think that [Caldwell] is an ill-used, but respectable man, while others do not share this opinion, but so long as he comes and says 'I can get the murderers' we can give no other answer than 'we are glad if you can.'"

Meanwhile, his family of Hong Kong's first true Eurasians was growing up. His son Daniel Edward Caldwell was the first bilingual, Hong Kong–born, and Hong Kong–trained lawyer, and a founding partner of Wilkinson and Grist (a still-independent law firm in Hong Kong). He blotted his record by fleeing the colony due to debt. A brother, Henry Charles Caldwell, was the third partner of Deacons admitted to the Hong Kong Bar, forming a legal partnership with the fourth, W. H. Brereton. The signatures of Caldwell and Brereton are found throughout the documents underpinning the China-Asia trade. At least three of the Caldwell children married Westerners; their descendants are far-flung to this day.[13]

Many more mixed marriages were to follow the Caldwells' in nineteenth-century Hong Kong, although unfortunately we will never know the full amount. The patchy records exclude, for example, what the historian Guo Deyan called a significant amount of mixing between Parsis and Chinese, not only in trade and intellectual exchange, but in love. "In China as elsewhere, intermarriage between people of different nationalities is an age-old practice; there is nothing surprising in this fact itself. But in the early 20th century, and even earlier, marriages between Chinese and Parsees were not marriages of convenience; they served no political purpose. They were the results of a process of the two communities getting to know and appreciate each other over a long period of time."[14]

Most intermarriage took place among the middle and lower classes, such as that of the German auctioneer Christian Friedrich Rapp, who married Mei Ho and appointed her guardian over his six children in his will. Alfred Parker, chief engineer of a steamship ferry called *Tai On*, married a matron at the Hongkong Hotel. Edward Lewis provided for his widow, Ah Ching Lewis, and daughter, Yan Noi; he hailed from Kingston, Jamaica, arrived to Hong Kong in 1865, and worked in the Public Works Department (PWD) for thirty-six years. John Maxwell, a Scots ex-policeman from the Royal Naval Yard, also joined the PWD; he had his first child baptized at the London Missionary Society Chapel, where they persuaded him to marry his lover, Wong Ah Hing. Thomas R. McBean, usher and interpreter in Hindustani and Bengali at the Supreme Court for twenty-five years, married Francesca Brigitta Cruz, but left her and their seven children entirely unprovided for on his death.

The taverns of western Hong Kong Island were home to multiple liaisons, many of which led to the altar. William Godwin of Middlesex married the Chinese widow of Christian Jensen; he worked at the Land We Live In tavern. John Humby married Ms. Wong and had two daughters; after a policeman's career he bought the British Tavern in 1872, changed its name to Empire Tavern, and ran it until 1891.

Christian Fredrick Petersen, who established the German Tavern, married a Chinese girl and their children were baptized in the Chinese To Tsai Church. His brother Peter Petersen also had a Chinese wife, Lum Sing. Born about 1852 in Macao, she had been a student of the noble Miss Harriet Boxer and so learned good English. She was only seventeen when she became Petersen's "woman"; his tavern-keeping career took him from the Land We Live In to the City of Hamburg and on to the Royal Oak, where he died in 1876. After leaving $500 to his mother back in Sweden, the rest of his estate went to Lum Sing. Now calling herself Mrs. Jane Frances Petersen, she kept the business running, at a price. The Licensing Board preferred men's names, and perhaps because of this, she soon married a J. J. McBreen, an unhappy match that did not last—she had to pay for him to get out of police custody and cover his debts. She went to Singapore and opened a boardinghouse, also giving birth there to McBreen's child, for whom he paid no maintenance. She returned to Hong Kong and signed a formal deed of separation in July 1884, with the Anglican missionary Reverend J. B. Ost acting as trustee for her and her children. Moving back and forth between Singapore and Hong Kong, she had minor brushes with the law but at least she had money.

The will that her first husband, Petersen, made in her favor had been executed by his good friend, another tavern keeper with a Chinese wife, John Olson. Of Swedish farming stock who left the land after successive crop failures in favor of shipyard work, Jons Olson reached Hong Kong in the 1860s, and soon anglicized his name to John. By 1867, he held the liquor license for the National Tavern and was also managing the Oriental Restaurant; he appears to have owned or leased the Star Hotel and later the Stag Hotel. The Jury List of 1888 even has him running a Temperance Hall. He died in 1918, and "Ellen Olson" died on October 20, 1915, aged sixty-one. Olson descendants have concluded that she was his wife, Ching Ah Fung. However, there was also an infant son of "J and Y Olson" who lived only a few months in 1879, raising the question as to who was "Y." John's surviving offspring included daughters Elizabeth and Ellen (Nellie) Kerstin, sons John and Charles William—and a daughter, Hannah Mabel, whose mother was a Chinese woman, Yau Kum—thus, presumably, "Y." In other words, John Olson had two Chinese women: first, Yau Kum, with whom he had a daughter called Hannah; then he marred Ching Ah Fung. Yau Kum's fate remains unknown.

Ching Ah Fung and John Olson were public partners for thirty-four years and had four children. It seems Hannah grew up with her four half siblings in the family home. With her half sisters, Hannah went to the Diocesan Girls' School; the sons John and Charles to the Diocesan Boys' School. Hannah went on to marry an Englishman, Charles Warren, who ran a construction company that also sold sanitary ware, tiles, and plumbing requisites. He was joined by his brother-in-law John Olson junior, who married Annie Louisa Moore Burke under Catholic rites in Kowloon, a location suggesting she might have been Eurasian-Portuguese.

Sadly, the first John Olson's will, made in 1890 and never revised, left his estate "in trust for all my children by the said Ching Ah Fung whether born before or after wedlock both classes being hereafter included in the terms child and children." Hannah was somehow left out, as from a different mother. It's unclear why or how exactly, but after John's death, the family split and the business partnership broke down. Perhaps tensions over race had something to do with it, suggests one descendant: "It wasn't only to do with the fact that Old John didn't include my grandmother [Hannah] in his will, written when she was only 10. Both our families managed to hush up their Chinese inheritance but in Hong Kong, the Olsons were much happier in their Eurasian skin than the Warrens," noted a present-day descendant and researcher, Jill Fell.[15]

The family story, key parts of which are still disputed by descendants, highlights the ready intertwining of British, Chinese, and Eurasian worlds at a time when such mixing was, in theory, frowned upon. It also highlights how class mattered as much as race: the younger John Olson and all his generation were happy to reference the family's seafaring past but didn't mention the family's financial roots in a tavern.

But we cannot be left with the idea it was only barmen and -women who got together. The Shearman Bird family challenges most clichés.[16] Shearman Godfrey Bird was a British Army officer, aged just twenty-two, in Canton, in late 1858 or early 1859. He was the fourth of fifteen children of a rural vicar, with an extended family full of senior military men, architects, and civil servants. Young (Winchester-educated) Shearman was sent to China in 1857 as part of forces due to fight the Second Opium, or "Arrow," War. Luckily, he wrote—of the mosquitoes, the prickly heat, the military actions and treaty ports. He was learning Chinese at the same time as he was busy helping to burn down Chinese villages; he took up photography, bird hunting, and sailing, and then he met eighteen-year-old Amy Chun. No marriage certificate was ever found but the two claimed marriage on June 1, 1859. Amy was baptized as an Anglican in 1863, after two of her children had already been baptized.

His descendant the researcher Naomi Ridout believes Shearman resigned his commission (in 1862) because the relationship had become or was about to be made formal and/or public. She notes that the head of the Imperial Maritime Customs, Robert Hart, was typical in having a Chinese partner who bore him several children, whom he later left behind in China when the soon-to-be-ennobled Hart went home on leave to find a "proper" wife. By contrast, Shearman chose to marry his wife with formal Anglican rites—even at the cost of his military career, his prospects, and his finances. Shearman Bird had made no effort to hide his tie with Amy—they went out together publicly and strolled in Howqua's gardens. It seems more likely that he resigned from the military to pursue a more lucrative civilian career.

Moreover, Amy was no "flower boat girl." Her father was possibly a builder or contractor for the British and the family may have been at least recently wealthy. In any case, Amy brought some material substance to the union. As had Caldwell, perhaps Shearman Bird was simply moving closer to the local community, with his eye on a rich life in the East. He was soon made surveyor with the Hong Kong government, notably after he had a publicly acknowledged Chinese wife.

Life for the young couple, in both Canton and Hong Kong, was not easy. His diary reveals, however, the social life possible for a mixed-race couple of those times. There was a round of dinners, picnics, and teas, almost invariably with members of the Protestant missionary world; there was also the friendship between the Birds and the wealthy broker Granville Sharp and his wife, Matilda, of Matilda Hospital fame. The Sharps knew Rev. Fred Turner of the London Missionary Society, a noted opponent of the opium trade, and the Turners were Shearman and Amy's neighbors in Canton. Matilda was herself an adventurous woman, a linguist in French, German, Dutch, and eventually Cantonese. Granville was a stalwart of The Hong Kong Club thanks to his career as an accountant in several banks and then a bullion and bills broker. The Sharps would later help Amy the widow when money was short.

The Shearman Bird children were baptized at St. John's Cathedral (where Shearman audited the accounts on the side). In 1865, his brother Sotheby arrived from Taiwan; it was Sotheby, not Shearman, who played a founding role in what would become the leading architects' firm of the China coast, Palmer and Turner. Shearman's working life (and pay packets) were improving but not his health, and by 1867 he was heading homeward with Amy, five children, and an amah; he died soon after arriving in Canada in 1869, leaving a total of eight children to be reared almost single-handedly by Amy, all of them integrated into Canadian or British society.

———

Each of these growing, mixed families formed part of the fabric of Hong Kong—a city built not just by a handful of white men and Chinese coolies, living in different worlds. Rather, the energy and lubrication that Hong Kong brought to world trade came from the people who stepped over the limits of their colonial, class, or racial fencing to help build a new world.

5

THROUGH THE SCREEN

The American Rev. Lucius N. Wheeler found Hong Kong in 1866 to be "one of the most unique and beautiful of oriental cities." He was impressed by the remarkably clean and tidy streets and noted the harbor was "one of the finest in the world, and floats an immense commerce." But what really fascinated him was the motley throng:

There are people of almost every nationality and color, in costumes odd, antique, and many-hued: on foot, on horseback, in sedan chairs, in phaetons; here and there a military or naval officer, proudly bearing the insignia of his rank, with groups of common soldiers and jolly jack-tars sauntering in and out of the curiosity shops, or bantering with fruit-venders; now and then a foreign lady, dressed a la Parisienne, riding in an open carriage, or in her chair, borne by men in uniform; some hurrying to and fro, as if pursuing important business engagements, some walking leisurely, with cane in hand; haughty Parsees, worshippers of the sun, sporting the Persian habit, and distinguished by their tall glazed hats; half-naked coolies, carrying heavy burdens with their bamboo poles, in contrast with the Celestial gentry, who appear in long robes, gracefully waving the ever-present fan; and native women in gay apparel, attracting public attention by their various arts . . .

Over all this strange scene, more heterogenous and fantastic

than perhaps any other city in the world can present, the air is reso-
nant with the jargon of many languages, the twang of the banjo, the
song of the minstrel, the indescribable plaint and whoop of burden
bearers, the cries of men hawking their wares, the din of countless
rattle-boxes, and the rush of wheels—sounds mellifluous, discordant
and ear splitting.[1]

New arrivals settled where they could and such was the overcrowding that life was lived on the street. Hawkers touted goods, shops spread
over the footpaths if there were any, workers made meals or entertainments or rattan baskets in the street, where men had haircuts and their
ears cleaned, walked their birds (in cages), or simply hung out.

Some chroniclers chose to lament that while it might have looked
exotic, all these different peoples really didn't get along. J. S. Furnivall,
the influential historian of Southeast Asia, is often quoted with his im-
mortal lines on plural societies, where different peoples meet "only" in
the marketplace.[2] Dare we ask for more of any time or place than such
a pluralism? And how can his description be a limitation on a place
such as Hong Kong, which must have been the nearest thing existing
to a marketplace incarnate? Rich examples abound, however, that the
mixing went far beyond the market, into bed, home, and families over
generations.

———————

One man illustrates all the contradictions of mid-century Hong Kong.
His roots go back to the glittering port city of Venice although he
arrived in Hong Kong from Calcutta and went on to huge financial
success and philanthropic achievements, notably in girls' education.
He sat at the peak of respectability as an early board member at the
Hongkong and Shanghai Bank (1868–88) and on the Legislative Council. Yet he ran a known double life with two families, one Jewish and
one Chinese, the latter rising to prominence. His name was Emanuel
Raphael Belilios.[3]

From Venice, his father had managed close ties to Baghdadi traders in Syria, operating a lucrative trade among Europe, the Middle East, and India. His mother, Salha Lanyardo, was from a prominent Aleppo family. Once in Calcutta they quickly became wealthy there, too. Based around Howrah, north of Calcutta, they owned half the district where rail was inaugurated in 1854 carrying jute, cotton, and wood—and opium. Young Belilios (born in 1837) married Semah Ezra from the top Baghdadi family in Calcutta (related to the famed Sassoons) in 1854, the same year he joined his father's firm as a clerk.

He arrived in Hong Kong in 1862 on his own; his first godowns (or warehouses) were on Lyndhurst Terrace, that so-called marginal zone that was in fact the center of bare-knuckle commerce. Some parts of town were clearly more European than others—the Peak Reservation of 1904 would later be the most egregious example, though affecting only the merest handful of people rich enough to imagine ever living on the Peak—the geographic as well as social summit of the city. Most ordinary Hong Kong people, without privilege, just doing what it took to get by, could be found where Rev. Wheeler was sitting—his view, after all, was from the Stag Hotel rooftop, just west of the central business district. This is also where the Protected Woman Ng Akew held her properties, in Soho, or more properly, Sheung Wan, a zone "populated by a mixed and polyglot group composed of middle-class or wealthy Chinese, Chinese prostitutes serving non-Chinese, European prostitutes, Indian, Parsee and Muslim merchants and shopkeepers, a few scattered Portuguese and Macanese and Protected Women."[4] In fact, there were settled communities of Portuguese here, not mere scatterings, holding their Catholic masses at a church on the junction of Pottinger and Wellington Streets in the heart of this zone. The buildings were a mixture of Chinese and European style, with rows of connected houses facing the streets, their ground floors mostly taken up by Chinese carpenters, washermen, provision stores, and bookbinders. It was a convenient spot for all in-between people, with warehouses, shops, homes, places of worship, and brothels packed closely together. No wonder Belilios started here.

He came from a world in which knowledge of Judeo-Arabic and Hebrew as well as English had long facilitated global trade. Grabbing an early foothold in the opium trade from Calcutta to Canton and Hong Kong, he diversified into property and public companies. Key to his success—and that of so many others—were his multiple, fluid identities. The British saw Belilios as Indian or Portuguese Jewish, whereas, he said, "the native Chinese make no difference between a Jew and a Christian. Both are foreigners in their eyes, but, if anything, they are better affected toward the Jew, whom they regard as an Asiatic like themselves." He was both successful man of public affairs and domestic man of parallel homes.

He took up with his Chinese lover (who is known only as Ms. Li) sometime between 1869 and 1872. It's unclear when Belilios's Jewish wife appeared in Hong Kong from Calcutta but it's thought to be around this same time. With his wife, Belilios had a stillborn son in 1871 at Seymour Terrace. In 1872, he built the impressive mansion he called Kingsclere on Kennedy Road (after his first Kingsclere at 13 Caine Road), all these roads being destinations for the up-and-coming bourgeoisie. His summer residence, the Eyrie, where he kept a pet camel and other animals, was next door to the governor's on the Peak, home to the elite. Straddling the ridge it offered sea views both ways; a small open-air pavilion on the top had a 360-degree view.

In 1880, with his wife, Semah, he had a son, Raphael Emanuel. Two years later he was appointed to the Legislative Council and made a justice of the peace. His mistress gave birth to his first daughter in 1885, named Marie Felice "Paw Paw" Lee Wai Yin, on March 3. Two more daughters with his Chinese partner followed, "Yee-paw" Mabel and "Saam Yee-paw."

It's clear the exotic behavior of Belilios in Hong Kong was no bar to worldly honors and success. He rented three of the sixty-two telephone lines available in 1889, sat on the highest councils in the colony, gave large bequests to charity, and expressed his obsessive admiration for the British prime minister Benjamin Disraeli (Earl of Beaconsfield) in his construction of Beaconsfield Arcade behind the bank on Queen's Road. "Every Friday I commission my butler to distribute fowls and bread among the necessitous families . . ."[5] As for his camel, the *Hongkong Telegraph* reported on July 24, 1897: "We are informed that the animal belonging to the Hon E.R. Belilios strayed away from his stable at the Peak yesterday afternoon. A long search during the afternoon proved fruitless but this morning, the poor animal was found dead about 100 feet below Mountain Lodge, having apparently jumped or fallen from the wall there."

Belilios's private life was no hindrance to his growing influence. When at last the Government Central School for Girls was founded (in 1890), it was thanks to Belilios that it got new premises in 1893. It gave a middle-class English education to daughters of Chinese, European, and Indian residents; in 1891 it taught twelve English, two Spanish, forty-six Eurasians, nineteen Chinese, and one Jewish girl; by 1898 the renamed Belilios School for Girls had 539 pupils, of whom about 233 were British. This (and the Diocesan Girls' School) reinforced the fact that, contrary to earlier fears, Eurasian girls had alternatives to merely drifting into concubinage.[6] Belilios also endowed scholarships, a reform school for boys, several hospitals, medals for bravery, and more. The Belilios Medical Scholarships were for boys "who are Chinese on the mother's side," a clear opening to children of mixed race.

Belilios seemed to be more liberal than his fellow leading Jews of the colony, the Sassoons. Just as his father had donated land for a synagogue in Calcutta, so did Belilios offer part of his Kennedy Road site. But the offer soon morphed into a legal fight with the Sassoons, who claimed in court in 1897–98 that Belilios had promised the whole site and was now reneging. The judge ruled in Belilios's favor but behind this ran a deeper schism. The Sassoons were Baghdadi Jews, tracing their lineage back to Sephardic (and thus Iberian) roots; they would marry into the Spanish and British aristocracies. Belilios was a Sephardic Venetian but open to Ashkenazi as well as Sephardic Jews. Ashkenazi generally hailed from Eastern Europe and were poorer migrants, fleeing the pogroms of the Pale of Settlement and other horrors. Behind the schism was thus a hint of class warfare.

Hong Kong's earliest Jewish migrants—and still the most prominent—have been Sephardic. The colony's first synagogue had been one of Arthur David Sassoon's houses on Seymour Terrace; later, his brother Solomon David Sassoon gave a house on Shelley Street; in 1882 Sir Jacob Sassoon bought the defunct Cosmopolitan Club on Staunton Street. The local press now claimed they had in fact been opposed to the Belilios site all along: "They seemed to have considered that the place was too public for certain persons of the Jewish community who were in poor circumstances . . ."[7] Even though Sephardim had first appeared as humble seamen, the later growth of the community was fueled by Sassoon wealth and patronage. Caroline Plüss believes this produced a Sephardic relationship with poor Jews "characterised by distance, disapproval, embarrassment and the refusal to integrate mendicant co-religionists."[8] In contrast, the new phenomenon of desperate Ashkenazi refugees left our cosmopolitan Belilios unfazed. Ashkenazim, also, held their worship in Hebrew, rather than in the Judeo-Arabic of the Sephardim. When the Sassoons settled on the (still-current) synagogue site, Belilios refused to lend his name to a tablet enshrining gratitude to the Sassoons and the naming of the Ohel Leah Synagogue after the Sassoon matriarch; he resigned as a trustee.[9]

Though Jewish, Belilios's idea of himself did not rest on that identity alone. The Carl T. Smith Collection, an indispensable archive on Hong Kong personalities, shows that Belilios was in frequent business dealings with other leading in-between men who were neither wholly British nor Chinese, such as the Armenian Catchick Paul Chater, Jews back in Calcutta, Lee Chin, "gentleman of Canton," Portuguese Hong Kongers, and members of the Parsi community. The Jardine Matheson archives show he was on close, collegial terms with all the leading hongs of the day, confident enough to tell them how to go about his business. He was trading in opium but in cotton, too, and frequently fought over insurance and interest rates.[10]

Double life notwithstanding, by 1893, Belilios earned his Companion of St. Michael and St. George honor from the British queen. David, his second son with his wife, died of bubonic plague in 1898.

Two years later, Belilios left both his wife, Semah, and his Eurasian family in Hong Kong, and "retired" to England with his son Raphael Emanuel. He secured a coat of arms for his family in 1901; these heraldic designs once graced the shields that knights wore in battle but now granted a royal seal of approval to a family's identity and achievements.

He died on November 11, 1905, at Green Park House, 134 Piccadilly, aged sixty-seven. An obituary in *The Times* described Belilios as merchant, legislator, and landed proprietor, one "largely interested in many public companies," with a special interest in education. His marriage to Semah is recorded but no mention is made of his parallel Chinese lover and family. Instead, note was made of his admiration for Lord Beaconsfield, and his sending of large wreaths to Disraeli's statue in Parliament Square each year, as well as primroses and violets to his grave.[11]

Belilios's will named only his son Raphael as heir. Back in Hong Kong, Semah lived in the King Edward Hotel, continued her extensive philanthropic work, and died on November 28, 1926, aged ninety, leaving the residue of her estate to the poor of Jerusalem and Calcutta. She was buried beside her son David in Hong Kong's Jewish Cemetery. Meanwhile, their son Raphael Emanuel married Vera, daughter of Sir Israel and Lady Hart, in England (in 1904), had two sons at Park House, Piccadilly, and became a Member of Parliament.

The whitewashing of Belilios's double life was just as normal as the existence of the second family in the first place. This pattern has had the effect of simply writing out of history up to half of what was actually going on. Many are the histories and sweeping claims made about racial segregation in empire, asserting that the British and the Chinese had no intimate connection—yet they were sleeping together most nights.

—————

Deeper than business ties were the family webs created by cross-faith and cross-racial congress, in this case, Belilios's relationship with his Chinese woman. Intermarriage would tie the Belilios name to those of Lam, Tyson, Heard, Lobo, Overbeck, Kotewall, Ho Tung, and Botelho—a roll call of the names that would form the core of Hong Kong's prewar elite and the nexus of old money. Just this one strand of multicultural relationships linked the worlds of overseas Chinese from Malacca in Malaya, via Jews from Venice and Calcutta, to German, Spanish, British, Portuguese, Dutch, American, and Parsi worlds.

How this happened involves tracing more women from the same neighborhood of higgledy-piggledy tenements just west of the central business district. Four sisters—Lam Fong-kew, Lam Kew-fong, Lam A-shui, and Lam Tsat-tai—were born to a woman named Lam and a man named Bartou. It's thought that the prolific lover Bartou was Spanish consul in Macao and Manila in the 1840s and '50s. From the Lam sisters' liaisons came the men and women who would form the basis of an influential Eurasian network in the closing decades of the nineteenth century.[12]

The first and second sisters, Lam Fong-kew and Lam Kew-fong, were the Protected Women of George Tyson and Albert Farley Heard, although, perhaps unsurprisingly, the records do get muddled over the twin sisters' names. George Tyson arrived in Canton from Boston as a clerk with the American trading firm Russell and Co. in 1854.[13] After Tyson's death in 1881, his land in Hong Kong went to a clerk in the magistracy, called Chan Kai Ming, George's half-Chinese son with Lam Fong-kew. Young Chan was placed in the Diocesan Home in 1870 and won scholarships at Central School, before becoming secretary of the all-important Opium Farm (not an agricultural farm but a tax-collecting arrangement). He would become one of Hong Kong's leading men, following the traditional trajectory of success in the non-British world.[14] He joined the Chinese Chamber of Commerce, chaired the Tung Wah Hospital Group, was a founding member of the Bank of East Asia, donor to the University of Hong Kong and other educational causes, and an acting member of the Legislative Council.[15]

Albert Farley Heard was in China from 1854 to 1873, after which he married a Mary Livingston. But before he left China, land records show the depth of his liaison with Fong-kew's sister, Lam Kew-fong. He gave her a valuable site in Hong Kong, and another in Macao. She subsequently expanded her property empire, buying and selling lots for profit, building herself a new house, and leasing sites to other Protected Women. The fourth sister, Lam Tsat-tai, was first "protected" by Gustav Overbeck, partner in Dent and Co. (before transferring her affections to an American, Edward Constant Ray). Overbeck married an American woman in 1870 but the previous year had conveyed two lots to Lam Tsat-tai "to provide for her and her children" (she later sold the sites). She, too, developed an extensive property portfolio.

Meanwhile, the third Lam sister had a daughter, Chan Quay Neo, who married Choa Leep-chee (sometimes Lap-chee). His Fukien family had settled in Malacca, on the Malayan Peninsula, and boasted an ancestor who had been leader of the Chinese community, or "Kapitan Cina," under Dutch colonial rule there. He also had an uncle in Hong Kong since the 1870s, Choa Chee-bee, comprador to a sugar firm. After joining him there in 1874, Choa Leep-chee rose to great riches and lived in luxurious style. His home high on Hong Kong's slopes, Burnside, bloomed with hundreds of English and European flowers.

His progeny blossomed, too. His son Choa Po Sien married Belilios's daughter Marie Felice; one of their two children, Margaret, would marry Rogerio Hyndman Lobo, the future Sir Roger, a man of influence in late-twentieth-century Hong Kong (the Lobo Amendment of 1984 required any deal signed by China and Britain over Hong Kong's future to be debated by the Hong Kong Legislature). Meanwhile, their son George married Maisie Kotewall, one of the nine children of Sir Robert Hormus Kotewall and Edith Lowcock. So far, the mix engendered from the four Spanish-Chinese Lam sisters had encompassed American, European, Chinese, Malay Chinese, Venetian Jewish, and Portuguese roots. Now it came to include Parsi blood, too, because Sir Robert was the eldest son of the Parsi trader Hormusjee Kotwaj and his Chinese wife, Cheung A-cheung.[16]

Meanwhile, Choa Leep-chee had another wife, and with her an-other half-dozen children, one of whom was Trixie, born in 1909, who married a Portuguese called Arnaldo Botelho. At the Diocesan Girls' School, Trixie made friends with other Eurasian family networks, such as the Churn and Leonard families. Trixie's daughter Pat Botelho re-calls that some Choa cousins looked down on the Portuguese Botelho line, which, considering the Choas were also products of one of the Lam sisters, seems unnecessary. At the same time, "My mother never wanted us to be in touch with the Singapore and Malacca family," says Pat Botelho.[17] Despite the snobbery, Portuguese identity would prove useful during World War Two as Portugal's neutrality allowed the family to stay at their mansion on Robinson Road largely un-scathed, where many Choa cousins soon arrived to share sanctuary.

———

Contrary to twentieth-century assumptions that being Eurasian was a blight on one's life or a fatal impediment to success, countless life stories show both the failures of obviously British or Chinese people and the successes of others. Part of the reason for this variation is that almost all the Chinese first making homes and businesses in Hong Kong were also migrants—from at least Canton and its surrounding districts, if not farther afield.

The London Missionary Society had its own particular view of all this: "The Chinese here, having left their native villages to engage in trade or obtain employment under a foreign government, are as a rule a more adventurous and independent class than those who stay at home. They are likely to lose some of that tenacious bigotry which is so hostile to the search for truth and to become a little more liberal-minded through their intercourse with foreigners. This gain is, I fear, more than counter-balanced by the sad example which a great number of nominal Christians from England and elsewhere set before their eyes. To this must be added the unwise action of our government. The three great vices of conduct of the Chinese—opium smoking, fornica-

tion, and gambling—are all carried out under the licence and regulation of [British] government."[18]

Yet in the same year as this lament at the lack of proper European
role models, China's economic migrants were showing they needed
no such thing. In 1868, they grouped themselves into Hong Kong's
first formal business organization, Nam Pak Hong, literally, the South
North Trading Group. Originally this was taken to mean the trade in
products from north and south of the Yangtze River in China; however, this soon came to mean the trade in products from Southeast
Asia—primarily forest and marine products such as birds' nests and
herbal products—to China.

Just up the hill from there was founded the Tung Wah Hospital
Group (in 1872), which would become the central focus of Hong
Kong Chinese philanthropy, medical care, and community organization. Under its auspices, the District Watch Committees would take
shape. These were another venue for neighborhood-minded Chinese
to take care of their property, and at the same time show leadership
qualities that would endear them to the British government. (As a sign
of its role as a breeding ground for the Chinese elite, its membership
by 1941 would include the five Chinese members of the Legislative
and Executive Councils—Sir Shouson Chow, Sir Robert Kotewall, Lo
Man-kam, Dr. Li Shu-fan, and William Ngartsee Thomas Tam—three
of whom were in fact Eurasian.) Just as the Tung Wah Hospital Group
was so much more than a hospital, the District Watch took on jobs far
beyond its initial remit, becoming census takers, helping to trace run-
away girls, acting as detectives for welfare societies, arbitrating civil
cases and family disputes, controlling queues at water shortage times,
and still making sure to catch pickpockets, thieves, and loiterers.

Under Tung Wah auspices, too, was formed the Po Leung Kuk,
to stop the kidnapping of women and young girls. Its well-meaning
patriarchs saw no problem with the purchase or "rescue" of impoverished, redundant daughters from poor families and the placing of
them in wealthier Chinese homes as "little sisters" or mui tsai, thus

unpaid household help. But it did actively work against the trafficking of grown women into prostitution. The Po Leung Kuk was forced into being after the vociferous Chief Justice John Smale suddenly discovered in 1879 that all those women working in the sex industry or as child domestic workers were in fact slaves. It had taken more than thirty years for the British administration to choose to notice the abuses built into a society reliant on the selling of children to ameliorate extreme poverty, and the many variants of the sale of women.[19]

His basic point was that in British laws, no one person can acquire any right over another person. There had been no doubt about this in 1867, when Tang San-ki appeared in the Magistrate's Court fighting to stay in Hong Kong rather than be returned to her "owner" in Canton; she won.[20] Smale had a head of steam, however, likening the underbelly of Hong Kong life to that of the Confederate States of America under slavery. The government then called on its China expert, the German missionary Ernst Eitel, to explain that the Chinese version of slavery was quite different, and anyway a necessary support to Chinese patriarchy, and so was morally impossible to condemn.

This was an unbridgeable chasm between notions of individual rights. Chinese patriarchy as an organizing principle meant that individual rights and ideas of personal liberty as understood in the West were completely alien. In Chinese society, anything from betrothal or marriage to concubinage, adoption, or servitude also involved the exchange of money. Thus the right of a patriarch to sell his children was unquestioned, and selling girls and indeed boys (for adoption) was totally normal and done without fuss.[21] The Po Leung Kuk did rescue and escort women home (to China) if desired, or house and hopefully find honest work or even husbands for them. It ensured the continuation of the mui tsai system, however. Not until 1923 was free will made the genuine reason to regulate prostitution. Not until 1970 was concubinage made illegal. But already back in 1921, a British government commission reported to the Colonial Office: "The [Po Leung Kuk] home is largely used as a recruiting ground for cheap supplementary wives by members of the Committee . . . The Committee have luncheon parties there on Sundays, and the marriageable girls attend on them."[22]

Organizations such as the Tung Wah, the District Watch, and the Po Leung Kuk were avenues of advancement for Chinese, and others who chose to identify as Chinese, to gain respectability and to support burgeoning wealth in Hong Kong's colonial society. They were venues in which people of mixed origins could prove their "Chineseness."

Belilios was exceptional in not feeling any need to pander to the expectations of others—not his immediate Jewish community, nor the wider Hong Kong crowd. He had an ego and certainly wanted his name on things and the honors that went with the philanthropy. But he wasn't trying to be anything he wasn't and felt no need to dissimilate. For his various offspring, such casual insouciance would prove harder to achieve.

6

CONSTRUCTING IDENTITIES

Mary Louise Emily Angell, who would call herself Maria Louisa Emily Angele after her education with the Canossian Sisters, was born in Hong Kong on November 10, 1880. She gained a competent education from the Catholics, based in the property that Leonardo d'Almada e Castro, our first Portuguese fresh off the boat four decades earlier, had donated to the Sisters. Tuition was in English, Portuguese, and Chinese; there were also Malay and Irish girls—and girls of mixed parentage.

When she came of age in 1902, Maria Louisa received a letter from Victor Hobart Deacon, Hong Kong's leading solicitor of the time. In this, he explained her situation to her: "Soon after my arrival in this Colony in the year 1880," wrote Deacon, "I made the acquaintance of one with whom ever afterwards till his departure from Hong Kong I was on terms of intimate friendship. I allude to the late Charles David Bottomley, your father, and one of my greatest friends. He was a Merchant in the firm of Messrs Douglas Lapraik and Co."[1]

The archives do not make clear if this is the first inkling this young woman had that she was not an orphan; she still didn't know who her mother was, but she was now a woman of substance with property and income to her name. Her father had left a trust, the proceeds of which were "for her sole and separate use and benefit and free from the control, debts or engagements of any husband of hers." Deacon explained how his firm had collected the rents from her properties until, in 1894, plague caused the government to condemn most of the congested Taipingshan area, pulling down her flats among others, to tackle the infection. Deacon itemized the value paid by the government for the property and how he had almost doubled this fund on her behalf. (His most profitable play had been the purchase of twenty shares in the Hongkong Ice Co., managed by Jardine's, while his purchase of China and Manila Steamship Company shares netted a loss.)

Showing that her education with the nuns had achieved some practical benefit, Maria Louisa pondered the options before her and asked first that all the shares be put in her personal name. She then agreed with Deacon that the best way forward was to invest the extra cash in property. She wrote to Deacon in January 1903 that "indeed you could not have done it in a better way." It remains unclear if she read further into her deceased father's papers; if so, she might have guessed the identity of Bottomley's mistress and thus possibly her own mother. Bottomley had arranged that if his daughter died before coming of age, the trust and income should all go to "Kan Shun Tsoi of Victoria aforesaid Single Woman."

―――――――

Maria Louisa's future was secured not just by money but by education. The schools of early Hong Kong would form a key institutional route for many such in-between people to get ahead.[2] Through these schools—vital engines of competition and class—a distinctly motley generation with few natural advantages learned how to rise to great heights of wealth and status. Maria Louisa's schooling, unusually, was paid for by her absent father. That of most mixed-race children was often thanks to their uneducated mothers: "In fact these women understand the value of education and prize it far more than respectable Chinese women do."[3] We have already seen how the various offspring of the Belilioses, the Lam sisters, and other clans almost all found their way through something called the Central School.

At first Hong Kong had just a handful of local Chinese-language schools for the offspring of fishermen. These were augmented by the arrival of missionaries such as Robert Morrison, who introduced the more Western-style Anglo-Chinese College, which he transferred from Malacca up to Hong Kong. It closed in 1856, followed a few years later by St. Andrew's School, which, despite its name, had offered secular, multiracial schooling for girls as well as boys since 1855. Financed from public subscriptions led by Andrew Shortrede, editor of the *China Mail*, St. Andrew's taught Portuguese, Chinese, Parsi, and other children.

No failure of the mixed-culture education idea caused the demise of St. Andrew's, but rather its success. The far larger Central School, founded in 1862, was specifically intended to be multicultural. (This became Victoria College in 1889, and Queen's College in 1894, the name it has to this day.) Half the school day was spent on Chinese language drills and the traditional Confucian curriculum; the other half was spent on more modern Western subjects and the English language. The goal was the creation of people to help develop Hong Kong, and perhaps eventually, China. These people would be intermediaries, or to put it more bluntly, a Westernized local elite. The vast majority of boys were Chinese or Eurasian, yet there were enough students of varied backgrounds to require classes to be taught in Urdu and Portuguese as well as English, Latin, and Chinese. (Schooling expanded under religious auspices, too. The Church of England's Anglo-Chinese School of 1848 reemerged as St. Paul's in 1851. St. Joseph's College was born in 1876, out of a Roman Catholic school first opened in 1860.)

But what about the girls? Governor Bowring lamented that "a large proportion of children of native mothers by foreigners of all classes is beginning to ripen into a dangerous element out of the dunghill of neglect . . ." Would they, as he feared, be doomed to careers in the sex trade as their mothers had been? Back in the 1860s, fueled not by feminism but by moral fervor, missionaries sought to avoid this fate. Alongside the Canossians, the Protestant Harriet Baxter set up an independent Chinese girls' boarding school, a school for European orphans and children of mixed race, and a boys' day school in the early 1860s. Separately, the Diocesan Native Female Training School (DNFTS) from 1863 was intended for middle-class Chinese "small-footed" girls (meaning their feet were bound, indicating higher status), in contrast to Miss Baxter's vernacular education for the poor. The DNFTS taught Chinese and English reading, writing, plain needlework, geography, and Bible history, plus "moral habits." It was all about creating women who would support future generations of Chinese men as wives and mothers. Thus, girls' education was limiting in its conception of traditional roles, but also revolutionary for the opportunities it opened up for young women. Quite how threatening this was can be seen when, in 1864, the DNFTS superintendent Mary Winefred Eaton was stoned by a Chinese mob who saw her teaching of English as akin to the degradation of Chinese girls.[4]

The problem, again, was the hypocrisy surrounding sex and its price. A first DNFTS graduate was the seemingly perfect Lydia Leung, who went on to marry a church assistant and spread the Word in Foochow. But she was an exception. Families more typically retrieved their now-English-speaking daughters from school to sell them for a higher price as a result; most of them became mistresses kept by Europeans. This quickly led to a wholesale shutting down of girls' education for a generation, justified on so-called moral grounds by men of the church and of business, including those whose sex lives had brought the girls into being.[5] The apparent "failure" of this early effort at educating girls ignores the reality that, for many young women, becoming the mistress of a rich white man may well have been a preferred option. The buyers of women were left unchastised; instead, girls were punished through the withholding of education. Young Chinese, Eurasian, and other boys were allowed to garner the benefits of a Westernized education; girls were not.

The DNFTS became the Diocesan Home and Orphanage, mainly for European and Eurasian children, including boys, in 1869. By 1878, it had become the Diocesan Boys' School, the next most important institution after the Central School for the creation of Hong Kong's non-British elite.

Maria Louisa was the product of a beneficent Western father and an otherwise engaged Chinese mother. Hong Kong's most famous, and fabulously rich, Eurasian, Ho Tung, was made the other way around.

The Ho Tung clan has been described in fictional or incomplete versions, although younger generations are now more boldly picking up the challenge of tracing the family's lineage, and one biography of Ho Tung has at last emerged.[6]

Arnold Wright, in his 1908 compendium, claimed that "no man amongst the Chinese has borne his part in local, commercial, and social life with more conspicuous ability, or with greater credit to himself and his nationality than Mr Ho Tung."[7] This is the standard tone of reporting on Ho Tung—lavish admiration, crediting him with incredible ability and (as if it were connected) moral uprightness. Perhaps it's true, as one family account has it, that he shared with his staff the bonus he earned on a big early deal as comprador. It is true, too, that he gave a large amount of money to a wide range of good causes. It might be less true, however, to portray him as a campaigner for racial equality, or one of the most "public-spirited men in the island," possessing great foresight and courage, as Wright put it. Certainly, it's true he became exceedingly rich.

His mother, known only by the surname Sze, was the Protected Woman of a Dutch Jewish businessman, Mozes Hartog Bosman, known in Hong Kong as Charles Henry Maurice Bosman.[8] Bosman arrived in 1859; three years later he formed Bosman and Co. with Cornelis Koopmanschap and Henry Edwards, who had been supplying the Californian goldfields with labor; Jardine's archives show Bosman trading in quicksilver (the liquid form of mercury), chartering ships, and exchanging currencies. Sze had a daughter before she met Bosman, named Ho Pak Ngai, who would marry Choy Sing Nam, a Jardine's comprador. Sze then had four sons with Bosman—Ho Tung, Ho Fook, Kai Mun, and Kai Gai (Walter)—interspersed with another son, Ho Kom Tong, who cannot have been conceived with Bosman, who was away at the time. Two more daughters were probably fathered by her post-Bosman companion.

Through Bosman's business partnership with Cornelis Koopmanschap, a window opens onto the trade that saved Hong Kong's faltering economy—the California gold rush. News reached Hong Kong in 1849, spurring a huge flow of voluntary migration through Hong Kong across the Pacific to California. With it went vital supplies of Chinese food, opium, and women in one direction, and wealth, offspring, and often the bones of the dead coming back the other way. As the historian Elizabeth Sinn has detailed, "Like other frontier towns, where the social structure was still fluid, the young colony allowed marginal people with energy and daring—those adept at seizing opportunities as well as creating them—to get ahead." She described a common culture of greed among Hong Kong's early British and Chinese people and notes: "Though never a level playing field, Hong Kong as a British colony provided enough flexibility and openness for people of different backgrounds to exert their entrepreneurial vitality and not be ashamed of growing rich. It was just waiting for the big break."[9]

That break was gold. The American gold rush made and destroyed many fortunes; the sums of money in play were simply enormous. It drew in numberless migrants from around the world, especially Chinese, many of whom ended up finding not pots of gold but lifetimes of backbreaking toil. One of those busy handling Chinese goods and ships in California was Koopmanschap. By 1861, his company with Bosman was responsible for chartering half of the ships plying the Pacific, but the risks taken started failing to pay by the second half of the 1860s and the two men had fallen out by 1869 when Bosman was declared bankrupt and left for England.[10] Thus did Robert Ho Tung become fatherless.

Ho Tung's life followed almost the identical path to that of his fellow Central School graduates, compradors, and Chinese committee members. But he surpassed them all. Ho Tung was the oldest son; perhaps, when Bosman disappeared, he took the desertion hardest. Or perhaps he felt in tune with this anonymous letter, signed "Eurasian," to the editor of the *Hongkong Telegraph* in 1895:

> *Our lot is anything but a happy one . . . Practically without home or blood relations in true sense of the term . . . deserted in nine cases out of ten by heartless fathers who seldom give us even a fair grammar school education; thrown at an early age on the slender resources of our fine mothers who . . . are not in a position to rear us up in the same manner as our heartless fathers were reared . . . and the wonder is, truly, that we are as well off and as educated as many of us find ourselves today. It certainly reflects the utmost credit on our unfortunate mothers and stimulates one and all of us to leave no stone unturned to render the existence of our mothers as happy as it is possible under the peculiar circumstances . . . I cannot shut my eyes to the fact that many of us have cause to curse the memory of our fathers and say in the bitterness and anguish of our souls, it were better we had ne'er been born . . . I freely admit some of our fathers act like men and have either settled a dowery on our mothers and have left us the means of keeping the family respectable but there are, unhappily, many shocking cases calling aloud for the closest inquiry by the authorities and for justice.[11]*

Whatever the reason, the young Ho Tung developed a determination early on to make very sure that he and his family would never be so vulnerable again. Family legend has it that in twenty years as comprador with Jardine's, he accumulated HK$2 million on the side, a huge amount in the year 1900. Throughout, he insisted on identifying as Chinese. Despite his half-European roots and blue eyes, he wore Chinese clothes, followed Chinese habits of family piety, claimed China as "the land of my fathers," and formed notions of Chinese patriotism.

Ho Tung's start at Jardine's came through the man his older sister had married. He had been smart at school, and done a clerical job for a couple of years (in his case with Chinese customs in Canton) before joining Jardine's in 1880. He was a loyal and clever servant to the British conglomerate and parlayed local knowledge, alongside skills in handling foreigners, to good effect and high profit. Perhaps his first marriage, to Margaret Mak, daughter of Jardine's partner Hector Coll Maclean and his Chinese love, helped Ho Tung up the promotion ladder. On his own account, however, he was clearly brilliant in business and made sure he was known for integrity and hard work. After twenty years with Jardine's, he used his chronic digestive complaint as reason to hand the compradorship to his (half) brother Ho Kom Tong, after which he actively managed a vast and international investment portfolio.

Naturally Ho Tung was chairman of the Tung Wah Hospital Group, the seat of Chinese community leadership and power. He funded its extension with a quarantine ward capable of handling victims of the plague, which struck in 1894 and 1896. He owned fine residences in Hong Kong such as Idlewild on Seymour Road, and in Macao. He became a director of a score of companies, including the Humphreys Estate and Finance Co., Hongkong Reclamation Co., Hongkong Hotel Co., and Hongkong Land. In 1890, he was made justice of the peace; he traveled extensively in Europe and the United States. He was a personal friend to governors, sat on committees, and donated funds to anything from the Diamond Jubilee or South African War funds to the Kwangsi Famine.

He became astonishingly rich. It is the scale of his wealth, coupled with his seemingly deliberate creation of a dynasty, that marks him out from his contemporaries. His wealth gained him entry to sanctums previously reserved for the white colonial elite. Ho Tung was always sensitive about his parentage and set out to create a set of interlocking clans in which strategic marriages and shared advancement would present an invulnerable, albeit mixed, face to the world.[12]

As his daughter Jean Gittins would record, "Father chose to be Chinese as he thought the Chinese would not disown him openly."[13] He took a Chinese surname, Ho, and persuaded his brothers to follow suit. He then took on the role of patriarch, making sure his brothers and half brother had jobs, jointly running shipping, sugar trading, and banking businesses; his brothers Ho Fook and Ho Kom Tong would succeed Ho Tung as Jardine's comprador and set up their own private businesses with his support. Ho Fook was on the Legislative Council; Ho Kom Tong was busier in Chinese affairs through the Po Leung Kuk.

When his wife, Margaret Mak, found she could not conceive, she adopted Ho Fook's son Ho Shai Wing, then arranged Ho Tung's second marriage to her cousin Clara, who proceeded to give him ten children. How consciously Ho Tung plotted which marriages of his brothers and those of his and their offspring is not known, but a series of unions did then take place that achieved the clear strategic benefit of tying Ho Tung's people into Hong Kong's leading Eurasian networks.

Ho Kom Tong had a son and daughter who each married a daughter and son of Choa Leep-chee. Another daughter, Elizabeth, married Tse Kan-po, scion of a Macao comprador's family; their son Andrew would marry a granddaughter of Ho Fook. Two sons of Ho Fook married two daughters of Sin Tak Fan, the legal mind who helped birth the venerable firm of Lo and Lo Solicitors. Meanwhile, Ho Tung's sister Ho Sui Ting married Wong Kam Fuk, highly successful comprador to the Hongkong and Kowloon Wharf and Godown Co.

Thus did his siblings tie Ho Tung into the docks of this port city, and into the commodities from sugar to opium that passed through them; they all had footholds in the burgeoning professional class of Eurasians in law and banking, too.

Then it was the turn of his children, where a series of intermarriages with the family of the prominent comprador Lo Cheung Shiu would shape a next generation of wealth. Ho Tung's eldest daughter, Victoria, married Lo's son Man Kam, or M.K.; another daughter, Grace, married M.K.'s younger brother Lo Man Ho. Meanwhile, a sister of M.K. married Ho Fook's son Ho Leung.

So began what the Dutch historian Geert Mak found when researching the multiple generations of wealth and power of the Jan Six family of Amsterdam: the oligarchization of power. In a family's search for certainties, family is put before everything else; "the family fortune and the family collection had to be carried through time as intact as possible, for the sake of future generations and out of respect for previous generations."[14]

Almost all these marriages were arranged and lasted long enough, tying the Ho Tung family into a multiplicity of other Eurasian family lines, including Rothwell, Fuhrmann, Kew, Bush, Zimmern, Kotewall, Hung, Gittins, Hall, Churn, Anderson, Overbeck, Baker, Fenton, Broadbridge, Ahlmann, Wong, Lowcock, Shea, Laing, Frith, and of course Tyson, Choa, and Belilios.[15] Unsurprisingly, this ever-expanding web of family ties resulted in a great deal of shared market intelligence and wealth generation—some of it overt through the passing on of comprador and other positions in the Hongkong and Shanghai Bank, Jardine's, E. D. Sassoon and Co., and other banks—some of it less overt but just as important, as in the family-backed establishment of the Tai Yau Bank.

Despite his constant profession of "Chineseness," Ho Tung played with multiple identities. He carried a British passport and nationality, he worked for British firms and sought British honors. He also lauded certain Western values such as a worldly as opposed to purely Confucian education. Would he have managed the same career of great riches and honors (from both British and Chinese states) if he had identified as Eurasian, or even tried to be British? His looks allowed him to carry off any of these identities. The famous photo of him and George Bernard Shaw, both in Chinese garb, highlights how very similar their faces were.

Ho Tung's embrace of so-called Chineseness was not without its problems. Ho Tung's youngest brother did just what Ho Tung did—denied half his heritage—but chose the other half, taking an entirely Western name, Walter Bosman, and identifying as English, securing a brilliant engineering career, working in England and South Africa, and having adventures such as traveling overland from Europe to Asia through Cairo, deserts, and more. Yet Ho Tung rejected him utterly, precisely for not being "Chinese." In another identity crisis, when Ho

Tung's son Eddie went radically off grid and secretly married an Irish Catholic maid from their house in Belgravia, Mordia O'Shea, Ho Tung firmly rejected both Mordia and, for many years, Eddie. It is fascinating that Ho Tung, the deeply filial son of a prostitute (he left money for her indigent relatives, and paid obeisance to her grave), found it impossible for his son to marry a maid. It was a racial rejection as well as class, as much "better" wives had been held in mind for Eddie back in Hong Kong, all Eurasian or Chinese.

Ho Tung's failure to ever achieve a government position is unusual and rarely commented upon. His former employers at Jardine's, being themselves on the highest councils of government, knew of this but in semiprivate correspondence clearly thought he had little chance of acquiring such a role.[16] Ho Tung's political career never really took off. He spent a lot of time and money in the 1920s on his quixotic idea to bring all of China's warlords together for a "roundtable discussion," as if that was going to bring unity to China. Perhaps this was a ruse by which Ho Tung secured mainland contacts to advance his business interests. If so, it was wasted energy.[17]

Ho Tung and his brothers were much more successful in celebrating the 1887 and 1897 Jubilees of Queen Victoria. He was also to have his cake and eat it when he became the only exception to the 1904 law that aimed to bar non-Britons from living on the Peak. Portuguese, Jews, Armenians, Parsis, Japanese, Chinese, and Eurasians all lived in Mid-Levels, halfway up the hill, not at the top. Racism was sometimes dressed up as a moral stricture against Chinese habits of multiple wives and families, but there was also fear of property price escalation, which would force Europeans back down the hill.[18]

Men such as Ho Tung wanted it all—the approval and influence in the British world, but also a world in which they could truly be on top. So they created a parallel world. They already had their Nam Pak Hong, Tung Wah Group, District Watch Committees, and Po Leung Kuk charity. Indeed, active roles in these were a clear route to British respect. Then, when failing to gain entry to British sanctums, they made their own.

Ho Tung was a founding member of the Chinese Club in 1899. Members would include compradors, lawyers, and the newly professional classes of Chinese and Eurasian worlds.[19] A Chinese Recreation Club would also be established, in 1912, mimicking the same strict entrance requirements and dress codes of its exclusively European forebear. It offered cricket and tennis, with food served on Western tableware.

It is arguable now, in hindsight, whether Ho Tung's choice to identify as Chinese was necessary to his giddy ascent into wealth. It may even have been an impediment if it aggravated the serious digestive problems that plagued him all his life, through the stress of constantly trying to be something that he was (half) not. Leaders of the Tung Wah were not averse to marrying their sons to his daughters; Jardine's was not averse to hiring Eurasians or Chinese. All the honors he garnered, from both the British and the Chinese, came as a result not of his nationality but of his great wealth. It would be silly to pretend that the Chinese presidents giving him mandarin buttons and feathers did not know he was not entirely Chinese but, to this day, even a scrap of Chinese blood is enough for the Chinese state to claim one as their own.

Perhaps race was quite irrelevant to Ho Tung's rise—other than in how it motivated him to ever-greater money accumulation. Once he had money, it really didn't matter what race he was or claimed. Perhaps the trick was to be Eurasian but claim to be something else. After all, Eurasians seemed more adept than either "pure" Chinese or British at straddling cultures, languages, and worlds of experience. They could employ the best of all worlds to their own advantage.[20]

When the Republican Revolution in China in 1911 overthrew the last Chinese imperial dynasty, the Qing, men such as Ho Tung appeared even more ambivalent, or perhaps simply more subtle at negotiating their multiple identities. Ho Tung was no overt backer of the revolution but he proudly had its leader, Sun Yat-sen, to lunch. Ho Tung's son Edward was the University of Hong Kong student union leader who hosted Dr. Sun's famous 1926 speech in which he traced the roots of his revolutionary ideals to his education in Hong

Kong. Another son, Ho Sai Lai (Robert), became a prominent general in the Chinese nationalist Kuomintang (KMT), later fleeing to Taiwan, which he represented as a diplomat abroad. At the same time, Ho Tung was still the Confucian-style patriarch at home.

Perhaps one of the ultimate ironies is that this great investor and financial brain, Chinese patriot and British knight, entirely failed to understand the threat of Chinese communism. He would lose all his properties and investments in China after 1949—despite warnings from his son Eddie.

———

Politics was a less comfortable arena for the first generations of these core Hong Kong families. Their training at the Central School had focused on language and commercial skills, taught largely by rote by British schoolmasters to row upon row of orderly young boys seated at long benches for hours on end. Some young men, however—those sent to mission schools—seemed to get larger ideas.

One such was Ho Amei, one of six sons of an Anglo-Chinese School alumnus and ardent Christian who had set up a printing business next to the London Missionary Society chapel in Hong Kong and accumulated a valuable clutch of real estate. Other sons entered diplomacy and journalism, but Ho Amei took a first group of Chinese miners to the New Zealand goldfields and embarked on building a fortune.[21] Marking a break with the more reticent generation of his father, Ho Amei wrote in English to the *Hong Kong Daily Press*, on October 16, 1878, of the gross discrimination against Chinese at a public meeting called ostensibly to consider new security measures (but also to discredit Governor Pope Hennessy's administration). Ho Amei's letter stressed that the Chinese present at the meeting were not shop coolies but members of the better classes, with large stakes in the welfare of the colony—and yet Europeans at the meeting had thrown out the Chinese and offered "a gross insult to our intelligence . . . I think we are equal in intelligence and common sense to those foreign gentlemen at the meeting."

The "British"—who were and are invariably called foreigners but saw themselves as the true settlers and builders of Hong Kong—found it hard to imagine that the "Chinese" had a genuine loyalty to Hong Kong. It was assumed the "Chinese," seen as an undifferentiated mass, were either in cahoots with or easily corrupted by the Chinese in China. Many leading British traders in the colony were also appalled by Governor Pope Hennessy's then-unusual ideas about racial equality.[22] Ho Amei soon led a public meeting at which Robert Ho Tung would also emerge, to protest against the Light and Pass regulations, which required all "Chinese" to carry a pass, and a lantern, if they were out on the streets after dark.[23] Gradually, Hong Kong's indigenes were daring to step out beyond a simply Chinese sphere.

Another local man soon to share that stage was Ho Kai, son of another successful mission product, Reverend Ho Fuk-tong, who had also managed to combine religious fervor with a knack for making money.[24] In 1862, Ho Kai's sister Ho Mui Ling married the man who would be the first Chinese barrister in Hong Kong and the first Chinese to enter the Legislative Council: Ng Choy.[25] Five years after Ng Choy qualified in London in 1877, Ho Kai followed suit. While in London, Ho Kai took the unusual step of marrying an Englishwoman, Alice Walkden. Her name and that of his sister were immortalized in one of his earliest philanthropies—the Alice Ho Mui Ling Nethersole Hospital.

Later knighted and a Freemason, Ho Kai was "Chinese at heart," yet promoted Western medicine and education among the Chinese, helping to found the Hong Kong College of Medicine and the University of Hong Kong. He also cared deeply about reform in China, writing regularly in both the English-language *China Mail* and the Chinese press, before offering secret support for the revolution in China.[26] His multiple identities made him a beneficiary and backer of colonialism at the same time as he expressed a Chinese personal and political identity. Attempts to describe him as either British imperialist or Chinese revolutionary have foundered, as the roles overlapped: it was his Western exposure that fueled his desire for change in China. Of course he wanted the best of both worlds, just as Ho Tung did.[27]

Ho Kai's notion of where the local elite should sit in Hong Kong was revealed when, in March 1891, he led a petition of prominent Chinese. They described themselves as "an important and influential section of the Chinese Community" in need of an English-language school for the children of the upper-class Chinese. They didn't like Queen's College and its precursor the Central School because of "the indiscriminate and intimate mingling of children from families of the most various social and moral standing." They wanted "a suitable English School for the education of the children—both boys and girls—of the upper classes of the Chinese resident in this Colony," and got St. Stephen's College in 1902.[28] This was Chinese elitism in action against Hong Kong's cosmopolitan core.

Ho Tung, perhaps because of his own mixed roots, had a different vision. He offered money for a new school open to everyone but—in what would become King George V School in Kowloon Tong—he initially got the exact opposite. Just like Ho Kai's Chinese friends, the British also wanted a school free of all that indiscriminate intermingling and so the government pressed Ho Tung to let his money be used for that. Only after a couple of generations did it become the school of choice for Ho Tung's original constituency, the English-speaking mixed races of Hong Kong.

Some British, like some Chinese, claimed that only a mess arose from the mixing of races: "European children in this Colony have been ruined irretrievably by intercourse with and contamination from the mixed races with whom they have had to associate in the elementary schools," opined the *China Mail* of January 30, 1901. But the British, too, were not an undifferentiated mass. The British headmaster of Queen's College, G. H. Bateson Wright, firmly refuted all this exclusionary talk, stating that the parents' desire for "British" schooling was based on entirely baseless prejudice. Perhaps, he said, the hidden problem was that the "Chinese, taking them all round, are more apt and willing pupils than European boys." He was busy teaching every-

one, including American, Hindu, Japanese, Parsi, and Portuguese, so
was qualified to speak of the difficulties inherent in trying to educate
"a large, mixed, cosmopolitan community, the bulk of which belongs
to the most conservative of nations on the face of the earth," by which
he meant the British and the Chinese.[29]

As leading Chinese and Eurasians—such as Ho Amei, Ho Kai, and
Ho Tung—aimed to join or even supplant the exclusive British elite, a
genuinely cosmopolitan education would be provided only by Jewish
generosity through the Ellis Kadoorie Chinese Schools Society. This
ran multiracial schools popular among Indian, Eurasian, and Chinese
students. The language of instruction was English, with Hindi, Urdu,
and Cantonese offered as second languages; admission was free. The
schools were "historically reserved for non-Chinese speaking locals"
and were taken over by the government just before World War One.[30]
Some Catholic schools also helped nurture more mixed communities. After St. Saviour's came St. Joseph's College, one of Hong Kong's
most advanced schools, which still educates a mixed-race elite of boys.
Bateson Wright vigorously praised the "generous unpaid zeal of the
Christian Brothers, who, in a truly catholic spirit, admit Jews, Turks,
Heretics, and Infidels to the benefit of their high-class education."[31]

Thus, by the late nineteenth century, be they cosmopolitan or elitist or often both, Hong Kong's Eurasians were central to the emergence of a distinct culture of educated professionals. They were not
just bilingual but genuinely bicultural. They did not all need to be intellectuals but were alert to new ideas, technologies, journalisms, and
diplomacies. From being merely in between they were now on their
way to becoming central.

7

HONG KONG PEOPLE MAKING HONG KONG

Egerton Laird sailed into Hong Kong on June 12, 1873, as a self-declared globetrotter. He loved the harbor at night, waking to the view of dwellings along the narrow shore beneath the rising Peak, and thinking of Genoa.

> *We reached Hong Kong this evening at half-past eleven; it was a splendid moonlight night . . . we had a lovely sail across the placid waters of the bay, occasionally passing a junk, with its picturesque latteen sail gliding slowly onward with the tide. When we arrived opposite Victoria Peak the numerous lights of the shipping, and those of the town, which extend far up the side of the mountains, shone out brightly, and added to the fairy-tale character of the scene . . . I had no idea that the harbour was of such size; it is eight miles long, and one to five in breadth . . . The bay is encircled by bold and rugged ranges of hills, varied by spots of scanty verdure . . . The harbour, in fact, resembles in some degree one of the Scotch Lakes . . . the buildings undoubtedly remind one of those of Genoa, or one of the Italian sea-ports. The streets are narrow, and there is not much level ground at the base of the Peak . . .*[1]

By the start of the twentieth century, his allusion to old-world glories would no longer hold. The buildings were still ornate and gracious in a style dubbed locally "Compradoric"—a play on the Doric columns appropriated in an oriental setting by the compradors, or middlemen. The harbor was, however, a new shape, with contours now shifted farther out to sea and a large new chunk of city brought into being.

Hong Kong was becoming a larger, busier, more vibrant port city—barely recognizable from when the royally named town of Victoria, with its one main thoroughfare called Queen's Road, marked the narrow sandy shore beneath a towering, precipitous, jungle-clad peak. Those vertiginous slopes plunged deep below the waterline, attracting seafarers for centuries before the British claimed it as their own. The city's first builders had created a line of imposing trading houses, the courthouse, the club, and eventually the cathedral—all symbols of an imperial outpost on the up. Now British power seemed unassailable around the world, and the Suez Canal had drastically shortened travel times for steam shipping between West and East; telegraph cables snaking along seabeds were joined by radio wave innovations and eventually the telephone, too. Where there were hinterlands, there would be new railways to traverse them. If commodities were discovered—from gold to tin to coal and more—new machines would appear to exploit them. This high time of industrial, technological, and commercial explosion, in places around the globe, offered a world of opportunity.

In Hong Kong, new land was created, as were electricity, land reclamation, telephone, mining, and property companies. Facilitated and funded by Hong Kong's Eurasians and others, neither the sky nor the ocean depths would be the limit. It was an exciting time to be alive and Hong Kong was in fine fettle. Celebrations of the royal jubilees (Golden in 1887 and Diamond in 1897) had established the colony as a shining light of the empire in the East. Japan's defeat of Russia in the far northeast in 1905 had established its status as an ally of Britain. The odd whiff of revolution in China was largely ignored—after all, there was always some sort of chaos going on over there. Few had any inkling that a couple of world wars and Communist revolution would follow; it was startling enough to some that opium divans were to be closed by 1910.

Perhaps the greeting of Governor Sir Henry May in 1912 by a Chinese shooting a gun at him (and missing) was a clue to the future. There would indeed be a lot more shooting going on and the natives—as colonialists called the Chinese then—were most certainly restless. A quarter of a million people in 1895 grew to around 450,000 by 1911, despite the bubonic plague in the 1890s. Within those numbers, "as the Chinese population doubled, the non-Chinese trebled."[2] The 1911 population (which excluded the British military establishment) comprised 5,185 Europeans and Americans, 2,558 Portuguese, 3,482 Indians and others, 55,157 Chinese on boats, and the rest Chinese on land.

The Portuguese were described, in a local newspaper's special issue, as different from the British in that they were "settled in the tropics, thoroughly acclimatized, and apparently not recruited to any extent from Europe. In one sense therefore they are indigenous; but in another alien, as they retain their allegiance to their own country, and their connection with the Portuguese Colony of Macao . . . The Indians, like the English, are an alien and unstable element. But a considerable number have married, sometimes to Chinese wives, and settled here quasi-permanently. Their sons do well at school and afterwards in business . . . The Others classified with Indians are Filipinos, Asiatic Jews, Japanese, Eurasians, etc., to whom no special reference need be made." As for the Chinese mass, it was described as being attracted to Hong Kong "in the main not as to a home but as miner to his camp, a place where gold is won to be enjoyed elsewhere. The average urban Chinese never regards Hongkong in any other light: he returns to his village every festival day of his life, and if he dies here, retires thither for burial."[3]

Who among this medley of settled Eurasians and other Asians, sojourning Europeans and itinerant Chinese, would grab this moment of opportunity? As Hong Kong neared the end of the nineteenth century, it would either get stuck at an early provincial phase, catering to a limited amount of traffic and appealing to few people as a home for the future, or some new ideas and people would have to come along to catapult it into greatness. Who in small, snobbish, and insalubrious Hong Kong would have the chutzpah to commit?

Luckily for Hong Kong, a teenager, Paul Chater, arrived and gathered around him his Parsi friends, dynamic Chinese, a bevy of Portuguese, a handful of Scotsmen, and a core of Baghdadi Jews. Together, they made Hong Kong ready for a new century.

Catchick Paul Chater, later Sir Paul, arrived in Hong Kong just two years after Belilios, a bright eighteen-year-old fresh off a ship from Calcutta. Born in 1846, orphaned aged seven, and one of thirteen children, he was sent in 1855 to La Martiniere School for Boys, where he became prefect and captain of the cricket team. His graduation to enter the India Survey Department meant he had a neat legible hand, a thorough knowledge of arithmetic, square and cubic roots, geometrical progression, fractions, and logarithmic calculations, algebra, trigonometry, and a knowledge of plan drawing; he also had "a healthy and vigorous constitution, and good eye-sight for observing." (These were among the requirements as laid out in the 1855 Manual of Surveying for Revenue in Bengal and the North-Western Provinces.)

Those skills, especially the plan drawing, would be seminal to his later success. So, too, were his roots in the Indian Armenian aristocracy. The East India Company's interlocutor, the eminent Armenian merchant Khojah Phanoos Kalandar, was the great-grandfather of Begoom, who married Agah Catchick Ariel; their granddaughter was Paul Chater's mother. A eulogy on the death of Agar Catchick Arrakiel[4] had noted his "liberal spirit," adding that he "possessed the regard of the whole Settlement, unsullied by the enmity of a single individual . . . [was] looked up to as a guide and director . . . He died lamented . . . and especially by the Greeks, to whom he rendered the most essential service . . ." This cosmopolitan influence spread from Julfa to India and through his descendants to all of Asia and beyond.

It also meant that when young Chater turned up in Hong Kong, he was not a waif of few prospects. He had lineage, from which some of his vaunted confidence no doubt derived. "He often put his money into enterprises that seemed risky, but his supreme confidence was usually vindicated in their success."[5] He also had networks. These were initially Armenian but quickly encompassed Indian, Parsi, Chinese, and Jewish, and eventually the heart of British power in Jardine's, The Hong Kong Club, and Government House.[6]

Chater sailed to Hong Kong on an Apcar ship (the *Lightning*). Arratoon Apcar (born at Julfa in 1779) had founded Apcar and Co. in 1819; the family intermarried with other Armenians such as the Seths and the Sarkies. Apcar began modestly, with a small fleet of vessels traveling from Calcutta to Rangoon, Penang, and Singapore. By the mid-1840s the *Arratoon Apcar* was plying the Calcutta-to-China circuit, calling in at Penang and Singapore nearly every second month, carrying, along with large numbers of people, wedding cakes and tombstones for the Armenian community flung far and wide.[7]

On arrival in Hong Kong, Chater stayed with his eldest sister, Anna.[8] He probably met the Parsi Hormusjee Nowrojee Mody at his first job in Hong Kong (in 1864), where they were both clerks with the Bank of Hindustan, China and Japan.[9] Mody's Parsi forebears had been trading with the Portuguese before the British arrived in northern India, and had come to Hong Kong thanks to his uncle by marriage Jehangirji Faramji Buxey. Within three years, Chater had quit his bank job and become a broker on his own account. Mesrovb Jacob Seth, the Armenian historian, believes this move was made with backing from the Sassoons: "One day he plucked up the courage to ask the head of Sassoons whether they would help him if he started as an Exchange broker. The reply being in the affirmative, Chater tendered his resignation . . . With the help of the Sassoons, he started auspiciously, and cleared $600 in the first month as a broker. Thenceforth Fortune smiled on him."[10] At the same time, circa 1868, Chater entered into a business partnership with Mody, cementing a friendship that would last their lifetimes and outweigh even his links with Jardine's.

Chater and Mody shared interests in mining and electricity, in horse racing and philanthropy, and in building. Mody could be changeable and quick in temperament, Chater was steady and outgoing. They both had large ideas and would make them real, not in India but in Hong Kong.

The Li family, meanwhile, came from closer by, having sided with the British during the Second Anglo-Sino, or "Arrow," War of 1856–60 after arriving in Hong Kong in 1854. The Li family's firm, Wo Hang, established in 1857 by the former artist Li Leong, was a typical Gold Mountain firm, meaning its focus was not on the traditional trade in marine and forest products between South and Southeast Asia with China, but on servicing—with labor, opium, and money transfers—areas opening up through the discovery of gold.[11] The family won the opium monopoly in 1862–63 and 1873–79 in Hong Kong, and so got a lock on the market for high-quality prepared opium in North America and Australia; they also traded extensively in rice. In between, on Li Leong's death in 1864, his cousin Li Sing took charge. He pioneered the first Chinese-owned insurance companies and in 1882 set up the Wa Hop Telegraph Company to lay a cable from Canton to Hong Kong. Li Sing was Hong Kong's twelfth-largest taxpayer in the 1870s and a leading man of the colony.[12] His youngest son, Li Po Chun, founded a primary school in his father's name and greatly expanded the family real estate business.[13]

Chater had already done business with the On Tai Insurance Company, set up by Li Sing and Poon Pong. These men had all known one another other since the 1860s. A triangular pattern emerged—where the Armenian Chater, the Parsi Mody, and the Chinese Li Sing would change the shape of Hong Kong. Out of this nexus came the development of the stock exchange, the Jockey Club, the central business district, the docks of Kowloon, mining in the New Territories, the birth of the Star Ferry, the University of Hong Kong, and the establishment of most of the leading companies: the Hongkong and Kowloon Wharf and Godown Co., the Hongkong Land Investment and Agency Co., the Dairy Farm Co., Hongkong Electric, Hongkong Telephone, and much more.

Only in the 1880s did the Scots of Jardine Matheson and Co. wake up to their importance, and a next vital relationship was forged by Chater with John Bell-Irving, the oft-overlooked taipan of Jardine's. Bell-Irving was succeeded by his cousin J. J. Keswick in late 1889, so that much of the credit for developments such as the founding of the Land Company went to Keswick when in fact they had grown out of the far deeper tie between Chater and Bell-Irving. It was said: "Where Chater goes today, Jardines goes tomorrow."[14]

Chater was a personable, kindly, charming man and made friends easily with all kinds of people. As Austin Coates put it, "With his high broad forehead and wide-spaced, friendly eyes, he radiated kindness. Everything he did in his long life was for the public benefit as well as his own . . . Chater never did anything drastic. He simply contrived to make things happen."[15] A rare hint of discord is raised by a letter to the editor of the *China Mail* (January 14, 1893) that strongly criticized the economic perils of the "gambling mania" induced by the listing of the Hongkong Land and Wharf companies, in both of which Chater played a leading role. A letter to the *Hongkong Daily Press* lamented that "the community has seen a considerable portion of its accumulated savings swept away and is now appreciably poorer than it was a few years ago."[16]

Having set up the Mr. Paul racing stable in 1872 when Mody set up his Mr. Buxey stable, Chater would later become chairman of the Jockey Club. Like his forebears of Bengal, he was a lavish enthusiast for royalty and for British rule.[17]

From the first land sales of 1841, marine lots—those fronting the harbor—were most in demand. Traders on the foreshore could have the latest news and commodities off ships in the harbor, brought by small boats to their door; they usually built their own jetty from their office into the sea, and hoped for the best when typhoons thundered in. A decade later, in 1851, a fire in the Lower Bazaar destroyed more than four hundred Chinese houses. This forced the first reclamation with rubble from the ruins used to fill in the adjoining creek, creating a new road called Bonham Strand.

As more people arrived in Hong Kong, a debtors' jail and police station were built and thoughts turned to drainage and roads. Governor John Bowring managed the next reclamation in an area called Happy Valley. But when he tried to persuade holders of those cherished marine lots to make room for a road, he met entrenched resistance. He had proposed that lot holders not only lose the expansions they had claimed, and their wharves, but also pay for construction of a seawall and then pay rent on any new land created in their lots. The merchants bucked. A wall along the Praya was built in bits and pieces only to be regularly destroyed by typhoons throughout the 1860s.

Chater began experimenting in land creation in the 1870s by extending his lots in western Hong Kong, in an area called Kennedy Town. This involved leveling a cliff, hurling it into the sea, and providing a public road at his own expense. Kennedy Town was developed in the 1870s largely by Chater, Li Sing, and Meyer Sassoon. They were entering a fraught field of endeavor and making it their own.

Now Chater's early training in surveying techniques would prove useful, alongside his ability to think big. After his Kennedy Town success, Chater hired a small sampan for nights in a row, so that he could let down a plumb line over the side and measure the depth of the harbor along its central shore. He was collecting data, privately, as he worked out how to reshape the city.

This was the genesis of the Praya Reclamation Scheme, which Chater finalized by 1887. He was the pivotal figure—with his surveying skills, investor's courage, knowledge of how to persuade the government to support the plan (from his membership of the government's top advisory councils)—and, unlike Governor Bowring before him, his design of a finance scheme to keep the merchants (of which he was one) on his side. The innovation of Chater was, in effect, to give the rights to reclaimed land to the nearest marine lot holder. Successive meetings with lot holders were chaired and charmed by Chater; Bell-Irving or Li Sing would then propose motions with the other seconding it, thereby securing approval from all.

Chater even went to London and met the top colonial officials to persuade them of his scheme's indispensable worth. Through his Freemasonry network, he got the Duke of Connaught to lay the foundation stone in 1890. Land was quarried farther afield and brought to be dumped into the sea; as it settled and strengthened, Chater's Hongkong Land Co. then developed the central sites. He persuaded the prestigious Hong Kong Club, which he now chaired, to place its imposing clubhouse across the new square, on which he arranged to place statues of royalty.

By 1902, work on the Praya Reclamation had already been under way for thirteen years, and Chater's Land Investment Co. had acquired a large stretch of the Wan Chai waterfront with another reclamation plan in mind. (Objections to this Praya East scheme were not surmounted until 1923 and works not completed until the 1930s.) But even Chater could not move the navy from its Admiralty, so the dream of a continuous road from the western to the eastern end of the island remained just that.

While the vision was Chater's, the building of Hong Kong's new central business district could not have succeeded without the support of his friends. It so happened that Li Sing and his brothers and sons had stakes in almost a dozen key marine lots, just next to those owned by the Sassoons. All were good friends in business, and were joined, through Chater, by Jardine's man Bell-Irving. These sites became—by 1905—the heart of central Hong Kong, where Prince's Building, the Mandarin Oriental Hotel, Alexandra House, and Chater House now stand. In today's language, the reclamation scheme begun in 1889 created most of the land from the tram line to the shore, where some of the most expensive real estate in the world is found.

Chater's own financial interest came through his acquisition of the Sassoons' key central marine lots. It's never been spelled out by chroniclers of the Sassoon empires quite why the family quit Hong Kong around 1902. Several of David Sassoon's sons who had moved outside Bombay were now moving to England and joining the British aristocracy, through friendships with royalty, lavish hospitality, support of horse racing and politics. Perhaps opium was no longer a good look? The Society for the Suppression of the Opium Trade had been formed in 1874; in 1895, the British government stated it planned to control the trade, at some unspecified point in the future; China's imperial leaders, in decline, claimed in 1906 that the trade would be abolished in ten years but they were themselves abolished in just five. By 1909, the Hong Kong government forbade the export of opium to any country that banned its import, and by 1913, consumption in Hong Kong was beginning to decline.

Or was the Sassoon departure because there were no male heirs left and David Sassoon's widow, running the business in Bombay, was not taken seriously enough to keep it going? One wing of the eastern enterprise had already moved to Shanghai—that of E. D. Sassoon with his trading company and later bank, which would fall to Sir Victor Sassoon, and then to war and communism. The Sassoon retreat from Hong Kong was eased, anyway, because close ally Chater was ready to lighten their load. Without his Chinese business partners, men like Belilios could not have achieved the success he did. Without the Parsi Jamsetjee Jeejeebhoy of Bombay, young William Jardine could never have become the lord of all he surveyed on the China coast. Without his Jewish and Parsi friends, the Armenian Chater could not have rebuilt Hong Kong's land- and seascapes, its clubs and churches, its gardens and trading halls.

Chater then secured control of Kowloon's waterfront along what is now called Canton Road.

It will be recalled that when "Hong Kong" was ceded to the British Crown back in 1842 this referred simply to the island of Hong Kong. In 1860, the tip of the peninsula across the harbor, a small part of Kowloon up to Boundary Street, was also ceded in perpetuity. Not until 1898 would the far larger swath of land including the mountain range, Lion Rock, and far beyond become part of Hong Kong. Called the New Territories, this was not ceded forever, but merely leased for ninety-nine years—prompting the handover almost a century later in 1997.

When first ceded after a short battle that killed hundreds of villagers, Kowloon was rugged, marked with many small hills, ravines, marshes, and rice fields, and ringed with sandy beaches. The government calculated the population was 5,105 persons, in perhaps ten villages. Most of the inhabitants were Hakka, with Cantonese more dominant as one moved north. The building of Victoria across the water had prompted the growth of a granite-extraction industry—in 1871, there were eighty-one stone quarries in Kowloon, with quarrying a traditionally Hakka occupation. The Taiping Rebellion spurred entire families to move to Kowloon from China, including one alleged Taiping general who rejoiced in the nickname "Seven Legged Heavenly Flying Tiger."[18] Mong Kok and Ho Man Tin were old Hakka villages, each with two hundred to three hundred inhabitants; there was both intermarriage and fighting between Hakka and Punti Cantonese. If there was not enough room to grow rice, then pig farming and vegetable growing were the norm. No colonial administrators or magistrates were yet based there in the nineteenth century; police appeared only in emergencies.

Ownership of vital Kowloon marine lots was initially split among the Sassoons, Mody, and Chater, but by September 1887 they were assigned by Chater to the Hongkong and Kowloon Wharf and Godown Co., his first venture with Jardine's. Reclamation works began soon after 1860; they were expanded massively when more land was needed for the Kowloon Canton Railway, which would open in 1910.

Chater was a first buyer of land in Kowloon, building a "bungalow" (in fact a huge mansion), then granting the land and money needed to build St. Andrew's Church. (He had already, in 1899, secured the Conduit Road site on Hong Kong Island on which he

would build his famed Marble Hall.) He would host everybody from
the king of Hawaii at his Kowloon bungalow to Lord Kitchener at
Marble Hall.[19] He married only in 1910, when he was sixty-four
years old and his Swedish bride, Maria Christine Pearson, was thirty-
one. That prompted great gossip about Chater's possible affinities
with men rather than women—or was he simply homosocial? There
was also gossip about Maria Christine, who may or may not have
been dropped by a fiancé or been working in a brothel, or was simply
good company for a man who now had just about everything.

Like Chater, his good friend Mody "had special faith in the development of Kowloon at a time when it was almost an empty area,
and invested heavily in real estate there,"[20] recalled in the naming of
Mody Road.

———

Alongside supporting Chater in all his endeavors, Mody's biggest contribution was his funding of the University of Hong Kong. Since the
1880s, Hong Kong had become home not only to traders of all kinds,
but also to what might be called intellectuals. Men such as Patrick
Manson and James Cantlie were socially engaged professional men.
Dr. Philip Ayres, a Hong Kong Club member and friend of Chater, was
exceptional for his regular visits to the plague warrens of Taipingshan.
Along with Chater's nephew Dr. Gregory Jordan, and Ho Kai freshly
returned from his London studies, these men helped found the Hong
Kong College of Medicine in 1887. New life was coming to drama,
choral, literary, sketching, and debating societies, including the Odd
Volumes Society, formed in 1893 to develop "a community of men
striving for the truth." Little wonder that the idea of a university took
off in 1908, with the arrival of Frederick Lugard as the new governor.
He had a brutalist reputation from his Nigeria days to live down, and
an erudite wife, the foreign correspondent Flora Shaw, who is credited
with personally persuading Mody to make his pivotal contribution
that brought the university into being.

Even as clouds gathered on the century's horizon, mixed and multihued Hong Kong produced a unique institution. The list of early donors to the university is a map of the burgeoning elite. Here are the Chinese men trading in the Nam Pak Hong, that association centered around Bonham Strand which specialized in the forest and marine products of Southeast Asia and their markets in China. Naturally, Paul Chater was the university's honorary treasurer, and there was Robert Ho Tung, fretting as usual about whether his name would be prominent enough and his gifts adequately honored. Hardworking men, active in the Tung Wah Hospital and the Po Leung Kuk charities, such as Lau Chu Pak and Ng Li Hing, Sin Tak Fan, Chan Kai Ming, and Tso Seen-wan, not only gave money but time to attend HKU Council meetings and fund scholarships. The Anatomical Laboratory was backed entirely by the Chinese guilds, not only the trading associations but guilds for the trade in opium, gold leaf, salt fish, pigs, hemp, cattle, and rice, and even the pawnbrokers guild.

Alongside the wealthy Chinese and Eurasians stood the Portuguese, Jews, and key figures from Southeast Asia. These included Tseng Shek Chau of Saigon, Eu Tong Sen of the Straits Settlements, and Loke Yew and Cheung Pat Sze of Penang. Another major chunk of money came from the viceroy of Canton—invited to Chater's Marble Hall to meet Mody and so be persuaded to contribute. The only British trading family to make significant pledges was John Swire and Co., the recently arrived Liverpudlian firm that was reshaping the way East Asian shipping was practiced. The university's historian, Peter Cunich, believes that British merchant opposition to the project stemmed mainly from the (indeed justified) fear of creating a class of educated, brighter, and cheaper Chinese who would supplant many Europeans at work.[21] Eventually, donations came from the Hongkong and Shanghai Bank and Jardine's, but the next-biggest corporate donors were the (Jewish) Sassoons and (the Armenian and Parsi) Chater and Mody Co. Mody eventually paid about $365,000; thanks to him the university, established on March 30, 1911, was opened on March 11, 1912.[22]

Thereupon the university began to build a small, tightly knit campus

life; all students lived on campus unless exempted for religious obser-
vances such as Ramadan. The student body included Portuguese names
as well as Parsi, Muslim, and Eurasian. The largest group of non–Hong
Kong students came from Malaya, but then as now, openness on race
far pre-dated equality of gender: no women were admitted for the first
decade. The first woman student in 1921, Rachel Irving, happened to
be the daughter of the director of education; she was joined by Irene Ho
Tung, daughter of the biggest Eurasian donor.

The university struggled constantly with finances but was saved by
Sir Robert Ho Tung and a stunning interest-free loan worth $500,000
from Penang's tin magnate, Loke Yew. Donors also included characters such as H. M. H. Nemazee, a dealer in Persian opium; university records show that discussion of the origins of his wealth was not
allowed to get in the way of the donation.[23] Chinese donors were
especially keen on an arts faculty, pressing to go beyond medicine
and engineering into ethics, international and constitutional law, and
moral philosophy.[24] Fung Ping-fan said his father, Fung Ping-shan,
another key donor, saw the university as a "lighthouse of the Far East"
and wanted it to be "the centre of learning in South China."[25]

Graduates became part of a bilingual, bicultural elite in China,
Hong Kong, and Southeast Asia. After all, this frontier town was made
by migrants, and virtually everyone had roots elsewhere.[26] It was also,
thanks to the quirk of British rule, a haven from cross-border political
struggles. This was a free-fire zone through which could flow books,
movements, and ideas. Not until the 1920s did the British rulers of
Hong Kong try to fence off the colony from dangerous thoughts,
choosing the Chinese conservatism of an old elite over its revolutionary spawn.

With Chater, Mody indulged in donating statues of royalty, collecting art, racing horses, and other lavish hobbies of the coming
man of the early twentieth century. When he popped back to Bombay in 1907 for his daughter's wedding, he entertained the entire
Parsi elite. The party was lit with myriad multicolored electric lamps
in trees, which, given there was no other electricity in Bombay at the

time, was all achieved with human-propelled dynamos. The bride's sari was studded with pearls, her shoes with diamonds. Her father gave her diamond and emerald jewels once owned by Queen Marie Antoinette.

Both Chater and Mody gave regularly to good causes. Mody gave largely to the Seamen's Institute in gratitude for the sailors' role in making Hong Kong such a base for commerce and prosperity. A particular bond with the Lugards inspired his eight "Lugard Scholarships" to Hong Kong schools. He donated the fountain at the Parsi Cemetery thanks to an idea from Lady Mody; its six ornamental iron benches and a huge entrance door were all made in England and shipped out. He also donated sixteen hundred feet of pipe to supply regular water to the marble fountain and the cemetery. Like Chater, Mody was also a Freemason and keen on cricket; he built the Cricket Pavilion for the Kowloon Cricket Club in 1908. He was president of the Hong Kong Canton and Macao Zoroastrian Association for twenty-five years from 1886.

Sadly, Mody died on June 16, 1911, just before the university opened formally; his funeral was attended by the governor; stock exchange, banks, and government offices were closed for the day. His descendants remain in Hong Kong to this day.

When the home contents of Mody were auctioned after his death in 1912, more clues to this mixed-up Hong Kong style can be found. Items ranged from marble-inlaid Chinese blackwood to Japanese weapons and watercolors, to Austrian vases and Moroccan armchairs. A full British billiards room, Axminster carpets, and Queen Victoria were there, but so was Buddha in brass. The auction inventory filled out a 39-page booklet and included such gems as a lavatory with a Viennese seat and spittoon, thousand-piece sets of silver cutlery, Waterford crystal, and Wedgwood crockery. The wine cellar was lavish, and the library held twenty volumes of "famous literature" next to three volumes of Parsi literature, all standing in oak bookcases, surrounded by statuettes and fireplaces with full sets of fender tools. Perhaps most important to Mody, however, were the Silver Cups won

by his horse-racing stable, the mere listing of which covered half a
dozen pages.[27]

————

Above all stood Chater—a man of many parts, with multiple layers of
identity. He traveled frequently, from New York to Shanghai, San Francisco to Port Said, to Honolulu, Sydney, California, Washington, DC,
Vancouver, and Paris. He was British and Indian and Armenian, but
more than anything, a man of Hong Kong.

In 1899, he had sponsored the journey to Hong Kong of six young
Armenians and arranged jobs for them at the post office while setting
them up to find their own ways to fortune. One of them, Mackertich
Cyril Owen, married Phyllis Seth, daughter of Court Registrar Ara-
thoon Seth. The most original of Chater's young imports was Nazareth Malcolm Manuk, who left the post office for the Chartered Bank
of India and then the Dairy Farm, a company that Paul Chater had
helped to start, where Manuk became secretary and director. An excellent marksman in the Hong Kong Volunteers, Manuk was also a
devotee of Theosophy, founding the Hong Kong branch of this faith,
which, he explained, was based on the "express idea of drawing together men and women of every race and every creed." By the 1920s,
he was running the office of the Theosophical Society from a room
in the Hong Kong Club building (where he was also a member); he
reportedly was also a fan of nudism.

Yet Chater was still sometimes sniffed at by people who didn't
know any better, such as the callow young Charles Hardinge Drage,
aide-de-camp to Governor Sir Reginald Stubbs (and future spy). His
diary entry for December 1, 1923: "Woke up feeling rather the worse
for wear and with a busy day ahead of me. With H.E. to lunch with
Sir Paul Chater, a coloured magnate and the multi-millionaire of
Hong Kong. He has a lovely house full of wonderful china, and gave
us an excellent meal with superlative wine . . . His collection of china
is well-known and, though much of it is said to be faked, the pieces

are really beautiful, but the furnishing of the rest of the house is in atrocious taste."[28]

As well as "coloured magnate," Chater was also "British," according to the Member of Parliament T. P. O'Connor, who met Chater at Vichy in 1924. He wrote in the *Sunday Times*:

> *Sir Paul Chater is perhaps the least known and at the same time one of the most powerful and, what is more important, one of the most beneficent figures in the Empire . . . He is at the head of everything there; no enterprise gets on without asking his assistance. Shipping, banking, international companies with their heads in London or in Paris he is in them all. And he has accumulated one of the largest fortunes in the Empire. He is the father of everything in Hong Kong, by long residence and service. He is the oldest British settler, he is the oldest member of the Executive Council. From his immense wealth he has given most generously to every cause.*[29]

Whatever identity he chose or was given, it was Chater who brought Hong Kong into modern times. Governor Sir Cecil Clementi said on May 27, 1926, the day after Chater's death:

> *It is difficult for me to speak without emotion of the grievous loss sustained by this colony through his death. When, as a young cadet, I first landed in Hong Kong, I stepped ashore upon ground which under a most successful scheme, devised by Sir Paul, had been newly reclaimed from the sea . . . [his] sage advice . . . wonderful foresight . . . breadth of vision . . . remarkable financial skill . . . unbounded enthusiasm . . . above all he has bequeathed to Hong Kong development schemes of great magnitude . . . which have changed the face of the land, which have vastly increased the prosperity of the colony, and which will inure to the comfort and contentment of present and future generations of its inhabitants. While Hong Kong and Kowloon endure, so long will his work remain as his imperishable memorial.*

8

A COSMOPOLITAN PLACE

It was in a Hongkong school that the following conversation took place.
Is your father Eurasian? No, sir. Is he a Parsee? No. A Jew? No.
Then what is he? A broker, sir.[1]

Similar questions could be asked of Hong Kong itself. Just what was its personality as it entered the twentieth century? A British colony, attached geographically to China and umbilically through trade to the world—was it a cosmopolitan mosaic bustling with possibilities or a tetchy, arrogant bore constipated by discrimination and division along lines of race, gender, and class?

Writing in 1909, John Stuart Thomson decided that Hong Kong worked because of a willingness to adapt and adopt. He enjoyed the "kaleidoscope of dress and a College of Languages. Here are good Scotch names like Mathieson; Japanese like Mitsui; German like Melchers; Portuguese like De Mello; Netherlands like Stoomvaart Maatschappij; Parsees like Cawasjee Moosa; and Indian like Matab . . . Here are Koreans with tiny black bamboo-fiber hats . . . An Episcopal bishop passes in regalia which conceded something to the East, while he remains reminiscent also of the Occident; a sun-topy crowning a black morning coat, knickerbockers, silk stockings and pumps. His Catholic confrère . . . wears the familiar long black gown of his ilk and a cross, but notice his sun-helmet and that his beads are of native jade."

Thomson recorded "the powdered and carmined wives of a native banker of Bonham Strand . . . a silk merchant once of Calcutta—

and his wife, who wears a wonderful one-piece silk sari . . . Following, is an Indian officer of the Baluchis . . . a Mahratta from Bombay." Here, too, "Chang, the coolie, with his string of goats, which he milks at the doors of his customers . . . Japanese courtezans from Ship Street, dressed in their blue-figured kasuri cloth, shuffle by on wooden shoes . . . A Hebrew . . . drifts by on the wind behind the only cloud of whiskers east of Calcutta . . . A chimney-hatted Parsee, looking very confidential in black, and sporting a pink ruby of faultless water."[2]

Concepts of cosmopolitanism naturally change over time. The hosting of former American president U. S. Grant, hero of the Civil War, to a state dinner at Government House in 1879 was taken as a sign of how cosmopolitan Hong Kong was becoming. There were St. Patrick's Day festivals that year, and the hosting of Prince Thomas of Savoy, the Duke of Genoa, and Prince Heinrich of Prussia. By 1885, the *China Mail* was enthusing that the annual Belilios Scholarships for St. Joseph's College went to two Portuguese—J. P. Braga and L. G. Barretto—explaining this was because Belilios had been nurtured in "that spirit of liberty and fair play which disregarded the distinctions of creed and nationality."[3] By 1902, the *Hongkong Telegraph* noted the Zoroastrian New Year: "Hongkong is certainly a very cosmopolitan city, enjoying the benefit of being the home of useful men with different customs and religions . . . Each is of service to the other, all exchanging knowledge . . . Though . . . most of us are not holding any celebration today, the Parsees have their new year's day to keep up, and we hope they will enjoy many returns of it."[4]

The historian Philip Mansel described the Levant's port cities as both cosmopolitan—in governance, associations, individuals of mixed antecedents, skills, and interests—and communal, in that distinct communities also pursued their own interests.[5] So, too, with the port city of Hong Kong.

Hong Kong's cemetery at Happy Valley hosted a multitude of faiths, and Parsis, Eurasians, and Muslims could choose their own cemeteries or this "colonial" resting place at will. All races mixed at the most popular recreational ground, the horse-racing track. The

Freemasons admitted anyone of any hue happy to pledge faith in one God: alongside Chater and Jordan were Polycarpo Andreas da Costa, Chan Tai Kwong, Sir Kai Ho Kai, and Wei Yuk. Chinese members were frowned upon in an 1899 statement by Brother O'Driscoll Gourdin: "Grand Lodge is . . . strongly opposed to the admission of Chinese into Freemasonry, and though we have the misfortune to have one or two of such nationality attached to one of our lodges, their number is not likely to increase."[6] He was soon proved wrong.

Rhoads Murphey said cosmopolitanism is integral to port cities, seeing it as not necessarily sophisticated, but hybrid. "A port city is open to the world . . . In it races, cultures, and ideas as well as goods from a variety of places jostle, mix, and enrich each other and the life of the city." Ports flourished by being as open to as many peoples and products as possible; naturally, they became "centres of ferment, social mobility, innovation, and stimulus, open doors on the world and major crossroads of its traffic in ideas and people as well as in goods." Most people here lived mixed-up or in-between lives, living in homes, playing sports, and going to schools that were at least part Western in style and content. Most were not only "arrivistes but parvenus, people whose origins were humble or obscure but who made their way rapidly upward in the dynamic and fluid situation of the port cities where change was concentrated."[7]

A measure of just how cosmopolitan Hong Kong had become can be found in the story of one women's hostel, opened to give single "white" European women visiting the colony somewhere respectable to stay. Surely such an obscure project had no hope of funding? Yet The Helena May Institute for Women and Children was born thanks to deep Jewish and Eurasian pockets. The same names keep recurring across each fresh idea, highlighting how the creation of Hong Kong society was due as much to the apparent outsiders as it was to the Chinese who had arrived from across a closer border. A cynic might say these newly wealthy men were simply buying a place in society, seeking favor with the colonial power structure, or indulging in other similarly nouveau riche self-indulgences. Who can say? The record of contribution shows that both motives and beneficiaries were diverse.

Take Ellis Kadoorie. He came from Baghdad via Bombay to Hong Kong and, among a vast range of philanthropies, made the keystone donation to The Helena May, a club where women find accommodation and inspiration through its excellent library, events, and facilities to this day. Its birth in 1916 was spurred by Helena, the wife of Governor May, and by the fact that "respectable" European women then arriving in the colony could not stay at hotels and expect to keep their reputation (and other things) intact. The future Sir Ellis was a member of the University Court since 1914, a role in which he was followed by his nephew Lord Lawrence and Lawrence's son Sir Michael Kadoorie. Such a range of giving suggests more than mere currying of favor. This looks like a genuinely inclusive kind of mind.

Ellis Kadoorie was the youngest of three brothers to arrive in Hong Kong in the 1880s, offspring of the philanthropist patriarch Silas Kadoorie of Baghdad with his Sassoon-related wife, Reemah Yacoob Elaazar Yacob. His eldest brother, Moshi, was followed by Eleazar Silas "Elly" Kadoorie, who had joined E. D. Sassoon and Co. in Bombay and moved with his job to Hong Kong. Both Elly and Ellis used Kelly as a surname for several years before reverting to Kadoorie. The middle brother, Elly, became best known, not least because his sons Lawrence and Horace followed in the footsteps of his philanthropic capitalism. Elly got ahead by getting sacked—when working for E. D. Sassoon and Co. up the China coast in Ningpo he broke open the stores of disinfectant to combat plague. When reprimanded, he left, annoyed. Moshi gave him $500 to make his own way and the result was the Benjamin, Kelly and Potts brokerage.

This firm rapidly became central in the market, combining the substantial talents of Kadoorie, Sassoon Benjamin, and the British character George Potts. From this vantage point, Elly Kelly took a stake in the Hongkong Hotel—founded by Chater, Ho Tung, and the Parsi Dadabhoy Rustomjee—which was proud to offer "hydraulic ascending rooms," otherwise known as elevators. Meanwhile, China Light and Power Co., founded in 1901, was growing so fast it needed a second power station in Kowloon and more funding—provided again by Ho Tung and the Kadoories. From this came the Kadoorie family's generations of wealth production: control of China Light and Power Co. and the Hongkong and Shanghai Hotels group. When its Peninsula Hotel opened in 1928 in Kowloon it was seen as too far away across the harbor, until Sir Robert and Lady Margaret Ho Tung celebrated their golden wedding anniversary there in 1931, making it achingly cool.

Elly Kadoorie moved to Shanghai in 1911, encouraged by the Hongkong Bank to help save a rash of flailing rubber companies. A neighbor of Marble Hall, the huge, imposing Kadoorie residence built there in 1924, recalled that despite all the money, Elly Kadoorie was a humble man. "He would just come out and just put his hand on our head and talk to us quietly and gently, and he never pushed himself to the forefront, he was always taking a back-seat, and people would come and kiss his hand, but that was a mark of respect."[8] The Jardine's archive makes clear that the Kadoories were formidable competitors; the correspondents could not help but admire Kadoorie success and almost feared the arrival of a Kadoorie on any of their company boards for the investigative determination that would follow.[9]

Meanwhile, in 1897, Elly married Laura Mocatta, an adventurous traveler, painter, and diarist from a prestigious family of Portugal that had fled the Inquisition to Amsterdam in the late fifteenth century and become bullion dealers for the Bank of England in the seventeenth century. Their first son, Lawrence, was born in 1899; Victor, born in 1900, died in infancy; Horace was born in 1902. As the Sassoons gradually drifted away from Hong Kong it was the Kadoories who took on their mantle as leaders of the Jewish community, for alongside the cosmopolitan was also always the communal. Kadoorie money and activism has seen the synagogue through the twentieth century (with major redevelopments, disputes, and expansions); in 1905, it endowed the adjacent Jewish Club and its expansion in 1909.

Wrote the traveler Israel Cohen in 1925:

> The Club was the finest Jewish institute of the kind I have ever seen . . . equipped with something of the comfort and characteristics of a social or political club in the West End of London. There was a large and tastefully furnished room with a grand piano, which could serve as a drawing room, concert hall and lecture theatre; there was a reading room, supplied with a select library and several select Jewish newspapers; there was a billiard room . . . a bar presided over by a white-jacketed Chinese mixer who could dispense you any cocktail that you chose . . . most of the members of the Community belonged to the Club and visited it almost every afternoon, and its popularity as a social rendezvous tended to make it a more efficacious racial preservative than the synagogue which adjoined it.[10]

As with The Helena May and other gifts, the Kadoories saw their world as far larger than that of the synagogue alone. After their mother, Laura, died when their home in Shanghai burned down in 1919, Lawrence and Horace went through formative years in London—where their home was host to King Faisal I of Arabia and Emperor Haile Selassie of Ethiopia—before returning to the open-minded city of Shanghai.

That world demanded education, health, and other help which the Kadoories gave irrespective of religion and, surprisingly, gender. Kadoorie charities are still legendary, from schools for girls in Baghdad or Indian boys in Hong Kong to agricultural training for Gurkha soldiers to pig-rearing research and the grant of farms to Chinese refugees reaching Hong Kong. "We Kadoories know everything about pigs but the taste," said Lawrence.[11] The Kadoories backed the Hebrew University in Jerusalem but also non-Jews with schools and hospitals in Iraq, Iran, Syria, France, Turkey, India, Britain, and China;

they also endowed a synagogue in Portugal. In 1901, Ellis founded the Ellis Kadoorie Chinese Schools Society with his good friend Lau Chu Pak, to build schools in Shanghai, Canton, and Hong Kong.[12]

Lawrence became the colony's first baron. His brother Horace led the Kadoorie Agricultural Aid Association as it helped villagers get their produce to markets and underpinned agricultural innovation, even finding a fix for swayback pigs. Denis Bray was a young district officer in Tai Po and, having calculated how much cement he needed to link a vast spread of villages, realized it would take twenty years of his budget just for the basics. Happily, he was referred to Horace Kadoorie, who gave him all the cement at once; Bray, the junior civil servant, was left in awe at this prominent industrialist doing so much for poor farmers.[13]

Perhaps the point about the Kadoories is that they shared the vision of many in-between people—that Hong Kong was home. Speaking in 1986, Lord Lawrence told me: "Hong Kong is far less class- or race-dominated than it used to be . . . The Chinese have got to know those families which have been here a long time. And I think there is a feeling of 'better the one you know than the one you don't.' Perhaps we're more trusted." Lawrence saw Chinese clan structure as more important in the shaping of society than whether someone was rich or poor. He added: "In the old days for the Europeans, class was just a matter of how far up the Peak you lived. But that attitude has almost disappeared."[14] Speaking in 1997, Lawrence's son Michael said: "We will not run off in different directions. We are Hong Kong people."[15]

––––––––––

Once Michael's great-uncle Ellis Kadoorie had put up half the money for The Helena May Institute for Women, his gift was matched by that of a leading Eurasian, Ho Kom Tong. Ho shared a mother with Sir Robert Ho Tung and followed in his half brother's footsteps through Central School and Jardine's into private business, largely in Hong Kong's opium monopoly. He quite outstripped Ho Tung, however, with the complexity of his private life. At least twelve concubines and numerous mistresses were housed in Sai Uk, the so-called Small House. His wife and her children lived in the smaller Dai Uk, or Big House. Ho's wife, Edith Sze Lin-Yut, was also Eurasian, daughter of a Jardine's tea merchant in Shanghai, Archibald McClymont, and a part-Chinese, part-Parsi mother. Their eldest daughter, Elizabeth, educated by the Italian Canossian Sisters, was Catholic and so married the prominent Macao businessman Tse Kan-po, who would become one of the first owners of a cine camera in 1930s Hong Kong. In a reminder of how closely intertwined Hong Kong's leading families were, Ho Kom Tong's son Ho Sai Kit married Winnie, the daughter of Choa Leep-chee, our Malacca-linked sugar tycoon ultimately connected back to Belilios. Another daughter of Ho Kom Tong married Winnie's brother Choa Pu-yiu; two more family weddings would later link them to the Zimmerns.

Ho Kom Tong had style, wit, and even flamboyance. One of his favorite ways to raise money was to sponsor—and then take leading roles in—Chinese theater performances. Funds raised went to flood victims in China, the London School of Tropical Medicine, public dispensaries, widows and orphans of soldiers of the Russo-Japanese and Boer Wars, Lord Kitchener's Memorial Fund, myriad schools and hospitals—and The Helena May Institute (as did contributions from the Chinese Lau Chu Pak and the Eurasian Chan Kai Ming).

Most of all, Ho got ahead on audacity. He and his brother Ho Fook were among the owners of a cotton and yarn company, Sang Cheong Fat. One story is that in 1900, during the turbulent times when the United States took the Philippines from Spain, the U.S. Navy blockaded the seaports, causing the price of sugar to plummet in Cebu and demand for it everywhere else to skyrocket. Ho Kom Tong decided to run the blockade, took a fleet of ships to Cebu, somehow got through, and loaded up with cheap sugar. Then he heard that in the Boxer Rebellion foreign troops had entered Tianjin and Beijing and desperately wanted sugar. So Ho changed course, sailed north to Tianjin, where he sold the sugar at a huge profit, then loaded his ships with more than three thousand refugees out of Beijing, thus converting a blockade-busting sugar run into a charitable endeavor.[16]

Hong Kong's biggest landowners and ratepayers were now Hong Kong Chinese, Eurasian, Jewish, Armenian, and Parsi. Many of them went through Queen's College (the successor to Central School) or the Diocesan Boys' School; they almost all worked their way up in the respectability stakes by joining the Tung Wah Hospital Committee, the Po Leung Kuk, the District Watch, the Chinese Permanent Cemetery Committee, the Chinese Club, and the Chinese General Chamber of Commerce. Once they became justices of the peace, they joined more government advisory bodies, of which there were many.

These families were now choosing to stay in Hong Kong, already in the 1910s, not least because conditions in China were entirely unconducive to the kind of peaceful profit-making available in Hong Kong. Some new Hong Kongers had fled China a generation earlier for Australia or beyond, and chose to return not to China but to Hong Kong. Forebears of the Gockchin, or Kwok, family were market gardeners in Australia before returning to Hong Kong to open the Wing On department store in 1907. According to the firm's official history,[17] eighteen-year-old Gock Lock left Guangdong for Australian goldfields but instead found compatriots working the nursery gardens from which he saved enough to branch out on his own, selling fruit and vegetables from a barrow in the Sydney market, even going to Fiji to buy bananas. In 1897 he opened his own store and called it Wing On ("Perpetual Peace"). His younger brother Gock Chin had worked in a lawyer's office in Hawaii before joining his brother in Sydney. Gock Lock was the tough entrepreneur, Gock Chin the calm administrator; both converted to Christianity.

Their exposure to the optimistic, confident, and pioneering spirit of New World commerce offered a stark contrast to the torn, despairing last years of dynastic rule in impoverished China. Hong Kong was the nearest homecoming possible where business could be pursued in safety. By 1925, Wing On was the major Chinese department store in Hong Kong, with an adjoining hotel, and a Shanghai branch which opened in 1917.

Their fellow fruit-and-vegetable merchant Ma Ying-piu had helped the young brothers in the Fiji banana breakthrough. Ma's founding in Hong Kong of the Sincere Department Store in 1900 had inspired the Kwoks to follow suit. Ma, too, was Christian, and his innovations included the hiring of women shop assistants—which caused a near riot in the store's first days; he offered the novelty of fixed prices and receipts for each sale; his stores closed on Sunday and staff were given improvement classes in the evenings. His wife, Fok Hing-tong, daughter of the vicar of St. Stephen's Anglican Church, had contributed key ideas to the new store, even working behind the counter to prove it was possible for a woman. While her husband was active in the Young Men's Christian Association (YMCA), she co-founded the Young Women's Christian Association (YWCA) in Hong Kong in 1918, and was its chairwoman in 1920–23 and director in 1920–28 and 1948–57. Alongside giving birth to thirteen children she gave strong support to the Anti-Mui Tsai Movement, a statement of early feminism and concern for workers' rights.[18]

When trouble arose, this mixed elite staked their fortunes on British rule, backing the colonial government's measures against the workers, such as during the 1912 Tramway Strike, or the 1922 Seamen's Strike, and British refusal to succumb to leftist pressures during the far more devastating Strike and Boycott of 1925–26. Some individuals veered more to the left or right, choosing to work with this or that political figure on the mainland at times. But this crowd, just as Belilios, Chater, Mody, Kadoorie, Ruttonjee, and others before them, were now stayers. Hong Kong was their home.

———

Another of Hong Kong's diverse communities had meanwhile been making Kowloon their own—the Portuguese. What is now the heaving shopping and residential area of Yaumatei had once been known only for its snipe-shooting until, in the 1870s, boatbuilding and repair yards moved there. At Tsim Sha Tsui, whose name means "sharp, sandy point," what is now the crowded Chatham Road was once a sandy bathing beach. Junk parties from Hong Kong would go there in late afternoons, erect matsheds and changing rooms for the ladies, enjoying cherry brandy, tea, and dinner on the launch.[19] Both these areas would benefit from Portuguese middle-class ideals of happy, garden-filled homes.

Of Yaumatei's twelve farm lots, mostly on the seafront, seven went to Chinese and five to foreigners, in 1869 and 1870. These "foreigners" were Marcos do Rozario and Delfino Noronha, R. A. do Rozario, Fredric Sander, Henry Charles Caldwell, and J. M. d'Almada e Castro. Garden lots were different, intended purely for gardens, but were eventually reassigned as Kowloon Inland Lots. Not just Chater but nearly forty non-Chinese names appeared on the original leases for garden areas that covered the whole of the middle of Kowloon, mostly east of Nathan Road, especially between Kimberley and Jordan Roads.[20]

They were joined in Kowloon by the Kadoories, who, in a link to J. P. Braga (related by marriage to the earlier Kowloon man Noronha) built what became the Kadoorie Hill district of luscious 1930s mansions. Braga had been editor of the *Hongkong Telegraph* from 1902 until 1911 and later became the first Portuguese member of the Legislative Council. A close associate and friend of Robert Shewan, the Scottish founder of China Light and Power, Braga joined that company's board in 1928, the same year as Elly Kadoorie joined it. Together, Kadoorie and Braga won the contract to supply electricity to the New Territories. Braga helped Sir Robert Ho Tung to set up a New Territories Agricultural Association. As managing director of the Hong Kong Engineering and Construction Co., he led the Kadoorie Hill project, financed by Sir Elly Kadoorie.[21] The naming of Braga Circuit attests to his influence.[22]

The Portuguese of Hong Kong are a good example of both a cosmopolitan sensibility and a coexisting communalism. They lived with their own but also worked, mingled, and developed beyond that community.[23] Separate to the Kadoorie Hill initiative, Portuguese were leaders in other garden suburbs in the early twentieth century. Frederico "Jim" Silva says that for his people, "everyday pleasures took place in a satisfying and simple middle-class milieu. Club life with cards and mahjong, family gatherings and weddings and funerals, jaunts to Macao, weekly outings to the beaches in summer, food and gossip, movies and sports. These were an integral part of the Filho Macao life."[24] Kowloon offered space for the community to grow, especially once land prices and rents in the Mid-Levels started rising out of the middle-class reach.

Another favored destination for the middle-class peoples of Hong Kong was the distinctive neighborhood of Kowloon Tong (originated by a Constantinople-born insurance man called Montague Ede). Once St. Joseph's School opened premises nearby (in 1924), it drew in more Portuguese and other mixed families; then St. Teresa's Church emerged.[25] A more cosmopolitan, less purely Portuguese ideal motivated Francisco Soares, a future consul to the Portuguese, into building yet another garden city in Kowloon where he named streets after Peace, Liberty, and Victory, as well as himself and his wife, Emma.

One hobby in particular would bring diverse peoples together from both Hong Kong Island and Kowloon: gardening. From the middle of the nineteenth century onward, local newspapers regularly carried reports of the annual horticultural shows, displaying a range of names from Peak-resident Britons to Kowloon Portuguese, from Mid-Levels Eurasians and Armenians to Parsis.

The Parsi hotelier Dorabjee Nowrojee's glorious garden of flowers, fruit, and vegetables helped spawn a multicultural obsession in parts of Hong Kong. The Star Ferry was born when he lent his private boat to family and friends who wanted to cross the harbor to visit friends' gardens; heavy demand required a second boat, which he called the *Morning Star*. Demand grew so that it became commercial in 1880 and he was running four boats by 1890, averaging 147 crossings a day.

Other avid gardeners included J. J. dos Remedios at Pokfulam on the Hong Kong side, and Mathias Soares, who claimed to have introduced the root of the ginger lily to Hong Kong. Noronha and Rozario's garden at "Delmar" featured Australian fir and pine trees, as well as Malay areca palms, coconut palms, fruit trees, flowering shrubs, vegetables, and more. Among Noronha's keen horticulturist friends were Soares and Charles Ford, superintendent of the Botanical and Forestry Department—the three moving spirits behind the foundation of the Hong Kong Horticultural Society.[26] Confirming elite support for the pastime, both Chater and Mody built fantastical gardens around their mansions on the Peak; society members were honored to be invited to visit.

———

Being both cosmopolitan and committed to one's own community was always a balancing act in early-twentieth-century Hong Kong. Clubs showed how it was done—many of them drew in members of just one ethnic group to dominate or even exclude others, but some deliberately chose to cross those boundaries. Relationships would both solidify into self-centered ghettoes and broaden to include unexpected connections. Wealthy Europeans, more English than American or Antipodean, already had their Hong Kong Club. Rich Armenians and even a Parsi were members there, and a look at a 1924 membership booklet puts an end to assumptions that Jews were banned from those elitist halls. D. E. Sassoon joined in 1886, M. S. Sassoon in 1894, S. A. Levy in 1894, A. J. Raymond in 1898, D. M. Nissim in 1899, C. S. Gubbay in 1905, E. S. Kadoorie in 1905, Dr. R. A. Belilios in 1907, H. H. Solomon in 1910, and A. S. Gubbay in 1911.[27]

Less besuited recreation could be found at the sailing and swimming clubs. Cross-cultural playtime was well under way at the racecourse, and on cricket grounds or football pitches. Cricket, rifle shooting, football, golf, wild birds and game, lawn bowls, alley bowls, racquets, hockey, lawn tennis—all were on offer.

The Parsi community had their Anjuman, or community center with a temple, which had moved with them from Canton via Macao to Hong Kong. Parsis initiated their own Parsee Cricket Club in 1897 before playing a key role in the founding of the Kowloon Cricket Club, whose president was none other than our old friend Sir H. N.

Mody, who opened the KCC on January 18, 1908. By the 1930s, KCC membership was almost entirely Eurasian.[28] The Kowloon India Tennis Club was formed in 1907, and was also used by the Indian Muslim Society (established in 1924). Within the not strictly white world were further delineations. Eurasians went to school at the Diocesan schools (DBS and DGS) or St. Paul's, and played sport at the KCC; those identifying as Portuguese would more likely attend Maryknoll and La Salle colleges, play games at Club de Recreio, and worship at the Catholic St. Teresa, St. Joseph, and Rosary churches.

The "Chinese" Eurasians led by Ho Tung had their Chinese Club. The Jews had places of worship but would not get their Jewish Recreation Club until the start of the twentieth century. The mid-nineteenth-century City Hall had allowed only limited access to non-elite and non-white groups, but this was opening up by century's end. More uniform-minded men could have joined the Hongkong Volunteer Regiment in 1862, although it lasted only four years in this incarnation until revived in 1878. Masters of the mercantile marine had the Phoenix Club, born in 1907 out of the Hong Kong Bowling Club, founded in 1898. St. George's Club, set up in 1905, was purely social. Club Germania was serving Germans from 1859. The Nippon Club was founded in 1903.

For enthusiasts of a different sort there was the YMCA, formed first for Chinese in 1901, with Sir Ho Kai in attendance at the stone-laying ceremony for a hostel on Bridges Street. An international wing opened the next year. This was consciously not an elite organization. Initial prejudice against its religious background faded quickly as many Chinese became donors, impressed by its educational work.

Interestingly, the goal of the international YMCA was to attain a "higher standard of morality . . . amongst the Europeans and thus remove one of the great hindrances to the progress of Christianity among the Chinese."[29] As J. L. McPherson, YMCA general secretary, saw it, "Our membership is largely made up of what might be termed the middle classes. We have to a large extent left out the soldiers and sailors, while bank clerks, assistants in the large shipping firms and government officials, who think themselves the highest grade of society, have left us out. The soldiers and sailors are by no means a neglected class as two well-equipped institutions are at work among them, but the class which tries to hold itself above us is indeed a needy one, which we cannot afford to let go without the greatest effort."[30] The YWCA started for Chinese women officially in the 1920s, but long before that, Lucy Eyre, who educated Eurasian and impoverished girls, spoke of the need for a center for women. By 1913, Miss Eyre's YWCA had merged with the Hong Kong Benevolent Society.

The Victoria Recreation Club was often described as cosmopolitan, meaning, it seems, that its membership was open, mixed, and cheerfully unpretentious. It did not mean inclusion of Chinese members unless they carried foreign passports, until rules changed in 1964. Its roots and early activities lay in the Regatta Club of Canton (birthed back in 1832), then the Victoria Regatta Club of 1849. In 1872, swimming, boating, and gymnastics activities were amalgamated under the new name of the Victoria Recreation Club, with the governor as its first president. Its first clubhouse, close to the waterfront in Central, suffered typhoon damage in 1872 and 1874; its Kowloon premises were wrecked in the 1906 typhoon. The VRC hosted annual cross-harbor swimming races, rowing, water polo, and gymnastics competitions. A look at its 1892 accounts and membership lists shows that out of 403 members, guessing from the names alone, there were at least forty-six Portuguese, twenty-three Jews, four Parsis, two Armenians, and a dozen Indians. Many more will have been of mixed origins in many ways, perhaps identifying as Eurasian. Names ranged from Belilios and Botelho to Castro, Chater, Gubbay, Joseph, Kew, Levy, Lopez, Madar, Manuk, Nowrojee, Remedios, Sassoon, Sherazee, Stopani, and Wodehouse.[31]

Club Lusitano has been serving the Portuguese community since 1866. Its membership has always overlapped with that of the Club de Recreio and the VRC. The two main sources of funding for the founding of Club Lusitano came from J. A. Barretto and Delfino Noronha, the printing tycoon who was one of the first migrants to Hong Kong and settler of Kowloon. The club offers balls, theater, fine dining, and a quiet place to gather with one's own. This both raised Portuguese standing in Hong Kong and helped integrate the Portuguese community.[32]

No doubt clubs divided as much as they brought together; many people of mixed race have stories to tell of exclusion from this or that institution based on notions of race or class.[33]

Therein lay the hitch, as a specifically nationalist republican revolution convulsed China in 1911, and World War One appeared on the horizon.

The rise of the nation-state and the unleashing of ideas about nationhood had their impact on ideas about race, as always with any general increase in insecurity. These wider forces at work would have an impact on Hong Kong's in-between people as the twentieth century advanced.

9

IMAGING COMMUNITIES

When the republican revolution overthrew the Qing dynasty in China in 1911, it was easier for a Chinese or Eurasian to cut off his queue, that long pigtail of hair down his back, than it was to adapt to a new nation-statist world. Sun Yat-sen and his Four Desperadoes had been meeting in the twisted back streets of Hong Kong, as part of their preparations for the republican revolution, garnering support from many of Hong Kong's great and good; after all, this was part of a march toward modernity aimed at helping China to progress. But modernity carried perils for in-between people. The 1911 revolution was a nationalist struggle, with clear racial undertones. Although Sun Yat-sen would later praise his education under British rule and the inspiration gained from the tidy drains of Hong Kong, he and his fellow leaders called specifically for a racial uprising. This was for the Chinese. It was not a time for people who were half or three-quarters Chinese, or who felt a different Chineseness, informed by time abroad or in bed with the Other.

Medical science was tossing out strange ideas, too, of an alleged inherent weakness of those with mixed blood, or the eugenicist notions of breeding "better" people. New ways of classifying people harden distinctions, tighten definitions, quantify difference. In his survey of how newly republican Chinese culture brought with it a decline in Confucian authority and a rise in "science," the historian

Frank Dikotter found that "the biological category of 'race' and the administrative category of 'population' were heralded by modernizing elites as objects worthy of systematic investigation." A popular slogan arose: "To strengthen the country, one first has to strengthen the race; to strengthen the race, one first has to improve sex education."[1] Assertions of Chinese racial pride made it more difficult to be different. Dikotter noted that one well-known reformer, Tang Caichang, thought amalgamation of races was the way to go, using the intelligence and strength of mixed-race people in Hong Kong to prove his point. But his was a lonely voice in this new century. More commonly, Hong Kongers were looked down on by China's new nationalists precisely for their hybridity, with women's loss of chastity related directly to Hong Kong being colonized.[2]

Attorney General Sir Challoner Grenville Alabaster's "Some Observations on Race Mixture in Hong Kong" warned of the onset of a race problem in the wake of the revolution.[3] He expressed surprise at the lack of any laws "bearing upon the problem of race mixture, certain laws declaring marriage between certain races invalid or a punishable offence, or at least certain decisions as to the degree of blood making a particular person a member of one race or of another." He thought this might be because "until as recently as 1911 the Eurasian problem did not exist; or perhaps it would be more accurate to say that before that year classification could be effected easily without too close an inquiry into a person's pedigree."

Before 1911, Eurasians were Portuguese, Chinese, or British.

The grouping would depend on many things, the least of which would be the quantum of blood admixture. A man with such a name as Remedios, Xavier, or Silva, who was a Roman Catholic, educated at St Joseph's College, with relatives in official positions in the neighbouring Portuguese colony of Macao, and who was a member of the Portuguese staff of a British firm, besides being a member of the Club Lusitano, would never be regarded as Chinese, even though he was Oriental in feature and had only a fraction of European blood in his veins. Again, one would have no difficulty in giving a Chinese classification to a half-caste, even though his father were English, who wore Chinese clothes and a queue, who passed under the name of Wong or Chang, who had married according to Chinese custom a "Kit Fat" (wife) and three concubines, and who after some years' business training in the compradore department of a foreign firm was trading on his own account under a Chinese "hong" name, besides being a member of the Chinese Chamber of Commerce. At the same time a Eurasian with an English surname who dressed as a European and lived as such, both in business and in his home life, would not be regarded legally as a Chinese, although his parentage might affect him socially.

After 1911, events had "gone far to bridge the pre-existing gap between the Chinese and British Eurasian." Alabaster noted the emergence of a "better class Chinese," more Western in hairstyle and dress. "A further and less obvious effect was the awakening in the pure Chinese of a spirit of nationality which is resulting gradually in forming in their minds the idea that the Eurasian Chinese should no longer be classed as Chinese, or at any rate as the leader of the Chinese community and the exponents to the British of Chinese thought and sentiment." So "the race problem has been brought into existence," requiring legislation in a "broad and sympathetic spirit." But, he noted, "it will not be easy— to give an imaginary case—to classify Major Long of Eton, Corpus and the Rifle Brigade, and his father, Mr Leung, the chairman of the Chinese Chamber of Commerce and ex-representative of the Chinese community on the Legislative Council." Tiresome though Alabaster's British smugness was, and his conceit that now he had noticed an issue (race) thus had it begun to exist, he was highlighting an important historical moment in the development of Eurasian consciousness and conditions.

World War One only brought such tensions more to the fore. Within the European world of Hong Kong, suddenly drastic new divisions emerged as businessmen who had played bowls, smoked cigars, and drunk together the night before became British officers locking up German enemies the next day. People were shocked when the German ship *Emden*, whose band had given concerts at City Hall, began capturing allied shipping around the region, attacking Penang and shelling oil tanks at Madras. The war caused a massive redistribution of wealth as Chinese and Eurasians snapped up businesses now available as Germans were interned and the British went to war. Other changes were more subtle, such as when Cafe Weissmann changed its name to Wiseman in 1914.

The ferment of ideas continued, as after the revolution there came the 1912 Hong Kong Tram Boycott—in protest against a perceived insult of the Chinese in the tram company's rejection of mainland Chinese coinage—followed by China's May Fourth movement of 1919. The war had left patriotic Chinese outraged as Britain's ally Japan had marched into German concessions in China and kept them. Once the Versailles Peace Conference of 1919 confirmed Japan's landgrab, Chinese protests, boycotts, and strikes exploded.

While the war itself may have touched Hong Kong only lightly, the aftereffects were profound for in-between people the world over—including many of the leading lights of Hong Kong. One was the return of the passport, now a marker of modernity. Formerly sprawling and often cosmopolitan empires—the Austro-Hungarian, the Ottoman, the Tsarist—were now a mass of individual states in the process of becoming. They wanted borders to define themselves, bringing to an end a laissez-faire approach to national identity and freedom of movement. France, Britain, Germany, Italy, and others also passed laws requiring foreigners to carry identification documents. In the years after World War One this trend for nationalist self-definition took off such that this "extraordinary expansion of the capacity of states to control the migration of populations using documentary means . . . was, in fact, one of the central features of their development *as* states."[4]

These shifting sands would prove particularly irksome for many of Hong Kong's peoples, as seen in the shift in status of the "British Protected Person." This had been a loosely defined category of people—such as Baghdadi Jews—and included those who might have been of British origin but were not British subjects, in places where Britain exercised extraterritorial or capitulatory rule (such as Turkey and China). It was sometimes a short hop from BPP status to full British nationality—but this could no longer be assumed after the war, when the national mood everywhere became more intense.

So much for the promise of a new century.

———————

In about 1920, guests at Hong Kong's fanciest hotels—the Repulse Bay Hotel, Hotel Mansions, and the Hongkong Hotel—were told that the city's "ideally picturesque surroundings contribute to produce a rare scenic harmony with panoramic land-and-seascape not to be surpassed anywhere in the Far East."[5]

Such scenic harmony was not reflected in its populace, however. The decade opened with a mechanics' strike, the first in a string of victories for organized labor. The seamen followed in 1922, demanding equal rights to those of non-Chinese seamen. At first ignored, they went on strike with devastating effect. A port city cannot last long if the ships arriving and departing are hindered. Heavy-handed colonial rulers banned the union and moved to crush the strikers but failed; bakers, butchers, waiters, and domestic servants joined in, apparently prompting a run on Mrs. Beeton's cookbook as expatriates discovered their kitchens.[6] When a large group of strikers set off on foot for Canton they were shot at by British police and troops; five died on the spot. After fifty-two days, the government had to cave in, relegalize the union, and agree to a substantial pay hike. It was a humiliating comedown for the governor, Edward Stubbs, who would be criticized for being out of touch and unable to speak Chinese.

The event served as an eerie dress rehearsal for a more far-reaching strike and boycott in 1925. Politics across the border in the new republican China were beginning to intrude on Hong Kong's claimed, but never complete, tranquility. Local demands for pay, improved work conditions, and even democracy combined with the ambitions of the left wing of the nationalist Kuomintang and of the fledgling Communist Party in Canton, creating a perfect storm for colonial rule. Trouble began in Shanghai in May 1925 when Sikh police under British command in the International Settlement opened fire and killed at least nine Chinese demonstrators. The news spread like wildfire, and by June, most of the students at Hong Kong's Queen's College had heeded the call to strike. Soon cargo carriers, tram drivers and conductors, seamen, typesetters, and other union members followed suit. Later that month, during a heated public demonstration in Shameen— the foreigners' island off Canton—fifty Chinese protesters were killed by the foreign troops based there; anti-British placards appeared in Hong Kong to rise up against the colonialists and their Chinese "hunting dogs." By June 22, Governor Stubbs had again declared a state of emergency, and by early July, Hong Kong was a ghost town. Many thousands of Chinese had left for Canton, the banks tottered, and the economy entered dire straits that would last for more than a year.

On whom could the government rely through this time of trial? On its local elite, peopled by many of the Chinese and Eurasian men we've already met.

Two particular figures stand out. One was Shouson Chow, whose family—unusually—went back to the 1600s on the south side of Hong Kong Island. His father was comprador to the Hongkong, Canton & Macao Steamboat Co., based in Canton, and young Shouson, after starting at Central School, was selected by the Chinese government in 1873 as part of a first batch of pupils to study in the United States. Educated at Phillips Academy and Columbia University, Chow returned to be Chinese consul in Korea, managing director of the state-initiated China Merchants Steamship Navigation Co. (in 1903) and of the Peking-Mukden Railway (in 1907), earning many decorations from the Chinese imperial government. He returned to Hong Kong, aged fifty, after the 1911 revolution in China toppled the last imperial dynasty, to embark on a new career of business (banking and real estate) and government service. He was a founding partner in the Bank of East Asia and a director of most of Hong Kong's leading enterprises.

He followed the usual route to prominence via the Tung Wah, Po Leung Kuk, and District Watch Committees, and was invited onto the Legislative Council in 1921. Chow was a rare combination of genuine Hong Kong roots, Western education, and Chinese conservatism—he despised any hint of "bolshevism," such as seamen asking for a living wage, while being a keen philanthropist, including to lepers. He was also a member of the League of Fellowship, which advocated good fellowship within the Colony irrespective of race, class, or creed.

The second key man was Robert Kotewall, the son of a Parsi—Rustomjee Hormusjee Kotewall—and his Chinese woman, Cheung A-cheung. The elder Kotewall had been a cotton and yarn dealer for the great Parsi firm Tata and Co.[7] He brought up his family on Peel Street, then part of a bustling business and residential district inhabited by people of all races, often with their local partners. When H. R. Cotewall, often rendered as Kotewall, died in 1895, A-Cheung was gifted property in her name in time-honored fashion, and made sure her children got a good education. Robert Kotewall later admired his father's willingness to flout convention "when in an environment such as ours, British prudery and Parsee bigotry were superimposed on Chinese conservatism."[8] In a memoir, Robert described dressing, speaking, and in every way living as Chinese.[9] A mere government clerk, he joined the multiracial, wealthy, and multitalented elite by jumping into commerce, running the Hong Kong Mercantile Company for the well-connected Eurasians Chan Kai Ming (manager of the Opium Farm, the purchased monopoly on distribution of the popular drug), Lau Chu Pak, and Ho Fook.[10] Kotewall was invited onto the Legislative Council in 1923 to represent "the Chinese," a role he clearly treasured, despite or perhaps because he was not wholly Chinese himself.

The unrest from the Strike of 1925 brought British rule perilously close to the edge of economic collapse. Total trade in Hong Kong fell by half, with shipping tonnage and share values dropping 40 percent, property prices and rents down 60 percent. More than three thousand bankruptcies had occurred by the end of 1925, and the devastating physical losses, personal crises, and political quarrels were unprecedented. Although clearly fueled by Canton-based politicians, in Hong Kong the strikers' six demands were clear: freedom of speech, publication, assembly, and organization; universal suffrage for direct election to the legislature; legal equality with Europeans; labor protection laws including an eight-hour workday; rent control and provision of adequate housing; and the right of Chinese to reside anywhere in the colony. Ultimately, the mainland-based leaders of the nationalist Kuomintang and the Chinese Communist Party (CCP) failed to stand up for these demands; Hong Kong had to wait another sixty-five years before even limited voting was allowed.

The government, again, grossly underestimated what it was up against, and some of Stubbs's emergency measures intended to calm things did exactly the opposite. All transportation stopped, Chinese compositors left their newspapers, waiters and bakers walked out, as did domestic servants once again. The Hong Kong Volunteer Regiment was called on and limited ferry and tram service resumed, but the strike spread through schools, university, most private clubs, and even some hospitals.

Yet the local elite, led by men such as Kotewall and Chow, never wavered. Seeing the strike as a direct threat to their position, and to that of Hong Kong, they mustered their own forces against it. The historian John Carroll believes, "One reason these men collaborated so actively with the colonial government to end the strike was to protect their own class interests. But fighting the strike also meant preserving the colony they had helped to build. It furthermore enabled the leaders of this bourgeoisie to prove themselves to the colonial government as loyal Hong Kong Chinese."[11]

Soon Stubbs would be replaced by a new governor, Cecil Clementi, who arrived in 1925, ready to parley with the men in Canton. Clementi, a brilliant India-born, Oxford-trained colonial administrator, was fluent in Cantonese. He formed a Chinese Committee to handle the strike and put Chow and Kotewall in charge.[12] Kotewall's Bureau of Counter-Propaganda established the *Kung Sheung Yat Po* newspaper to counter strikers' news; he also advocated the creation of a strike-busting gang of "intimidators," little short of thuggery, called the Labour Protection Bureau. Kotewall's report on the period admitted the men had to be "a bold type," no doubt having had "a somewhat adventurous existence." Posters warned that Canton's adoption of outright Russian Bolshevik principles presaged "a reign of unspeakable terror . . . if assistance is not speedily given this poisonous tide of Bolshevism will steadily grow until it engulfs the whole of China beyond the hope of redemption."[13] By October 1925, the worst was over, but the strike and boycott continued for another year.

The strike finally ended when its mainland leaders decided it could. Meanwhile the government had recognized the importance of its "Loyal Chinese." As Governor Stubbs had reported: "In the first panic, when the Chinese might have been likened to a herd of frightened sheep, they [Chow, Kotewall, and others] immediately came forward and shamed and compelled their fellow countrymen into at least a semblance of courage. Anonymous letters threatening violence and murder were received by them daily, a reward for their heads was posted in Canton, and still they worked incessantly, gathering at first a few of the more venturesome spirits, who in their turn brought in others, till in a short time the whole Chinese Community had forgotten its fears."[14] Secretary for Chinese Affairs D. W. Tratman stressed "the wonderful spirit of loyalty and solidarity shewn by the Chinese intelligentsia of the Colony in the face of this great crisis." Shouson Chow was the first Chinese appointed to the Executive Council, in 1926.[15]

The death of Sir Paul Chater the same year, with the governor at his bedside, only reinforced a sense of times changing. "In his dignified person he stood for the Colony's heart and soul . . . he typified Hongkong, its success, its philanthropy, its hospitality, its culture. He was patron and doyen of almost all our activities."[16]

———

As so often, while elite figures thought they understood their supremacy, the dynamic and heaving life of this Asian port city was surging along regardless. An airfield had opened at Kai Tak, offering flights to Penang, from where one could fly to London, and a first broadcasting studio opened at the post office in 1929. Of more global impact was the founding—in Hong Kong—of the Vietnamese Communist Party by Ho Chi Minh. A generation later, of course, his leadership of the Viet Cong would lead first to the French withdrawal from Vietnam and then the debacle of American military involvement there, a geopolitical event that would reverberate for decades to come.

The logic of a port city, even at a time that might already be seen as post–peak empire, made Hong Kong a gathering place for people from all over the world. Many of them, as we have noted, played key roles in building the society of Hong Kong—its universities, schools, hospitals, clubs, legal system, financial world, and even a brewery. Names long-established, such as Belilios, Chater, Mody, Kadoorie, Ruttonjee, and more, would be joined by poor English boys, such as the fifteen-year-old Noel Croucher working as a clerk in the post office in 1905 who, after a chance chat with the great Sir Paul Chater, became a wildly successful broker and quiet philanthropist.[17] Marjorie Matheson's father was a stockbroker who went bust in the 1920s, so she became a housekeeper at the Repulse Bay Hotel, poor but very respectable. Other impoverished Europeans made their way running boardinghouses or shops, working as seamstresses or car mechanics. Some of those with rare skills or lucky contacts could get ahead.

Women such as Rosie Weill arrived from Harbin, with her family's Sennet Frères jewelry business; her daughter Sophie would marry the impresario Harry Odell. Despite his seemingly Irish surname, he had been born in Cairo in 1896 as Abadovsky, his father a Russian Jew, before moving to Shanghai. A failed career as a tap dancer led him via the U.S. Army into trade that brought him in the early 1920s to Hong Kong, where he became a wealthy stockbroker before starting to bring in live shows to his Empire Theatre, revolutionizing Hong Kong's entertainment scene. The arrival of Austro-Hungarian (thus Ashkenazi) Jews from the 1880s on was a new factor in Hong Kong; they had less pretension than some Baghdadi Jews and often went into running pubs, such as the Land We Live In, Globe, Criterion, and others. Aaron and Amelia Landau arrived from Constantinople in 1916 and, via Shanghai to Hong Kong, established the iconic Landau's and Jimmy's Kitchen restaurants. A teacher at the top Diocesan Girls' School was Irma Last, originally of Czernowitz, a place variously found in Poland, Ukraine, and Russia.[18] George Smirnoff arrived out of the White Russian diaspora of Vladivostok and became an architect and renowned watercolorist in Hong Kong and Macao.[19]

Many more, of course, did not get ahead in the conventional sense, managing merely to survive until the next rupture, be it war or revolution. "The life of a low-paid European in Hong Kong cannot have been very pleasant. Many found solace in drink"—and apparently fewer than half of these lowly Europeans actually survived to enjoy their police or prison pensions, thanks to the demon drink.[20] A literature exists on why it was considered wrong for "white" people to be poor; it was "letting the side down" and deeply injurious to notions of British prestige. Those attitudes mattered only to a tiny cohort of British imperialists who still busied themselves with the notion that they were running the world. Most people, most of the time, were more intent on getting by.[21]

Later chroniclers sometimes called these people "white trash"— until they became rich, that is. Beyond the narrow boundaries of class came many white men of varied origins who, like their Indian or Portuguese, Parsi or Jewish counterparts, started with nothing but, in Hong Kong, made something of themselves. Thomas Lane and Ninian Crawford, for example, were low-level arrivals. Perhaps Thomas was related to Edward Lane, a butler for the East India Company in Canton, or to William Lane who opened a ship's chandlery and bought a tavern. Thomas was a clerk in 1843, then an auctioneer and shopkeeper; in 1850 he owned a ship's chandler with Ninian Crawford (a former clerk and, briefly, secretary at The Hong Kong Club). Their enterprise evolved into the now-expensive department store Lane Crawford. George Duddell was another lowlife, engaged in dubious land dealing and shady auctioneering. But, somehow, he became a government auctioneer by 1857, built a property empire, and had a street named after him.

Scots migrants were particularly plentiful, with the diaspora across Asia prominent in trade, Christian mission, journalism, law, brokerage, banking, and manufacturing. Small in numbers, their impact was huge. Scots had a stronger network than the Welsh or Irish through their roots in the East India Company. Behind them back in Scotland was shipbuilding on the Clyde, where engineering firms were providing turbines and pipes for irrigation, and sixty jute mills in Dundee were providing the world market for burlap, matting, rope, and other jute products. Scots, too, ran an insurance industry active in Asian markets by the 1850s. Thomas Sutherland (1834–1922), from Aberdeen, began as a clerk to the Peninsular and Oriental shipping company before becoming its vice chairman and co-founding the Hongkong and Shanghai Bank in 1865, the precursor to today's banking behemoth HSBC.

Histories usually focus on the big names and leave out the majority of the lesser-known, whose lives more genuinely form the bedrock on which a society is built. Many of these people were also extraordinary in their own ways. Consider the Sikhs imported by the British as watchmen (preferred for ammunition duty as they did not smoke) back in the 1860s. By the early twentieth century these had their own community of expanding families and dedicated prayer at their Khalsa Diwan (built in 1901 and still on its original site today). Through their long trading history linking Greek, Persian, Arab, and Sindhi mariners, Sikhs brought another global dimension to Hong Kong; more recent networks included a diaspora spread out from Malaya, Fiji, New Zealand, and Australia to Canada. There remained a fluid boundary between Hindu and Sikh, especially abroad, so that they often shared places of worship. Muslim Punjabis also came, many living around the Shelley Street Mosque first built by Shaikh Moosdeen in the mid-1800s. These communities kept to themselves in matters of faith and practice, but also intermarried and remain a part of the Hong Kong mosaic. Almost all led humble lives, but exceptional stories also emerged, such as when Allah Ditta died. He had been watchman of a building near the stock exchange and was found to be worth more than a million Hong Kong dollars, which he left to the Incorporated Trustees of Islamic Community Fund, and to a charity in Pakistan.

The Guests' Guide given out free to elite guests of the Hongkong Hotel in the 1920s eulogized not only what proved to be an illusory harmony, but Hong Kong's world-famed curio shops, museum, theater, library, banks, clubs, markets, and Sincere's great department store, "with its fine roof-garden from which a very extensive view is to be obtained." It recommended tours around the island but especially along Queen's Road, of which it says, "There is probably no part of Hongkong in which the traveller will find a more fertile field for exploration and sightseeing . . . It runs the whole length of the City." Such praise was printed opposite an advertisement for "The Eastern Bazaar, Proprietors Wassiamull Assomull and Co, The Premier Silk House of Hongkong, Established 1868, Wholesale and Retail Dealers in Oriental Silks, Piece Goods, Embroideries."[22]

The advertisement highlighted another community of Hong Kong, which became gloriously present in glittering technicolor by the 1920s, the Sindhis. They formed a worldwide trading network of "Sindhiworkies," typically trading in lacquerwork, quilt covers, embroidery, and brass items. In Hong Kong, their presence manifested in the stunning shopwindows offering fabrics of a sheen and silkiness to rival anything from the Chinese Middle Kingdom. Riotous color, rich deep reds, blues, and purples, with weaving and embroidery to dazzle, became regular treats for many a society lady. As with their Sikh and Punjabi predecessors, the Sindhiworkies were forced abroad due to the British annexation of Sind in 1943. One of their first destinations was Egypt, but the trade in trinkets and fabrics grew fast on the back of this new industry called international tourism. Thanks to the Suez and Panama Canals and steam shipping, the demand for "curios" and oriental textiles only grew through that high noon of imperialism.[23] From Egypt,

Sindhis joined Armenian, Levantine, and Jewish merchants and spread far from home into Africa and East Asia, stopping along the way at Colombo, Calcutta, Singapore, Penang—and Hong Kong. The pioneers included Pohoomull, Chellaram, Chotirmall, Harilela, and Assomull, descendants of whom remain in Hong Kong today.

––––––

Seeing this wild mixture of peoples, professions, colors, and belief systems might lead to the romantic notion that this was an integrated and open society in which people of many races and cultures mixed deeply and meaningfully, where lifestyles mingled, where East not only met West but where each became entangled with and changed by the other. But was that so? Chater, as we saw, was still called "a coloured magnate" by a sniffy Briton. So was Hong Kong indeed that stuffy, divided place where racism flourished and exclusion triumphed over desire? Certainly, many varied cultures and people met in the Hong Kong marketplace. They also met frequently under the mosquito net in bed, at church, on sports grounds, and at the horse races. Among the wealthy and influential elite, they met constantly at formal events, from weddings and funerals to industry openings, to university committee meetings and much more.

True, few Parsis married outside their community; among the elite names, only Ruttonjee and Kotewall had done so. Some Jewish families preferred to keep marriage and procreation within the faith. But many others didn't care. Muslims became more intermingled with Chinese families through their wives. The families of Moosdeen, Arab, Rumjahn, Curreem, and Sadick all intermarried with Chinese.[24] Hong Kong's Muslims did not come only from South Asia, either. Chinese Muslims were among the first refugees, in their case from repression in the Panthay Rebellion (1856–1873), a separatist movement of Hui Muslims in Yunnan. As so often, Hong Kong was a haven.

Conventional Chinese families mixed least of all. They circumscribed their daughters' choice of partner, all the more so if there was a chance that money was involved. Power over who produced the sons who would carry the family name and wealth long overrode any other consideration. In what its inhabitants like to see as the elite European world, the mixing was also severely curtailed, at least in public, and more so in the early twentieth than in the nineteenth century. For those intellectuals or clerks, many from the Eurasian world, who sought careers in government, they had the attitudes embodied in the Crewe Circular of 1909 to contend with. This had been issued from London to deal with a scandal in Kenya, where the wife of a British official had expressed her outrage at an acting district commissioner living with a local woman. The Circular was not formalized in law in Hong Kong, but the attitude was clear. It stated that moral objections to concubinage were "self evident," and besides, it damaged government efficacy. No administrator could tolerate such behavior "without lowering himself in the eyes of the natives, and diminishing his authority to an extent which will seriously impair his capacity or useful work in the Service in which it is his duty to strive to set an honourable example to all with whom he comes in contact."[25]

Perhaps more relevant to Hong Kong was the rising fear among Europeans about the economic competition now presented by the existence of a strong, wealthy, and sophisticated local elite. The European establishment feared rising property prices—hence the Peak Reservation of 1904, restricting residence there to Europeans—but also a more existential threat to their superior position. Such fears were given a scientific veneer by Dr. James Cantlie and others who claimed mixed-race offspring lacked endurance, were prone to illness, and worse. Eurasian beggars on the streets were seen as "bearers of the stigmata of imperial decline." Health, particularly of children, was used to justify the Peak Reservation too,[26] against a backdrop of eugenicist arguments then current in Europe and the United States.

Governor Frank May had expressed the hope that the growth of a Eurasian population would be limited, if not altogether stopped by his plans. But he was entirely mistaken. Even as his wife, Helena, ran with men of mixed race but deep pockets to found her women's institute, he was fighting to prevent British policemen, security guards, and sanitary inspectors from marrying out. Though not expressly forbidden, intermarriage was discouraged; one risked losing free government accommodation, contract renewal, and promotion. Governor May's reasoning, if such it may be called, was that any Chinese or Eurasian women willing to marry Europeans were bound to be of a low class; they wouldn't consider it otherwise. There was also the ever-present fear—apparently nonexistent if the spouse was non-Chinese—of influence by the wife's relatives. Only by the 1930s were some of these strictures beginning to be relaxed.[27]

When May tried to extend his anti-mixing fervor into banning Ho Tung's children from attending the Peak School, however, he was more firmly quashed. He feared that the school would not be successful if permission was granted to the seven children but had to admit that "Eurasian" was hard to define. If they were "Europeanized Chinese" it might be all right, he wrote. But other voices in the correspondence poured scorn on his "fears": "As there is only one family in the Peak District and that the family of a man so well known, I think the Governor is a bit fanciful. I would express regret [to May] and say we cannot think that the admission of one family and that the family of a man of such standing can prove detrimental to the school," came the message back from London, which insisted the children should be admitted. It was a triumph for Ho Tung, although he eventually sent his children elsewhere anyway.[28]

Yet the Portuguese who kept the banks and businesses running were routinely underpaid and confined to clerk status. As a Jardine's manager put it: "I rather think funeral expenses are a charge on the Firm, Europeans a first class affair, Portuguese second." Yet they were respected, too: "here in Hong Kong [they are] as good as I remember it to be bad at Shanghai . . . But they all commit matrimony at an early age and they all have enormous families. They are, as you know RCs [Roman Catholics] . . . Hence the Portuguese live on a very narrow margin and sickness or any form of bad luck puts them down the drain . . . we have to tread delicately."[29]

As for the prospects of in-between people, or men who married them, at the formidable institution of the Hongkong and Shanghai Bank, an earlier tolerance, or at least neglect, again gave way to racist exclusion in the years between the two world wars. Chief manager of the bank in the 1930s, Vandaleur Grayburn, was determined that at this "British" bank his staff must marry "British" wives. His name has been enshrined in a halo since his genuinely heroic death from the results of Japanese torture when he was found funneling money to prisoners of war during World War Two. But in the years before then, his views would shock a modern mind:

> These youngsters are beyond understanding; both presumably had decent relatives & upbringing, yet one falls for a Russian Jewess of doubtful origin & the other for a half-caste Japanese . . . These young fools make me quite sick & it disgusts me to think they can so quickly forget their British standing & home upbringing . . . We welcome the marriages of our men when their allotted time arrives, but to British girls, and we do not want Russians, dagos & half-castes attached to our staff . . . I want you to realise that the question of suitable wives for Bank men is becoming acute and I will not tolerate "mixed" marriages with Russians or half-castes, and I look with disfavour on most marriages with non-British women.[30]

The idea that Hong Kong attitudes were somehow worse than Shanghai's is spurned by the historian of empire John Darwin, who noted, "The conviction that a wide civilisational chasm separated Europeans from Chinese remained the leitmotif of British attitudes, especially, perhaps, among Shanghailanders . . . Communal loyalty was enforced through residential and social segregation as far as possible, and by taboos against intermarriage."[31] The British were also not alone in their prejudices. When Richard and Harold Lee, son of the land and opium tycoon Lee Hysan, were sent off to England for an education they were told they would be instantly disinherited if they made the cardinal error of marrying a non-Chinese. But British cultural imperialism was not equivalent to biological racism, found Darwin. Despite arrogance and prejudice, "in both the French and the British empires (by contrast with the United States) the potential for equality among persons of all races remained the formal position in law, in institutions and in official ideology."[32]

Non-elite Europeans were perhaps the freest of societal strictures to love where they chose, in a continuation of that pattern of European men marrying locally from the earliest days of Hong Kong. Perhaps their relative freedom from religious orthodoxy was the key, and the oft connected relative freedom accorded to women. Marriages did not need to be arranged by their elders to fit preconceived notions of caste or faith. Nor was there any money at stake around which so much stress and unhappiness over inheritance has swirled.

———————

Hong Kong, as we have seen, was always a place where it was possible to play around with one's identity to commit fraud, or, in the case of Ho Chi Minh, to escape a French death penalty. The Vietnamese revolutionary had been in Hong Kong in 1930 to bring together several groups to found the Vietnamese Communist Party there. After a trip to Siam (Thailand), he was back in Hong Kong in 1931, but two years earlier he had been sentenced to death in absentia by a French-run court in Vietnam. The French were now pressuring the British colonial government to send Ho back to French Indochina. In Hong Kong, Ho now claimed to be a Chinese gentleman, Sung Man Cho, and secured the services of a British solicitor, Frank Loseby, to get him through habeas corpus hearings to prevent his deportation. Reports the historian Christopher Munn, "Although they knew all along who he really was, the failure of the British authorities to establish his real origins in court was a key factor in the decision to compromise and allow him to go to Moscow instead."[33]

The case unearthed by Munn of one Carvalho Yeo is even more interesting. First Yeo chose to be Portuguese in order to be hired as a clerk by the bank he intended to defraud, then he chose variously to be Chinese, Siamese, and British in order to escape justice. In 1928, the Treasury discovered that more than a quarter of a million dollars had disappeared from its account at the Hongkong and Shanghai Bank. A sensational trial of this man of "mysterious antecedents and doubtful nationality" ensued. Many trials by jury "were microcosms of multicultural life revealing relationships across communities that complicate conventional ideas of a city segregated by ethnicity," noted Munn.[34] Yeo's jury comprised three Portuguese, three Europeans, and one Eurasian (Ho Kom Tong). Yeo was convicted of using ("uttering") checks he knew to be forged and given ten years hard labor. When the government later sued the bank, the jury included four Europeans, one Eurasian (S. M. Churn), and a New Zealand–born Chinese (B. Wong Tape). Munn concluded that the "strategic adoption of ethnic identities, particularly by people of mixed ancestry," was a running theme in Hong Kong history, citing men such as Ho Tung and Kotewall who busily stressed their Chineseness "even though they were probably never seen as Chinese by other Chinese."[35]

Yeo had looked at 1920s Hong Kong and chosen an "Asiatic" or "local Portuguese" identity as the one most likely to facilitate the crime he had in mind. This, says Munn, "underlines the role of the Portuguese and other minority communities, as well as the permanent Chinese community, in what Henry Lethbridge sees as a coalescence of the middle classes into a plural society, its members bound together by a network of trust and contractural arrangements—even the beginnings of a Hong Kong identity."[36] After all, this middle class is what settled the unrest of 1922–25, not the government's emergency measures. New forms of civil society emerged during the 1920s that would enable Hong Kong's different communities to more assertively express their identities. Clubs, societies, self-help groups, and activities proliferated such that billiards competitions were held between European and Chinese teams at the Chinese YMCA, and the founding of the Hong Kong Society for the Protection of Children was led by the barrister-businessman T. N. Chau and the solicitor T. M. Hazelrigg. For Munn, despite the racism and discrimination, Yeo's trial and people around it "suggest a diversity and fluidity that complicate the usual colonial stereotypes." When a (Chinese) clerk in the Treasury was threatened by Yeo's crime, his bosses defended him strongly due to an "implicit trust built on long experience, mutual respect, and common interests that transcended cultural differences."[37]

Whatever the naming rights, labels needed to be malleable and capacious, as did the idea of Hong Kong itself. Many preferred the label "Portuguese" as sounding more sophisticated. But "Portuguese" in the East was Eurasian, mostly being a mixture of Chinese and Portuguese blood—as well as Goanese, Indian, Malay, Timorese, Indonesian, Japanese, and European—from hundreds of years back in Macao, thus "Macanese." But today many don't like to call themselves Macanese. Their insider name is FM or Filhos Macao—meaning "sons of Macao" (including its daughters)—and celebrations of this unique culture frankly enjoy the varied influences on language, families, and, most important of all, food.

That diversity and fluidity were badly served by the government, its bureaucrats, and a blinkered elite. As Governor Stubbs saw it, during the unrest of 1922, "We can rely on nobody except the half-castes and even they will throw their lot with the Chinese if they think they will be on the winning side." He fretted about "excessive" Eurasian influence.[38] Yet as the historian David Pomfret notes, the deep divide between British and Chinese elites "perpetuated the government's continued reliance in the crises of the 1920s upon elite Eurasians to represent 'responsible' Chinese opinion."[39]

Robert Kotewall was a standout example: half-Chinese, half-Parsi, Chinese scholar, and adept bureaucrat, all at once. Watching the first films (shot by Ho Kom Tong's son-in-law Tse Kan-po) of "the leading Chinese" in the 1920s and '30s, it is striking how Kotewall looked different, and that probably mattered.[40] The very slipperiness of the Eurasian identity made him useful, but also vulnerable.

10

THE EURASIANS

Eurasians were, by the 1920s, into their second or third generation. Now was the time not only to survive but to increase their security through education and wealth. Eurasian success now made the discriminatory practices scratch deeper. It was a time of rising consciousness of a specific Eurasian identity as something no longer to be ashamed of. It is during this interwar period that the steps were taken that would embed Eurasian networks and consciousness as something that today's generations are—at last—proud of.

Of course there were divisions, competitions for status, arguments over varied origins, and stark fights over money. Every family produced at least one difficult character per generation who gambled away the family fortune, married wrongly, or sparked conflicts among multiple mothers, or worse. Sometimes these struggles were expressed in racial language—one might be derided or praised for being more or less "European" or "Chinese." And there were class divisions as the products of Protected Women and their Western merchants of the mid-nineteenth century seemed to accrue wealth and power, while legitimate offspring of the earnest, well-married hotel manager or lesser civil servant rarely scaled the heights of this elite.

But by the end of this decade, through confusion of names and relationships, business ties and social competition, this group that had once dared not speak its name would come together publicly, declaring themselves both Eurasian and truly of Hong Kong.

———

Take the extended Churn-Macumber-Leonard family with its Chinese, Scots, Portuguese, Belgian, and other roots, for example. Descendants puzzle over two gravestones for one great-grandmother. Is Ms. Cheung the right one, or Ms. Yip, and where does the name Lily Brown come in? William Macumber was a Scots merchant in Shanghai in the 1880s when he met the mystery woman who would produce Samuel Macumber Churn aka Cheung Kit Tsoi in 1887.[1] Samuel was one of Hong Kong's coming men in the booming interwar decades, a British intelligence officer in the next war, and a doyen of China coast business after that; the Union Trading Co. name remains in family hands today.[2] He married Lena Johnsford (1894–1940), another Eurasian of probably Swedish extraction, and had six children: Molly, Eddie, Mabel, Eva, Doris, and Samuel "Charlie" Churn.[3] Along the way, Samuel accumulated Lena House, the comfortable home Pinecrest, in the New Territories, and a beach house; he lived the life of an English, albeit part-Chinese, gentleman.[4]

Samuel formally dropped his Chinese name in 1913. Charlie, his youngest son, recalled his father claiming to be 70 percent European because his mother, Lily Brown—a surprise name to today's descendants—had mixed blood. "There's a story that my father went back to America to meet his *real* father, who told him: 'Son, I now have my own family. I will ask "certain friends in Hong Kong" to give you a helping hand.' Was it Macumber? We don't know. They were very secretive in those days about the parentage. I think this happened after I was born but before the war," said Charlie. His father was "a very tough, autocratic man," and well connected. "He was successful because he was in the right place at the right time, and yes, he knew the right people. Father never said we were Eurasians, we were English-Chinese. He was proud of what he was, never mind Eurasian or not."[5]

He was not alone. The first chronicler of this evolving Eurasian world, Peter Hall, called it the Web when he published the myriad connections among a long list of interrelated names.[6] When he began his research, he faced obstruction and ignorance at almost every turn. One generation further, there is now a pride in tracing linkages that show how a Churn or a Leonard ties into a Botelho or Fenton, Baker, Soares, Zimmern, Kotewall, Ho Tung, and beyond.

"Growing up was very hard—my Chinese cousins used to call us half-breeds! But we Portuguese couldn't care less," recalled Pat Botelho, the granddaughter of Choa Leep-chee, whose daughter Trixie had married a Portuguese. Two different forebears had each married a so-called pure Chinese. The products of one union were accepted as Chinese while the others were called "half-castes."

> Apparently they didn't look like bastards, but we did. We Choa and Botelho grew up together, but they slagged us off—they said, don't play with them because they're half-caste. Yes, we were Catholic, and the Choa said they were Chinese. But we had the best of two worlds—we celebrated Christmas, midnight mass, presents, and then when we came out of mass we had a bowl of congee and roast duck waiting for us. At Chinese New Year we were dressed in padded jackets and full-length cheongsam and we got our lai-see [Chinese gift envelope of money]. Marrying a Portuguese was seen as marrying down but my mum worked it in such a smart way—she was Chinese in many ways. Just as Chinese did every Chinese New Year, she took us first to eldest son of her "First Mother," i.e., Dad's first wife. Then to second brother, third brother, etc. She followed the Chinese hierarchy. You know where you stand.

"But everyone just stayed in their own clique," said Pat Botelho, agreeing that a few families were still fighting status wars two generations on. "That whole family thinks they're different," she said about one well-known line. "They still don't have much to do with the rest of us. But did I care? No! We all bleed the same, and shit too."[7]

Many are the stories of separate family lines being just a little bit too close. Cousins often married cousins, and there are highly respectable families to this day whose antecedents either never married or who married more often than they divorced. This community was both deeply divided and tightly linked. Much has been made, for example, of the three daughters of Sir Robert Kotewall marrying three sons of Adolf Zimmern. Their descendants are the repository of some of the greatest wealth and influence in twentieth-century Hong Kong.

Yet the tie-ins between the two families began three generations earlier, through two brothers, one of whose liaisons created the Zimmern clan, and the other the Kotewalls. Back in the 1870s, Henry W. Lowcock, a British merchant and partner in one of the earliest big firms in Hong Kong, Gibb, Livingston and Co., served on the colony's Legislative Council in 1872 and 1875–79. He married Annie Loftus Russell in 1873; their one child, Henry Christopher, died in the year of his birth, 1874.

Two decades earlier, however, Henry had a deep and lasting relationship with a woman whose name and ethnicity, though probably Chinese, remain unknown. That union produced at least two sons: Charles in 1853, and George in 1864. Charles was father to a vital woman called, among other names, Mary Lowcock. And she married a half-Chinese and half–German Jewish man called Adolf Charn Kwong Zimmern. His parents were Adolf Hermann Christian Anton Zimmern and Lai Kim Ip, or Yip.[8] The elder Adolf Zimmern (1842–1916) had come to Hong Kong in 1868, and worked for the trading firm Reiss and Co.; he was made partner in Shanghai in 1867 and served on the Shanghai Municipal Council in 1871–72, the same year he was listed as being on the General Committee of the prestigious Hong Kong Club alongside the cream of society.[9] His son, young Adolf, and Mary Zimmern produced Andrew, Ernest, Frederick, Francis, Nora, and Archibald. Young Adolf was on the Hong Kong Stock

Exchange in 1914, alongside names already familiar to us, most of them Eurasian, Jewish, Armenian, Portuguese, and Indian.

On to Charles's younger brother George, and the pattern is similar. He, too, had a Chinese or Eurasian lover (perhaps with Parsi blood); among his offspring was Edith Lowcock, born in 1889. She would marry Robert Kotewall, our man of government knighted in 1938, and they would produce Esther, Phoebe, Doris, Helen, Bobbie, Maisie, Cicely, Cyril, and Patsy.[10] Meanwhile, Edith had a brother, named Henry after his grandfather. He married his sister's niece, meaning the daughter of Robert Kotewall's brother Samuel, Mabel Constance. Samuel Kotewall was the black sheep, long happy with gambling, wine, women, and song. While Robert was carving a path into the highest reaches of colonial governance, Samuel leaned on him for financial support and had at least two children; alongside Mabel was Dorothy, who married a Luigi Ribeiro.[11]

The permutations are endless. The Zimmerns and Kotewalls who married each other in the twentieth century had no idea their families were tied generations earlier. When Doris Kotewall married Frederick, they were wed by a cousin of the groom, Rev. George She; dignitaries present included top officials from the Chinese and British governments, and members of Hong Kong's leading families.[12] Unsurprisingly, perhaps, when Dr. Ron Zimmern, direct grandson of Sir Robert Kotewall, checked his DNA he found 29 percent Scottish/Irish/Welsh blood, 21.4 percent Chinese and Vietnamese, 15 percent Ashkenazi Jew, 11 percent South Asian and West Asian, 2.3 percent Middle Eastern, and 11 percent Filipino/Indonesian/Malaysian.

Doris Kotewall's sister Helen married Frederick Zimmern's brother Francis, a leading broker, and produced five daughters. Doris and Helen's sister Cicely married Frederick and Francis's brother Archibald Zimmern and produced Annabel (founder of Hong Kong's Oliver's Delicatessen) and Hugh (an architect). Francis Zimmern would later outline his roots deep in the Hong Kong–style aristocracy by listing his Zimmern father and grandfather as leading businessmen, his cousin

George the Anglican canon, Frederick the solicitor, Archie the barrister, Queen's Counsel, and first local high court judge. His wife's lineage through Sir Robert Kotewall warranted mention, too, because he had been on the colonial government's highest decision-making body, the Executive Council, "before and during the war." Francis Zimmern recalled stockbroking in the prewar days as relaxed, friendly, and rules-free: ". . . there were some clients who smoked opium as people smoke cigarettes today, and I often had to arrange only to visit them after they woke up from their opium daze."[13]

Meanwhile, another Kotewall daughter, Phoebe, married Walter Alexander Hung, whose sister was the wife of Sir Robert Ho Tung's son Robert Ho Sai Lai. The Kotewall daughter Bobbie never married; her sister Maisie married Dr. George Choa, the son of Choa Po-sien; while the youngest, Patsy, married John Fenton.

Their daughter Kim Fenton notes that despite Sir Robert's prominence, he was never that wealthy. "The money came later, from the Zimmern marriages, all the girls. Robert Kotewall had a lot of land in Stanley, so the girls, who were all very smart, sold off bits of land and the girls made millions . . . only Esther and Patsy married men who already had money." It's also believed by some in the family that Sir Robert had other children. When he died in 1949, his will made the usual provisions for his known legitimate offspring, but also specified the "remaining two equal parts for persons whose names I have in a separate letter to my trustees," suggesting the existence of people he preferred not to name in public.[14]

Such convolution was not a problem, believes Kim, because generations of Eurasians were now being "brought up loved and educated. We have no problems because we are so full of ourselves, and yes, we have money. There were hang-ups around the 1900s; it's when they got rich and educated that the hang-ups evaporated."[15]

If we step back in another direction, to Kim's parents, we find that the John Fenton who married young Patsy Kotewall in 1951 was the son of Solene Hung So Lin—the eighth child of Ms. Kan Shun Tsoi and Charles David Bottomley. Readers may recall Bottomley paying for a daughter, Maria Louisa Emily Angele, to be educated at the Canossian school (Chapter 6). "Solene wouldn't talk about family because her mother had so many men," remembered Patsy's daughter Kim.

Kim's mother, Patsy, has no such self-doubt. "I never thought about being different to others at all," she says, laughing. "I'm a Eurasian, and I have no problem at all, I'm quite happy. Lots of Shanghai Eurasians, they feel, ooh, they must say they are English, or Chinese. But in the case of my family, we didn't care at all because we were very well treated by everyone. Our family is quite different to other Eurasians—we have a road named after us!"[16] Having said that, even in cheerful circles, appearance made an impact on identity. Patsy recalls her husband, Johnnie, and his sister Doris as "quite dark, well, not dark, but not fair," and admits that in old photographs, "everyone looks Chinese, because of pigtails and Chinese dress, even if they are Eurasian."

In contrast to modern squeamishness about linking looks and roots, another family memoir described the Zimmern and Lowcock families as Eurasians who were "more Chinese than Western in their outlook. In fact they usually went by their Chinese names . . . They were well-to-do but in their household fortunes were made and lost with a certain regularity."[17] When Cicely Kotewall married Archie Zimmern she saw his mother, Mary Zimmern, as Eurasian "but her looks were the very antithesis of her manner. She looked Western, being tall and fair, yet her demeanour was totally Chinese. She barely spoke any English, always wore Chinese clothes, smoked a silver bubble water pipe and loved playing mahjong. She was nicknamed 'kum gai,' or golden bun (as in chignon) due to her fair hair."[18]

Young Zimmerns and Kotewalls played and went to school together, as did members of other related families. Patsy met her future husband, John Fenton, when her older sister Phoebe was marrying Walter Hung at the Kotewall family home, Hatton House, a wonderful mansion up on Hatton Path, later Hatton Road, adjacent to Kotewall Road. John Fenton's sister Doris married her aunt's son Tom Baker, a journalist in Shanghai—Doris's family were disappointed as they had hoped for a higher-status match, says one of their daughters, Vivienne or Vivi, who married a Portuguese, Frank Correa. She, too, was looked down on by some in her family for her choice. The schisms within the Eurasian community perpetuated the snobbery and divisions that they themselves suffered from. At the Kadoorie-run China Light and Power, where her husband worked, Vivi remembered three sets of washrooms, one for Europeans, one for Chinese, and one for "Local," meaning Portuguese and others.[19] Vivi's sister Gloria married John Hung, the son of Phoebe Kotewall-Hung (when her first husband, Walter, died, she married his half brother M. C. Hung).

With such complicated marital ties went not empires, but lucrative business positions, such as the compradorship to the Hongkong and Kowloon Wharf and Godown Co., which Phoebe's son John would enjoy. As John Hung said, "The only pure blood I know is mixed blood—we, the compradors, are the ones who melded Hong Kong together."[20]

Many more webs can be woven, some suggesting even the most prim and proper men of the elite had children with their Protected Women, such as the one who was mother to the future Sir Oswald Cheung, a leading figure of postwar Hong Kong.[21]

Behind the solicitors' firm Lo and Lo lies a long Eurasian trail, which highlights the interwar decades as critical for the Eurasian community's consolidation. The nineteenth-century Shanghai merchant Thomas Rothwell had three children with his Chinese woman; Jardine's helped his failing business by buying his Shanghai land in 1880, employing him, and moving to Hong Kong the children then known by their Chinese names: Lucy aka Lo Shiu-choi, and her brothers Lo Cheung Shiu and Cheung-ip.[22] Lo Cheung Shiu married Lucy Zimmern, and his sister Lucy/Shiu-choi married Ho Fook, brother to Robert Ho Tung. Lo Cheung Shiu became assistant comprador to Jardine's in 1894, a job long in the gift of Ho Tung, becoming top comprador in 1918.[23] One of Lo's sons, Man Kam Lo, was chosen by Sir Robert Ho

Tung to marry his eldest daughter, Victoria, and was co-founder with his brother Man Wai of the Lo and Lo legal firm—the first wholly Chinese law firm in the colony.[24] With his three brothers, M.K. would lead the next generation of professional Eurasians into a postwar era in which many realities would change.[25]

Their story overlaps with that of the American Club's country club facilities on the south side of Hong Kong Island. These stand on a spur above Tai Tam Bay that was previously home to three magnificent villas of Ho Tung's extended family.[26] Just above those three stood the Lo mansion—all of them with sweeping sea views and grass tennis courts.[27] Man Kam and Man Wai Lo were doubles tennis champions several times through the 1920s and '30s, and Man Wai won the singles title in 1929. By the time the club came asking to buy the land, old M. W. Lo would greet visitors, even uninvited ones, in shorts and an old rattan hat, often leading visitors to think he was the gardener rather than the host.[28] Ian McFadzean, the property dealer who found the lease loophole to enable the sale to the American Club, understood the Eurasian nexus: "The Los, the Hotungs, and the others, they did not mix with real Chinese and vice versa. And of course the Brits didn't see them as real Chinese. Who did [Jardine's ruling family] the Keswicks rely on, whether in China or Hong Kong? Their compradors. And who were they? Half-European. This half-world was run by Eurasian compradors."[29]

Some Eurasians who used Chinese names and lived according to Chinese cultural norms considered themselves more distinguished than Eurasians who used their English names.[30] Henry Gittins (alias Hung Tsin) was an entirely proper gentleman and keen churchgoer who worked with Jardine's until retirement. He had married the Eurasian Dorothy Ahlmann and had eleven children. But still Sir Robert Ho Tung had trouble giving his approval when his daughter Jean wanted to marry one of Henry Gittins's sons, Billy.

All these people linked by marriage and business above were many things at once—aspiring members of the British colonial elite, often "Chinese," yet also contributors to specifically Eurasian causes. They each straddled many worlds in which the sorry misery assumed to be the lot of mixed-race peoples was rarely the whole story.[31]

On December 23, 1929, these interwoven, incestuous, mutually supporting, and competitive clans decided it was time to combine, in public, as Eurasians, to help other Eurasians. They founded the Welfare League (which exists to this day), thanks to an anonymous donation for the care of destitute Eurasians. The league's committee, then and now, is a roll call of the Eurasian elite, covering all the names from Ho Tung and Kotewall to Churn, Grose, Ho, Hung, Gittins, Litton, Tse, and more.[32] Shying away from a hard and fast definition of "Eurasian," the league decided to help in the maintenance and education of permanent residents of the colony, and their families. "Of course, at that time, aside from the Eurasian Community, few considered themselves permanent residents of Hong Kong," noted Eric Peter Ho in his account of the league.[33] His comment highlights the extent to which Hong Kong's core community was neither entirely Chinese nor British but a mixture of both and more.[34] As Carl Anderson said at that first meeting:

> Gentlemen, it has been said of us that we can have no unity . . . this, though palpably absurd, is a challenge to be faced and an insult to be wiped out. Our detractors little know that if we have not coalesced sooner it is simply because the urge to do so has not been pressing. They do not realise that, after all, there is no gulf between a Chan and a Smith amongst us and that underlying the superficial differences in names and outlook, the spirit of kinships and brotherhood burns brightly. We Eurasians, being born into this world, belong to it. We claim no privileges but we demand our rights for which we must contest to the last ditch. With the blood of old China mixed with that of Europe in us, we show the world that . . . this fusion, to put it no higher, is not detrimental to good citizenship.

DANCING ON THE EDGE

I n the first week of December 1931, those who saw themselves as the great and good gathered at the behest of the man who had worked so hard to define a Hong Kong version of greatness: Sir Robert Ho Tung. It was his golden wedding anniversary. Lavish arrangements were made for the event, celebrated in great style at the Peninsula Hotel, that glossy new palace over on the tip of Kowloon, built by Sir Robert's good friends the Kadoories. Of course, everyone knew Sir Robert had two wives and countless other lady friends, but this event was to mark his marriage to Lady Margaret, his first wife. A booklet was printed with photographs showing the young Robert and Margaret fifty years earlier and their accrued status since then. Glowing purple prose from the local newspapers was reprinted in full, in case anyone might have forgotten how important, visionary, wealthy, romantic, intelligent, and downright heroic Sir Robert had been, so far.[1]

"Perhaps no Chinese resident of Hong Kong is better known throughout the world than Sir Robert. He has been royally received upon his visits to England and is personally known to many of the leading financiers and businessmen in Europe and America," lauded the *Hongkong Daily Press* (on November 30, 1931). It traced his meteoric rise from a humble home through education and into commerce, his true métier. All his company directorships were listed, all his philanthropies and all his honors and decorations. He was hailed as a wise adviser to government and even as a peacemaker for his failed efforts to convene a conference of Chinese warlords. His electrifying presence enlivened the British Empire Exhibition at London's Wembley Stadium in 1924 and 1925 and brought their majesties the king and queen into his orbit. The newspaper cited Sir Robert's belief that his astounding success was all down to "honesty, foresight, carefulness, courtesy, perseverance and hard work." The writer admitted to being amazed, in Sir Robert's private office, to see how "his active brain keeps several secretaries constantly employed."

As for Lady Ho Tung, she was a gracious and worthy helpmeet and companion who shared with her husband "his generous and philanthropic spirit." The nobility of this pair can hardly be believed. The *China Mail*, after columns of deathless prose, notes, "The subject is one on which, like Tennyson's brook, we could go on babbling . . . But in honouring Sir Robert Ho Tung and Lady Ho Tung, the Colony is but honouring itself, brimful of pride that this particular Colony and no other had been the chosen area for the multitudinous activities of our 'Grand Old Man.' Long may he and his yet be spared to fulfil the pleasurable role of worthy citizens of a worthy Colony!"

The Chinese General Chamber of Commerce gifted Scrolls of Eulogy: "Like sunshine that dispels all darkness, your sagacity and perspicacity enabled you to penetrate into the inner nature of men and of things revealing it in the light of your understanding. Cherishing an ambition that defies planetary influences . . . culturing your inner being and outer behaviour, you have won from your friends and the public the reputation for simplicity and truthfulness . . ." The Tung Wah Hospital sent poetry extolling Ho Tung's moral character, which apparently must go hand in hand with wealth and conjugal bliss. In the days following, long lists of all the guests were published, as were details of yet new philanthropies chosen by Ho Tung.

Speaking "on behalf of the Chinese community," the half-Parsi Robert Kotewall claimed to "see that the same romantic spirit as resides in the hearts of newly-wed lovers, still animates theirs." After citing Mark Twain he reached what was probably the main point of the gathering—the association of a newly built elite with the venerable, albeit ambivalent, character of Ho Tung. Said Kotewall: "Those who have known Sir Robert, as I have, for the last thirty-five years or so, can tell you that his intellectual powers have not shown the slightest diminution . . . he is still imbued with that adventurous urge . . . ever to go forward and to achieve . . . I count myself one of his admirers. I admire him for his wonderful foresight and unerring judgement, his tremendous energy and tenacity of purpose and, what appeals to me most, the perennial spirit of youth which he has evinced in his later years."

Throughout, he spoke "in the name of their Chinese friends who can be said to comprise the Chinese community." It was as if there were no Eurasians there that night in a hotel built by Baghdadi Jews, reached by a Parsi-built ferry, from a waterfront built by an Armenian.

Exactly ten years later, on December 2, 1941, a spectacular diamond wedding celebration for Sir Robert and Lady Ho Tung was held at the Hongkong Hotel—and one week later, Hong Kong would be at war. The 1930s was a wild decade when the living seemed easy—but family fortunes, including the Hos', crashed. Cross-cultural partying at the races, the hotels, or the beach was ever more accessible— yet when war threatened, non-white Hong Kongers found themselves disadvantaged, refused sanctuary, and paid less for an equal willingness to die for Hong Kong.

———

Dancing on the precipice is fun; not even seeing it's there is dangerous. The year 1933 offered both the dancing and the dark.

When Sir Robert and Lady Margaret traveled through Europe in 1933, what mattered was Ho Tung's "excellent receptions in various European capitals." He met the prime minister in Paris where he was made an officer in the Legion of Honor; in Berlin he was entertained by President von Hindenburg, the man who would appoint Adolf Hitler as chancellor of Germany, and Franz von Papen, Hindenburg's protégé; in Rome he had a private audience with the pope—and on the same day he was received by Signor Mussolini.[2]

Back in Hong Kong, a different journey was embarked upon by a fleet of one hundred cars carrying six hundred prominent citizens on a long twelve-mile drive from the comforts of the island to the distant reaches of Castle Peak in the New Territories. Thankfully, there was the promise of freshly home-brewed beer at the end of it on that mild day in August 1933, when a new brewery would open its doors, and vats. A jolly good time was had by all as the general officer commanding, Major General Borrett, usually busy running the military behind British rule over Hong Kong, toasted the new venture. It was a highly Hong Kong affair: the Hong Kong Brewers and Distillers Limited's directors included Sir Elly Kadoorie, the Hon. José Pedro Braga, Ho Kom Tong, Wong Kam Fuk, the Armenian theosophist Malcolm Manuk, and J. H. Ruttonjee. The key investor was Jehangir Hormusjee Ruttonjee, whose father, Hormusjee Ruttonjee, had traded in wines, spirits, and provisions in Hong Kong since 1884.[3] Interestingly for an enterprise funded by Parsi, Jewish, Eurasian, and British financiers, religious services on Sundays were provided by the Irish Jesuit fathers who happened to have a study house nearby. The Ruttonjee name would become better known for its philanthropy, which, unlike that of many Parsi families, was focused not on Bombay or Baghdad, but Hong Kong.[4]

As the beer was brewing, so, too, was the catastrophic fall of the second-generation Ho Tungs. Two nephews of Sir Robert—Ho Leung and Ho Kwong (father of the late Stanley Ho)—and Robert's adopted son Ho Wing had been buying up all the shares they could find in the Jardine's-managed Yee Wo (Ewo) Spinning Factory in Shanghai.

Family legend has it that one day the Jardine taipan in Hong Kong was talking with his comprador, either Ho Kom Tong or Ho Leung, but after a while was called out of the room. Ho looked around while he was waiting and saw a cable on the taipan's desk: "For the Eyes of the Taipan Only. Buy Yee Wo Spinning Shares." Such a deal could be assumed to send the price of those shares sharply higher, profiting those who were fortunate enough to already hold them. The boss soon returned, ended the meeting, and Ho dashed out to call in his brothers saying, "This is it! Let's buy big and make a fortune!" To raise cash, the brothers even liquidated shares in the Tai Yau Bank, owned by a majority of the Eurasian elite of the time. But the stock crashed and the Ho boys were left high and dry. They ran to their uncle Robert for help, but he chose to pluck only his adopted son from disaster, leaving Ho Leung to shoot himself dead on the cliffs below the gorgeous mansions of Tai Tam, while Stanley's father fled town.

Another family tale has it that the leaving of the cable for a Ho comprador to see had been a cunning plan on the part of someone at Jardine's to weaken the by-now-formidable economic power of the Ho Tung clan. A close reading of the Jardine's archive does not lend itself to this view. But it does show Ho Leung had long been heading for a fall. More cosmically, perhaps, it raises questions about the value of family succession in jobs as pivotal as comprador to such huge conglomerates as Jardine's, the Hongkong and Shanghai Bank, the wharf companies, and more.[5] Within Sir Robert's bedchamber, the scandal perhaps strengthened the hold of the now-leading woman in his life, the levelheaded, practical, and loyal Katie Archee. She was of Guyanese and Chinese ancestry and had been Sir Robert's lover since his 1910–13 illness, producing a son, George Ho.

Already, back in 1928, Jardine's bosses had fretted about the size of debts their comprador Ho Leung was carrying as he traded commodities on Jardine's behalf. By May 1929, they were trying to persuade his patron, Robert Ho Tung, to increase the guarantee (with more cash or shares) to support the Comprador Agreement, in vain. Jardine's in Hong Kong wrote to London: "Ho Tung says, and there is a certain amount of truth in it, that the more security he puts up the tendency would be for Ho Leung to exercise less care and zeal in his operations and in order to protect himself he is trying to force Ho Leung to put up some security of his own. Ho Tung maintains Ho Leung inherited a certain amount from Ho Fook but I think if he did it's all gone west long ago . . . ."[6] By 1933, it was found the rot had begun much earlier still: "I said in my private letter that Ho Leung went down the drain in 1925, actually it was 1922 when his father was still alive. From that time to this he has never been in a position to meet his liabilities."[7]

Detailed renderings of Ho Leung's debts were bad enough, but more were expected in the coming year, fretted Jardine's managers: "When I took over this office I knew I had a man of straw but what was the alternative? My predecessors had apparently endeavoured to nurse our Compradore through to financial sanity and I followed the same procedure . . . For a decade now Import business has been carried on here with the knowledge that Ho Leung was in a highly insolvent state . . ."[8] Some in the family trace the trouble to when Ho Leung's father, Ho Fook, had accompanied Sir Robert and Lady Margaret Ho Tung to the Empire Exhibition in London in 1924, leaving Ho Fook's sons free to lose about a third of their father's fortune in a year.

Ho Kwong meanwhile had become embroiled in a messy case of alleged abduction, transporting a woman to Canton who was apparently underage, after a similar episode with her older sister. The Jardine's boss in Hong Kong, chatting to his colleague in Shanghai in December 1933, observed pithily: "Local Chinese are wondering what all the fuss is about though many of them on general principles would like to see Ho Kwong impaled."[9]

Then came the shocking news that Ho Leung had shot himself. The year had begun with another son of Ho Fook, Ho Iu, killing himself on January 1. He had been comprador of the Mercantile Bank. According to family legend, which some family members still deny, he died by suicide, overdosing with sleeping pills or similar, because he was bisexual or a homosexual and was about to be exposed. Now, on December 21 in the same year, Ho Leung tumbled into the waters off the cliffs at Tai Tam.

Jardine's began circling its wagons. "It transpired yesterday that Ho Leung has been financing himself by drawing cheques on London with the intention we think carried out in some instances of remitting later before cheques arrived Stop Hongkong & Shanghai Banking Corporation queried these transactions and as a result regret to inform you Ho Leung shot himself Stop Bank informs us possible amounts outstanding £8000."[10]

In fact, the amounts were far higher and there began a long process of negotiation between the absent Sir Robert Ho Tung and Jardine's management about who was liable. Jardine's expected it would have to cover half the losses and, more than a year later, that was the result. The process was nonetheless labyrinthine. Jardine's had immediately retained legal advice and was prepared to take the matter to court, forcing a forensic look at just how Comprador Agreements were constructed and to what extent their guarantees could be enforced. But it much preferred not to expose itself.[11]

It knew Sir Robert was a formidable counterpart, noting his nickname in Canton was "the wily Scotsman." Complicating the matter completely was the fact that when the news broke of Ho Leung's suicide, Robert Ho Tung was in Switzerland having lifesaving thyroid surgery and was told by doctors to eschew all work, correspondence, and shocks of any kind. Lady Margaret thus refused to tell Robert the news for fully six months. At least that was the public line, but some Jardine's managers were not entirely convinced. They knew Ho Tung was collecting ammunition, too.[12]

By June 1934, Jardine's claim was $1,183,565.03 while Ho Tung admitted a total liability of just $100,000; with M. K. Lo mediating, this was raised to $500,000 by October. The Jardine's boss, W. J. Keswick, now handling the matter, wrote to London saying his inclination was to accept the offer, "but I'd like to try a final tortuous manoeuvre through M. K. Lo . . ." He added:

> One cannot help admiring the old man's cleverness in offering a sum which is materially less than what we might consider a reasonable compromise yet cannot be turned down without the most serious consideration.
>
> I wish I had Peter Fleming's powers of describing to you our interviews, how we whispered at each other sitting huddled together on the most uncomfortable Victorian sofa in an immense room hung

with extremely bad portraits of halfcaste concubines, how when things became too strained we switched to shares—always oil on the troubled waters of a Ho Tung mind—how we fenced with a profusion of flattery, insincerity and jibes . . . and so on. The dramatic effect was magnificent, even the chorus was good—nurses, boys, inquisitive offspring sidling in with blankets, smelling salts, milk and impudence.

But underneath it all was that clear cold mind of Shylock immovable. Pathos and playacting are all very well, but what we want is more than a million dollars![13]

A month later, Ho Tung had been pushed to $600,000, and so a deal was done. Meanwhile, Sir Robert resigned from the boards of seven Jardine's companies.[14]

————

Another alignment took place in 1933 that would shape the fate of Hong Kong's local elite for generations to come. It was a wedding, in fact, a double wedding. Back in January 1919, a new enterprise had been born by combining Chinese wealth and connections with Western banking practices: the Bank of East Asia. This brought together the financial heft of the Li, Kan, and Fung families, the elder statesman Shouson Chow, and others. Several of these men would form a property syndicate, too, buying the Kennedy Road site once owned by Belilios, and backing Chow when he wanted to develop his home village on the island's south side.

Why was a new bank necessary? Its historian, Dr. Elizabeth Sinn, points out that World War One had spurred rapidly growing Chinese trading and industrial power; Chinese-owned fleets were in big demand, and the rice trade was crucial. One look at the harbor was enough. Tall ships jostled for space, dockside jetties were covered with coolies, and the brokers of the goods being landed were not far away. Human cargoes reached Hong Kong from mainland China, too, by train into the heart of the harbor, where the terminus punctuated the Kowloon waterfront.

Chinese status was rising, as was the property market. There were new department stores, palatial Chinese restaurants, and large godowns, which all "testified to this new opulence. So too, the Census Officer claimed, did the increasing number of concubines counted in the census!"[15] The money needed somewhere to go and grow, but native banks were too small, and the Western banks too Western. "Chinese businessmen felt strongly that foreign banks did not understand their business practices and were insensitive to their special needs . . ."[16] The Bank of East Asia was not the first but would prove to be the longest-lasting solution.

Its roots lay, as did so much of non-Western business in Hong Kong, deep in the Nam Pak Hong, a trading association based to the west of the central business district, focused on channeling Southeast Asian products (rice, timber, medicinal products, birds' nests, and more) into China, and Chinese goods (silk, tea, porcelain, etc.) out. "Some of the largest Nam Pak Hong firms, the Shiu Fung Hong, the Ng Yuen Hing and the Cheong Sing Hong, were owned by the Bank's Directors, Fung Ping-shan, Ng Chang-luk, and Wong Yun-tong, respectively."[17] The bank's founders were aware that a growing chunk of Hong Kong trade had little to do with China. Rice was moved from Siam and Indochina—through Hong Kong—to Japan, the Americas, and the Philippines, or Japanese-manufactured goods—through Hong Kong—to Indochina, Siam, Malaya, and the Dutch East Indies. The families of Kan, Fung, and Li would solidify that knowledge into generations of riches.

Kan Tong-po hailed from Shunde in Guangdong Province; his father was comprador to the Hong Kong branch of the Yokohama Specie Bank. Young Kan worked in the firm's Kobe head office and learned about banking. He would stamp his cautious, paternalistic style on the Bank of East Asia, and on his seven sons and five daughters. Four of his sons followed him into the bank.[18]

Fung Ping-shan left Guangdong in 1874 aged fifteen to work in Thailand at his uncle's firm, dealing in silk and general merchandise. Back in China, he set up a three-way trade among Chungking, Canton, and Hong Kong. In 1909, he established the Shiu Fung Hong with a large shop house, pier, and enormous warehouses storing dried marine products, mushrooms, and herbal medicine. Nowadays it specializes in abalone from Japan. In 1932, Fung's son Fung Ping-fan (later Sir Kenneth) inherited the firm, which is now run by his granddaughter Christine King.

As with many Nam Pak Hong pioneers, Fung Ping-shan did not stick to the produce trade. He owned extensive property and had interests in native banks. He joined the committees of the Tung Wah, the Po Leung Kuk, the District Watch—and the University of Hong Kong (donating its Chinese library); he also believed in the education of girls: four of his daughters earned PhDs. His son Fung Ping-fan followed in his father's footsteps in virtually every respect, joining the Bank of East Asia as a sub-accountant in 1937 and succeeding his father-in-law as chief manager in 1964. He, too, served on the Urban, Legislative, and Executive Councils and was a key figure during the mid-1960s bank runs and unrest.[19]

Li Shek-pang, youngest son of a refugee from the Taiping Rebellion in China, seeded five generations of businessmen, bankers, senior officials, legislators, advisers, the first Chinese Court of Appeal judge, and the post-1997 chief justice. The Li family's historian, Frank Ching, likened the Li family's wealth to that of the Rockefellers and its influence to that of the Kennedy clan. "Though at various times others have surpassed it in terms of wealth or power, this family is unmatched on its staying power."[20]

Shek-pang went to Catholic missionary school and learned enough English to handle officials and business. Then he bought secondhand ships to sail between Saigon and Hong Kong, making a fortune importing rice from Annam during World War One when his ships escaped requisitioning. His death in 1916 made each of his six sons independently wealthy. (Interestingly, when he sought British natural-

ization, as after the Shipping Act of 1894 only British subjects could
own ships, his interview was with a young civil servant named Cecil
Clementi, the future governor.) Shek-pang's direct successor was his
son Koon-chun, who was soon joined by his brothers: Li Tse-fong
helped run the shipping, and Li Siu-pang handled the rice importing.
Their little-known firm, Wo Fat Sing, also took a lease on number 2
Queen's Road, Central, which, fatefully, allowed for use of the premises for residence, business, "or as a bank."

Li Koon-chun was the real brain, frugal, wearing often old and
worn clothes; he was impatient, exacting, and a frequent guest (with
his brothers) at Government House, the home of the governor and
seat of British colonial power. Li Tse-fong was not just banker and
horse owner but politician. He was an activist investor, instrumental
in forming the China Underwriters Co. and Hong Kong Tugboat and
Lighter Co., and galvanizing the boards of the China Provident Loan
and Mortgage Co. and the Hongkong, Canton and Macao Steamboat Co. By the 1930s, he was active, too, on various government
advisory boards, and was appointed to the Legislative Council in 1939.
(Li Siu-pang gambled away a life of leisure with three concubines,
many horses, and stylish jade-studded clothes.)

Li Tse-fong, a Queen's College award-winning scholar, had studied the theory of banking while at Hong Kong University; his family
also had experience with the Banque de l'Indochine and the Mercantile Bank of India. He soon met Kan Tong-po, just back from Japan,
also a Queen's College graduate. Thus, Li Koon-chun (thirty-one)
and Tse-fong (twenty-nine) joined forces with Kan Tong-po (thirty-
six); Shouson Chow was the oldest at fifty-nine. The Bank of East
Asia was born. Kan and Li Tse-fong would later be managers for
life. These bright men forged a network of relationships in Europe,
Japan, and North America, with branches in Shanghai, Saigon, and
Canton.

And so to that double wedding. Fung Ping-shan (who had died
in 1931) had twin sons, Kenneth Fung Ping-fan and Fung Ping-wah.
On December 13, 1933, Ping-fan married Ivy Kan, eldest daughter of

Kan Tong-po, and Ping-wah married Doris Wai-yin, eldest daughter
of Li Tse-fong. Though clearly a well-organized match, the couples
were also reputedly close. Kenneth and Ivy were seen as a loving, in-
separable couple; he died just over a year after his wife of sixty-eight
years. Doris Wai-yin Li said she was the first woman of her family
to choose her own husband.[21] The brides both wore silver satin with
draped sleeves and long georgette trains trimmed with pearls. Their
silver-embroidered veils were weighted with pearls and orange blos-
som; their bouquets were of white roses and gladioli with asparagus
fern. The lavish reception served a thousand guests.

Four years later, Japanese bombs were dropped on central Shanghai,
sending floods of refugees to Hong Kong. The portents had been there,
if anybody happened to be looking, as Japan's long-held designs on
China were clearly becoming more pressing. Controls were imposed
on entry to Hong Kong, and censorship was stepped up; food supplies
were under strain and tuberculosis, cholera, beriberi, dysentery, and
leprosy cases rose. But staggeringly, once the bombs stopped, many
of the foreign trading community returned to Shanghai, even pouring
more money into fixed assets in the city, locking up land and wharf
areas in some vision of a stable future, even as the forces of World War
Two gathered on the outskirts.

Part of this blindness to the precipice was the natural urge to
enjoy the crazy fun and wealth while it lasted. Behind it, however,
was a feeling prevalent in the highest British circles, that Japan's ag-
gression against China had a silver lining—it would stop China from
uniting and becoming a formidable trading and political force of its
own. The chief manager of the Hongkong and Shanghai Bank, Vandaleur Grayburn, in a letter to London agreeing with a colleague's
analysis of the situation, said: "While no-one wants to see Japan in
complete possession of China it would be infinitely worse, as Hench-
man says, if China beat Japan, for life in China for a foreigner would
be impossible."[22]

The director of medical services, Selwyn Selwyn-Clarke, saw this, too:

Though the sky was full of warnings in that twilit phase, there was a tradition of "business as usual" while orientals fought each other, and an ambivalence of attitude which allowed some mercantile minds to approve the weakening of Chinese nationalism at the hands of Japan . . .

From October 1938, after the landing at Bias Bay which ensured the fall of Canton, the Japanese had had outposts along the colony's land-frontier with China. But one soon got used to that, and picnic-parties in the border hills made relaxed and even amiable contacts with the Japanese sentries . . . the pleasures of life appeared to suffer little interruption . . . The British had made their usual comfortable provision for all their sports, from golf and cricket to yachting and surfriding, and the Chinese entertained them with fireworks and dragon-boat races. Around the island, away from the crowded wharves and docks of the harbour, there were delectable beaches for bathing and barbecues and moonlight parties . . . in the evening was the endless exchange of dinner-parties, drinks and dancing in the big hotels, or excursions among the exotic attractions of Chinese, Portuguese and Indian restaurants and cafes.[23]

The sardonic Jardine's taipan J. J. Paterson, writing to his colleague Keswick in August 1937, summed up local preparations: "Meanwhile grave apprehension exists in the minds of the Chinese Chamber of Commerce here that its members may be forced to subscribe to ambulance services in the North . . . However Ho Kom Tong has stated he personally will subscribe heavily and will go North to see the money reaches the right sources . . . the old gentleman contemplates travelling with a bevy of hospital nurses. Sir Robert on the other hand has offered to help if a statue of him will be put up at Nanking by Nanking."[24] Bad feeling toward the Japanese was slow in coming but then resulted in a rash of discoveries—that the barber at the Peninsula

Hotel was a Japanese spy, as were barmen and masseurs. Conscription of all Hong Kong men was made compulsory in July 1939 but already the many peoples of Hong Kong had joined the Hong Kong Volunteer Defence Force, which had companies named for specific groups who, then, were proud to be identified as members of Portuguese, Chinese, and Eurasian companies.

The government architect Leslie Wright, a third-generation Hong Konger, recalled how race was treated differently then. "Hong Kong was based on racial differences before the war without being racial in the modern sense. I used to play cricket, not very good cricket, for the civil service cricket club. We played the Indian Recreation Club, and Club de Recreio, which was Portuguese, and Craigengower Club, which was basically Eurasian. We all enjoyed playing the Indians because we got very good curry puffs at tea time. The Volunteers were extraordinary, where Number 1 was English, Number 2 was Scottish, No 3 was Eurasian, Nos 5 and 6 I think were Portuguese, and 7 was Chinese. This was not looked upon as racial classification. The Scots were proud of their Scottish company. The Eurasians did the best of all, they fought a terrific battle against the Japanese at Wong Nei Chong Gap. I think they did a great job for the Eurasian community because people realized how well they had fought in the Battle of Hong Kong. This was not being racial. It was just a fact of life."[25] Solomon Bard told the historian Paul Gillingham that the Volunteers "was one of the few institutions in Hong Kong where the gap between the races did not exist. While in training Chinese and Europeans were as one. Only when the uniforms came off did the barriers return."[26]

That pride soon took on a bitter taste. One could put one's life and the safety of one's family at risk the same as the next man. But when Governor Northcote announced (on June 28, 1940) that all British women and children should be evacuated, it was left unclear as to who, precisely, qualified. The departure was described as compulsory, and due next week; only nurses and others in essential services were exempt.

Among the European community, the frantic packing and planning was shot through with anger that families were being divided, the men left behind; some women went through interesting permutations of career to suddenly make themselves "indispensable" to the war effort. On the other hand, many women, including Eurasian, Portuguese, or Indian British people, whose men were fighting for Hong Kong, found they could be excluded. What did "British" mean, after all? Was it holders of British passports? If so, then the families of many endangered volunteers from the Eurasian, Portuguese, Indian, and other communities of Hong Kong would qualify. But if it meant "white," then the problems were obvious. On July 5, 1940, the *Empress of Asia* sailed from Kowloon wharf first to the Philippines, where some evacuees report being filtered out and sent back to Hong Kong. The problem was the "White Australia" policy of the planned final destination, which banned people of non-European ethnic origin from immigrating to Australia. Eurasians and others were not barred from leaving Hong Kong, but no one in the Hong Kong administration had thought through the fact that they might not be allowed entry at the other end.

When pressed in the Legislative Council, the government claimed its aim had been merely to help people with no real domicile in Asia. It apparently hoped non-whites would find their own sanctuaries in India, Macao, Indochina, and China. This meant the Hong Kong taxpayer was paying for a tiny elite to reach safety, leaving 99.9 percent of the population unprotected. Council leaders said the government had, with this measure, lost the respect and confidence of the community, and put a heavy strain on the loyalty of a large part of the population.[27]

"Registration will be undertaken of the families of Chinese, whether British or Chinese subjects, who are considered to have rendered service to Britain or the Colony. However, there is no definite guarantee that those registered will be evacuated." So explained the newspapers as registration centers opened, one of them "for Chinese" under the supervision of Samuel Macumber Churn.[28] Another member of his Eurasian world was the young Joyce Anderson, who would marry Robert Symons, and become postwar headmistress of the Diocesan Girls' School. Her memoir recorded how she and her sister were confronted by a registration official saying he didn't know what to do "with the likes of you."[29] The Bliss sisters were also turned back for not, as they put it, being racially "pure."

In the first days of July 1940, the government sent away 3,334 women and children evacuees until protests caused the program's suspension in November. But that didn't mean those already evacuated could return, nor could those who still wanted to go do so at government expense. The issue turned on what the government called "domicile"—the assumption that white/British residents of Hong Kong were only ever temporary, bound by the husband's job, and due to go back "home" when the job ended. Anyone looking at the reality of lives lived through Hong Kong's first century would see that many "pure" British people did nothing of the sort. They spent their whole lives in Hong Kong, birthed babies there, grew up there, and always returned there, even dying there. Hong Kong officials tried to correct London's assumptions on this front, in vain. The *South China Morning Post* was led to conclude (in an editorial on August 2, 1940) that *domicile* was just another word for racist discrimination. It was clear, the newspaper noted, that race somehow determined domicile in London minds, even when it clearly was not the case on the ground.

The historian Vivian Kong found that letters to the newspapers reinforced a "vision in which Britishness transcends the boundary of race," but official views from different parts of the empire demonstrated a "historical reality in which Britishness was reserved to those of 'pure European descent' at the time of war." Kong notes that the Hong Kong government did try to arrange evacuation for its non-white British subjects but racism elsewhere in the British Empire got in the way: when it asked the governments of Fiji, Ceylon, Burma, and India to receive about 2,393 Portuguese, Chinese, and Eurasian British subjects, only Fiji agreed to take the Chinese.[30]

The episode was the most egregious example yet of the failure of bureaucracy to keep up with Hong Kong's multicultured and multicolored population.

Hong Kong's harbor quickly drew in shipping from around the world, here gathered around a New York–built steamboat plying the Pearl River up to Canton, circa 1865.

1

Soon, the harbor was lined by the solidity and status of major merchant houses.

2

Central to the port city's growth was the mixing of peoples, spurred not least by the exploitation of young women as sex workers or, as seen here, domestic helpers.

3

By 1868, Queen's Road wound westward between temples of commerce, the clock tower, and (back left) the cathedral.

4

The wealthy Parsi community erected a ceremonial arch and lanterns to celebrate the visit to Hong Kong of HRH the Duke of Edinburgh in November 1869—as Chinese traders nearby advertised their peanut oil and good wine for sale.

5

This trading free-for-all helped Hong Kong grow into a bustling harbor town in the 1890s.

6

7

8

"Big Number Brothels," here seen on Spring Garden Lane in the 1920s, served a well-traveled clientele. Other brothels from Queen's Road West to Shek Tong Tsui catered to specific groups—Chinese, European, and others—with varying degrees of sophistication.

9

As people kept coming from around the world, they needed money changers, pharmacists, jewelry stores, tailors, dentists, and transport, as seen here on Queen's Road in the 1910s.

10

Precipitous "ladder" streets, seen here in the 1920s, climbed out of the harbor and up the hillsides.

11

Homes were small, dark, cramped, and often unsanitary, and life was often lived on the street, where hawkers offered anything from lychee fruits to cigarettes—and a lucky few could grab opportunities to get ahead.

Out of this melee emerged dynasties, especially if sons—such as the Ho Tung boys here, in the 1920s—built on the education and commercial opportunities needed to straddle East and West.

As their wealth and status grew, so did the lavishness of gowns to adorn wives and concubines.

The Ho Tung clan built gracious summer homes in the early twentieth century—such as the one seen here at Tai Tam Cove in faded 1980s grandeur (before demolition to make way for the American Club's country club).

15

Patriarch Sir Robert Ho Tung, here third from left, always wore Chinese clothes as if to obscure his half-Dutch heritage. By now rich and powerful, he hosted world figures, such as George Bernard Shaw in 1933, here third from right, where the resemblance between them was remarked.

16

Ho Tung, front left, was part of a wider Eurasian elite in the 1930s that included the part-Parsi Sir Robert Kotewall (third from left, front row) and other leading officials.

Hong Kong's leading merchant, the Armenian Sir Paul Chater, made a fortune through savvy brokerage, land and property deals, and investments in industry.

17

18

Chater built his Marble Hall on the Peak in European grandeur with an oriental flourish to enjoy the view and entertain in style.

Chater's best friend and business partner, the Parsi Sir Hormusjee Nowrojee Mody, lived no less lavishly in a city both men had helped to build.

19

20

The colony's wealthiest and most powerful men gathered to mark Queen Victoria's Diamond Jubilee in June 1897, here gathered around the governor, Sir William Robinson, in dark garb with plume and sword. On his left hand is Sir Paul Chater and over his right shoulder is the top-hatted barrister Ho Kai. On the far left is another leading Chinese businessman, Wei Yuk, and third from left is the Jewish merchant and philanthropist Emanuel Belilios; on the far right is a future governor, Henry May.

By the 1920s Hong Kong was a buzzing city, now served by the Kowloon Canton Railway, which deposited travelers on the tip of the Kowloon Peninsula, next to the Star Ferry terminal.

21

As ever, the harbor brought in new people, here Filipino seamen, circa 1911.

22

Rising 1,200 feet above sea level, the Peak Tram had been built in 1888 to serve the European elite seeking higher, cooler climes. At its foot, the open ground was home to cricket games next to the Hong Kong Club on the waterfront; further up, on the left, with cupolas, was the former grand home of the merchant Emanuel Belilios.

23

24

Views from the top of the Peak, also in 1924, stretched from the business district below and across the harbor to the Kowloon Peninsula, where new wharves and residential areas were being developed.

Lascar Row, otherwise known as Cat Street, was initially home to boardinghouses for less wealthy traders and sailors of all origins. Its stalls evolved from serving the needs of such travelers into an antiques market.

25

26

Wyndham Street, also known as Flower Street, offered all manner of services amid a thriving mixed trading community in the 1920s.

Patsy Kotewall was the last daughter of Sir Robert and Lady Edith Kotewall. When she married her fellow Eurasian John Fenton in 1951, her wedding at St. John's Cathedral was attended by top government figures such as the secretary for Chinese affairs and the chief justice, and their wives.

27

28

Li Sui Ling, left, second wife of Choa Leep-chee, a sugar tycoon from Malacca, gives a hint of the style that would come through in her daughter Trixie, center below, who married Arnaldo Botelho, on the right. The shift from Western velvet to imperial Chinese costumes illustrates just how diverse were these families sharing Chinese, Portuguese, Spanish, and other blood.

29

Hatton House was home to the vital Kotewall clan, perched on Kotewall Road halfway up the Peak.

30

The mansion was the product of the hard work of Robert Kotewall, the Parsi-Chinese government servant and merchant, and his lovely wife, Edith. A refuge for the family during World War Two, it was let go amid postwar travails.

31

32

That three of Kotewall's daughters married three Zimmern sons is well known. But generations earlier, another level of connection existed when Adolphe Zimmern (of German-Jewish stock) left his Protected Woman, center, flanked by her two sons, Andrew and Adolf; two daughters; and two daughters-in-law.

The view from a bomber plane in 1945 showed a city flattened by deprivation and the flight of its people. A prewar population of about 1.6 million had been shrunk by starvation, killings, and sometimes forced flight to just 600,000.

33

The successful businessman and leading Eurasian philanthropist Major Samuel Macumber Churn, whose parentage remains wreathed in mystery, worked for British military intelligence during the war.

34

Some people who could not flee found shelter and food thanks to the International Committee of the Red Cross's brilliant wartime representative, Rudolf Zindel, who set up the Rosary Hill home for dependents of imprisoned Britons and a varied crowd of "third nationals."

35

36

By 1952, Hong Kong's recovery was so profound that tourists could pose in front of the Hongkong and Shanghai Bank headquarters and the slimmer Bank of China.

37

Within a few short decades, the Hong Kong Stock Exchange had taken off; some degree of wealth and stability now seemed possible for many.

38

Among the many success stories of early-twentieth-century Hong Kong is the Harilela family. From selling toothbrushes out of suitcases, Hari Harilela and his brothers rose through tailoring to become cosmopolitan hotel and property tycoons.

39

When Little Red Book–waving cadres overflowed from China's Cultural Revolution into the streets of Hong Kong in 1967, the vast majority of Hong Kongers backed their police force's firm measures to quell them. Few wanted to relinquish the capitalism enabled by Western rule.

Fast-forward to 2014—long after the British deal to relinquish sovereignty over Hong Kong to China in 1997 in return for the promise of continued freedoms—and Hong Kongers were on the streets for a record seventy-nine days in their self-styled "Occupy" movement. They were peacefully angry at the perceived loss of those freedoms, and the breaking of promises to allow a free choice of leaders.

40

The growing pro-democracy movement took a new turn through the summer of 2019, when the government's attempt to legislate extradition of Hong Kongers into China's opaque legal system backfired. One million people marched against the government one week; two million marched the next. The marchers kept coming, rain or shine, until quashed by a now far less popular police force.

4

The Covid-19 pandemic inspired the government to ever greater heights of surveillance. It was impossible to do as it was told by Beijing—achieve zero transmission through heavy social distancing and quarantine regimes—and keep the city alive. So the city started to die: hundreds of thousands of its bright, educated people, including those now fearful for their future following the national security crackdown, simply left.

42

Meanwhile, the Ho Tung diamond wedding party went ahead, as did a "Tin Hat" ball at the Peninsula Hotel thrown in aid of the allied war effort. One lady dancing on that precipice was Gwen Priestwood. She remembers the orchestra playing "The Best Things in Life Are Free" after she had been at the races that afternoon amid "crowds of Britishers, Americans, and wealthy Chinese, winning and losing bets; the pretty frocks of the women; the gay little groups sipping Gimlets and whiskey-sodas . . ." She later reflected that it was precisely her years of living on the China coast through all manner of perils that had made her blasé this time. "Having lived since 1919 in China, where wars and rumors of war are so prevalent, and also having seen the bombing of the outskirts of the International Settlement in Shanghai in 1932—watching the bombs drop across the road from me, yet still living through them—I had somehow become a little disbelieving . . . This time—well, would it be any different?"[31]

Yes, it would. All of Hong Kong's peoples fought desperately for just over two weeks, before the government surrendered to Japanese occupation on Christmas Day. The fighting had begun on December 8, 1941, the same day Japan bombed Pearl Harbor (where locally it was December 7). Britain had dithered about whether to reinforce this colony, and its wartime leader, Winston Churchill, made clear he knew it would fall; the hope was a gallant defense would delay further Japanese advance. British, Canadian, and other Allied forces suffered around 2,000 men killed or missing, and perhaps the same number of wounded (the counts vary). The toll for "Indian Other Ranks" was at least another 1,000 men. For the next three and a half years, almost 11,000 Allied soldiers were held in grisly prisoner of war camps where another almost 300 died; of those who survived, many never fully recovered from the ordeal. In addition, 2,400 British and Allied civilians were detained in Stanley Internment Camp, where hunger and disease ruined lives. Several gruesome atrocities were perpetrated by Japanese troops before and after the British surrender.

"The sybaritic life of pre-war Hong Kong faded into a dream," noted the historian Paul Gillingham.[32]

One particular battle of that war brought to light the willingness of Hong Kong's Eurasians to, literally, die for Hong Kong if need be— the Battle of Wong Nei Chong Gap. This is the dip in the high ridge dominating Hong Kong Island and thus the route from one side of the island to the other. By mid-December 1941, Japanese troops held the New Territories and Kowloon. With Hong Kong's defenses now focused solely on the island, Wong Nei Chong was "the valley that the Japanese must surely attack (with their excellent intelligence) in order to split the defending brigades"; indeed, "by chance or good planning" No. 3 Company was "on the exact path that the Japanese would choose for their move inland."[33]

No. 3 (Machine Gun) Company comprised almost entirely Eurasian volunteers from the Hong Kong Volunteer Defence Corps. Several members of the largely British No. 1 Company suggested forming their own Eurasian company. They were all Eurasian men, and all graduates of the Diocesan Boys' School.[34] Evan George Stewart, orphaned son of China missionaries and headmaster of St. Paul's Co-Ed, was the officer in charge. He presided over three platoons (numbered 7, 8, and 9). Commanding 7 Platoon was Captain Leslie Holmes, who, along with his wife, was a crack shot. Commanding 8 Platoon was the first local magistrate of Hong Kong and older brother of the renowned educationalist Joyce Symons, Donald Anderson. But of Stewart's three platoon commanders only Lieutenant Bevan Field, commanding 9 Platoon, survived the war. He worked at Hongkong Land.

The men under them included lawyers, accountants, civil servants, engineers, teachers, salesmen, storekeepers, clerks, brokers, and even a journalist,[35] and several university students. Such men and their families formed the bedrock of prewar Hong Kong society.[36] After initially separate deployments, the three platoons were united by December 14 at Wong Nei Chong Gap and Japanese troops were soon directly on the attack. The first short, sharp encounter cost ten lives from No. 3 Company. The grenades, shells, and other fire poured onto their positions, and the machine gun volleys that No. 3 Company sent back, have been reconstructed by diaries and ground evidence; the pillboxes they defended still stand on Hong Kong's hillsides.

By the end of a days-long dramatic fight and defense, thirty officers and men from the company had died in and around the Gap, with two more killed later and many of the survivors wounded. Several of those who survived—including Douglas Hung, C. S. M. Quah, and the brothers George and Jimmy Kotwall—managed to evade capture and joined the resistance British Army Aid Group (BAAG); others joined clandestine or commando units such as Force 136 and Mission 204; yet others were sent into the India-Burma theater and joined the Chindits, the British-led guerrilla force fighting behind Japanese lines. Major-General C. M. Maltby (General Officer Commanding, Hong Kong) remembered them in his *Dispatches*, a supplement to the *London Gazette*, in 1948: "I should like to place on record the superb gallantry of No 3 (Eurasian) Company at Wong Nai Chung Gap."

Most members of No. 3 Company were taken as prisoners of war, and amid great privation they achieved a higher survival rate than others. "While familiarity with Hong Kong's dubious pre-war sanitation and the accumulated immunity may have helped, no doubt personal motivation was also a factor."[37] By 1943, several were shipped off to tough labor camps in Japan. Many never recovered fully after the war but most returned to and built on their prewar Hong Kong lives.

12

WARS WITHIN AND WITHOUT

Within months after Hong Kong fell, the Japanese-controlled *Hongkong News* reported that Jimmy's Kitchen, the Parisian Grill, and Ruttonjee's brewery were back in operation. But the city had deteriorated, Japanese shipping was under pressure and had failed to bring supplies, and repression was intensifying. By 1944, food shortages would become acute; the populace was starving and the economy had atrophied. A population of 1.6 million before the war was reduced, also by flight, to around 600,000 by its end.

The Japanese governor Rensuke Isogai was keen to play the racial card, encouraging Asians to rise up against their British colonial masters by backing Japan in a war of the colored races against the white. But the daily details of life under the Japanese—the huge number of rapes and looting, the lack of food and work, the infliction of petty humiliations, the corruption at every level, the atrocities—soon stripped the Japanese option of any appeal. The sudden British collapse in Hong Kong and across Southeast Asia had grossly damaged British prestige, as had a prewar scandal in Hong Kong when the girlfriend of the officer in charge of air raid precautions made money by supplying substandard concrete,[1] but there was little to stop a gradual resurgence of local preference for a past normality.

Within a year, the Japanese had shown they could be more racist, bossy, and brutal than anything previously experienced in the colony.

The atrocities began early—when Japanese troops rampaged through Queen Mary Hospital raping and killing any women they found; survivors staggered bloodied to an internment camp to tell their tale. Looting was endemic and civilians were ordered to bow low to any soldier they met; if they forgot or otherwise failed to do so they would be slapped, or worse. While professing benevolence, the Japanese failed to feed the people. An uninterned Swiss resident recalled one day during the war: "The Japanese would stop the tram . . . and probably one man did not have his certificate on him so he tried to jump to the other and immediately they took a gun and shot him."[2] Meanwhile, efforts by the Japanese to recruit Eurasians who, they assumed, must have suffered discrimination at the hands of the British met with negligible success.

Despite a history of distrust, of being seen as second best, or derided as "not British enough," it was the crucible of war and occupation in which the mettle of the true Hong Kongers was displayed. This was a motley bunch. Young women from good Eurasian, Portuguese, British, and other homes worked as confidential assistants to military men, as air raid wardens and nurses. Young men lined up to shoot and be shot at; families sought ways to bury wealth or hide their daughters; many fled to Macao, where they formed a contingent of Hong Kong people committed to supporting the resistance against Japanese occupation and envisaging a different future.

They included the obviously British gentlemen of The Hong Kong Club who patriotically drank as much of the alcohol stocks as possible to stop them falling into Japanese mouths. When later interned in the Stanley camp for civilian prisoners of war, these same men ran their company boards on camp stools and empty stomachs, authorizing money for the club housekeeper, and plotting actively for life after the war. Some future executives grew up in the Stanley camp, such as Peter Hall, future company secretary for Hongkong Land and the chronicler of the Eurasian "Web"; others were born there.[3]

Those who were excluded from or had a way to choose to avoid internment had a different set of complicated choices to make. One such was an American journalist, Emily Hahn, who claimed a Chinese husband to stay out of camp. Harder questions would follow. How far does one go to get food on the table for one's family? How could one survive if one's wage-earner was dead or interned? Should one flee overland through to "Free China," meaning the nationalist-led Chinese government now based in Chungking? Intelligence operations were based there, and men such as Keswick from Jardine's led Special Operations Executive work behind the lines, as did Hong Kong University's Dr. (Col.) Lindsay Ride, who set up the British Army Aid Group. Or would that put others at needless risk?

Those who couldn't get away suffered "the agony of the Japanese occupation, when tens of thousands died in the streets and boats and the crowded dwellings of the poor, and cannibalism stalked among a kindly and industrious people." So described Dr. Selwyn Selwyn-Clarke, director of medical services before and partway through the war. He saw when hospitals flying the Red Cross flag were violated, Chinese stretcher bearers with Red Cross armbands were killed, and scores of nurses were raped. In 1942 alone, said Selwyn-Clarke, 83,435 burials of Hong Kong residents were recorded, some of these from fighting or reprisals, but many from starvation. Bank accounts were frozen; people had to sell belongings for food. Third-grade rice increased in price more than twelvefold before the end. One tactic the Japanese found to cope with the lack of food was forced evacuations: people were rounded up, put on boats, towed out to sea, and left to sink or swim, perhaps seeing their boats burned by the Japanese.[4]

Selwyn-Clarke soon discovered that Japan was not a signatory to the Geneva Convention. That meant he could run only an Informal Welfare Committee, which, nonetheless, made sure medical supplies reached many in need. Once citizens of Britain and its allies were interned near Stanley Beach on the south side of the island, on January 21, 1942, he could get more organized. Internees lacked beds, bedding, clothes, diapers, infant foods, kitchen utensils, and much more, including drugs; he even managed to smuggle a dentist's chair into the Stanley camp. He appreciated the spontaneous generosity, at great risk to themselves, of Chinese, Indians, Portuguese, and others who were living outside.[5] Selwyn-Clarke was eventually arrested on charges of passing secret messages to British spies in China, but survived the war.

Inside Hong Kong, the Japanese had settled after an orgy of looting and rape to rule along the lines of their East Asia Co-Prosperity Sphere. This overtly anti–Western imperialism plan targeted anticolonial independence movements in the region (to some effect in Burma, Indonesia, and India). In Hong Kong, Indians and other Asians were given positions of control over the interned Europeans. The Rehabilitation Committee, leadership of which was imposed on Hong Kong's senior Legislative Council members Sir Shouson Chow and Sir Robert Kotewall, was kept busy "trotting off to Japanese celebrations and making polite, deferential remarks about the virtues of the new regime . . ."[6] In March 1942 came the Chinese Representative Council and the Chinese Cooperative Council. These had no power at all, but presaged a proliferation of district affairs bureaux. Participation in such pro-Japanese performances would cause great angst during and after the war.

No one knows how they will react under such extreme stresses, when the outcome of any decision could mean death, torture, or triumph. Hong Kongers, as anyone, responded in diverse, startling, scurrilous, and inspiring ways. Western histories of the war have focused on the privations, starvation, and despair suffered by civilians interned at the Stanley camp and military men at the POW camps in Kowloon. Less attention has been paid to how the majority of Hong Kong people, of all kinds, ducked and weaved their way through the minefields of war.

———

As Japanese troops poured over the hills and into Kowloon, a young Lawrence Kadoorie got a handful of transport passes for all senior staff of China Light and Power (thanks to a government secretary whose brother worked at the power station). Frantically signing them as the ferry brought him to Kowloon, he commandeered a small bus. Passing La Salle College he heard shouts of "five somewhat terrified European nurses at their wits' end and wondering what to do. I adopted them and put them in my bus . . ." At the power station, all was under control: explosive charges were in place, it was ready to blow, and key parts already adorned the harbor floor. On his way back to the pier, he met his Portuguese accountant Remedios, who gave him one Mrs. Wookie carrying a baby, saying she was the common-law wife of a British sergeant. Collecting a further three American sailors, he got everyone Hong Kong–side. There he managed to off-load the nurses onto a grateful Dr. Selwyn-Clarke, and "after heated argument" persuaded the American consulate to take the sailors. Then, with Mrs. Wookie and baby, Lawrence went to his home on the Peak, now filled with Canadians. "Mrs Wookie and her baby, not being considered 'enemy subjects' were found accommodation elsewhere," recalled Lawrence, implying she was Chinese or Eurasian; her fate would become clear as the war progressed. Lawrence, meanwhile, interned at Stanley, reckoned he became skilled at scrubbing toilets and living rough. It no doubt helped that his family was rich and prominent—after just five months in Stanley they were allowed back to Shanghai.[7]

Barbara Anslow was a young British woman in Hong Kong who had signed up for Air Raid Precaution duty and remembers working long hours in the last days of the war, and being billeted in Dina House, a building in central Hong Kong still owned by the Ruttonjee family. She recalled sharing rooms with Eurasians and British women. She was beginning to live beyond her previously small British world. By the end of the war, she felt the change in herself: "How did the time in camp affect my life? It altered my outlook on racism and religion. Pre-war I had no Chinese, Portuguese or Eurasian friends or acquaintances; our ways didn't cross. In Stanley I had close connections, mainly through R.C. church activities, with all three races and made many friends among them . . . I like to think camp made me more tolerant."[8]

The Ruttonjees already knew there was a wider world, and they instantly put that knowledge at the service of Hong Kong and its peoples, at great personal risk. In 1942 Japanese guards surrounded their buildings, both Dina House and Ruttonjee Building, for several weeks; in 1944, both Jehangir Hormusjee Ruttonjee and his son Dhun were accused of engaging in anti-Japanese activities, thrown into prison, and tortured, only to be freed at war's end. Meanwhile, Mrs. Ruttonjee slowly eked out her savings and sold pieces of jewelry to stretch the stash of tinned foods and other goods on which she, and many hangers-on, could survive.

Lachman Narain's father was a messenger for many Hong Kong Indians as his father's brother owned a store in Macao and could send letters overseas; others in the community were ambulance volunteers or contributed funds and food. A core of British bankers was kept outside camp for some months by the Japanese in order to keep the banks working and issuing currency, later recognized as duress notes. One of these was G. A. Leiper: "My two colleagues and I, and many others, were especially indebted to the late Hon Dhun Jehangir Ruttonjee CBE; his father H.H. Ruttonjee; and to Dr the Hon Sir Sik Nin Chau CBE, who also gave his professional services and supplied medicines free on many occasions. After the war none of these gentlemen would accept any form of repayment for the financial and material help they had given to us."[9]

Life outside camp moved slowly, as businesses died and daily rounds became focused solely on food and security. A Sindhi businessman, U. S. Chellaram, described the Japanese attitude to Indians as "honey on the tongue, dagger in the heart."[10] He and his family escaped overland by pretending to go on "holiday" to Vietnam; when they got to Chungking the British authorities refused assistance, so they trudged on to Guilin to get a flight to Calcutta with the help of the U.S. Army.

Shapurji Fakirji Jokhi, like Ruttonjee a Parsi, was jailed by the Japanese for eleven months of torture and solitary confinement for supplying food and medicine to camp internees. Due for execution, he had a dream that if he survived he would build a housing colony back in his native Navsari, India. "When a new commandant came to the camp he reviewed all the death sentences and asked Jokhi if he had indeed supplied such parcels and why. Jokhi said that he would do the same for a Japanese prisoner because his religion required him to feed the sick. 'We are,' he said, 'Asiatic religious people.'" The commandant was moved and commuted the death sentence to imprisonment; three months later Jokhi was freed. He then built housing for more than two thousand people back in Navsari. Fellow Parsis such as Minoo Master, and the Canton residents Behram C. Tavadia and Jal Patel, his brother-in-law, were also tortured, Patel fatally.[11]

Japan's imperial dreams of an Asian Co-Prosperity Sphere were doomed to fail despite their initially rapid takeover of most of the region. Certainly the United States, Britain, and other Allies aimed to regain power in a part of the world likely to grow in importance, due to its richness in trade and people; World War Two was not only about defeating Nazi Germany but also forging networks to counter the rising threat of Soviet and other Communist foes. Bankers in Hong Kong before the war feared what a united China would mean for their profits, fearing (rightly) that they would be banished from a lucrative market.

But these were not the only reasons why Japan would lose this war. Just as important was the flawed nature of Japan's idea of uniting the region under its leadership in the first place—"Asians" were never a homogenous bunch, ripe for the picking, but a hugely diverse jumble of cultures, countries, economies, and peoples. No one power, be it Chinese, Japanese, or Western, could ever get it all under control. Influence was what mattered, and that could be nurtured from a spot central to the region: Hong Kong.

———

It may be recalled that when the opium trader Belilios left both his Chinese woman and his Jewish wife in Hong Kong in 1902, the latter, Semah Belilios, made her home in the King Edward Hotel until her death in 1926. Why there? Because it was another place where the outwardly "colonial" shell of prewar Hong Kong disguised a cosmopolitan core. It was, after all, founded by a Parsi (Dorabjee Nowrojee, founder, too, of the Star Ferry, which plows the waters of the harbor to this day[12]), and hosted the Parsi philanthropist Mody when his lavish Buxey Lodge was being renovated in 1910. The hotel's guest list for the opening on October 6, 1902, was led by Abdoolally Ebrahim, head of the oldest firm in Hong Kong still operating today.

Here was another relationship that would attain sudden significance in this war: Ebrahim's firm topped the list of clients in the earliest ledger of the Hongkong and Shanghai Bank (in 1865); this was, said the bank, "a respectable firm with whom our dealing [sic] have been very satisfactory and whom we consider would not enter into any engagements they could not see their way to fulfil."[13]

Ebrahim was not Parsi. With his founding business partner back in 1841—Seth Ebrahim Noordin, who had earlier survived a shipwreck on a bale of cotton—he was part of the Dawoodi Bohra community, an Ismaili sect that moved first from Yemen to India in 1539. The word *bohra* is Gujarati for the verb "to trade," and, while following Koranic rules against the charging of interest, the tiny but long-lasting Bohra community was and is deeply enmeshed in business. The Bohra speak their own language, an Arabized form of Gujarati, and practice their own pattern of worship.[14] They are members of Hong Kong's Incorporated Trustees of the Islamic Community Fund. The men wear sweeping gowns and white pillbox hats or topi with gold hand embroidery; women wear long dresses topped with matching capes to cover neck and shoulder.

Ebrahim's company dealt in spices, silk, art, imported cotton goods, and raw cotton from India; it diversified into shipping, real estate, and manufacturing. It ran the very first ferries across the harbor before the Star Ferry was established, small boats still called "walla-walla," a name originating in India, as *walla* means "person from," explained Zafir T. Ebrahim, a fifth-generation Hong Konger.[15] Many of the Bohra were schooled—alongside Portuguese, Eurasians, and Chinese—at the Catholic St. Joseph's College and the Anglican Diocesan Boys' School. They have been adept at survival, being careful and small scale, adapting to local mores and languages though never relinquishing their own style; their refusal to drink alcohol disadvantaged them with the British, they joke.

"For a long, long time we have seen Hong Kong as our only home," said Norman Hoosenally, one of the community elders who first came to Hong Kong in 1930. "We are almost more local than many of the Chinese. It's just that we don't have Chinese faces."[16] When the fifty-second dai (the intermediary between the Prophet Muhammad and the Bohra people) visited Hong Kong in 1997, a full-page newspaper notice recorded that about a million Bohra lived in India, Pakistan, the Middle East, East Africa, and the West: "A community eager to explore avenues of trade in the East were encouraged to come to China over 150 years ago by the 47th Dai. They remained and prospered. The 52nd Dai now arrives . . . His guidance remains: 'Be loyal to your land of abode.'"[17]

And so they proved.

Both the Barma and Ebrahim families had friends and relatives interned in the Stanley camp during the war—and in the resistance. When a couple of Hongkong Bank employees, Luis Souza and Charles Hyde, needed help, it was to Ebrahim's office that they came. The two men had been put up by the Japanese at the "bankers' hotel," the Sun Wah, where it was too dangerous to keep their radio. When the bankers asked the Ebrahims to hide it for them, they immediately agreed. They also lent money for food and medicine for camp internees, including one Uncle Saleh, also known as Shanghai Taipan. "Yes, we kept documents for the bank and a radio," Ebrahim confirmed. The researcher Brian Edgar adds: "Hiding the radio meant death if it was discovered, but even making a loan was dangerous—a Turkish restaurant owner and his wife were brutally tortured after incriminating documents were discovered. A quick-thinking Abdoolally employee ate a promissory note from HSBC man Hugo Foy when he realised the Kempetai were entering the premises."[18]

———

Across the harbor in Kowloon, a different sort of heroism was afoot when the acting Portuguese Consul, Francisco Soares, decided it was time for all Hong Kong Portuguese who might have seen themselves as British until now, and indeed had just fought on the British side in the war, to now reclaim their Portuguese identity for sanctuary under neutrality nearby. He had allowed his home on Liberty Avenue in the garden city part of Kowloon to become a refuge that doubled as the consulate, frantically issuing Portuguese passports. About 85 percent of Hong Kong's Portuguese would flee to Macao. On their way, about four hundred of them crowded into the Soares mansion, where chickens were reared on the roof and many of those staying had their own guns and guarded the whole area at night against looters. Sanitary waste was a problem, but then a beautiful mango tree in the garden that had never blossomed suddenly, thanks to a fresh sewage trench, burst into fruit.[19]

Living nearby was the Gosano family—another name to watch as the war progressed. Mrs. Gosano had a powerful religious faith to sustain her as she single-handedly brought up nine children and four orphaned nephews. Also nearby, the Braga family, parts of it working with the Kadoories, had resources enough to make several trips to Macao to make sure it was a suitable refuge for older family members. One member wrote to another telling how it was only when three boys from the Soares house turned up that they realized how they could escape, by emphasizing their Portuguese identity. "They told us they were able to creep about like this by slipping down side-roads and avoiding the Japs as much as possible, and when accosted, pointed to the flag of a neutral country—their fatherland. This gave us courage to go out so the girls got out some green, red and yellow bits of cloth and sewed most excellent Portuguese flags. (We had become 'Our People' indeed!)" Jack Braga, already in Macao, "had been sending secret messages by members of the crew of the Jap ship coming to HK, urging us all to come to Macao where he could arrange for our keep. The only reason why I think we were all so stupid as not to trust his advice is that we must have been 'effected' . . . All sense of reasoning seemed to disappear, giving way to a stupid behaviour of stubbornness and the desire to 'see the war through' in Hong Kong." That gave way to the realization that Macao, with its sleepy colored houses and enclosed verandas, its hawkers and Catholic fathers, was still, even with its overcrowding and "off-duty" Japanese, a safer prospect.[20]

Another family to find refuge there was that of Margaret Choa. Her grandfather had been the Malacca Chinese who came to Hong Kong to trade in sugar.[21] Margaret had a privileged upbringing in a mansion in Happy Valley, but that all changed when British troops requisitioned it during the fighting, then the Japanese advanced. Her family threw what they could into large bedsheets and carried them on the walk to Central. They had no idea where to go but "there was a wonderful shop owned by Indians which was Kamali [sic: Kayamally?] . . . a very old Indian establishment, and they gave us two rooms upstairs of their own building. I think they must have seen us coming up looking for a place and we stayed in those two rooms to start with. But being Eurasians we were not put in camp or given any problems and we were given passes to leave Hong Kong . . . and gradually my family in batches went into Free China because there you could find jobs with the American army and the British army in consulates and so on . . ." It is thanks to this escape that Margaret met the man who would become her husband, Roger Lobo, a hero both in the war and to Hong Kong many decades into the future.[22]

Roger's father was Pedro José Lobo, one of two key middlemen who—along with the British consul John Pownall Reeves—kept supplies and support moving for the growing refugee flows into Macao. Pedro Lobo had been born in another Portuguese colony, Timor, but had arrived in Macao young and married into the Hyndman family. Meaning it in the nicest possible way, the historian Geoffrey Gunn says Pedro became the major "collaborator" and savior of Macao. With his "oriental psychology" and the "skills of a Kissinger," Lobo made numerous interventions with the Japanese.[23] He was head of the powerful Macao Central Bureau of Economic Services, and manager of the Macao Water Co. Now he led the Companhia Cooperativa de Macao, a joint Macao government–Japanese Army private venture. Portuguese surplus, such as tugboats or telephone equipment, was exchanged with the Japanese for food from the mainland. Lobo, father and son, used an old generator and diesel engine found in the naval dockyard to start milling flour acquired in this way; they traded or bartered everything they could lay their hands on, from gasoline or church bells to metal frames, wire, nails, and more. At the same time, Lobo senior helped refugees with schooling, and young Roger Lobo worked periodically with British intelligence.[24]

There's no doubt that personal fortunes were made, with the late billionaire Stanley Ho being a good example. "I was in charge of a barter system, helping the Macao government to exchange machinery and equipment with the Japanese in exchange for rice, sugar, beans . . . I was a semi-government official then; I was the middleman," Ho said.[25] Ho got to Macao aged twenty just before the invasion of Hong Kong; by 1944, he had bought a launch, the *Coloane*, and his future as casino and transport king of Macao was set.

In Macao, a revitalized branch of the Portuguese Red Cross was run by another leading Macao merchant, Fernando de Senna Fernandes Rodrigues. Though officially neutral, Macao had been pro-British for years. Portuguese leaders knew that if the British were entirely ousted from China, their own time in Macao was likely to be short. So its practice of neutrality was highly ambiguous. The Macao Red Cross of 1943 mainly helped the British Portuguese Eurasians fleeing Hong Kong. Rodrigues made deals for provisions, and had large storage facilities and a wide net of contacts useful not only for foodstuffs but for intelligence, too. Then he was shot dead on a Macao street on July 10, 1945, for murky reasons including perhaps smuggling and refusal to cooperate with the Japanese. This incarnation of the Red Cross lasted only another year.[26] Rodrigues's daughter Norma was shot in the back when she attended, aged twelve, her father's funeral; she would live in Hong Kong from 1951, in a gracious Kowloon Tong home with many Portuguese neighbors. After marrying d'Almada

Remedios she had three children: the high court judge Sue; Leo, a lawyer; and José, who died young. "Yes, we all have Chinese blood. My grandfather was pure Portuguese and married a typical Chinese lady."[27]

Also in Macao was Sir Robert Ho Tung. After that silver wedding anniversary party at the Peninsula Hotel on the eve of war, he had retired to Macao "for a rest," staying at his lovely mansion with garden and high walls. Perhaps he'd been tipped off it was time to go. It was certainly a smart move; while men such as his son-in-law Billy Gittins, who fought in the Volunteers, was imprisoned, and eventually died in Japan, and Billy's wife, Jean, starved gently in the Stanley camp, Ho Tung was comfortable. His son Eddie had his feet and half a leg shot off as he sought food under fire in Hong Kong. A brother, Ho Wing, was jailed by the Japanese and tortured. Another brother, Ho Kom Tong, at last could be in charge of the Jockey Club, keeping the races going through the war. Ho Tung's concern was, apart from his digestion, his wealth. The Japanese Colonel Sawa visited Ho Tung in Macao, pressing him to join the governance councils being set up, promising help to retrieve confiscated properties. Ho Tung did not succumb to the blandishments but he did visit Hong Kong briefly in March 1942. He was described by the Japanese-run *Hongkong News*, under the headline "Ho Tung Expresses Earnest Willingness to Cooperate—Anxious to Assist in Bringing a New Era of Prosperity," as "looking extremely fit and well." He met the press at the Peninsula after a forty-minute chat with Governor Isogai. "Accompanied by a lady secretary, Mr Ho appeared in splendid spirits and, fanning himself meanwhile . . . ," explained he'd returned to Hong Kong to see his wife and injured son; the Japanese had been "most solicitous of his welfare. He could not adequately express his deep gratitude for their kind interest in him." Now his one wish was to help bring a new era of prosperity to Hong Kong, and he welcomed the advice of the Japanese, the press, and all. When pressed, he said he would "contribute his share towards the establishment" of the Co-Prosperity Sphere in East Asia. "This concluded the interview but before leaving, Mr Ho smilingly asked the Press representatives how he looked. When told that he was very healthy for his age, he appeared extremely pleased."[28]

Meanwhile, Carlo Henrique Basto was arrested at Club Lusitano in 1942 while playing bridge with friends—the Japanese thought his score sheet was coded message-making. He was taken out and killed.

Also executed for alleged espionage were the brothers Jimmy and George Kotwall (not related to the Kotewall family of Sir Robert). As had many members of the Volunteer regiments—Eurasian, Portuguese, and others—they joined the clandestine British Army Aid Group. The Kotwall brothers were neighbors of Saleh Ebrahim, of the Bohra radio-hiding family. With George Samuel Ladd, he joined the resistance network during 1943 and formed part of "K" Group alongside Jimmy Kotwall, as the historian Brian Edgar has traced. He notes that the young men were joining the network at its most dangerous time; George, Jimmy's brother, was executed on October 29, 1943. "Using code, the team sent a wide variety of intelligence to BAAG Field HQ at Waichow, detailing, for example, the movement of ships through Hong Kong harbor, damage caused by American bombing, conditions at Stanley, and the activities of the pro-Japanese Indian Independence League . . ." But they were betrayed and arrested in March 1944, and interrogated for thirty-eight days before being handed over to the military authorities at Stanley Prison. Jimmy Kotwall was sentenced to death and executed two days later. Mr. Ladd and Mr. Ebrahim received sentences of eight years, while a Chinese associate, Lau King Sing, was sent to prison for three years but died that year.[29]

Boris Pasco had arrived from Russia in 1919 via Vancouver, Montreal, Southampton, and Yokohama. He ran a book shop in central Hong Kong and kept getting sued, or suing others, for copyright infringement or even assault. During the war his shop was used to drop off money for the underground, and provisions for prisoners of war; he, too, was taken by the Kempetai.[30] In 1948, a plaque was erected at the synagogue for the Jews who died in defense of the colony.[31]

For many young men of the Volunteers who either avoided or escaped internment, joining BAAG was the next obvious step. Eduardo Liberato Gosano, more usually called Eddie, was one example. He was an HKU medicine graduate but, when made surgical officer in the government's medical department, was paid on a local scale—meaning no free housing or long paid leaves—rather than the "British" scale accorded his fellow doctors from abroad. Yet he risked his life for Hong Kong by becoming the famed Agent Phoenix for BAAG. He had been interned but, released as a "third national" by the Japanese, he went to Macao, joined his fellow Portuguese doctor Horacio Ozório, then working at the British consulate, and became a courier for the underground. He was also key to the rescue of the Hongkong Bank's records, which had been brought to Macao ahead of the Japanese invasion but now needed to be sent farther away, to Chungking.[32] Agent Phoenix would also help Leo d'Almada get to London to work with the Hong Kong Planning Committee, plotting the British return to Hong Kong.[33]

Earlier, Gosano, Albert Rodrigues, and Solomon Bard, all medical graduates from HKU, put their skills to work inside Sham Shui Po POW camp. They had been in the Field Ambulance of the Hong Kong Volunteers—and in the summer of 1940 Bard had just become naturalized as a British subject. Jewish POWs were not separated out or treated any differently and even managed to gather for Sabbath services using prayer books sent into camp by the YMCA. "Incidentally, the Japanese made no effort to isolate or distinguish Jewish POWs; Nazi propaganda had either not reached Sham Shui Po or was ignored by the Japanese," said Bard.[34] His wife, Sophie, was not interned, as she was British merely by marriage.

Camp changed lives and fortunes—such as when Bevan Field of the Hongkong Land Company met young Bob Baker and recruited him for a postwar career while reconstructing company minutes in camp. Baker's successor in the job, Peter Hall, was surprised that Bob was a Eurasian, too.[35] He was one of the eleven children of John Baker and Gladys Fenton, both Eurasians. Gladys was left bringing up the children when John deserted her, succumbed to opium, and died bankrupt before the war. Another of her sons, Thomas, a journalist, was recruited as press attaché at the British embassy in Shanghai and Chungking. Thomas's wife, Doris (née Fenton), and her son's wife joined him by the overland escape route out of Hong Kong and mingled with a high-flying social crowd during unsafe times, meeting General and Madame Chiang Kai-shek, and entertaining officers and diplomats.[36] Fluid relationships, across ideology and borders, are seen in the fact that few overland escapes succeeded without help from the Communist-based East River guerrillas.[37]

Clifford Matthews, the cricketer refused entrance to the "British" Cricket Club, nonetheless fought for Hong Kong and was interned for it. He tried sharing his calculus skills in camp but his guards thought it was code and stopped class; he was later among those sent to a shipbuilding yard near Hiroshima, but despite backbreaking work, bad food, and disease he survived.[38] Phylis Nolasco da Silva née Anderson (whose brother Donald had died in combat) took on the highly dangerous task of running BAAG agents, earning a King's Medal for Gallantry. Her sister Joyce taught English to refugee children in Macao. Douglas Hung worked in intelligence and Mary Suffiad in counterespionage. She and her sister Zaza retired to California, but said Hong Kong would always be home. Sam Gittins and Oswald Cheung were cipher clerks in the British General Liaison Office in China.[39]

Yet another Eurasian who committed wholly to his Hong Kong community was Osler Thomas. His father, George Harold Thomas, also known as Tam Ka-sze, had no idea who his real parents were; they had died of plague. George was adopted by a woman surnamed Tam who had no children of her own. She adopted another unrelated stray boy, too, who would run a lighthouse near Shanghai. A converted Christian, she sent her boys to Diocesan Boys' School, and George went on to graduate in medicine from HKU. Dr. George Thomas would work in medicine in Hong Kong for sixty years, much of it at the Tung Wah Hospital.[40]

During the battle of Hong Kong, Dr. George Thomas, now medical superintendent at Tung Wah Hospital, was able to send an ambulance to rescue his son Osler, who had been part of a group that surrendered to the Japanese only to be lined up for beheading. Young Osler, already a medical student at HKU, decided to fall into the ditch full of corpses before he was slashed to death. He survived a day and night under the putrefying mess before staggering out and being given new clothes from an old woman in a shack on a nearby hillside. Once he saw the signs of dysentery in his stools he knew he had to find a way back to town, and, through word of mouth, his father found him. Five weeks later he went back to the ditch and spoke to a gardener who said yes, the water had run red for a few days. Osler managed to retrieve his pips (shoulder decorations to indicate rank), which he had hidden in a niche, and, seeing he was a survivor, the gardener handed over the medals of the sergeant major who had been in charge and killed there. The bodies were exhumed and reburied in Stanley Military Cemetery.

Osler Thomas joined what became a group escape of HKU students into Free China in August 1942. Journeying by truck, sampan, river junk, and bribery, with long days of walking and nights of bedbugs, some went to complete their studies at various Chinese institutions. Some of the funding for this escape came from the tiger balm entrepreneur Aw Boon Haw. Others, like Osler, reached BAAG headquarters by November, and joined Force 136. He spent all of 1943 infiltrated back into northeastern Hong Kong helping mainly Indian escapees. He heard the Japanese surrender in 1945 on a pedal-powered radio. "I had been asked by Colonel Ride a few months before if I would like a period of leave and recreation in India, and had declined his offer, thinking the end was near and wanting to be 'in at the kill.' After all, Hong Kong was home," he recalled.[41]

––––––––––

Young Pat Botelho spent her wartime childhood skipping school, and eating broken red rice and yam leaves, which her mother had started growing on the dug-up tennis court. She remembered pushing a trolley to one of the Ho Tung family homes to collect water from its well.[42] Charlie Churn learned how to fiddle the gas meter to make it go backward, and how to chop trees for fuel.[43] Both Charlie and Pat remember taking some lessons from Hugh Asome, a teacher at St. Joseph's College.

Hugh had been born in Hong Kong, product of a Jamaican-Chinese father and a Liverpool British–Chinese mother. Taken to Hong Kong at a young age, he knew little of Chinese culture and grew up Eurasian. The Asome family huddled at St. Joseph's for safety; home to boys of all faiths and races since its founding, it, too, was a Portuguese refuge during the war. Hugh's son John recalls growing up alongside Jews, Muslims, Christians, and others. "Perhaps racially I should have felt more Chinese than anything else, but my grandparents were brought up in particular parts of 'the West' and we had western habits." They used sit-down toilets, ate Western food with spoons and knives, and sat on comfy sofas rather than hard-backed blackwood Chinese chairs. John concluded: "Being Eurasian is not just about race or class, it's a state of mind."[44]

Meanwhile his aunt Agnes Theodora Asome had become a nurse and was working at the French Hospital in Hong Kong when war broke out. The family heard that she was "interned" at some place called Rosary Hill, until she appeared one day after the war loaded with fresh fruit. Everyone gorged on it and fell sick, but freedom felt fine.[45]

So what was this Rosary Hill?

On April 23, 1942, the *Hongkong News* noted that a meeting of Eurasians would be held at St. John's Cathedral Hall on the coming Sunday, "for the purpose of formulating plans for communal relief and general welfare." This wartime edition of the Welfare League provided genuine help to some, but the larger issue of providing support to "third nationals"—anyone neither formally British nor Japanese—remained unresolved. These were the local wives or common-law partners, even stray loves and mixed offspring, of men who, now interned, had left their women and families destitute. Here, too, were stateless people of perhaps Latvian descent, or Peruvians with Chinese surnames; "Asiatic Iraqis" whose names such as Hardoon and Gubbay suggest they were Baghdadi Jews; people with Western surnames calling themselves Chinese to avoid the alleged "slur" of *mixed-race*; Portuguese, Irish, Americans, and people of British nationality who were too richly colored to be British enough to be interned at Stanley.[46] As well as racial minorities, they were also mostly women.

Not until May 1942 could permission be gained to open a Red Cross office to disburse allowances guaranteed by the Allies for people inside and outside the camp. It was specifically barred from caring for Filipinos and Indians left in the lurch by the war; these were the "Asiatics" for whom Japan claimed responsibility (and then largely ignored). It was only allowed to help those American-Chinese who had registered as Americans; this effectively eliminated all American-Chinese, as none of them declared their U.S. nationality to the Japanese for fear of anti-Western repercussions. As for helping Hong Kong's Chinese, this was impossible, as Japan said the Red Cross "must abstain from giving any assistance . . . even to those that had British papers, or to Indians . . . or to any other Orientals, except to those who were Dependents of POWs, or of men killed or missing, or of Stanley Civilian Internees."[47] By the end of January 1943, there were officially almost seven thousand "third nationals" in Hong Kong, not including internees or "Enemy-Nationals." As for defining who was of which race and which nationality—often not the same thing at all—the definitional complexities multiplied.

Their plight was only ameliorated through the initiative of a Swiss businessman named Rudolf Zindel.[48] He was a trader in Hankow and Shanghai for an export-import business, Arnhold Trading and Co. (the now-defunct relative of the still-existing Arnhold and Co.), before joining his company's Hong Kong office in 1939. Suddenly given the task of caring for the defeated of Hong Kong, he had no background in relief work and lamented that he had been dropped in it without even a basic manual from Geneva of dos and don'ts. He was constantly constrained by the Japanese, allowed only highly controlled, quick appearances in some camps. Money and relief parcels had to sail through hostile waters to be disbursed through the Red Cross delegation in Tokyo, itself working under the gun; parcels and thousands of messages were simply tossed into back rooms and ignored by the Japanese until after the war—all this before factoring in a high rate of pilferage along the way and outright pillage of internees' possessions.

Throughout it all, Zindel endured surveillance, threats, censorship, and an increasing risk of arrest and torture by the Gendarmerie, as he tried to find ways to navigate this vast minefield in such a way as to gradually improve internees' conditions. He also, at huge personal physical and financial risk, finally resorted to raising loans locally from three Belgian bankers and a Danish consul with which to buy gold in local (military yen) currency at black market rates, to be paid back in Swiss francs after the war. (One of those Belgian bankers was Pierre Mardulyn, linked to the Macumber-Churn Eurasian clan by his marriage to Mabel Churn.) Even more extraordinary: after horrendous pressure for three and a half years, Zindel stayed on and provided for 22,000 Japanese internees all those Red Cross services that these same Japanese had made it so hard for him to give their opponents.

Zindel's innovation for the many people outside camp was to pool the allowance funds he was disbursing individually into one fund with which he set up the Rosary Hill Home. It was a hostel that all stray dependents and other random people could choose to enter, bringing their own basic needs in clothes and household goods, but leaving any pretension of private life behind. No pets, no servants, no fancy habits or bad behavior would be allowed. This would be communal living, in an empty college halfway up the Peak (the use of which Zindel negotiated with the Spanish Dominican Fathers for a fee), surrounded by pine trees.

As always with people of mixed origins, identities, and relationships, deciding who was eligible for support was not easy. A set of medals, a wedding ring, or parts of a uniform might be genuine, but could easily have been faked or stolen. Did one include mothers-in-law, grandchildren, and adopted children? Explained Zindel to his colleagues back in Geneva: "This question of 'adopted children' particularly, is not, of course, an unusual one in Hongkong. Men in the Armed Forces, in time of peace, quite often lived with, or were married according to Chinese Customs, to Chinese girls, have children which perhaps were acknowledged by their fathers, but also left behind when they or their Regiments were transferred. In many cases, the Mothers of such children later on entered an alliance with some other soldier and the children of the previous marriage were taken in, but never really adopted. Their status now, with regard to our scheme of paying allowances, gave much cause for thought . . ." Common-law wives caused similar dilemmas, with little to prove their claims. Invariably he erred on the side of generosity.[49]

At Rosary Hill, by mid-1943, 1,104 "Dependents" had found shelter. The composition of this community gives an insight into the actual makeup of prewar Hong Kong society. Here were 143 British Legal Wives, 61 Common-Law Wives of British Subjects, 41 Portuguese Legal Wives, 25 Third National Legal Wives, 1 Common-Law Wife of a Third National, 28 Eurasian Legal Wives, 1 Eurasian Common-Law Wife, and 19 Chinese Legal Wives. There were also 166 Close Relatives of a former supporter now in Camp, 4 Fiancées (which interestingly added up to 5 beneficiaries), and 26 Wives of Men serving with British forces and/or the British Merchant Marine abroad. Many of these people had children, thus boosting the overall total of people to be fed and housed.[50] One of them was the woman with a child collected in Lawrence Kadoorie's mad dash through Kowloon as war began—Mrs. Florence Wookie, "Eurasian, British by Marriage," and so given sanctuary.

In correspondence after the war, Zindel explained more of what might be termed the *Eurasian dilemma*, through the case of young Egbert Charles Watson, a nineteen-year-old orphan in desperate circumstances. What should he call himself? To the Japanese, it was better to obscure one's British nationality and appear Chinese—but in young Egbert's case this almost killed him. His father was Gilbert Charles Watson, a British engineer in the Mercantile Marine who, as far as Egbert could recall, had died in October 1937 on his ship, leaving only a collection of postage stamps. Egbert's mother was Chan A Sin, a Chinese woman; of two brothers, he thought one was killed and the other missing. Once his father's burial expenses were covered, the widowed Ms. Chan got help from the harbormaster, who had the dead man's stamp collection sold in London for about $8,000. She managed to buy two properties with mortgages just before the war but then the Japanese demolished the first one to expand the airport (offering her military yen, which she refused to accept). The second house was also demolished by local outlaws who sold the wood for fuel.

Said young Egbert: "The reason why we did not register with and apply for assistance from the local branch of the International Red Cross Association is because my mother had ignorantly registered the whole family as Chinese nationals and given us Chinese names. After a long time, when she came to know about the work of this Association it was too late to do anything because any change of names and nationality would bring about long term imprisonment and corporal punishment for the whole family. Therefore throughout the war we passed as Chinese nationals." That status not only deprived Egbert and his family of Red Cross assistance, but made them vulnerable to periodic compulsory repatriation orders by the Japanese. One such forced expulsion in July 1945 caught up his brother George, never seen again, and then Egbert and his mother. Robbed thoroughly of even their outer garments by gangs on the junks used to deport them to Chinese territory, Egbert's mother died within three days and Egbert smuggled himself back to Hong Kong on foot.[51]

For some Eurasians, however, those educated and with more resources at hand, it was precisely their ability to morph identity at will, changing names and clothes when needed, that enabled them not only to survive the war, but to do good work. One such was Archibald Zimmern—future son-in-law of Sir Robert Kotewall and prominent barrister. Rosary Hill had a revamped Administrative Council in early 1944, which included the bakery, milk distribution, outdoor sports, safety services during air raids, fire prevention, boys' working crews, wood-chopping, and three kitchens run by a young Leopold Gaddi as chef in charge. Gaddi would become famed for his eponymous fine-dining restaurant at the postwar Peninsula Hotel, but for now, dependents would have the benefit of one of the Far East's top Swiss chefs![52]

The council also included one Mr. Y. C. She. His job was to run general stores, fuel, rations, medical stores, education, the sewing department, indoor sports, and entertainments. He was actually Archie Zimmern, who had been interned in Sham Shui Po POW camp but, on changing to a Chinese name and garb, was able to take advantage of a release of Chinese prisoners from the camp. There was at least one such release, in September 1942, when about 120 men were freed, in line with Japanese policy that they had no quarrel with Asian people and anyway the Chinese must have been forced to fight for the British. Recalled his fellow internee Solomon Bard, "As far as I recall, there was no resentment in camp at the release of the Chinese POWs, especially as most of them had families in Hong Kong or Macao. As we learned later, some of the released men managed to escape from Hong Kong and rejoin the Allied forces in China and India . . ."[53]

This is just what Archie She would do: when he resigned from Rosary Hill and escaped through southern China to Chungking, he was feted as a leading British citizen with vital information on conditions in Hong Kong. He was both Chinese and British and got the best out of both identities. At the same time, two elderly relatives, Mr. and Mrs. S. Y. M. Zimmern, aged seventy-four and seventy, respectively, and listed as "Chinese," were residents first of the French Hospital Red Cross Section and then briefly of Rosary Hill.[54]

Zindel noted how "unbalanced" his Rosary Hill community was, hinting at tensions over race, class, age, and gender. Certainly there were a lot of confused social mores due to this mass throwing-together of people. Most of the men were under twenty years old and had not previously been required to clean up after themselves. The majority of residents were women, and the Japanese rule that residents must be back in the home by dark caused its own challenges, noted Zindel: "We have a number of 'Ladies' in our midst, who, whilst they possess the necessary credentials as 'dependents,' find it apparently difficult to withstand the lure of their 'old profession.' Periodical 'roll-calls' have disclosed a number of such 'Absentees,' who are, however, never at a loss to explain their unauthorized absences by the sudden sickness of an 'Aunt' or a 'Grandmother,' or by an 'unexpected intoxication at a Birthday-Party.' We have now drawn a line under such excuses and future offenders will face the risk of immediate expulsion."

From early 1945, conditions everywhere were worsening dramatically. Food stocks would cover the Home only until about May 10; available cash was just about exhausted. "Our ship became less and less seaworthy and actually was in imminent danger of sinking early in April . . . drastic measures to 'lighten our ship' became unavoidable . . . ," wrote Zindel.[55] Such lightening occurred through the managed departure of 305 dependents, 281 of whom left for Macao in a complex transfer of 1,200 pieces of baggage. By the end of August 1945, there remained at Rosary Hill a total of just 135 persons. Looking back on his Rosary Hill venture, Zindel dared to write that "thanks to its existence many families have been able to celebrate a Happy Reunion at the termination of the War, instead of standing sorrowful at graves."[56]

13

TOUGH LOVE

Three men from Macao, dressed as fishermen, smuggled themselves into Hong Kong in August 1945, and over to the Stanley internment camp, to pass on a message. They were Roger Lobo, Dr. Eddie Gosano, and their fellow undercover operative, the comprador Liang Yun-chang. The message they risked death to deliver was a letter patent, a document from the British government to re-establish British authority in Hong Kong. The intent was to instruct the senior British government official in the Stanley camp, Franklin Gimson, to take immediate political control of Hong Kong as soon as the Japanese surrendered. The urgent fear was that Chinese Nationalist troops, backed at least in spirit by republican-minded anti-imperialist Americans, would dash across into "empty" Hong Kong and claim it as their own. In fact, Gimson had already planned exactly this move from his camp stool and had lined up colleagues to go with him. He even had a flag to hoist, in order to signal that Hong Kong belonged to the British. Perhaps more telling is that the refugees from Hong Kong who spent their war in Macao—predominantly Eurasian and Portuguese—had made the very same plan, too. There was no doubt in all these diverse minds that Hong Kong was a place separate to mainland China and should stay so.

Gosano had already helped get leading Hong Kongers to London to join that planning committee.[1] In Macao, the British consul, John

Reeves, oversaw formation of a committee for Hong Kong's rehabilitation. It included senior Chinese, Portuguese, Indian, and Eurasian
representatives of the Hong Kong community then in Macao. "We did
our best to prepare plans for the renaissance of that Colony."[2] They
had also formed their own British Eurasian Association.[3]

Given the discrimination and neglect faced by non-white people
who identified as British, the commitment to helping a British Hong
Kong into a postwar future is even more surprising. If a plan proposed
more than two years earlier by a leader of Hong Kong's Eurasian
community, Dr. Douglas Laing, for example, had been acted on by
the British, a far richer relationship among different kinds of British
people might have been reached.[4]

In Laing's memorandum of December 23, 1942, he had described
the Eurasians of Hong Kong as "natives of the Colony . . . many of
them are third and fourth generation descendants of the earliest British
settlers . . . they have always borne a strong loyalty to Britain. This loyalty has always been taken for granted, and proof of it has been given
in times of emergency, as in the Great Strike and Boycott of 1925, in
the Great War of 1914–18 and in the present war . . ." And yet "they
could discover no official interest or encouragement in their special
problems; and in the matter of livelihood, various posts in the Government . . . were closed to them, regardless of their abilities." He noted
the exclusion of Eurasians from the 1940 evacuation. Yet these men
and women "all served without stint and gave of their best . . . Among
the Volunteer defenders of Hongkong, the death rate among Eurasians
was high. The majority of the young male population was either killed
on active service or are interned as prisoners of war . . . Almost every
Eurasian family in Hongkong was left in an extremely awkward position. Few had any but the most limited means; many families had
lost their all and were entirely penniless . . . almost every family of the
community has a son, a brother, or father interned."

Those who wanted to flee couldn't afford to do so and lacked
support to learn how. Worse, the Japanese knew that most Eurasians
were British subjects and were at heart pro-British, and Eurasian girls

had been "insulted and man-handled." The answer, he pressed, was a mass exit for China or Macao, and the provision of shelter and work on arrival.

Colonel Lindsay Ride, the Hong Kong University vice-chancellor who had founded BAAG, gave wholehearted support: "For many years now I have taught them, worked with them, lived with them and played with them and from that experience alone I would strongly support any move to help them. But the big point about them, I think, is that when the real test of war came they not only served to the best of their ability, but throughout their post-surrender suffering (and as a class I think they have suffered most) they have remained absolutely loyal. There can be no doubt that Hong Kong is for them of all people their home . . ." He was strongly in favor of a plan to get them out of Hong Kong—"We have done it [helped their escape] for many Indians (and it can be truly argued they were much less deserving) and I don't see why we could not do it for the Eurasians. We have the organization and I feel it could legitimately be used for this purpose because a large percentage of the Eurasians are families of those who served with us."[5]

H. D. Bryan of the British consulate general in Kweilin forwarded Dr. Laing's letter to the British ambassador in China at Chungking on February 15, 1943. He, Bryan, had known Eurasians in Hong Kong and was "strongly in sympathy with their case . . . ," he wrote. "They are, like the members of other communities, not without their faults and weaknesses, and there are some black sheep among them, but in general they have been a loyal and hardworking, if comparatively small section of the population, who have in the past not received the consideration they deserved . . ." Laing's letter, wrote Bryan, referred to those who "have, by reason of blood ties, education and general upbringing, clung to their British connexion [sic], in the face of continual disappointments and rebuffs." Bryan said the paying of such men of equal education much less "would appear difficult if not impossible to justify . . . on broad grounds of equity. The social discrimination against Eurasians which obtained generally in Hongkong, being doubtless characteristic of many other colonies, needs no emphasis." However, Laing's suggestion of a full-scale evacuation of Eurasians— even if "necessary or desirable"—would be pointless if there was no work or support for them on arrival.

Indeed, it was not to be. A cable on April 22, 1943, to British diplomats in Kweilin, Macao, and the Foreign Office in London stated the clear opposition of the government of India and Army Headquarters, India, to proposals for assisted wholesale escapes or walkouts of "Anglo-Chinese and Eurasians" from Hong Kong. This was "owing to the danger of enemy agents, transport difficulties and impossibility of absorbing these people in India even if guaranteed from security angle."

The failure to repay the undoubted loyalty of most Eurasians continued long after the war. On September 28, 1945, the newly arrived British Military Administration (BMA) promised repatriation or cash benefits to former members of the HK Volunteer Defence Corps. But this turned out to apply only to "pure" Europeans. "In a gesture of racially tinged ingratitude, the BMA decided that all those Chinese, Portuguese, and Eurasian volunteers who had fought for the British in December 1941 should be deemed to have been demobilized from the date of the British surrender to Japan and, therefore, would not be eligible for any further pay or allowances."[6]

Persistent discrimination, with the volunteers not treated as equal to British regulars, despite their equal suffering, was deadly. Volunteers were not automatically granted medical care or pensions after the war. Frank Correa recalled that twenty years after the war, his uncle Mem Soares was suffering from kidney failure developed from his time as a prisoner for three years and eight months at the Sham Shui Po prisoner of war camp. He was denied treatment by the British military hospital and could not even access dialysis machines to treat his kidney failure at government hospitals. Frank wrote a letter to the papers to complain, but it was too late and Soares died in Queen Elizabeth Hospital.[7]

Britain also refused to pay compensation to Eurasian civilians and others for their internment during the war; they were deemed "not British enough." Diana Elias, aged eighty-three, finally won her case in Britain when a court agreed the British government was guilty of racial discrimination. Her family of Iraqi Jews had arrived from Bombay, and Diana was born in Hong Kong in 1924; her grandparents, parents, and herself all held British passports. Interned for being British—a process that led to the death of her father from wartime illness and her mother's nervous breakdown—and denied war pensions by the government made her angry. She had joined the Association of British Civilian Internees, Far Eastern Region, when she moved to Britain, filled in her forms, and heard nothing until the details of her forebears' births were requested. Six years of legal fight later, Diana got her money, but wondered why it had to be so hard.[8]

After suffering two atomic bomb attacks by the United States on the cities of Hiroshima and Nagasaki, a shocked Japan surrendered on August 15, 1945. On August 30, Rear Admiral Sir Cecil Halliday Jepson Harcourt entered Hong Kong's harbor on board the cruiser HMS *Swiftsure* to accept the Japanese surrender and to administer the colony until the civilian administration was back on its feet. That second half of August was when Gimson and his team held the high ground for the empire. Once Harcourt brought the naval force, mass revival could be embarked upon. Police returned to duty; bankers lent liberally to get Hong Kongers back in business. The government was bulk buying rice and fuel, prisoners of war had to be sent home, volunteers had to be demobilized. Transportation was in ruins, so trucks took on new roles as buses.

In the Stanley camp, the interned biologist from the University of Hong Kong, G. A. C. Herklots, had plotted cooperative marketing of the fishing catch; Andrew Gilmour had ideas about shipbuilding and cargo. A report in the camp by the Committee of the Social Service Centre of the Churches outlined a series of measures for rights, trade unionism, and much greater participation of women in the postwar

colonial order. There was even talk of a primarily Chinese police force
at last. Renaissance men such as Solomon Bard hoped that a postwar
world would be more generous and tolerant. He would help found
the Sino-British Club in 1946, and the Sino British Orchestra (which
would become the Hongkong Philharmonic Orchestra in 1957).

The motives from London were mixed—desirous of restoring British prestige after its ignominious defeats by the Japanese, and perhaps,
too, the shoring up of a community against potential encroachments
from a reinvigorated mainland China. Gimson said he thought it important "to secure enhanced political contentment" and to provide a
basis for Hong Kong citizenship, and "thereby the conception of the
colony as a distinct entity from China would be created."[9] President
Roosevelt, meanwhile, against any perpetuation of colonialism, had
long favored returning Hong Kong to China.

On May 1, 1946, a new civilian administration took charge under
Governor Mark Young—now back from his war spent in Japanese
internment in Manchuria. He, too, had been thinking about the future. By July 26, 1946, the government had at last repealed the Peak
District Reservation Ordinance (of 1904), which had barred Chinese
from living on the Peak. Planning units in London had been promising
a "new angle of vision" since mid-1943, with more democratic governance and a speedy localization of jobs on the table. Young's plans
were far-reaching, promising the beginnings of universal suffrage and
genuine participation in Hong Kong governance by all its peoples. The
historian Felicia Yap wonders if the fact that both Gimson and Young
had served in Ceylon was significant. There they had overseen a broad
local franchise, and the task had been to prepare a post-independence
elite. These men had ideas of imperial citizenship where people of all
races were equal British subjects.[10]

This idea of a colony ruled by popular consent (albeit without full
voting or universal suffrage) survived the diminution of immediate
threats to Hong Kong's Britishness. After President Roosevelt died, he
was replaced by the less anticolonial Harry S. Truman, who accepted
British control of Hong Kong. But the consensual ideal did not survive

the onset of the early Cold War, when it became apparent that the Chinese Communist Party might win control of a united China, posing an existential threat to all of Westernized East Asia. Once Governor Grantham took charge in Hong Kong in 1947, Young's plan for a more inclusive future died.

Grantham lacked the background of Hong Kong's resident communities from long before the war, and so was ignorant of that specific Hong Kong identity that had led so many diverse people to build multigenerational homes and families, and even risk their lives for it. Perhaps he listened too much to the newly arrived wealthy Shanghainese who brought money and industry but no Hong Kong history with them. He simply decided that Hong Kong was a Chinese port and its people would never develop pro-British tendencies. As it would thus never become a self-governing state, in his opinion, he backed the vested antidemocratic interests in his ruling councils, particularly the local Chinese elite. This rich clique, with its family and business ties through every major colonial institution, was unwilling to forgo its own position of unelected privilege. Hong Kong's chance of an independent, self-determining future was lost.[11]

Lawrence Kadoorie, meanwhile, had managed a dramatic return through Free China in a cargo plane sitting on a pile of fresh currency. His family soon plunged into helping scores of Jewish refugees, most of whom wanted not to stay in Hong Kong but to move on to Australia and elsewhere. "Hong Kong was the most looted city in the world," he recalled. "Having run out of fuel, everything that could be burnt, wood flooring, doors, window frames, even the case of a grand piano, had been broken up for use as firewood. Large rats had come up from the sewers . . . and wild dogs roamed. These eventually had to be rounded up and shot . . ." But it was not all the fault of Japan: "My recollection of Chiang Kai Shek's troops and their camp followers passing through Kowloon reminds me of a plague of locusts. Houses left intact by the Japanese, who had prevented looting, were stripped bare in twenty-four hours."

For Kadoorie, the postwar revival showed "a genuine and heartfelt desire on the part of Government and of the citizens to return Hong Kong to normal as quickly as possible, delays due to bureaucracy did not exist. Rank was entirely secondary, insofar as I was concerned. Everyone did their best to assist in cleaning up the place and getting things going."[12] "The new Hong Kong didn't wait. People didn't say, 'Someone else must pay for this desolation.' They sat down immediately, to get things going. It's normal to work hard, to take work as something given, to climb the tower, getting better and better."[13] At the same time as he generously put up almost six hundred stranded Jews in dormitories in his hotel while they waited seven months for a ship, he was nonetheless firm in his belief that benign rule by an interested elite, not democracy, was the best way forward.

Alongside the rebuilding was the need for justice. As in any war, there were scores to settle—the punishment of those who had aided the enemy and the war crimes prosecutions of some of the enemy themselves. Inevitably, as the archetypal middlemen, some of Hong Kong's in-between people, Eurasians and Chinese, were caught in this new crossfire.

War crimes trials were held in Hong Kong between March 28, 1946, and December 20, 1948. In the view of the legal expert Suzannah Linton, they were a genuine effort to do justice fairly, and, despite failings, were remarkable for the time and place. She thought the treatment of Hong Kong by the Japanese had been genuinely shocking, particularly the forced displacement program that removed a million people from the city, and the famine and starvation that preceded it. She found it disturbing that large-scale sexual violence against civilians was almost invisible in the tribunal reports. There was textbook Japanese military police abuse in the police stations, including what is today called waterboarding alongside burning, beating, and more. Linton also found that most people did not choose to dwell on these recent horrors after the trials.[14]

By contrast, the treatment of what Britain's foreign office records called "Colonial Renegades and Quislings" was more ambivalent.[15] Discussions were under way well before the war ended about how to treat various people and deeds, not only in Hong Kong but in India, Burma, and Malaya. Three categories should be prosecuted if possible: those who had prominently engaged in conducting propaganda on behalf of the enemy; those, whether prisoners of war or not, who, during the war, had voluntarily engaged in activities calculated to assist the enemy's operations or to damage the Allied cause; and those who had applied for, and obtained, enemy nationality during the war. Any prosecutions would be conducted speedily. And yet they needed "to be founded on a tolerant view of their conduct, if by so doing it may be found possible more readily to enlist the loyal support and cooperation of the men of education, ability, initiative and authority upon whom we must necessarily depend, but who, by virtue of their position have in the past been employed by the Japanese." In other words, some men had blurred lines during the war, but the British would still need them to bolster their rule.

Indeed, a secret communication of October 4, 1945, titled "Quislings & Collaborators," reported: "On return to Hong Kong we were made aware of prima facie evidence that nearly all the leading Chinese in the Colony collaborated in one way or another with the Japanese. The only public figure who appears to have entirely clean hands is Mr T.N. Chau, the senior ranking Chinese member of the Legislative Council, who very early in the occupation slipped away to Macao." The report went on to note that prosecutions would be difficult, not least because British officials had asked Hong Kong's leading Chinese to cooperate with the Japanese. The report added: "Present charges of Quisling activities are being widely used to pay off old scores and to satisfy personal enmities contracted pre-1941 among the several contending parties and personalities in Hong Kong."

However, while it was not possible to indict everyone, nor could they be invited to receptions and ceremonies. "It just does not seem possible to have them shouting 'banzai' in August and singing 'God Save the King' in September."

Under consideration for trial were men such as Darrell Drake, a teacher in Japan who had married a pro-German Norwegian lady. He was a heavy gambler and drinker and, when he went on leave to Shanghai and then Hong Kong in September 1937, was reported to have business connections with the Japanese, and with a known German arms smuggler; he then worked for a Japanese news agency in Hong Kong and during the war worked on the pro-Japan *Hongkong News*. There was Timothy E. Dunn, a Eurasian British subject, formerly with Thomas Cook Co. in Shanghai, where he had been let go for embezzlement. British intelligence thought he was actually Edward Dunn, a half-British, half-Japanese agent for the Japanese, born in China, "a well-behaved perfect gentleman." Joseph Carroll, also Japanese-Eurasian, had collected tungsten and grease for Japan's navy; Joseph Richards trafficked watches, cameras, and radios, and then supplied Japanese officers with wine, brandy, whisky, and gin.[16] Richards, also Eurasian, stood accused by British intelligence of picking out "undesirable" third nationals for Japanese detention. He was known to have worked for the Japanese for a long time; he had been interned by the British authorities at the outbreak of hostilities but freed by the Japanese. He was reported to have been entrusted with the examination of documents, alleged to be Macao's British consular archives, discovered on the riverboat *Sai On*, which had been seized from neutral Portuguese waters by the Japanese in 1943.

Victor Vander Needa, a well-known amateur jockey, was lauded for conspicuous bravery against the Japanese invasion. But his sense of grievance at slights from his British clients and rulers helped rouse him to "a state of trembling hope and even occasional exaltation by the rediscovery of his Japanese blood," reports the historian Philip Snow, who adds that Needa became a "flourishing merchant" employing many to collect iron, bronze, and aluminum for the Imperial Japanese Navy.[17] At the same time, his brother-in-law Norman Broadbridge was serving in the Volunteers and helped save the life of Bevan Field, a future manager of Hongkong Land. So Needa's wife, Janet, enjoyed reasonable rent for her flower shop (Jeanette's) in Central for decades after the war.[18]

Snow found that "several hundreds of Eurasians and Portuguese managed to recreate their traditional intermediary role by setting themselves up as 'brokers' to traffic between the conquerors on the one hand and the Hong Kong Chinese population on the other." He also offered the example of the (Sindhi) Harilela family, which, among other survival tactics, traded rice from the Japanese, to show that "the brokerage boom enabled some vital goods to flow down to the desperate masses."[19]

Men such as C. M. Faure, a former Royal Navy commander with a Chinese wife, were also hard to judge. He became head of a Eurasian and Indian propaganda team at the *Hongkong News*, but in some chroniclers' eyes successfully subverted his role from within.[20] In all, about sixty locals were tried for collaboration and twenty-nine found guilty: fifteen Chinese, six Indians, one Japanese with Canadian citizenship, and seven "Europeans or Eurasians."[21]

Concluded the historian Anthony Sweeting: "On the whole during the Japanese occupation, Eurasians participated in resistance *and* collaboration. Some Eurasians were, at different times, active in both— for example, as gallant defenders of their homeland, especially prominent in the Hong Kong Volunteer Defence Force and eventually in the BAAG, and, later, being involved in the black or grey markets. In the main, most Eurasians who did cooperate and even those who collaborated with the Japanese did so for simple, pragmatic reasons—to keep themselves and their families alive."[22]

It was the case of Sir Robert Kotewall that burned hottest, however. The prewar attorney general Sir Grenville Alabaster, the secretary for Chinese affairs R. A. C. North, and the defense secretary J. A. Fraser had explicitly asked him and Shouson Chow to cooperate with the Japanese, a request that Kotewall felt unable to refuse despite his misgivings. On January 10, 1942, the Japanese invited Kotewall, Shou-son Chow, and others for lunch at the Peninsula Hotel, which was now their headquarters. Chow and Kotewall thanked the Japanese for not "harming the people of Hong Kong or destroying the city." They agreed to cooperate given that the Japanese goal was to "release the races of East Asia." Then Kotewall offered a "Banzai!" and Chow agreed heartily. Kotewall, Chow, and Li Tse-fong all expressed hope for an early end to the war between Japan and China, which Kotewall described as "more like a family quarrel between two brothers due to a momentary loss of temper."[23] The Chinese Representative Council created by the Japanese occupiers included Kotewall as chairman, with Lau Tit-sang of the Communications Bank and chairman of the Chinese Bankers' Association, Li Tse-fong of the Bank of East Asia, and Chan Lim-pak, a former comprador to the Hongkong and Shanghai Bank. The Chinese Cooperative Council was chaired by Shouson Chow and had twenty-two members including Lo Man-kam.

It was well known that Lau and Chan had strong pro-Japanese views; Chan had even been imprisoned by the British during the Japanese invasion on charges of aiding the enemy. Participation on the councils by others, however, was not seen as a great crime at the time.

The historian John Carroll believes: "That there was so little Chinese resentment toward the two Chinese councils during or after the occupation suggests that most Chinese understood that the Chinese and Eurasian leaders had to cooperate."[24] By 1944, Kotewall and Li Tse-fong had withdrawn from public duties on health grounds; M. K. Lo also frequently avoided meetings on claimed grounds of ill-health. Shouson Chow, now in his eighties, was excused on the grounds of age. Just about the only tangible achievement of the councils was the setting up of the Chinese Charity Association in September 1942 to help donate and distribute relief goods.

After the war, however, it was Kotewall who was singled out for attack. He would eventually be asked to resign from public roles while some figures still wanted his head. Lindsay Ride was a particular critic, calling Kotewall the "Japanese banzai-boy," feeling that the British government's decision not to prosecute him for treason after the war "did irreparable harm to British Colonial prestige" in Asia.[25] A view promoted by the journalist Emily Hahn, who spent a few months out of internment after the invasion, was that Kotewall was manufactured from "cheap material" and went on "fulfilling his destiny as a genuine talking doll, now that the Japanese instead of the British are winding him up."[26] Yet others who had been on the same councils and signed the same statements were left unscathed. When Kotewall's daughters Bobbie and Maisie went to visit friends in the civilian prisoner of war camp they could feel "that all was not well. That [a university professor] was too nice to us and somehow I just felt a little uncomfortable and the two of us left," said Maisie.

Yet when Maisie went to a tailor after the war, and the tailor realized she was a daughter of Kotewall, he gave her a huge discount because he said he and his family had been in Macao during the war and had always waited for speeches by Kotewall in Chinese from Hong Kong. He said the Japanese probably didn't realize the full message, but that he could read between the lines and had gained sustenance from that.[27]

In Kotewall's own 66-page account of his war, he said that when he was taken by Japanese officers to an office three days after the British surrender, Shouson Chow and young M. K. Lo were there before him and had already proposed Kotewall as their spokesman. Kotewall claimed that he wanted to leave town but had a large family, knew he was being closely watched, and besides, had been advised by government officials to stay. A statement issued on January 1, 1942, written above all the local leaders' names, including those of M. K. Lo and Kotewall, had been checked and approved by the British government.

None of these men knew, at that time, that Japan would ignore the Geneva Conventions, make playthings of local government bodies, and rule as brutally as they did. But how long should it have taken before Kotewall and his colleagues realized there was no chance of negotiation, or any coincidence of goals, with this regime? One sympathetic chronicler of Kotewall's war wrote of the naiveté: "There is a kind of pathos in this part of his narrative as Sir Robert, utterly decent and a believer in British fair play seems to believe that he can negotiate with the head of the Kempetai . . ."[28] Kotewall said he kept arguing for search and arrest warrants in advance and for families to be informed of arrests, and for the sending of food to those arrested—all in vain.[29] Wrote Kotewall: "I served the Chinese community throughout the Japanese occupation—a period of three years and eight months. It was the hardest and most distressing period of my life. While I was compelled by the Japanese to do things that were positively repugnant to me, and was constantly subject to rebuffs, indignities and secret surveillance, my actions were misunderstood by the British, some of whom I counted as friends."

A memo from a British official, N. L. Smith, dated March 22, 1945, noted, "It seems to me that it might be difficult to apply too strictly the European standards in the case of persons of Chinese race who (generally by a geographical accident of birth) are technically British subjects . . . The smaller fry who let their names appear as Members of the Council (Li Tse Fong and his brother Kwok Chan, Thomas Tam and the rest) seem to me not a great deal worse than the postmen or sanitary employees who carried on the machinery of the government. This opinion is fortified by the inclusion in that list of the name of M. K. Lo who is known, from other sources, to have been quite violently anti-collaboration. The most difficult case will probably be that of Sir Robert Kotewall who has undoubtedly praised by voice and pen the Japanese figment of co-prosperity . . . The evidence may be difficult to collect." Another note pointed out there was nothing that could bring Kotewall under the Treachery Act. Any prosecution "needs proof of something more serious than propaganda work . . ." Mr. Smith in London was pleasantly surprised when he finally saw a transcript of a Kotewall speech, calling it "Harmless stuff!"[30]

David MacDougall, a pre- and postwar government official, now fresh back to Hong Kong from the London Planning Unit, summed it up when he saw that virtually everyone was besmirched by contact with the Japanese, but that Kotewall was both "unabashed" and "impenitent." More, "The Kotewall business is a mess. So far as I can see no one has a scrap of real evidence, and all I have seen so far would not stand up in court for two seconds. This does not stop people pressing for his immediate arrest and trial. (K. was always a man who inspired violent personal dislike.)" This last sentence is perhaps the most interesting. Why did Kotewall inspire such dislike? Was it his combination of arrogance and naiveté? Was it, too, perhaps an anti-Indian strain of racism that had infected other Eurasians' and Chinese views of him?

Any prosecution of Kotewall was firmly quashed once the prewar secretary for Chinese affairs, R. A. C. North, wrote to Commander Trythall, naval secretary to the commander in chief. He stated, "Kotewall showed very marked resource, energy and determination throughout. He was primarily responsible for the measures which frustrated the Japanese plans for a rising in Hong Kong on the day on which they reached Kowloon . . . he even tried to organise a force of Chinese guerrillas to assist in the defence of the island, and was manifestly disappointed when I opposed the scheme on the ground that the employment by ourselves of *francs-tireurs* would invite a massacre of civilians by the Japanese." North pointed out, "Hong Kong was the first British territory to fall into Japanese hands," and he had so firmly believed it was possible that "they would follow the usual practice of civilized nations in protecting life and property and in allowing the Civil Government to continue to function to some extent" that he offered himself to the Japanese as someone who could represent the interests of the Chinese community. When they said no, North offered up Kotewall. Never, said North, had he ever doubted Kotewall's loyalty to the British Empire.

North then outlines three reasons for the particular level of vitriol directed personally at Kotewall.

What follows is highly confidential and I include it reluctantly. It appears necessary however in order to explain the extreme bitterness of the attack on Sir Robert . . .

(a) The General Strike in Hong Kong in 1925 and the boycott of

*1925–27 were part of the nationalist movement in China which led
to the elevation of Chiang Kai Shek. On this occasion Kotewall led
the local Chinese in the defence of the Colony and his services then
were rewarded by the grant of the CMG* [a British honor, sometimes
preliminary to a knighthood] . . . *Chinese nationalists have never for-
given him for this service to the Empire and would be glad to see him
replaced by advisers who might be less shrewd or more amenable.*

*(b) Personal dislike of Kotewall has for many years been fostered,
particularly among European business men, by slanders spread by a
Chinese merchant (recently deceased). This campaign was inspired
by personal enmity due to a fancied slight, but, equally had its origin
in local politics behind the scenes.*

*(c) There has existed for some time an unfortunate conflict be-
tween Sir Robert Kotewall and Mr M.K. Lo. I saw the beginnings of
this long before 1941 and am fully aware of the reasons for it. The
motives are mixed. I do not believe that Mr Lo would admit even
to himself that the vehemence of his criticism has any relation to the
removal of an influential rival, or to the diversion of attention from
his own yielding to Japanese pressure; but there is such a thing as
wishful thinking.*

*I suggest that when these peculiar reasons for enmity are taken
into consideration there is no essential difference between the case of
Kotewall and that of the other "collaborators."*

This defense saved Kotewall from prosecution, but not from an
earlier-than-planned retirement. Trythall wrote to Kotewall on October 5, 1945, saying the commander in chief "is satisfied that there
are no grounds upon which any major charge could be based. He
has, however, formed the opinion that you made an error of judgement in the degree and in the manner in which you interpreted the
advice given you by senior British officials to cooperate with the Japanese authorities. In these circumstances, and pending any further
evidence which may come to light through the War Activities Committee, the Commander-in-Chief considers that you must withdraw

from public life." Kotewall resigned from the Executive Council in May 1946.[31] Kotewall died just three years later, on May 23, 1949.

The British could now move ahead with a new Legislative Council, carrying little baggage from the war. The government was intent on getting the economy back on track with trade flowing, and building a more subtle line of defense against a new kind of enemy—communism in mainland China. That also meant finding ways to house, employ, and educate the millions of people fleeing China to the anti-China represented by colonial Hong Kong.

14

THE HONG KONGERS

In the 1950s, the Cold War came to Asia. The decade opened with the Korean War—ranging the United States and its allies (including Britain) behind South Korea, and China with Russia behind the North. Only a stalemate was reached in 1953 along the 38th parallel (today's border between North and South Korea) after three years of vicious fighting. That war included the imposition of UN and U.S. embargoes on trade with China, suggesting that British Hong Kong would be stymied, barred from trading with its nearest neighbor. But in many ways, thanks to Hong Kong's hybrid nature and the wheeler-dealer instincts of its people, the tensions only raised risks—and profits. Goods crossed borders regardless but, more important, Hong Kong's prewar homegrown industries now had a chance to shine. They already produced goods ranging from beer to batteries and from toys to jewelry; soon Hong Kong would be producing plastic flowers, luxury watches, and high-end jeans. It benefited, too, from those Shanghai arrivals bringing textile and other industries, grafting nouveau riche ambition onto a native economy.

When China's civil war ended in 1949, few outside the core of the Chinese Communist Party understood just how much would change. Impoverished and struggling, China would be led by Chairman Mao Tse-tung through the devastating and misguided push to industrialize that he named the Great Leap Forward, followed by the mass-murdering famine and then the Cultural Revolution—the purging of intellectuals and the middle classes in the name of Communist purity.

Meanwhile, Hong Kong under British rule, backed by the burgeoning projection of American military might, including its missiles, planes, and aircraft carriers, was carving a new future. There were growing pains: the 1952 and 1953 squatter fires that rendered tens of thousands of mostly new arrivals homeless and prompted the acceleration of a public housing scheme; the 1956 riots resulting from the overflow of Nationalist-on-Communist tensions from the mainland; and the 1967 riots sparked by economic inequity. More than a million mainlanders had fled communism, and the pressures on Hong Kong's social provision were immense.

Amid the frenzy, Hong Kong was changing in more subtle ways. After a first century developing its own Eurasian identity, it was now forced into a newer, wider world. The historian G. B. Endacott noted: "More important, Hong Kong became virtually autonomous, administratively and financially, in 1958, as was announced by Sir Robert Black, the Governor from 1958 to 1964, in the Legislative Council in March of that year; while Britain still exercises sovereignty, she has in practice restricted herself to control of Hong Kong's external relations."[1] It felt in Hong Kong—through these decades—that Hong Kong was indeed largely running itself, shut off from China, often ignored by Britain. Hong Kong's homegrown cultural capital was also gaining traction, with Cantonese music (Canto-pop) and the films of Bruce Lee telling the world this was a stunning and distinct place. Would Hong Kongers' sense of self, forged through generations and the crucible of war, survive?

An answer may be found in the work of Ackbar Abbas, the Hong Kong–born California-based academic and influential author whose roots go back to India, Malaysia, and China.[2] Said Abbas: "[My mother] looked slightly more Indian than I do, I don't look Indian or Malaysian at all. You know, I have this name, and I have this face, and the name don't go together with the face. So I feel like I am a living example of an allegory. And I identify with nowhere. It helps in the sense that you are inside and outside at the same time." The Abbas multifaith, multiracial, and geographically dispersed family has roots in Hong Kong's very earliest years.[3]

In his 1997 book, *Hong Kong: Culture and Politics of Disappearance*, Abbas explored nostalgia and collective memory in Hong Kong identity, introducing the concept of hyphenation for a culture or nation without sovereignty, dependent on another place to survive. "Hong Kong is not a nation, it's a hyphenation," he says. Colonialism "pioneered methods of incorporating pre-capitalist, pre-industrial, and non-European societies into the world economy and found ways of dealing with ethnically, racially and culturally different societies," Abbas wrote, giving Hong Kong a relatively benign version that seems "to contradict more orthodox understandings of colonialism as necessarily exploitative."[4]

Perhaps that's because there wasn't much to exploit, he wonders. "Its very lack of resources or means of being independent was always curiously enough a factor in its favor: it meant that more could be gained all around by making the city work as a port city . . . This was a position that both the colonizer and the colonized could agree on, a position of cute correspondence or collusion . . ." This made possible, or indeed required, that "lack and dependency were somehow advantages . . . dependency has been turned into a fine art . . . Hong Kong seems to have been built on contingency, on geographic and historical accidents, shaped by time and circumstances beyond its control and by pragmatic accommodation to events . . . a tendency to live its own version of the 'floating world' without the need to establish stable identities."[5]

Abbas admires the Hong Kong filmmaker Wong Kar-wai's romantic comedy of 1994, *Chungking Express*, for showing that "Hong Kong is not so much a mental or psychological state as it is a visual and spatial paradox, a skewed space that characters have to adjust to emotionally, with comic results. Far from being the habitat of one social group, many different groups feel equally (not) at home in it;

notice how in the first part of the film, Cantonese, Mandarin, English, Urdu and Japanese are all spoken."[6]

The prose and poetry of Dung Kaicheung and of Leung Ping-kwan are similarly focused on the distinctness of Hong Kong's past as a port city, open to all comers, and productive of a splendid mishmash of multiple heritages. Dung's work in translation (from Chinese) includes his *Cantonese Love Stories* and *Atlas: The Archaeology of an Imaginary City*, in which the lead character is Hong Kong itself. He writes of how disparate elements in Hong Kong converge to create a unique culture.

In his 2009 *Postcolonial Affairs of Food and the Heart*, Leung was inspired by his many Hong Kong friends

who are not particularly British-colonial or not particularly revolutionary, but just simple people living in Hong Kong, and all kinds of problems they encounter. I don't want to just write political stories, so I concentrate on food and love, matters of the heart, and I think in these situations I think people are more natural, more expressive of themselves, and why they love someone, what sort of thing they see in the other people that they want to have a relationship with or what kind of food they want to eat.

Food is an interesting entry point because Hong Kong makes changes. It appropriated, adopted some Chinese cuisine but then the imperial kind of cuisine will become the food on the street for common people. You have the British tea, but then when you move to Hong Kong you have milk tea, which later developed into tea-coffee, a mixture of tea and coffee which is not British at all, it's for the coolie, for the common worker, when they want strong tea they have that. So this is not Chinese and not British as well. I'm interested in all these different kinds of food . . . The early Western food when they came into Hong Kong is called soy sauce western cuisine [because] instead of using butter or cheese, which is not good for the Chinese stomach, they used soy sauce . . . Like there's a soup called comprador soup, [named after] the go-betweens, the people who make profit by dealing with business . . . it's shark fin soup with cream, so it's a Western-Chinese mixture in a very strange way.

People talk a lot about East meets West. Of course, the meeting itself is worth looking into—it could be a power struggle, it could be a domination, it could be a friendly relationship, it could be a lot of opposition as well. So I always see a simplification when people give slogans like "East meets West" and "Hong Kong is lively urban city," a cosmopolitan city, and so on. What actually is happening, how are people living and dealing with everyday life? I'm interested in wanting to know . . . Hong Kong people are very receptive of other kinds of things, of course they like Cantonese soup, but also they enjoy Malaysian curry, Indian curry. In a way Hong Kong has always been very open to all kinds of culture, and that is a good thing.

Speaking just ten years after the handover, he saw himself and fellow Cantonese as another minority in Hong Kong, as Mandarin-speaking mainlanders arrived at the rate of at least one hundred a day. He lamented that the colony's new rulers could not imagine Hong Kong could have developed its own culture and so failed to take it seriously.[7]

Clearly it makes sense to think of Hong Kong as a place of no single identity, but several. Its people have, from the start, epitomized so much more than an East-West binary; the mixing has created something greater than the sum of its parts.

The writer Han Suyin saw the writing on the wall just a few years after the war, insisting on what she called her "foolishness" in lauding her mixed identity. She wrote that being deeply cross-cultural, in her case as a matter of race as well as learning, was the way of the future. "We must carry ourselves with colossal assurance and say: 'Look at us, the Eurasians! Just look. How beautiful we are, more beautiful than either race alone. More clever, more hardy. The meeting of both cultures, the fusion of all that can become a world civilisation. Look at us, and envy us, you poor one-world people, riveted to your limitations. We are the future of the world. Look at us.'"[8]

"It's almost as though the city is Eurasian, just like us," says a character profiled in Kirsteen Zimmern's photographic and oral history of Hong Kong's mixed peoples, *Eurasian Face*.[9]

These in-between people might be impossible to keep down, to count, and to categorize. Yet one clear thread throughout the myriad different war experiences, choices, and outcomes is that the core of people who saw Hong Kong as home before the war held on to that belief and lived by it during the horrors of invasion and occupation. That belief in Hong Kong as home was shared by a far wider group than imagined or allowed for by British (and Australian) bureaucracies when they plotted their evacuation plans. It was also far wider than imagined by the Japanese, for whom the logic of their Greater East Asia Prosperity Sphere implied that all "Asians" would fall happily into their embrace. The "Asians" did not, because that's not how they saw themselves, and because Japanese military governance was repulsive.

What comes through in one memoir after another is that these people saw themselves as Hong Kongers. Whether born there or recently arrived, this place was worth holding on to. It is that imagined community of Hong Kongers that survived the war despite immense privation and despair. It is what led Hong Kong into a new, almost post-imperial world and held it together through the decades of massive refugee influxes, local unrest, and uncertainty that followed.

This might seem a bizarre claim, given that so many ordinary Hong Kong people—indeed its thriving middle class, too—of Chinese, Eurasian, Indian, Jewish, Parsi, and people of other descent had suffered the discrimination and snobbery doled out by an arrogant British Empire. Expressing the typically simplistic view of colonial life, the sociologist Henry Lethbridge claimed, "Hong Kong's population in 1941 was split into two main groups, Europeans and Asians, poised against each other."[10] He described the prewar Hong Kong as "rigidly stratified,

Victorian-colonial . . . dominated by the Peak . . . and the 'Peak' mentality," enabling him to pronounce the collapse of "the British Mandarinate" in 1941. Yet in the same essay he is forced to admit that there was in fact "very little racial bitterness or political agitation" perhaps because governance was "widely consultative."

The historian James Hayes, too, sees Hong Kong as a tale of two cities that worked together because what he calls simply the Chinese and the Europeans lived separately and ran themselves: "Two very different races and cultures have somehow contrived a mutually acceptable co-existence . . . mainly, it seems, by leading largely separate lives." Middlemen were useful functionaries between the two communities, but "Chinese society in Hong Kong, with its own leadership and intermediaries, was matched by an equally self-contained European community . . . The desire to live a separate life was a characteristic of both communities and fortunately for Hong Kong each possessed the capacity as well as inclination for it."[11]

And yet—most people, most of the time, lived somewhere in between.

Yes, Eurasians and others were outraged when they were barred from evacuation, and yes, there were clear historical reasons for each minority group to feel badly treated. But most of them, most of the time, held on to their idea of Hong Kong as home. That Portuguese, Eurasians, Parsis, and others risked their lives for their vision of Hong Kong, and returned in 1945 ready to implement it, suggests that their loyalty was to Hong Kong. In all their family's generations of living in Hong Kong this place had been officially "British," whatever people chose that to mean at varying times and places. That loyalty was often expressed as a kind of Britishness (which, as many would discover, had in fact very little to do with life in Britain). But this loyalty was to a Hong Kong imagined among these communities. It might have been an inchoate, nebulous reality but it was tangible enough to fight and die for and return to build. There just were not yet the right words (or leaders) to embody it.

It is telling that the moment when many of these diverse peoples did give up on Hong Kong was not 1941 or 1945 or 1949. It would be 1967. This was when many Portuguese and Eurasian families spread into their global diaspora.[12] In 1967, it seemed as if Hong Kong's distinct, separate status as an autonomous place was most directly threatened as cadres of the Chinese Communist Party's Cultural Revolution spread through town spurring protests and riots. In 1967, the Hong Kong Chinese police force stood up for Hong Kong. British chroniclers have said they stood against the red hordes in the name of British rule. Perhaps it would be more accurate to say they stood and fought for non-Chinese-state rule. For so long as Hong Kongers have been able to convince themselves that their home was special and different, then they have stayed. Certainly their idea of Hong Kong as home survived Japanese occupation, World War Two, and even the return of British colonial rule.

As Jürgen Osterhammel has made clear, domination by foreigners was not necessarily perceived by its subjects as illegitimate; indeed, in Hong Kong a long history of local collaboration is what made it work. Osterhammel also says *collaboration* is not always a dirty word.[13] Most Hong Kongers were collaborators in that they chose to come to Hong Kong, they were self-selected. They went on to become proud active players, getting ahead. These people existed thanks only to the colonial system, yet turned that system on its head. The result, unsurprisingly, is a vast spectrum of experience, from racism and violence at one end to creative innovation and true love at the other, with many, many variations in between.

After reading classics of imperial fiction from Kipling to Conrad, Douglas Kerr concluded that colonial mythology required both those who ruled, and the characters who "went native." He calls it "one of the allegories of empire. The imperial project can come to nothing unless contact is made with the native, but contact is felt to risk disaster, loss of identity, even forfeit of the soul. And so they go on together, the lawman and the outlaw." There is "no profit without knowledge, no knowledge without contact, no contact without transgression." The outlaw and the lawman need each other, are closer to each other than either will admit—and the temptations of native life are invariably portrayed in the curvaceous shape of a woman.[14]

Of course the numerical majority of people in Hong Kong has always been some kind of Chinese. There were those who came from Southeast Asia, or from wildly different parts of China, or who arrived in Hong Kong after lives in California, the South Island of New Zealand, or even from the local-born families of Hong Kong's preglobal fishing villages. Lynn Pan found that not until 1981 was more than half of Hong Kong's population actually born in Hong Kong (other sources suggest it was the 1960s). And Hong Kong's Chinese are different, they are *sui generis*, neither ancestral nor overseas Chinese but "those who succeed in becoming truly bicultural, behaving in a Western mode without a debasement of their own. They are different from the Anglicized subjects of the British Empire in Southeast Asia . . . the treaty-port Chinese of Hong Kong are a world away from the people of China; while their Chineseness is denied by nobody, it is unlike anything you will find in China proper . . . The treaty-port Chinese are better able to do that difficult thing, snap the tough thread of Chinese history and achieve the happy balance which has always eluded their cousins in China: the balance between modernity and Chineseness, between moving with the times and remaining themselves."[15]

When we ask who was engaged in the making of Hong Kong, we cannot stop there. We must include those lawmen and transgressors, the dastardly imperialists, the thugs and soldiers, the pirates of all kinds. We must include the merchants only out for a fortune—and the missionaries and teachers, the seamstresses and horse stablers, the poorer members of an intensely, densely multifaceted place. We must include the many children of the inevitable liaisons that occurred—between all racial and religious groups—of Muslims loving Chinese, or Parsis mixing with Malay and Chinese, or half-Jewish Chinese marrying Belgians. If there was an exotic variation possible it is fair to assume that it happened somewhere along Hong Kong's steep streets at some time.

One cliché all too often takes the place of a whole world, so we think only about a prostitute being left with children fathered by an absent European, and attach some kind of shame to the woman in that arrangement and so to her children. We have seen the product of such homes achieve the highest echelons possible in society, and the greatest wealth. These and other less well-known but probably happier homes of mixed parentage, aspiring young people and the grasping of opportunity, have existed for generations, helping to make Hong Kong—while those purporting to rule the place have come and gone, leaving often little trace.

Long lasting, too, are those families with no Chinese "blood" but deeper roots in Hong Kong than the majority of Hong Kong's current population, most of which only arrived after 1949. European families, perhaps staying within their own world, be it British or Australian or Jewish or Dutch, have lived in Hong Kong for many generations and thus been part of its making.

As in every other port city dating from the premodern era until now, the people who did truly cross boundaries are those who moved beyond collision into collusion with one another. These are the people who crossed all the standard taboos (in both Asian and Western societies) of race, class, and faith, to truly meld with the Other. Daniel Caldwell did this first while a succession of free traders pursued varying kinds of relationships with women that inevitably produced mixed-race offspring who were, initially, much despised and neglected. Yet here were the beginnings of a Eurasian community that, by the start of the twentieth century, had become an elite of its own. From the pliable backs of their mothers and on the back of colonial education systems, this new breed became the leading adepts in translating the East to the West and back again. Such intermediaries have provided, over the centuries and around the world, the vital glue required by any port city for its traders to understand one another and for business to grow.

Perhaps this is where power truly lay—in the margins between British and Chinese societies, in a multiracial core that, though numerically small, was nonetheless pivotal to the "making" of Hong Kong? At least, their importance has been largely overlooked in the histories of Hong Kong to date. For Hong Kong was never "just another Chinese city." In its most dynamic times it ranked with the great port cities of the world, from Genoa to Smyrna, from Salonica to Calcutta, from Canton to Makassar to Nagasaki. It grew out of a specific chain of Asian port cities, first seeded by the Portuguese at Malacca and Macao, then with the Dutch at Batavia and Galle, and finally the British at Penang and Singapore. Only then did Hong Kong come into its own, growing out of those ancient trade routes that spanned the Mediterranean, through or around Africa into the Indian Ocean, and on to the Straits of Malacca and Sunda, perhaps stopping off at the Philippine Islands on the way.

This visceral connection of Hong Kong to its Asian trades, and thus to its Asian traders, has made it more than just an offshoot of a China trade that at the time of Hong Kong's birth was going through one of its regular periods of strangulation and depression. We know in retrospect that the China market was rich and could be sustained, but at that time, the vigor came from the south. Even those leading figures who married within their communal groups almost invariably had mistresses of other origins, and their offspring also made Hong Kong. Some lived in a limbo or exile, by choice or neglect. Others formed great family dynasties, engines of huge wealth, power, and prestige. Hong Kong was not a city before these people from the south appeared. And almost every one of them mixed, in some way, with other peoples. It was this mixing that made it.

15

EPILOGUE

In the harbor of Hong Kong, where it all began centuries ago, the ferries still puff back and forth, carrying commuters to and from their outlying island homes, and crisscrossing from the island—"Hong Kong side"—to Kowloon. When the restrictions surrounding the Covid pandemic are eased, those ferries will again take tourists to the bus to the cable car to ascend the Peak, that vertiginous viewpoint over all Hong Kong, and the destination for its constantly aspiring classes. In many ways, the view and the sound of the city are the same. That constant hum rises from crammed streets made into canyons by high-rise hotels, banks, and window-to-window apartment blocks. On a clear day the mountains marking out the natural border between Kowloon and the more distant New Territories, beyond which lies China, stand firm. There, too, can be found the shape of a crouching lion, which gives us Lion Rock and, inevitably, the Lion Rock Spirit. Tracing how the definition of that spirit has evolved already tells us how the view changes, depending on when you look.

It was in its earliest elaboration a Hong Kong version of pulling oneself up by the bootstraps, the sheer grit and determination to start from nothing and get ahead. Mid- to late-twentieth-century administrations loved it; a popular television soap opera, *Beneath the Lion Rock*, lauded it; most of all, Hong Kong's homegrown Cantonese took it as their own. Attempts by more recent governments to hijack that "spirit" have failed. Instead, the rock became a site for physically challenging and politically daring acts of civil disobedience: intrepid rock climbers managed to hang huge bright yellow banners from Lion Rock with simple messages such as "Democracy" or "Freedom." Each time, the huge banners—visible, yes, from the Peak across the harbor— were torn down. The banner-hanging climbers have not been caught.

Down on the streets of the city, there are more ill-fitting suits, more bad sunglasses and obvious earphones. Hong Kongers now know they are being watched. Victoria Park, once a site for annual commemorations of the Tiananmen Square massacre, is now a more circumscribed place. Highway construction has cut into one side, and the large basketball court areas where masses used to gather are more often fenced off.

It is now seventy years since those multihued characters of Hong Kong—be they Eurasian, Chinese, Indian, Jew, British, or Other— emerged from World War Two to reclaim Hong Kong as their home. In the decades following, Hong Kong recovered rapidly from the war and played an important role in providing services, including rest and recreation, to the American and allied militaries involved in the Korean and Vietnam Wars. Hong Kong, watching as neighboring China convulsed, developed its industrial base and became an international financial center, ranking among the world's top ports. Tourism boomed, bringing more international attention. The label "Made in Hong Kong" evolved from a derisory indicator of cheap and low quality into something said proudly by a Chinese migrant to the Netherlands—"I'm made in Hong Kong!"—when asked where she was from.

Hong Kong remained a draw, too, for people coming from China, Asia, and the wider world. Its international character only intensified through the postwar decades, with the 1970s an incredible boom time for the stock exchange. The year 1979 saw the first transfers of major commercial power from the old-style British trading firms of Hutchison and Wharf into the hands of Hong Kong Chinese tycoons (Li Ka-shing and Y. K. Pao, respectively). Key parts in those dramas were played by the old elite of Eurasian brokers—not least Francis

Zimmern, known as "the Bank's broker," meaning the Hongkong and Shanghai Bank's inside man—even as welcome mats were laid out for international merchant banks to come for the ride.

By 1997, it would be time for the long-anticipated transfer in which Hong Kong would be handed from British sovereignty to Chinese. Naturally, any transition of a freewheeling port city, nominally governed by a power located far away on the other side of the world, into an administrative region of a powerful neighboring state will be difficult. There was no doubt, however, that such a transition would have to take place. China has long believed that "Hong Kong has always been a Chinese city." If taken literally, this cannot be true; we have seen how Hong Kong became a city only after the wider world arrived and peopled the island with mixers and traders and "port city people." But China means that the treaties its leaders signed with Britain in 1842 and 1858 that gave away the island of Hong Kong and the Kowloon Peninsula in perpetuity were "unequal" and thus invalid. And China had a plan, as was made absolutely clear when China's first representative at the United Nations, Huang Hua, spoke there in 1972:

> *The questions of Hongkong and Macau belong in the category of questions resulting from the series of unequal treaties left over by history, treaties which the imperialists imposed on China. Hongkong and Macau are part of Chinese territory occupied by the British and Portuguese authorities. The settlement of the questions of Hongkong and Macau is entirely within China's sovereign right and does not at all fall under the ordinary category of "colonial Territories." Consequently, they should not be included in the list of colonial Territories covered by the Declaration on the Granting of Independence to Colonial Countries and Peoples.*

Hong Kong residents all blithely ignored the disappearance act of Hong Kong as a colony in international law, meaning Britain could not grant it independence under the decolonization procedures followed elsewhere. They chose instead to focus on the next bit of the statement: that "with regard to the questions of Hong Kong and Macao, the Chinese Government has consistently held that they should be settled in an appropriate way when conditions are ripe." This seemed to suggest that the future of Hong Kong remained open.

Perhaps port city people need a solid streak of determined optimism or wishful thinking to survive. Our Hong Kongers have thrived on that persistent search for the space between the lines, for any hint of opportunity out of hardship, the need to push ever onward and upward. The result was a few more decades of growth and enthusiasm in Hong Kong under British administration while China gained more strength on the world stage. There was, after all, an immense amount of money to be made through Hong Kong. Everyone seemed prepared then, through the heady 1970s and into the '80s, to coexist in a liminal gray zone. Sovereignty was something to be tackled some other day, but for now, to paraphrase paramount leader Deng Xiaoping: to get rich was glorious.

Those Hong Kongers who held their nerve felt that with the international oversight provided by British rule, and the throbbing economic success now oozing out of every back street and tenement, they would be safe. The character of the city had changed as millions of mainland Chinese fleeing communism in 1949 settled down in Hong Kong. These new refugees had raised families in a free society and open education system out of which their children could become professional members of an international middle class.

At the same time, many of Hong Kong's more marginal communities had long planned a sanctuary elsewhere, never quite trusting what the future might hold. Some Eurasian families had already moved to Britain, Australia, the United States, or Canada in the 1960s and '70s. Many sent their children abroad for schooling and then followed them to make homes in the West. This was possible only for those with money, and many of the oldest families had that from before the war. To this day, many of the families we have met maintain homes—and an enviable lifestyle—in Hong Kong, at the same time as having homes, passports, and extended families around the world.

When Governor Murray MacLehose went to Beijing in 1979 to talk with Deng Xiaoping about the problem of extending land leases beyond the 1997 lease expiration, Deng said to MacLehose: "It has been our consistent view that the People's Republic of China has sovereignty over Hong Kong, while Hong Kong also has its own special position. A negotiated settlement of the Hong Kong question in the future should be based on the premise that the territory is part of China. However, we will treat Hong Kong as a special region. For a considerable length of time, Hong Kong may continue to practise its capitalist system while we practise our socialist system."[1] Deng also said Hong Kong people should "set their hearts at ease." And again, the coda was taken as the main message, and on went that gray zone in the minds of Hong Kongers as they rested "at ease," awaiting "ripeness."

Behind the scenes, however, certain practical steps were being taken that would directly affect the people living across boundaries— the Eurasians and others with mixed roots. It is no accident that soon after MacLehose's Beijing visit, the British government chose to confirm in immigration law its exclusion of the majority of Hong Kong's population from full British citizenship. The process had begun, while few noticed, back in 1962 when the Commonwealth Immigrant Act stripped Hong Kong passport holders of their legal right to live in Britain. Hong Kong residents taking British citizenship were now designated as British Dependent Territories Citizens (BDTC), which from 1985 became British Nationals (Overseas), or BNO. Neither status conferred any right of abode in Britain.

Behind these legal moves was the century-long shift in the nature of the British Empire itself, from global dominance to second-tier status, with a navy that no longer ruled the seas. Back before World War One it was commonplace for anyone born in a territory over which the British flag flew to gain British nationality and citizenship. This right extended at least as far as grandchildren of the British passport holder, whether or not the grandparents had themselves been born in Britain or had British forebears. Thus Baghdadi Jews in Shanghai, Sindhis in Hong Kong, Malays or Chinese in Singapore, to name but a few, all believed themselves to be British and carried British papers. Few, if any, of them had ever been to Britain or had any close family ties there, but the imperial umbrella was understood by them as a genuine shelter. After World War One, as the old sprawling, cosmopolitan empires of Istanbul and Vienna crumbled, it became more important for anyone of "dubious"—meaning mixed, non-white, or non-British-born—origins to make sure they held official British passports. Britain, too, was slowly but steadily pulling up its nation-state drawbridges.

Many of Hong Kong's in-between people failed to notice the diminishing value of their passports as British law cleverly separated out citizenship (including the right to live in Britain) from nationality. The former came only if one could prove one's grandparents, and later only one's parents, were British-born. The implicit racism of the shift was clear. But in Hong Kong, the good times continued.

Prime Minister Margaret Thatcher arrived in Hong Kong in 1982, her nose streaming and head blocked by a heavy cold, on her way to meet Deng in Beijing to discuss Hong Kong's future. When she emerged from those talks only to slip and stumble on the steps of the Great Hall of the People, it seemed a dramatic sign of the changing of the guard over Hong Kong. Many months of tortuous negotiations later, the deal guiding Hong Kong's shift toward Chinese sovereignty was set—and markedly aligned to that plan first outlined by Huang Hua back in 1972. Promised another fifty years after the handover during which nothing would change, residents of Hong Kong felt hopeful once more. Many of those who had fled to gain passports elsewhere now returned, with that insurance in their top pocket, to enjoy many more decades of the special energy in Hong Kong.

The next landmark moment for Hong Kong took place in Beijing—in another sign of how much closer Hong Kong's fate was now tied to

China. This was the killing of hundreds, probably thousands, of pro-democracy demonstrators around Tiananmen Square on June 4, 1989. Hong Kongers by the million expressed outpourings of empathy and fear for the future. And again, the many once-influential people of Hong Kong with no other place to call home became the subject of intensified lobbying in London. Britain agreed to issue fifty thousand full British passports to residents selected by the Hong Kong government.[2] Work began on a bill of rights. The last British governor, Christopher Patten, arrived in July 1992, and by October had promised a broadening of the voter base. China began threatening to take over Hong Kong sooner if Britain did not behave.

The clouds were gathering but the port city people pressed on. What mattered was security of domicile, and the chance for one's children to get ahead. If that could be assured under Chinese rule as much as it ever was under British, all was well. But was it?

China declared, "All Hong Kong Chinese compatriots, whether they are holders of the BDTC passport or not, are Chinese nationals." What remained unclear was what this would mean for Hong Kong citizens who were not "Hong Kong Chinese." Many of Hong Kong's non-Chinese had other passports, but some did not—and the governments' exchanges of memoranda ignored this. Thus, many of Hong Kong's Eurasians, and the 4,500 Indians with BDTC documents, were not covered; they were neither "Chinese" nor "compatriots."[3]

Yet, for several years after the handover, most people were relieved that daily life didn't seem to change much at all. The fruit-seller still tended his stall every day, the newspapers were printed, free debates still happened at school and university, money was still made.

Beijing chose to embed its rule amid the tycoon class, appointing a committee that chose Hong Kong's first chief executive, the shipping tycoon Tung Chee-hwa. Yet even participants in the hybrid system of Hong Kong governance admit that its failure is systemic. Tung had to resign after a million Hong Kongers marched in 2003 against the idea of a National Security Law. His successor, the former civil servant under British rule, Donald Tsang, eventually left office under a cloud of corruption allegations (he was jailed and then cleared of all charges and released). His successor, C. Y. Leung, was particularly unpopular with the younger generation who led the seventy-nine-day mass civil disobedience campaign of 2014 known as Occupy.

What an outburst that was. It surprised an older generation of democracy advocates, and terrified Beijing's appointees in Hong Kong. Here was a fresh new young generation of Hong Kongers, born after the 1997 handover, keen to save what they saw as their identity in a free, in-between place. In no mood for compromise, they rejected an electoral system imposed on them in which they could choose neither the candidates nor who voted for them. This group of school-leavers, led by the now-famous Joshua Wong, Nathan Law, and Agnes Chow, among others, had already fought off attempts to inject more "patriotic," meaning pro-China, material into school curriculums.[4] They joyfully camped out for more than two months with banners and seminars, and study areas to keep up with school-work, dispensing stations for water and food and medical care—and platforms where they debated their hopes for a future in which they would have a say.

Crucially, Occupy had broad public support—beyond those upset at how the traffic was messed up. Middle-class parents made sure their offspring and friends were well fed and sheltered. Office workers and off-duty civil servants joined the throng after work and sang along to anthems including "Do You Hear the People Sing?" from the French postrevolutionary musical *Les Misérables*. Among those camping out were groups of Nepalis, Indians, Filipinos, and more, all proclaiming their part in Hong Kong's fight for a future.

Clearly the old shibboleth that Hong Kong was fundamentally a financial center whose people just didn't care about politics was not true. Indeed, throughout its history, Hong Kongers have shown a marked tendency to express themselves—from protests against dis-criminatory anti-Chinese laws in the nineteenth century, to the sym-pathy strikes and boycotts to support Chinese republicans in the early twentieth. Port workers and seamen, tram drivers and maids—all had joined mass actions for greater rights under British rule. Back in 1925, or in 1967, the mass movements were in the name of Hong Kong, not in favor of this or that ideology. Hong Kongers have kept up the habit under Chinese rule, too. Ignored by both governments in the talks over their future, they have kept insisting that Hong Kong has a time and place of its own and a history worth defending.

What that history is remains disputed. Lady May, wife of Colonel Sir Lindsay Ride who ran the British Army Aid Group resistance organization during World War Two, told me, *"My dear, we built this place!"* An Australian by birth, she was referring to "the British," a world of which she was a part. But we must not ignore the hundreds of thousands of Chinese who followed and were integral to making this city what it is today. And we cannot deny the many others—Jews, Armenians, Parsis, Nepalis, Southeast Asians—who, though lesser in number to the Chinese, often played vital, standout roles in the making of Hong Kong. Of growing importance, too, are the ethnic Chinese born and/or educated in the West who come back to Hong Kong because it is close to, but not quite, China. Some non-Chinese dynasties have been in the city far longer than the majority of the Hong Kong population. Few Chinese ever imagined they would choose to stay in Hong Kong, either. The difference from the twentieth century on is that most Chinese who fled to Hong Kong have stayed there, in a city like no other. Little wonder the insertion in 2014, for the first time, of the term *Hong Konger* in the *Oxford English Dictionary*.

––––––––––

For a few years after Occupy was crushed, some residents left, to be sure their children would get a better education, or because the living was easier elsewhere. Others were more determined to hold on to the Hong Kong they believed in. Then, in 2019, the latest mayor backed by Beijing, Carrie Lam, sparked the largest mass protests ever seen in Hong Kong when she planned a law allowing for the extradition of Hong Kong people to the Chinese legal system. First, one million people marched through the streets, then two million. Only when a tiny group attacked the legislature physically did the government agree to drop the planned bill. By then it was too late, and through a long, hot, wet summer the movement grew. The more its demands were ignored, the more it grew and the more violence ensued. Finally, the early-2020 arrival of the coronavirus pandemic cleared the streets, and a crackdown followed, bolstered by the imposition of a new National Security Law.

It was all a heady reminder of the spirit of a Hong Kong that refuses to bow down. Or it was the last foolishness of people who should have known better than to be so very provocative. Or both. Either way, Hong Kong now knows it is under new management. As if to underline that fact, the "Made in Hong Kong" label, which had once been a source of shame and then pride, was now set to be eliminated. The U.S. government said in 2020 it could no longer apply in trading rules of origin, on the judgment that there remains insufficient difference between the systems of Hong Kong and China. Instead, goods from Hong Kong would be labeled "Made in China." Whatever China thought about that, Hong Kong's Chinese manufacturers were furious, and their protest to the WTO was upheld.

A second shift, of more direct import for the in-between people of diverse origins, was made clear in early 2021, namely, that China's long-standing refusal to recognize dual nationality was now being extended to Hong Kong. In other words, if one was born in Hong Kong and had Hong Kong or Chinese passports, then the concept of consular protection by any other passport one might also hold would no longer apply. Western governments were soon warning their passport holders in Hong Kong that this carried risks for all holders of more than one formal identity.[5]

––––––––––

Hong Kong may never have been seen as fully a place on its own ground with its own personality—such notions of independent agency are anathema to all ruling nation-states. Yet Hong Kong people have lived more freely, openly, and with greater education and cosmopolitan sense than those on the Chinese mainland. Merging groups with such disparate values could never be easy. Precisely because of its different history—because of the mixing of peoples and ideas from the whole world that has helped to make Hong Kong—that fit would not be smooth.

Where does this leave today's Hong Kongers? Those who cherished Hong Kong as an open city, where people of many kinds could come together, have fun, make money, and enjoy family life, might feel that their time has passed. It's that melancholy feeling, knowing that once, your town and your port city was special and dynamic and marvelous, linking disparate parts of the world, gaining and giving riches from that engagement. Then, as the empires around you shift and change shape, grow weaker or stronger, your favorite place becomes more a backwater, less a cosmopolitan town and more an outpost or suburb of a new or more overarching power.

Much depends on the nature of the new power. Will it embrace genuine openness to diversity, difference, and new ideas, allowing Hong Kong to express its sometimes unruly personality? Or will it emphasize only control and uniformity, risking the loss of Hong Kong's essential character?

The gray zone that had allowed Hong Kong and its multiple, mixed-up peoples to thrive is becoming, step by step, more black-and-white. Just as Philip Mansel saw that the key to his Levantine port cities was their nonstate nature, so, too, for Hong Kong. It was formed by its mixed peoples, and by its place between the rich worlds of trade and other ideas to the north, south, and southeast. Now China's nationalism and nation-statism is overtaking it, when it has no claim to a nationhood of its own.

Others, of course, never subscribed to the idea of a cosmopolitan Hong Kong and spurn it as a romantic, overidealized vision of something that never was. Perhaps all this is merely an exercise in pointless nostalgia? One five-generation Hong Kong family's matriarch says, Well, so long as we are making money here, we don't care; our children will go to boarding school anyway. A gracious China coast aristocrat laughed sadly at the failure of democratic dreams in Hong Kong, knowing, from her family's flight from Shanghai in the 1940s, what little chance there had been.

And then came Covid-19. Suddenly medical science supported the banning of any gathering of more than two people. Jokes in the early days about what "Wu-flu" might mean—a name coined from the origin of the coronavirus in China's huge city of Wuhan—soon fell flat. Political life was closed down along with the schools and universities, the bars and shops and restaurants within which communities would usually gather.

Not that the government felt the need for any excuse—it had already raided the homes of democratically elected legislators and locked up, without bail or charges, almost fifty of them who, two years later, were still in jail awaiting trial. They had planned a primary vote across the democratic camp to produce candidates who could win the plurality necessary to gain power over the Legislative Council. This was deemed subversion; subsequent restrictions of candidates and voting choices are described by the government and its loyalists as an "improvement."

So, too, with the media. By arresting and then freezing the assets of Jimmy Lai, the man who owned the bestselling local newspaper *Apple Daily*, the government achieved its total closure and demolition of the most vibrant Chinese voice for a free Hong Kong. Jimmy Lai had swum to Hong Kong as a child and worked his way up to millionaire status with clothes groups, canny investments, and a media enterprise. What he loves about Hong Kong is its freedom, and, unlike many local tycoons, he joined the crowds on the streets to defend just that. His steadfast Catholic faith, his daring to call live on a BBC broadcast for people in China to stand up, his very success as a businessman—all this and more mean that Jimmy, already in his seventies, is facing charges for anything from fraud to subversion, for which the maximum penalty is a life sentence. Following his fall, a long string of Chinese-language news sites and enterprises folded. The government insists press freedom exists as strongly as ever.

With the pandemic requiring isolation and quarantine, a movement not yet crushed by other means was forced, quite simply, to stay at home. Perhaps the science supported that approach in the early months of 2020. But by the summer of that year even the beaches were closed down. Amid real doubts that the science could support such measures, it was as if any attempt by Hong Kongers to sustain a conversation were now off-limits.

If any further proof was needed that Hong Kong under newly direct Chinese Communist Party management had missed the boat on what Hong Kong is, it can be seen in the near-total closure of its airport. Long after other countries—particularly its competitor as Asian financial hub, Singapore—had decided to live with the virus and allow travel once more, arrivals in Hong Kong still had to go through hazmat-gear-wearing inspectors enforcing one- to three-week quarantines in separate hotel rooms from which one could neither open the window nor escape.

Once-throbbing hallways for arrivals and departures were now busy only on the nights when overbooked planes carried out a group of weepy Hong Kongers, especially its younger, educated, and ordinary people. They were carrying their cats, and perhaps bringing their grandparents—these people were not coming back. Hong Kong recorded a net loss of 130,000 residents in the first half of 2022 alone.[6]

This new regime was not only shutting down its thinking persons within; it was happily demolishing the raison d'être of Hong Kong as port city, as global waystation, as gathering place to all comers. All that mattered was the central government's determination to have its "zero-Covid" policy followed. More than that—a powerful narrative was developed, and believed by Hong Kong's many ready quislings, that all those political troubles were nothing to do with Hong Kong being made into China at all. The official line is that the recent years of unrest are the fault of foreign forces, of the United States and others funding subversion and even paying those millions to march on the street, of *collusion*, a new Communist buzzword. Said the senior government member Regina Ip in July 2022: "Colluding with foreign forces is a definite no-no because of the current geopolitical situation.

Some Western countries are targeting China. The U.S. is roping in allies to target China. Such action to contain China forces our country to stay vigilant."

This, to put it mildly, is an entirely new way of looking at Hong Kong's traditional openness to people, inspiration, and enterprises from around the world. It also willfully ignores the large extent to which today's Hong Kong was made by a multitude of non-Chinese people and ideas.

Meanwhile, some of our in-between people—of perhaps Eurasian, Jewish, Indian, or Portuguese heritage in Hong Kong—have awoken to the discriminations and brutalities of British rule in their family's pasts, even as they adjust to newer Chinese realities. One confided that his family had been treated as second-class citizens by the British and were now third-class under the Chinese. One must either have a route out or accept the need to adjust to a new Hong Kong, whatever it holds. He had no illusions that the Chinese would be as forgiving of his dark skin as the British had been. Luckily, he has a European wife and homes around the world.

Others have chosen to toss off that in-betweenness and embrace the (new) motherland. One scion of a Eurasian family that fled to Australia in 1967 chose to return to the thriving financial center of Hong Kong, where, he believed, his children could more fully embrace what he called the "Asian century." He understood his parents wanted more security with a young family half a century earlier, and appreciated his overseas education, but saw no need to flee again. Even when he took his family to Singapore to get them into school during Covid times, he insisted he would go back to Hong Kong. He refused to engage with the thought that it's tough on a place when the only way to vote is with one's feet.

Others say the future lies in a new version of Hong Kong's past— as an offshoot of the trading world focused in southern China, around Guangzhou and newer satellite cities like Shenzhen all over the Pearl River delta. Indeed Canton, now Guangzhou, has been engaged in global trade since at least the 900s, and today boasts a lively mixed community of Africans, Europeans, and others alongside the Chinese in business. China academics can prove that China has always interacted with the rest of the world, that it, too, has had its cosmopolitan eras and enthusiasms. Southern Chinese still dream, some days, that, as in the old adage, the mountains are high and the emperor far away.

Many in Hong Kong must hope that this will be true again and thus allow room on the new empire's periphery for a place such as Hong Kong, with its many diverse peoples and ideas. However, the longtime China expert Jamil Anderlini has described China's current regime as "ethno-nationalist authoritarianism."[7]

Who will be right? And does it make sense for the city's denizens to stay in Hong Kong, which, despite everything, is still home? Or is it better to accept that clashing visions of Hong Kong do not a peaceful life make? Hong Kongers now, as in past cycles of upheaval and opportunity, are trying to answer those questions—even as most of those peoples engaged in making the Hong Kong known and loved for generations are long gone.

ACKNOWLEDGMENTS

This book could not have been written but for the help of many people. Key friends and colleagues have been vital supports throughout.

Inspiration has been provided by luminaries such as John Darwin, whose stress on the interstices within colonies and empires seemed to justify this inquiry. In the Netherlands, I am particularly grateful for the intellectual support of Henk Schulte Nordholt, at Leiden's KITLV, Tim Harper of Cambridge, and Heather Sutherland. The historian Brian Edgar's explorations of his own family's past in his impressively researched blog led me down interesting pathways. Frank Dikotter clarified the challenge when he told me, "Just dig into the archives and let them guide you in telling the story."

The historian Christopher Munn generously gave a professional reading of the first drafts and improved matters immensely; his kindness in helping to track references from afar and his patience in listening to years of research questions is most gratefully acknowledged. Further stimulus and help came from Chiara Formichi, Vivian Kong, Patricia Chiu, Vicky Lee, Peter Hall, Stephen Davies, Robin Hutcheon, John Carroll, Elizabeth Sinn, Robert Bickers, Philip Bowring, Ian McFadzean, May Holdsworth, and many more.

In several cases, insights into some of Hong Kong's founding families have been possible only thanks to descendants of those families themselves. First in line stands Dawn Leonard, a great friend from our early newspaper days, who I only later realized was part of the Churn-Fenton-Kotewall matrix. She helped me reach other family members, including her impressive ninety-year-old uncle Charlie, as well as the fabulous Pat Botelho, her cousin Marion, and the Fenton ladies, Patsy and her daughter Kim Fenton Lamsam.

Just as generous about the entire Ho Tung-Tse-Ho-Hui-Wong matrix has been Andrew Tse, a descendant of Sir Robert Ho Tung's brother Sir Ho Kam Tong. His central Hong Kong eyrie packed with books, photographs, and his own extensive knowledge was immensely helpful. His brother Michael was good enough to take me through the Eurasian cemetery.

Of help, too, has been Anthony Correa, proud descendant of Portuguese, Eurasian, and many other bloods. Through him I was able to communicate with the fantastic Portuguese community's elders and historians: Anthony's uncle Bosco Correa, Henry "Quito" d'Assumpçao, Michael Noronha, and Alberto Guterres. Anthony introduced me to his mother, Vivienne Correa (née Baker), and he connected me to the Shroff (Neville and Burji) family of Hong Kong; he also put me in touch with the d'Almada Remedios family and their excellent Macanese Friday-night dinners.

I'm grateful to descendants of E. R. Belilios, including Tim Judah, Anthony Choy, and Simon Choa-Johnston; to Sir Michael Kadoorie and his pathbreaking Hong Kong Heritage Project; and to George Cautherley, with his ever-expanding family tree. John Asome, Jill Fell, Brian Rothwell, and Sean Olson have all done original research on their families and shared generously, as have Audrey Thomas and Veronica Needa. Barbara Merchant is doing important research on her Eurasian pasts in Shanghai and has been generous, too.

Jimmy Master kindly shared his uncle Jamshed Pavri's painstaking research, a unique and underused insight into the Parsi community of Hong Kong and Canton.

One of my biggest debts is to scholars no longer with us, which, for Hong Kong, means Rev. Carl T. Smith. Back when my parents used to bring him back from church at Jordan Road so my mother could "feed him up," they warned me I might have to work on Carl's notes in the future. After decades of journalism, I realized they were right. This book would be nothing without Carl. As Christopher Munn wrote in an introduction to a reissue of Smith's seminal work, *Chinese Christians, Elites, Middlemen and the Church in Hong Kong*: "Every so often a work of history appears that radically changes our understanding of people, place and period. *Chinese Christians*, first published in 1985, is such a work. This book asks questions about Hong Kong that have never been asked before. It shows that the leaders of Chinese society had a far greater role in shaping early Hong Kong history than earlier historians had believed . . . The picture that emerges is . . . one of men and women using the machinery of colonialism to launch professions, gather riches, secure political influence and build dynasties."

Carl Smith's methodology, informed by a background in genealogy as well as divinity studies, set new standards of research and found new sources. By training his magnifying glass on land registry documents, wills, letters, missionary archives, Chinese-language archives, and simply the birth, death, and marriage notices in the newspapers, Carl opened up a new world for the rest of us to dive into. I only wish he was still around to share all this with.

Archivists, meanwhile, are among my favorite people—such as Helen Swinnerton at HSBC Archives and Amelia Allsop at the Hong Kong Heritage Project, now co-directors with me of History Ink Limited. My thanks also to Garfield Lam of the HKU Archives, Bernard Hui of the Public Records Office in Hong Kong, Iris Chan and colleagues at HKU Library's Special Collections, and John Wells and colleagues at the Cambridge University Library. Other helpful archives have been the SOAS special collections, the Hong Kong Jewish Community Centre Library, the London Metropolitan Archive, the National Archives (UK), the archives of the International Committee of the Red Cross in Geneva, and the Bodleian Library at Oxford.

Thanks go to my wonderful agent Doug Young at PEW Literary

Agency. My thanks also to Colin Harrison, Emily Polson, and the team at Scribner in the United States, and to James Gurbutt and his team at Corsair and Little, Brown in Britain.

Most important, I need to pay tribute to Dr. Ron Zimmern, who, ever since he started discovering his own family history, has wanted to know more. He inspired and supported this first scholarly attempt to research and write a general history of Hong Kong's Eurasians and other interesting people. It was an extension of his encouragement for the establishment of the Hong Kong History Project based at the University of Bristol. This book is the result of his commitment to understanding Hong Kong and its peoples, and his determination that this story reaches a wide audience.

Above all, my thanks and all love go to Kees Metselaar.

NOTES

INTRODUCTION: THE DIFFERENT CITY

1   Government of Hong Kong SAR Fact Sheets, see www.gov.hk.

2   Textbook revisions imposed on Hong Kong schools in 2022 made this explicit, stating that Hong Kong had never been a colony, merely occupied territory.

3   Anthony Sweeting, "Hong Kong Eurasians," p. 84. The original Sweeting Archives held by the University of Hong Kong Archives have been consulted.

4   Stephen F. Fisher, "Eurasians in Hong Kong."

5   Charles Hirschman, "The Origins and Demise of the Concept of Race," p. 410.

6   Eric Peter Ho, *Tracing My Children's Lineage*, p. 7.

7   Ibid., p. 10.

8   Jean Gelman Taylor, *The Social World of Batavia: Europeans and Eurasians in Colonial Indonesia*, p. xxvii.

9   It was never simple, though. As the census report of 1901 put it: "It is a very difficult matter to obtain the true figures for this portion of the population. The large majority of Eurasians in this Colony dress in Chinese clothes, have been brought up and live in Chinese fashion and would certainly return themselves as Chinese." The report noted the far higher number of Eurasians reporting themselves as such in Singapore who were probably from Tamil, Malay, or Indian mothers, not Chinese: "They would most likely not have any objection to declaring themselves Eurasians. The Chinese consider the term as one of reproach." Hong Kong Government Sessional Papers 1902, *Report on the Census for 1901*. Perhaps that's why just 228 people listed themselves as Eurasian

out of 319,803 people in Hong Kong in 1906; in 1911, just 42 out of 456,739 did so; in 1932, 837 out of 849,751. The *Encyclopaedia Britannica* specifically linked Eurasians to Eurasia: "Following the geographical employment of the term Eurasia to describe the whole of the great land mass which is now divided into the continents of Europe and Asia, Eurasian has come to be descriptive of any half-caste born of parents representing the races of the two continents." *Encyclopaedia Britannica*, 11th ed., Vol. 9 (London: CUP, 1910), p. 900.

10   Heather Sutherland, "Treacherous Translators and Improvident Paupers: Perception and Practice in Dutch Makassar, Eighteenth and Nineteenth Centuries," p. 320.
11   Ibid., pp. 339–40.
12   Ibid., p. 352.
13   Email correspondence, Heather Sutherland, February 13, 2020.
14   Christopher Munn, *Anglo-China—Chinese People and British Rule in Hong Kong, 1841–1880*, pp. 57–60.
15   Carl T. Smith, "The Chinese Settlement of Hong Kong," p. 27. See also his seminal works: *Chinese Christians, Elites, Middlemen and the Church in Hong Kong*; *A Sense of History: Studies in the Social and Urban History of Hong Kong*; and "English-Educated Chinese Elites in Nineteenth-Century Hong Kong," pp. 65–96.
16   John Darwin in Robert Bickers and Christian Henriot, *New Frontiers: Imperialism's New Communities in East Asia, 1842–1953*, pp. 251–53.

1: THE WORLD TO HONG KONG

1   Sir George Staunton, translator and East India Company man, speaking in 1833. E. J. Eitel, *Europe in China*, pp. 53ff.
2   Ashin Das Gupta, in Blair B. Kling and M. B. Pearson, *The Age of Partnership, Europeans in Asia Before Dominion*, pp. 191–213.
3   D. Warres-Smith, *European Settlements in the Far East*, p. 180.
4   LMS South China Report 1880, "London Missionary Society, The History of the Hongkong District from 1870 to 1880" dated February 10, 1881, by John Chalmers. LMS Archive held at SOAS, University of London.
5   K. P. G. Lowe, "Hong Kong, 26 January 1841: Hoisting the Flag Revisited," p. 14.
6   Claude Markovits, *The Global World of Indian Merchants 1750–1947: Traders of Sind from Bukhara to Panama*, pp. 10–12.
7   Anthony Reid, *A History of Southeast Asia—Critical Crossroads*, p. 92.
8   Frank Broeze, ed. *Brides of the Sea, Port Cities of Asia from the 16th–*

20th Centuries. In Chapter 2, by Anthony Reid, he notes that freelance prostitution for a fee was never mentioned by travelers. Instead, there was temporary marriage, as described by a Dutch captain in Patani, in which foreigners were free to choose from women who presented themselves . . . "provided they agree what he shall pay for certain months. Once they agree about the money (which does not amount to much for so great a convenience), she comes to his house and serves him by day as his maidservant and by night as his wedded wife. He is then not able to consort with other women or he will be in grave trouble with his wife, while she is similarly wholly forbidden to converse with other men, but the marriage lasts as long as he keeps his residence there, in good peace and unity. When he wants to depart . . . she may look for another man as she wishes, in all propriety, without scandal." Reid's source is J. van Neck's journal of 1604, in H. A. Forrest and A. de Booy, eds., *De Vierde Schipvaart der Nederlanders noor Oost-Indie*, vol. 1, p. 225. See also research by Barbara Andaya, which adds nuance and exceptions.

9   *Hongkong Daily Press*, May 18, 1867—ordinance for new Mahmedan Cemetery [*sic*] October 10, 1858, to Shaik Moosdeen, Mahomed [*sic*] Arab, and Sheik Jumma, Inland Lot 582, Saiyingpoon.

10   Carl T. Smith Collection, Probate file No. 33 of 1887 (4/651).

2: FRESH OFF THE BOAT

1   Frederic A. "Jim" Silva, *Todo o Nosso Passado, All Our Yesterdays—The Sons of Macao, Their History and Heritage*, p. 28.

2   Stuart Braga, "Making Impressions: The Adaptation of a Portuguese Family to Hong Kong, 1700–1950," pp. 146–47. Grande-Pré became the first non-British superintendent of police. Ibid., p. 147, citing Norton-Kyshe, pp. 361, 434.

3   J. P. Braga, *The Portuguese in Hongkong and China*, p. 142.

4   HK PRO HKRS 149-2-133 and 149-2-216, both December 10, 1859.

5   Carl T. Smith, "The Establishment of the Parsee Community in Hong Kong," p. 395.

6   Guo Deyan, "The Study of Parsee Merchants in Canton, Hong Kong and Macao," p. 58.

7   The Jamshed Pavri Parsi Papers, privately held, pp. 39–40.

8   *Friend of China*, September 21, 1848; cited in Carl T. Smith, "The Establishment of the Parsee Community in Hong Kong," pp. 389–97.

9   Mesrovb Jacob Seth, *Armenians in India from the Earliest Times to the Present Day, a Work of Original Research*, pp. 458–69.

10   Carl T. Smith and Paul van Dyke, "Four Armenian Families," p. 49.

11   Anita M. Weiss, "South Asian Muslims in Hong Kong: Creation of a 'Local Boy' Identity," pp. 417–53.

12   *China Mail*, August 7, 1851. See Carl T. Smith, "The Early Jewish Community in Hong Kong," in *A Sense of History: Studies in the Social and Urban History of Hong Kong*, pp. 398–413. See also Solomon Bard, *Traders of Hong Kong: Some Foreign Merchant Houses, 1841–1899*.

13   Cecil Roth, *The Sassoon Dynasty*, p. 26.

14   Stanley Jackson, *The Sassoons*, p. 4.

15   Roth, *The Sassoon Dynasty*, p. 34.

16   Ibid., p. 36.

17   Ibid., p. 45.

18   See also William Tarrant, *Hongkong*, pp. 16, 69.

19   George Smith, *The Consular Cities of China*, p. 82.

20   Carl T. Smith, "The Chinese Settlement of British Hong Kong," pp. 26–32.

21   Carl T. Smith, "An Early Hong Kong Success Story: Wei Akwong, the Beggar Boy," pp. 9–14.

22   *Chinese Repository*, Vol. XII, January to December 1843, p. 549.

3: HONEY

1   Benjamin Ball, *Rambles in Eastern Asia, including China and Manilla, during several years' residence: with notes of the voyage to China, excursions in Manilla, Hong-Kong, Canton, Shanghai, Ningpoo, Amoy, Fouchow, and Macao*, pp. 78–96. This is the diary of Mr. Ball, August 1848; see pp. 90–91.

2   See Vaudine England, *Kindred Spirits—A History of The Hong Kong Club*. Jews, Armenians, and one Parsi were members by the late nineteenth century, but "members of the local community" were not invited until 1964. They were at first mostly Eurasian. Women were not allowed to join on equal terms until 1996.

3   Cheng Po Hung, *Early Prostitution in Hong Kong*, pp. 65–66.

4   Elizabeth Sinn, "Women at Work: Chinese Brothel Keepers in Nineteenth-Century Hong Kong," pp. 87–111; see p. 94.

5   Veronica Pearson and Ko Tim-keung, eds., *Sense of Place, Hong Kong West of Pottinger Street*, Chapter 8: "Opportunity Knocking: Female Brothel Keepers in Hong Kong," by Elizabeth Sinn, pp. 262–77; see p. 267. See also Susanna Hoe, *The Private Life of Old Hong Kong: Western Women in the British Colony 1841–1941*, esp. Chapter 13.

6   Sinn, "Women at Work," p. 91.

7   Philip Howell, "Race, Space and the Regulation of Prostitution in Co-
     lonial Hong Kong," in John M. Carroll and Mark Chi-kwan, *Critical
     Readings on the Modern History of Hong Kong*, pp. 37–58; see p. 53.
     A report to the governor before the 1867 legislation noted that some
     Chinese men used European brothels, and that at busy times, European
     brothels took in women from Chinese brothels to meet demand. See
     CO129/124, pp. 95, 115.
8   See Philippa Levine, *Prostitution, Race & Politics—Policing Venereal
     Disease in the British Empire*, p. 40.
9   The debate before this legislation was introduced is revealing of Brit-
     ish ambivalence in their distaste for the whole subject, disgust at the
     Chinese ways of treating women, and the ultimately overriding need
     to protect their sailors and soldiers from disease. See CO129/50, pp.
     73–92, 1855. See also CO129/50, pp. 219–29; CO129/50, pp. 340–51;
     CO129/50, pp. 366–67; CO129/55, pp. 230–69. Members of the Leg-
     islative Council, all of them men, spoke of their "repugnance" for the
     subject, their dislike of having to legitimize something "intrinsically
     immoral," yet they eventually recognized that the trade was probably
     unstoppable and needed rules. CO129/55, pp. 230–69; CO129/62,
     pp. 468–517; CO129/65, pp. 98–100; CO129/67, pp. 586–88.
10   Levine, *Prostitution, Race & Politics*, p. 243.
11   Dr. Philip Ayres told a government inquiry in 1877, "The Chinese treat
     syphilis as an ordinary sore which heals up . . ." Dr. Lum Chau Fan,
     senior doctor of the Tung Wah Hospital, said, "A quack doctor would
     use mercury, but a proper doctor would not employ it. The use of mer-
     cury makes the disease settle down in one part or other of the body,
     then it breaks out again and is very difficult to cure." Women often
     self-medicated with alum water and other remedies. Government of
     Hong Kong, *Report to Enquire into the Working of the Contagious
     Diseases Ordinance, 1867* (Hong Kong: Noronha and Sons, 1879),
     Appendix, pp. 14–16.
12   Sinn, "Women at Work," pp. 87–88. See also Pearson and Ko, *Sense of
     Place*, pp. 262–77.
13   James William Norton-Kyshe, *The History of the Law and Courts of
     Hong Kong*, vol. 1, pp. 101–2.
14   Hoe, *The Private Life of Old Hong Kong*, pp. 68–69.
15   Wang Tao, "My Sojourn in Hong Kong, Jottings of Carefree Travel,"
     trans. Yang Qinghua, in *Renditions*, Chinese University of Hong Kong,
     1988; cited in Cheng Po Hung, *Early Prostitution in Hong Kong*,
     p. 19.
16   Carl T. Smith points out, "Such women were the fortunate ones who
     had generous protectors who ensured their financial security and who

used their business acumen to add to their initial seed money," in "Abandoned into Prosperity: Women on the Fringe of Expatriate Society," Chapter 6 in Helen F. Siu, ed., *Merchants' Daughters—Women, Commerce, and Regional Culture in South China*, pp. 129–42; see p. 136.

17   "Excluded from expatriate society, they formed their own network on the basis of their peculiar position." Ibid., p. 141.

18   "In the inter-cultural setting of the China coast cities, the protected woman, under certain circumstances, could create her own place. If she had been locked into the traditional patriarchal domination of females in the Chinese family she would have been denied this road to independence," noted Smith in Maria Jaschok and Suzanne Miers, eds., *Women and Chinese Patriarchy: Submission, Servitude and Escape*, p. 229.

19   Peter Vine, "A Study in Loyalty—William Thomas Bridges," unpublished, p. 12. Vine was a war crimes prosecutor in Hong Kong in 1946 before joining Deacons.

20   St. John's Baptism 1838–1887 Register, Public Records Office, Hong Kong, with permission. See also Hoe, *The Private Life of Old Hong Kong*, pp. 69–70.

21   "Openly acknowledging an association with a protected woman would not have brought the same degree of social stigma as would later have been the case. It is doubtful if even a decade later a partner of Jardine's would have displayed a portrait of his Chinese woman in his home." Smith in Jaschok and Miers, eds., *Women and Chinese Patriarchy*, p. 222. See PRO HKRS Will File 79, 1847, 4/14.

22   Carl T. Smith Collection, Card 61-780—Memorial 5941, dated April 13, 1874, Inland Lot 584 Section B, in consideration of $4,200, Mahomed [*sic*] Arab and John Stewart, traders to Francis Francis of Oriental Hotel, hotel keeper. Registered April 14, 1874. Memorial 6370, dated September 28, 1875, Inland Lot 231A, 248, 248A in consideration $2,200, equity redemption John Stewart, boardinghouse keeper, to Lumbah boardinghouse keeper. Registered September 29, 1875.

23   Carl T. Smith Collection, Card 61-779, Probate File No. 1066 of 1877 (4/346), John Stewart of Victoria, Licensed Victualler, estate to Ng Shee, appoints A. R. Madar, Victoria, as executor June 7, 1875. Probate calculated February 21, 1877, for John Steward, who died in Hong Kong on January 22, 1877, Probate Abdool Razak Madar, sole executor, $3,000. Burials St. John's Cathedral, Vol. 2, 1877, No. 4277, John Steward of Lascar Row, January 23, 1877, aged fifty-six. *Hongkong Daily Press*, January 24, 1877—died Hong Kong, John Stewart, Boarding House Keeper.

24 Smith sources this to Hong Kong Land Records, Memorial 12699, October 4, 1883.

25 For an example of this approach, see Patricia Lim, *Forgotten Souls— A Social History of the Hong Kong Cemetery.*

26 Carl T. Smith, "Ng Akew, One of Hong Kong's 'Protected' Women," pp. 13–17 and 27; see p. 13.

27 One of the governor's sons, Dr. Zerubbabel Endecott (born 1635), fathered Samuel, who fathered another Samuel, who fathered John Endicott, grandfather of James Endicott. There was not only New England politics in his veins (with related forebears including the Massachusetts governor Endicott Peabody and the U.S. secretary of war William Crowninshield Endicott); his direct forefathers also had deep experience in the East Asia trading world.

28 *Friend of China*, October 13, 1849.

29 *Hongkong Daily Press*, March 29, 1878.

30 She was "a formidable opponent and a person to be reckoned with. She played her double role to the hilt. She was a woman of intelligence and independence, trading on her own, making her own decisions, and achieving results in a man's world." Smith in Siu, ed., *Merchants' Daughters*, p. 138.

31 Hong Kong PRO Probate File, No. 104 of 1870 (4/227). Thanks to Carl Smith.

32 Elizabeth Sinn, in Jaschok and Miers, eds., *Women and Chinese Patriarchy*, p. 146.

4: HOME

1 William Tarrant, *Hongkong*, p. 139.

2 *Chinese Repository* Vol. XVI, 1847, p. 237.

3 *Chinese Repository* Vol. XVI, January to December 1847, p. 242.

4 See CO129/39, pp. 177–79, March 18, 1852; CO129/42, pp. 274–79, June 3, 1853; CO129/64, pp. 430–33; CO129/37, pp. 92–102.

5 Unpublished original manuscript, at PRO, Hong Kong, May 13, 1850; cited in Patricia Lim, *Forgotten Souls—A Social History of the Hong Kong Cemetery*, p. 120.

6 Marriage and Baptism Registers, St. John's Cathedral, PRO, Hong Kong, with permission. On Caldwell in general, see Christopher Munn, *Anglo-China—Chinese People and British Rule in Hong Kong, 1841–1880*. See also May Holdsworth and Christopher Munn, eds., *Dictionary of Hong Kong Biography*. In Robert Bickers and Christian

Henriot, *New Frontiers: Imperialism's New Communities in East Asia, 1842–1953*; see Chapter 2, "Colonialism 'in a Chinese Atmosphere': The Caldwell Affair and the Perils of Collaboration in Early Colonial Hong Kong," by Christopher Munn, pp. 12–37. See also Susanna Hoe, *The Private Life of Old Hong Kong.*

7   Henry Lethbridge, Introduction, in Albert Smith, *To China and Back: Being a Diary Kept, Out and Home*, pp. xiiff.

8   Ibid., p. 63.

9   CO129/62, pp. 576–80, March 28, 1857.

10   CO129/59, pp. 218–20.

11   Munn in Bickers and Henriot, eds., *New Frontiers*, p. 20.

12   *The Times*, March 15, 1859, pp. 583–84.

13   Stuart Heaver, "Flagrant Harbour: The Sordid Affair That Cemented Hong Kong's Reputation for Vice and Corruption," *South China Morning Post*, February 22, 2014.

14   Guo Deyan, "The Study of Parsee Merchants in Canton, Hong Kong and Macao," pp. 51–69; see pp. 59–60. See also Madhavi Thampi, *Indians in China 1800–1949*, p. 77.

15   Correspondence with the author, May 2019. See also Sean Olson, "Hong Kong Legacy: A Swedish Connection," pp. 61–74. Also his monograph, shared with the author, "Hong Kong Legacy," and correspondence, early 2019. Important corrections and clarifications of this chronicle were kindly provided by another descendant, Jill Fell.

16   Naomi Ridout gave a talk about this in Hong Kong in August 2014, and wrote, "He has Given up an Immense amount for this Wife," April 2019. My thanks to her for sharing her family story.

5: THROUGH THE SCREEN

1   Rev. Lucius Wheeler, quoted in Hallett Abend, *Treaty Ports*, pp. 161–63.

2   In his *Colonial Policy and Practice: A Comparative Study of Burma and Netherlands India*, pp. 304–5, J. S. Furnivall depicted relations between diverse races as neither wholly distant nor as close as cosmopolitan idealists might wish: "In Burma as in Java, probably the first thing that strikes the visitor is the medley of peoples—Europeans, Chinese, Indian, and Native. It is in the strictest sense a medley, for they mix but do not combine. Each group holds by its own religion, its own culture and language, its own ideas and ways. As individuals they meet, but only in the market place, in buying and selling. There is a plural society: with different sections of the community living side by side, but separately,

within the same political unit. Even in the economic sphere, there is a division along racial lines."

3   This portrait of Belilios relies on materials generously shared by the Judaica Library at the Jewish Historical Society, Hong Kong; and the published works of Caroline Plüss, AnitaWeiss, and others. Thanks are due to Judy Green, Amber Gould, Howard Elias, Anthony Choy, Tim Judah, Simon Choa-Johnston, Andrew Tse, and Dawn Leonard.

4   Carl T. Smith, "Protected Women in 19th Century Hong Kong," Chapter 10 in *Women and Chinese Patriarchy: Submission, Servitude and Escape*, ed. Maria Jaschok and Suzanne Miers, pp. 221–37; see pp. 226–27.

5   Caroline Plüss, "Assimilation vs. Idiosyncrasy: Strategic Constructions of Sephardic Identities in Hong Kong," pp. 57–58.

6   Letter No. 41 from Eitel to the Colonial Secretary, July 5, 1889, in CO19/342, pp. 80 et seq.

7   *China Mail*, December 1897, covered the synagogue court case, as did the *Jewish Chronicle*, December 2, 1897, p. 3, and *China Mail*, December 3, 1897, p. 3.

8   Plüss, "Assimilation vs. Idiosyncrasy," p. 53.

9   *China Mail*, December 6, 1897, p. 3.

10 See Jardine Matheson Archive, MF 8940: Hong Kong, August 13, 1867, "To Jardines—Dear Sirs . . . The system you are now about to adopt, viz: to start the Steamer before the others by some days, will I am sorry to say be untenable . . ." The next day, see C14/10, 1866, he was answered: ". . . the matter shall receive fresh consideration with the view of meeting the wishes of yourself and other friends if possible." Also JMA C36/21 Canton Ins. Letter Book, February 1875–March 1876.

11 *The Times*, November 13, 1905, p. 7. *The Times* had noted Belilios's eccentric enthusiasm, on April 20, 1921, in its report on the annual pilgrimage of devotees to Disraeli's grave in Hughenden to which "violets were sent by Mr Belilios, of Hong Kong."

12 All this is thanks to Carl T. Smith, "Abandoned into Prosperity: Women on the Fringe of Expatriate Society," p. 134.

13 Jardine Matheson Archive, Microfilmed Letters Files, B7/2, B17/15, and B11.

14 *Hongkong Telegraph*, October 5, 1909. This reported that the winning syndicate of the opium monopoly for three years was led by Ho Shai Kit, and included Ho Kom Tong, Ng Li Hing, Leung Yan Po, Lau Chu Pak, and Mr. Chan Kai Ming, known for his "intimate knowledge of the opium trade in Hong Kong." Other leading men on a similar trajectory included Ho Tung, Ho Fook, and Sin Tak Fan. Born in 1856, Sin Tak

Fan was another Central School graduate who began as a government clerk before joining the Stephens and Holmes legal firm as interpreter, and then the solicitors Ewens and Harston.

15   May Holdsworth and Christopher Munn, eds., *Dictionary of Hong Kong Biography*, p. 71.

16   George Choa became a renowned ear, nose, and throat surgeon, council chairman of St. John's Ambulance for sixteen years, innovator of treatments for deafness, and recipient of a CBE. He was among an early batch of "Members of the Local Community" invited to join The Hong Kong Club in 1970, a place he saw as convenient for lunch. "I'm half Chinese but identify as Chinese. I don't say I'm Eurasian unless some stupid Chinese is saying I'm not Chinese; then I say I'm mixed blood." Author interview with George Choa, June 24, 2013. See also, Jardine Matheson Archive, J1/6/3, Letter to Sir Paul Chater, August 23, 1923.

17   Author interview, January 21, 2019, with thanks to Dawn Leonard.

18   London Missionary Society, South China Reports, Box 1, Hongkong February 6, 1868, from F. S. Turner to Dr. Mullens, London, p. 5. School of Oriental and African Studies Special Collections; CWM South China Reports Boxes 1–8.

19   See report by Chief Justice Sir John Smale (October 20, 1879, in CO129/194) on trafficking, child slavery, etc., and the Eurasian street urchin problem. See also the study by Ernst Eitel (November 1879), which blames Eurasian "degeneracy" on low-class European men and "disrespectable" Chinese women. For details on refuges for women, see Susanna Hoe, *The Private Life of Old Hong Kong: Western Women in the British Colony 1841–1941*, p. 169, and Chapter 15, such as the French convent sisters' Home of the Holy Childhood (L'Asile de la Sainte Enfance), Berlin Foundling Home, Hildesheim Home for the Blind, Victoria Home and Orphanage, and the Eyre Refuge (including how Lucy Eyre's work evolved into Hong Kong's first YWCA).

20   Jane Berney, "Writing Women's Histories: Women in the Colonial Record of Nineteenth-Century Hong Kong," pp. 211–24.

21   Elizabeth Sinn, "Chinese Patriarchy and the Protection of Women in 19th Century Hong Kong," Chapter 7 in *Women and Chinese Patriarchy, Submission, Servitude and Escape*, ed. Maria Jaschok and Suzanne Miers, pp. 141–70; see p. 142.

22   April 1921, p. 5, CO129/472, p. 360.

6: CONSTRUCTING IDENTITIES

1   Deacons Archive, Hong Kong University Library Special Collections.

2   Gwyneth Stokes in her history of Queen's College noted, "In 1893 separate classes were established in the Upper School only, for non-Chinese boys . . . The basis of selection for entry to these classes was dress; all boys not in Chinese dress were non-Chinese. Again it was a 'simple' way and avoided problems that might otherwise have arisen in the case of the numerous Eurasian students." *Queen's College 1862–1962*, p. 61.

3   Minute by E. J. Eitel, November 1, 1879, in the *Hongkong Government Gazette* 26, February 4, 1880, pp. 177 et seq.

4   The mob "apparently associated her with the teaching of English to girls and thereby with their degradation." Anthony Sweeting, *Education in Hong Kong Pre-1841 to 1941: Fact and Opinion, Materials for a History of Education in Hong Kong*, p. 152.

5   See Patricia Pok-kwan Chiu, "'A Position of Usefulness': Gendering History of Girls' Education in Colonial Hong Kong (1850s–1890s)," pp. 789–805.

6   Special mention must be made of Andrew Tse and his family's gorgeous presentation volume on their ancestor, Ho Tung's brother, Ho Kom Tong. May Holdsworth's biography of Ho Tung was published by Hong Kong University Press in 2022, as *Sir Robert Ho Tung: Public Figure, Private Man*.

7   Arnold Wright and H. A. Cartwright, *Twentieth Century Impressions of Hong Kong—History, People, Commerce, Industries and Resources*, p. 176.

8   Andrew Tse has traced Bosman back through five generations to Germany, with a Jacob Levy Bosman moving to the Netherlands in the eighteenth century.

9   Elizabeth Sinn, *Pacific Crossing—California Gold, Chinese Migration, and the Making of Hong Kong*, pp. 30 and 41.

10 Ibid., pp. 114–17 and 354n84.

11 Letter to the *Hongkong Telegraph*, September 24, 1895, signed "Eurasian."

12 Victor Zheng and Siu-Lun Wong, "The Mystery of Capital: Eurasian Entrepreneurs' Socio-Cultural Strategies for Commercial Success in Early 20th-Century Hong Kong."

13 Jean Gittins, *Eastern Windows—Western Skies*, p. 11.

14 Geert Mak, *The Many Lives of Jan Six: A Portrait of an Amsterdam Dynasty*, trans. Liz Waters, p. 348.

15 Two members of the Ho Tung clan were married into the Choa net-

work: Ho Kom Tong's son Ho Shai Kit married Winnie Choa, daughter of Choa Leep-chee; and a daughter of Ho Kom Tong, Elsie, married another son of Choa Leep-chee, namely Choa Po Yiew. Meanwhile, Ho Tung's sister Ho Sui Ting was married to Wong Kam Fuk, comprador of the Hongkong and Kowloon Wharf and Godown Co. The son of Lo Cheung Shiu, a prominent comprador, was Lo Man Kam, or "M.K."; he married Ho Tung's eldest daughter, Victoria. M.K.'s younger brother Lo Man Ho married Ho Tung's next daughter, Grace. One of M.K.'s aunts, Lo Shiu Choi (aka Lucy Rothwell), married Ho Tung's brother Ho Fook. One of M.K.'s sisters, Edna, married Ho Fook's son Ho Leung. Sin Tak Fan's son married the daughter of Chan Kai Ming; his daughter Flora married Ho Fook's other son Ho Shai Kwong. Another son of Ho Fook, Ho Shai Cheuk, married another of Sin Tak Fan's daughters, Florence. It was Sin Tak Fan who arranged the merger of Lo and Lo Solicitors with Ewens and Needham Solicitors in 1908, creating the vehicle through which generations of the Lo and Kan families have found legal, commercial, and political success. Meanwhile, the eldest daughter of Ho Kom Tong, Elizabeth, was married to Tse Kan-po, son of Tse Yat, another comprador family, with roots in Macao; their son Andrew married Priscilla Ho, daughter of Ho Kwong and thus granddaughter of Ho Fook, and they were the parents of Andrew and Michael Tse.

16 JMA J1/8/4, from David Landale in Hong Kong to Henry Keswick in London, December 18, 1914: "Ho Tung is very pushing just now and has ambitions in several directions such as the Legislative Council but so far his efforts in that direction have not been responded to by the Government." J1/8/5, June 4, 1915: "You will have heard that His Majesty has conferred the honour of Knighthood upon Mr Ho Tung who now designates himself Sir Robert Ho Tung. This honour I understand has increased his desire to be invited to a seat on the Boards of as many local companies as possible . . ."

17 His former Central School mate Ng Choy (Wu Tingfang), now in Peking, told Ho Tung in no uncertain terms to leave Chinese politics alone and enjoy his wealth while he could.

18 Chinese members of the legislature were recorded as seeing "the justice and reasonableness of the proposed legislation." At least, that's how the governor described it in CO129/447. The Chinese Chamber of Commerce protested but was ignored.

19 The *Hongkong Weekly Press*, February 25, 1899, listed the founding committee alphabetically: Chan A Fook, Chan Kai Ming, Chan Wieson, Chow Kam-wing, Fung Wa chun, Ho Fook, Ho Tung, Kuk King-fo, Li Hong-mi, Li Pak, Lo Tat, Mok Man-cheng, Mg Kwai-shang, Tse Tsan-tai, and Wong Hoi-pang.

20 They could also get quite tangled in conflicting loyalties. During the Coolie Strike, provoked by a tightening of Lodging House regulations in 1895, Ho Tung convened meetings of compradors in his office at Jardine's; both Chinese and European merchants were losing money, so in that instance their interests were in concert. It was similar to the Anti-American Boycott of 1905–1906, when Hong Kong's Chinese ignored pressure from Chinese communities elsewhere to join the boycott; economic considerations were more powerful than any call on a presumed Chinese nationalism. It was different with the Anti-Japanese Boycott and riot of 1908 when all Chinese joined in even at financial cost to themselves.

21 The first son, Ho A-lloy, seemed a promising mission recruit until he took a second wife. A brother, Ho Chung-Sang, edited the *Wah Tze Yat Po* newspaper until 1889. Two other brothers, Ho Low-yuk and Ho Mei-yuk (Ho Amei), went to Australia, where they were welcomed by the church and sent to goldfields to distribute Bibles to Chinese brethren. Ho Amei also opened tin and silver mines in China, helped organize the Wa Hop Telegraph Co. (with Li Sing), and was the first president of the Hong Kong Chinese Chamber of Commerce. Carl T. Smith, "Sense of History, Part I," pp. 213–64. See also Carl T. Smith, *A Sense of History: Studies in the Social and Urban History of Hong Kong*, pp. 50–63.

22 But it was also a senior partner of Jardine's, F. B. Johnson, who felt it was his duty, not merely as a legislator but as a resident of the colony, to show these articulate new Hong Kongers "every possible sympathy." Smith, "Sense of History, Part I," pp. 257–60.

23 *Hongkong Telegraph*, December 28, 1895. See also Smith, *A Sense of History*, pp. 58–62.

24 Smith, "Sense of History, Part I," p. 150. See also *China Mail*, August 28, 1891.

25 Other Chinese lawyers included the sons of the comprador Wei Ak-wong (Wei Wah-on and Wei Pui) and one of Ng Choy's brothers-in-law (son of Rev. Ho Fuk-tong), Ho Wyson. Several of these entered the Legislative Council after Ng Choy, such as another brother, Sir Boshan Wei Yuk (1896–1914), and Tso Seen-wan (1929–37).

26 Ng Lun Ngai-ha, *Interactions of East and West: Development of Public Education in Early Hong Kong*, p. 136.

27 Law Wing Sang, *Collaborative Colonial Power: The Making of the Hong Kong Chinese*, pp. 79 and 82. Paul Cohen, "The New Coastal Reformers," pp. 255–64. See also Tsai Jung-Fang, "The Predicament of the Comprador Ideologists," pp. 191–225, "Syncretism in the Reformist Thought of Ho Kai and Hu Liyuan," pp. 19–33, and *Hong Kong*

in Chinese History: Community and Social Unrest in the British Colony 1842–1913, pp.138ff, 153ff, 160. Tsai has argued that patriotism and compradorism were not mutually exclusive; he also highlighted factional rivalry within the burgeoning "Chinese" elite. Competition between Ho Amei and Ho Kai for the seat on the legislature to be vacated by Ng Choy was partly played out through attempts to prove a greater "Chineseness," a contest that Ho Kai won.

28   See John M. Carroll, *Edge of Empires: Chinese Elites and British Colonials in Hong Kong*, pp. 86–87, 197–204, 215–21, and 341ff. See also Law, *Collaborative Colonial Power*, pp. 50ff. And see Patricia Pokkwan Chiu, "The Making of Accomplished Women: English Education for Girls in Colonial Hong Kong, 1890s–1940s," pp. 71–72. She adds the founding of St. Stephen's Girls' College in 1906.

29   G. H. Bateson Wright (Oxon), "Education," in Wright and Cartwright, *Twentieth Century Impressions*, pp. 121–28.

30   Anita M. Weiss, "South Asian Muslims in Hong Kong: Creation of a 'Local Boy' Identity," p. 437. See also Barbara-Sue White, *Turbans and Traders: Hong Kong's Indian Communities*, pp. 212–16.

31   Bateson Wright in Wright and Cartwright, *Twentieth Century Impressions*, p. 123.

7: HONG KONG PEOPLE MAKING HONG KONG

1   Egerton K. Laird, *The Rambles of a Globe Trotter in Australasia, Japan, China, Java, India, and Cashmere*, Vol. 1, pp. 300–303.

2   John R. Hinnells, *The Zoroastrian Diaspora, Religion and Migration*, p. 154.

3   David Faure, ed., *A Documentary History of Hong Kong Society*, pp. 49–51. Faure is citing the *China Mail*, 76th anniversary edition, March 1921.

4   *Calcutta Gazette*, July 29, 1790.

5   Solomon Bard, *Traders of Hong Kong: Some Foreign Merchant Houses, 1841–1899*, p. 96.

6   Being Armenian meant being tied into regional ribbons of trade with strong Armenian communities in Penang and Singapore. Chater had business and property interests that allowed him to vote in Singapore's municipal elections for many years. A Catchick founded the *Straits Times* newspaper, because his Armenian friend Martyrose had overstretched when ordering a printing press from England. The Armenian A. L. Agabeg was publishing the *Daily Press* in Hong Kong in 1860.

As Chater marked his sixtieth year of residence in Hong Kong in 1924, he also donated to the Armenian Relief Fund of London. See Nadia H. Wright, *Respected Citizens: The History of Armenians in Singapore and Malaysia*.

7   Wright, *Respected Citizens*, p. 94. See W. G. Clarence-Smith, "Middle Eastern Entrepreneurs in Southeast Asia, c.1750–1940," in Ina Baghdiantz-McCabe, Gelina Harlaftis, and Ioanna Pepclasis Minoglou, *Diaspora Entrepreneurial Networks: Four Centuries of History*, pp. 217–44.

8   Although he never founded his own dynasty, Chater's first steps in Hong Kong were shaped by family connections. He was technically uncle to Dr. Gregory Jordan but there were only ten years between them. Dr. Jordan, though born in Calcutta in 1856, went to medical college in Edinburgh. Chater was in business with his brother Joseph and with Dr. Gregory's brother Paul. The three brokers lived in fashionable Caine Road, as did the colonial surgeon Dr. Philip Ayres and Port Health Officer Adams—and then Gregory moved in, too. All six were keen Freemasons. Chater and Paul Jordan were stewards of the Jockey Club. Chater, Ayres, and Adams were justices of the peace. Gregory Jordan would succeed Ayres as port health officer; he was one of four volunteer doctors behind the Alice Memorial Hospital (funded by Ho Kai), and his practice included care of the Ho Tungs. When he died in 1921, Chater endowed the library that Jordan had intended for the Students' Union, and so the Jordan Memorial Library was opened in 1922 by his widow. See Katherine Mattock, *Hong Kong Practice—Drs Anderson & Partners, the First Hundred Years*, pp. 3–4.

9   See Liz Chater, *Sir Catchick Paul Chater: A Brief Personal Biography*. That Mody also worked at this bank is uncertain, however; the 1865 *The Chronicle & Directory for China, Japan & the Philippines, etc.* offers only "Mody, H.N. (T. Janaran), Gough St." The 1861 *Chronicle & Directory* has no relevant Mody, and directories between 1861 and 1865 are unavailable. Arnold Wright said Mody arrived c. 1861 "to enter the service of a firm of Hindoo bankers and opium merchants." Arnold Wright and H. A. Cartwright, *Twentieth Century Impressions of Hong Kong—History, People, Commerce, Industries and Resources*, p. 128.

10   Mesrovb Jacob Seth, *Armenians in India from the Earliest Times to the Present Day, a Work of Original Research*, p. 553.

11   Elizabeth Sinn, *Pacific Crossing: California Gold, Chinese Migration, and the Making of Hong Kong*, pp. 33, 110–19.

12   He would later finance a housing scheme on land once held by the Tang clan—evidence exists to confirm the Tang claim to the island of Hong

Kong, all of British Kowloon, Tsing Yi Island, and swathes of the New Territories; Li Sing's front man in the Tang land projects was Ho Amei. Chunks of the Tang lands had been sold off through the centuries, and neither the Chinese nor the British governments backed the Tang. But there were still some ancestral claims, mortgaged by one young Tang clan member to Li Sing and his family.

13   In 1865, Li Sing had invested in an ill-fated venture in the jungles of Borneo. Two Americans in Hong Kong, Joseph Torrey (editor of the *Hongkong Times* and the *China Mail*) and Thomas Harris, had bought two concessions in Brunei and secured Li Sing's firm, Wo Hang, as partner in the American Trading Company of Borneo. This shipped in laborers, placing Torrey in charge as "Supreme Ruler," and tried to develop the land: "Sailing north from Brunei the little expedition settled at the mouth of the Kimanis River . . . hacking at the jungle mangrove to build a flimsy stockade and precarious jetty." The settlement slowly starved. New backers included Baron von Overbeck, the Austrian consul general in Hong Kong, but the Brunei adventure never worked. See K. G. Tregonning, *Under Chartered Company Rule, North Borneo 1881–1946*, pp. 7–10.

14   Dan Waters, "Hong Kong Hongs with Long Histories and British Connections," pp. 219–56; see p. 225. Jardine Matheson Archive material shows Jardine's seeking Chater's business in 1880, writing that they had heard of two lots coming up for sale that might suit Chater, so what would he like to offer—JMA, C14/13: 1880. Ties deepened through intensive collaborations over the years but the comment from Jardine's head office at 3 Lombard Street London was measured: "for many years he has been a good friend to the Firm and he will be much missed in Hongkong"—JMA J1/2/20, June 3, 1926. The firm then engaged in making sure a statue of Chater was built, see J1/2/21 and J1/2/22.

15   Austin Coates, *China Races*, p. 133. Robert Nield wrote in Holdsworth and Munn's *Dictionary of Hong Kong Biography*, p. 80: "Chater had a kindly face and was well liked. There was no evidence that he ever made an enemy. He died as he lived, deeply admired and respected."

16   Both reports are cited in the *Hongkong Government Gazette*, 1893, 0603, pp. 479–80.

17   Again the narratives of colonial stuffiness and exclusion don't quite hold. He was an Armenian from India but race did not prevent him and Mody from becoming members of the proverbially exclusive Hong Kong Club. Chater was its chairman for years and recruited many members from his diverse worlds of freemasonry and trade. He and Bell-Irving were unofficial members of the Legislative and Executive Councils. He chaired the Queen Victoria Golden Jubilee and Diamond

Jubilee committees (1887 and 1897), was knighted in 1902, and was honored by France following his investment in coal mines in French Tonkin.

18 James Hayes, "Old British Kowloon," pp. 120–37.

19 Marble Hall was described in purple prose in the *Hongkong Telegraph*, December 22, 1904. See Liz Chater's privately published *Marble Hall Hong Kong—A Pictorial Review*.

20 Bard, *Traders of Hong Kong*, p. 87.

21 Swire's engagement could be traced not only to the family's Quaker roots, but to its desperate need for a better image after a Swire's employee allegedly kicked to death an elderly Chinese passenger on one of their coastal ferries. Peter Cunich, *A History of the University of Hong Kong*, pp. 119–20.

22 Given the rich list of donors, it can hardly be surprising that passage of the University Bill through the Legislative Council was held up when its provision for "one Parsee and one Mahommedan representative" on the court was thought to imply an unnecessary distinction of religion. Opposition to the wording was a sign of how an active community was far ahead of its blinkered bureaucrats. "Representatives of Asiatic races other than Chinese" wouldn't work, either, as that could exclude Jews, several of whom had given generously. At last, the governor was empowered to nominate "two additional members" without mentioning race or religion. My thanks to Frank Ching for alerting me to this.

23 Cunich, *A History of the University of Hong Kong*, pp. 226 and 497n100. The Hongkong and Shanghai Bank in Shanghai found that Nemazee later traded in real estate, raw silk yarn, cement, cellophane papers, "etc.," and advised "Great Caution" but noted he was "sole proprietor of M. Nemazee of Princes Bldg Hongkong, who is favourably reported on by our office there. He is possessed of large means and is considered good for his engagements." HSBC Archives (London), Bankers Opinions, HQ SHG II 688. Jardine Archives saw him as a respectable tea trader with an avaricious market in Persia. JMA: J1/12/4, April 26, 1934.

24 See HKU Archives, Minutes HKU Council, 1911–1941, 17th meeting, September 6, 1912; 23rd meeting, May 30, 1913; 25th meeting, January 15, 1914.

25 Cunich, *A History of the University of Hong Kong*, p. 317. Fung's son Fung Ping-fan said his father saw the university as a "lighthouse of the Far East" and wanted it to be "the centre of learning in South China."

26 "It was not a Chinese city with its own citizens and its own civic institutions and traditions that was ceded to Britain; rather, it was a city built by Chinese colonists under British sponsorship . . . not unlike the

overseas Chinese communities of Southeast Asia." Bernard Luk Hung-kay, "Chinese Culture in the Hong Kong Curriculum: Heritage and Co-lonialism," p. 653.

27 Deacons Archive 18/905, 39-page booklet "Inventory of Furniture &c., &c.," belonging to the Estate of the Late Sir H. N. Mody "Buxey Lodge."

28 Commander C. H. Drage, *The 1914–1933 Diaries* (manuscript), cited in Michael Wise, ed., *Travellers' Tales of Old Hong Kong and the South China Coast*, p. 194.

29 Seth, in *Armenians in India from the Earliest Times to the Present Day*, cites the *Sunday Times*, September [no date] 1924, pp. 553–54.

8: A COSMOPOLITAN PLACE

1 *Hongkong Telegraph*, March 3, 1894.
2 John Stuart Thomson, *The Chinese*, pp. 14–15, 16, and 17–18.
3 *China Mail*, January 9, 1885.
4 *Hongkong Telegraph*, September 15, 1902.
5 Philip Mansel, *Levant: Splendour and Catastrophe in the Mediterra-nean*, pp. 129–34.
6 Christopher Haffner, *The Craft in the East*, p. 73.
7 Frank Broeze, ed., *Brides of the Sea: Port Cities of Asia from the 16th–20th Centuries*, pp. 225, 236–37.
8 Manook Nissim, interviewed by Amelia Allsop for the Hong Kong Heritage Project, April 16, 2010, in San Francisco.
9 JMA J1/2/31, April 27, 1933; J1/3/5, November 7, 1935; J1/3/5, No-vember 14 and 28, 1935, Letter No. 1753; J1/24/54, October 31, 1935, Letter No. 1521; November 22, 1935, Letter No. 1529: "The Kadoories will not be 'handled,' and they are as relentless as they are patient. They try persuasion first, tortuousness second, and if necessary weight of shares third. They so often suggest steps which appear foolhardy, and are foolhardy, and yet they retain their wealth and add to it . . . Yours very truly, W. J. Keswick." Also: J4/2/2, February 4 and 23, March 30, and April 6, 1937.
10 Israel Cohen in his *Journal of a Jewish Traveller*, pp. 116–17.
11 Lawrence Kadoorie, in Debra Weiner, "Rothschild of the East," *Hadas-sah*, March 1983, pp. 36, 54–55.
12 See *Hongkong Telegraph*, March 4, 1913, for a report on when the governor opened a school extension in a stunning Chinese yamen-style building.
13 May Holdsworth, *Foreign Devils*, pp. 46–47.

14 Vaudine England, "Hong Kong Taipans—Lord Kadoorie," *Discovery Magazine*, March 1986, pp. 58–59.

15 *Asian Wall Street Journal*, June 27–28, 1997, p. 1. Two decades later, during Hong Kong's major political ruptions of 2019, Sir Michael noted that for more than 140 years, Hong Kong "gave us the opportunity to prosper . . . [and] instilled the Lion Rock Spirit in me and my children—that energy, ambition, drive and creativity has powered our prosperity and helped us to face many challenges. My faith in our home is undiminished. Now is a time for everybody to unite and be unswerving in our commitment not just to Hong Kong's special place, but to a peaceful solution to our current crisis for this generation, the next, and beyond." "A Letter to the People of Hong Kong," *South China Morning Post*, full-page advertisement, August 28, 2019.

16 Tse Liu Francis, *Ho Kom-Tong: A Man for All Seasons*, pp. 173–74.

17 Wing On official 100th anniversary celebration materials, 2007, in newspaper advertisements and the Wing On anniversary book, *A Modest Beginning*.

18 Their fourth son, Ma Man-fai, became a civil rights advocate and pioneer in the democracy movement. May Holdsworth and Christopher Munn, eds., *Dictionary of Hong Kong Biography*, pp. 293–95.

19 John Luff, *Hong Kong Cavalcade*, p. 42.

20 Jarrett lists the Garden Lot holders as including Daniel E. Caldwell, Joao L. Britto, V. I. Remedios, V. S. T. Engholm (Jarret thinks Engholm was female), J. D. Humphreys, C. F. A. Sangster, A. G. Morris, N. B. Dennys, H. J. Holmes, J. M. A. da Silva, A. F. Alves, C. F. Degenaer, Dorabjee Nowrojee, Andrew Miller, W. H. Brereton, George McBain, J. B. Coughtrie, T. D. C. and J. Parker, M. d'Azevedo, E. R. Holmes, M. J. D. Stephens, Mohamed Fakeera, E. G. Humphreys, F. X. da Chagas, J. A. dos Remedios, J. W. Torrey, F. V. Ribeiro, A. R. Madar, H. L. Noronha, Frederick Rapp, B. A. Eranee, James Craig, F. d'A. Gomes, H. L. Dennys, I. P. Madar, and James Henry Cox. Vincent H. G. Jarrett, *Old Hong Kong / by Colonial*, p. 605.

21 The Jardine's managers disliked the enterprise: "This Company gives me a pain. Their method is to acquire cheap land and after deduction for roads etc to sell the balance in small lots at very high rates, anybody else's method up to this point if they can get away with it but at the same time the Board pose as public benefactors. Ho Tung, you know Braga is his running dog, is I think mixed up in it." JMA, J1/24/48, June 2, 1932, from Paterson to Beith, p. 3.

22 With Lo Man Kam (son-in-law of Sir Robert Ho Tung), Braga urged in vain an end to government censorship in 1936. His son José Maria "Jack" Braga was a prolific collector and writer on the history of the

Portuguese. His collections are now held at the Australian National University. See Holdsworth and Munn, eds., *Dictionary of Hong Kong Biography*, pp. 45–46.

23 I am indebted to Philip Mansel's definitions of "cosmopolitan" and "communal societies" in his brilliant *Levant: Splendour & Catastrophe on the Mediterranean*.

24 Frederic A. "Jim" Silva, *Todo o Nosso Passado, All Our Yesterdays— The Sons of Macao, Their History and Heritage*, p. 31.

25 See James Hayes, Carl Smith, Helga Werle et al., "Programme Notes for Visits to Older Parts of Hong Kong Island (Urban Areas), and to Kowloon, in 1974," pp. 196–234; see pp. 221ff.

26 J. P. Braga, *The Portuguese in Hongkong and China*, pp. 226–28.

27 Resident members on February 1, 1924, included: A. H. Compton, 1915; E. M. Raymond, 1921; J. S. Gubbay, 1922. Absent members included, alongside Sir C. P. Chater, Kt. CMG, 1873, and W. H. Donald, 1904: E. Nissim, 1908; M. S. Sassoon, 1894, and E. Shellim, 1899. The 1911 Membership List included the Armenian Dr. G. P. Jordan, 1886; Dr. P. J. Kelly, 1910; and the Parsi Sir H. N. Mody, Kt., 1910. See also Vaudine England, *Kindred Spirits: A History of the Hong Kong Club*.

28 The 1935–36 cricket team included George Souza, Tinker Lee, Francis Zimmern, Bill Hong Sling, Ozorio, Hung, Gosano, and Fincher. By 1941, the names were Anderson, Lay, Mackay, Lee, Lloyd, Broadbridge, and two times Fincher and Zimmern. Ezra Abraham was club president from 1945 to 1954. One tennis star was Enid Lo (later Mrs. E. Litton, mother of Henry). In 1932, the Hong Kong vs. Shanghai tennis team included M. W. and M. K. Lo. See Peter Hall, *150 Years of Cricket in Hong Kong*.

29 Sue (Fulham) McPherson, "J. L. McPherson: Hong Kong YMCA General Secretary, 1905–1935," pp. 39–60; see p. 41.

30 Annual Report of the Foreign Secretary, 1909–10 (New York: Foreign Dept. International Committee of YMCAs). Cited in ibid., n. 22.

31 Jardine Matheson Archives, JMA-HK and CLUBS JM L6/7.

32 See *Club Lusitano, 150 Years of History, 1866–2016*.

33 Dawn Leonard recalls: "I know for a fact that my aunt Mabel, who was married to a Belgian banker, Uncle Pierre, was definitely refused entry to a club because she was Eurasian, and she was flatly denied the option to adopt a child when they couldn't have their own, on the same grounds." Dawn's grandfather Macumber Churn played down his Chinese blood. "My poor mother, who was the most Chinese-looking of all his children, was frequently kept upstairs when he was entertaining his business associates. She went on to be the only child of his to achieve academic success, which I'm sure was to prove a point to him," says

Dawn. She has concluded that the slights are "why the Eurasians got together to become such an economic force. To put the two fingers up to both sides—the Chinese and the Brits!"

9: IMAGINING COMMUNITIES

1 Frank Dikotter, *Sex, Culture and Modernity in China*, pp. 102, 109.
2 Lu Danglin, closely connected with the KMT, wrote: "The most unseemly sight one sees on the street is a Chinese woman walking with a westerner. These women love western meals—you may think they are prostitutes, but they may not be; on the other hand, if you think they are pure, some of them may indeed be prostitutes . . ." Translated in Law Wing Sang, *Collaborative Colonial Power: The Making of the Hong Kong Chinese*, pp. 114–18.
3 C. G. Alabaster, "Some Observations on Race Mixture in Hong Kong," pp. 247–48.
4 Jane Caplan and John Torpey, eds., *Documenting Individual Identity: The Development of State Practices in the Modern World*, p. 270.
5 "Guests' Guide to Hongkong," Compliments of the Hongkong Hotel, circa 1920. Compiled by California Directory Co.
6 Paul Gillingham, *At the Peak: Hong Kong Between the Wars*, pp. 31–32.
7 *The Chronicle & Directory for China, Japan & the Philippines, etc.*, 1868–1939. From 1868 until 1897, the directories record H. R. Cotwal as a clerk at D. C. Tata and Co., but in 1875 the spelling changed to Cotwale, in 1877 to Cotewall, and the company name to Tata and Co. From 1880 to 1896 the listing is consistent as Cotewall, H.R., merchant, Tata & Co., Hollywood Rd.
8 Christopher Cook, *Robert Kotewall, a Man of Hong Kong*, pp. 10–11.
9 He never went to Bombay or spoke Parsi-Gujarati. After tuition in Canton, Robert went to Queen's College aged eleven and then to DBS to improve his English. His first wife, his childhood sweetheart, Grace Hung, died in childbirth. His second wife hailed from an established Eurasian clan, the Lowcocks, and Edith would become a fixture at Robert's side as he moved rapidly up the government ladder, into elite circles of local business.
10 When Chan Kai Ming died in 1919, the mourners were led by Sir and Lady Ho Tung, Sir Ellis Kadoorie, Sir Boshan Wei Yuk, the Honourable J. H. Kemp, and the Honourable Lau Chu Pak, followed by various professors, doctors, and solicitors, including the Eurasian brothers M. K. and M. W. Lo, as well as Robert Kotewall. Other names included Kew, da Silva, Ellis, Razack, Hall, Ismail, Rumjahn, Samuel Macumber

Churn, Anderson, and Moraes. Wreaths came from the governor, the university, the Bank of East Asia, Dairy Farm, the Kadoorie Schools, the Italian Convent, and more.

11　　John M. Carroll, *Edge of Empires*, p. 132.

12　　When Cecil Clementi was made governor in 1925, Kotewall must have been pleased; back when Kotewall was First Clerk in the Magistracy in 1913, he had presented an illuminated address bound in full morocco to Clementi when he had been the departing assistant colonial secretary. Kotewall had led the expressions of admiration, and of great regret felt at the departure of Mr. and Mrs. Clementi.

13　　Kotewall's report, reproduced in CO129/489, p. 167.

14　　CO129/489, October 30, 1925, p. 428.

15　　Chow was replaced in 1936 by Kotewall; both men were knighted. In 1928, two new slots on the council were gifted by Clementi to the Chinese physician Tso Seen Wan and the Portuguese José Pedro Braga.

16　　*South China Morning Post*, Editorial, May 28, 1926.

17　　Vaudine England, *The Quest of Noel Croucher, Hong Kong's Quiet Philanthropist*.

18　　With thanks to Howard Elias, Hong Kong Jewish Historical Society, October 15, 2018.

19　　Stuart Heaver, "How the White Russian Refugee Crisis Unfolded in China a Century Ago, and the Lucky Ones Who Made It to Hong Kong," *South China Morning Post*, May 7, 2017.

20　　Norman Miners, *Hong Kong Under Imperial Rule 1912–1941*, pp. 79, 81.

21　　Aravind Ganachari, "'White Man's Embarrassment': European Vagrancy in 19th Century Bombay," pp. 2477–86.

22　　"Guests' Guide to Hongkong."

23　　Claude Markovits, *The Global World of Indian Merchants 1750–1947: Traders of Sind from Bukhara to Panama*, pp. 110–55; see p. 120.

24　　This was not just a nineteenth-century phenomenon: in 1934, the well-known tennis player H. D. Rumjahn married Miss Mary Leung of Canton; by the 1950s, a Rumjahn married a Mary Teresa Xavier at St. Margaret's Church; and a Rosie Rumjahn passed her senior exams at the Italian Convent in 1926. From early lives in trade or government jobs, some such as Ahmet Ramjahn became "broker" and "Gentleman," their lives recorded in the newspapers and remarked upon with respect. Ramjahn was survived by five sons who were renowned sportsmen and business figures. When Ebrahim Sadick married Miss Firdos Effiandie Rumjahn, the bridesmaids were Norah and Eillen Leonard (from a prominent Eurasian family), the page was Master Sydney Chow, and the flower girl was Thelma Gonzales, covering the Chinese and Portuguese communities, too. Rumjahns became champions in tennis, football, and lawn bowls; they worked for Deacons, ran the Jockey Club sweep, bought chunks of land in Kennedy Town in the early 1910s, and established industries (such as the Hong Kong Macao Mosaic Tile Factory of Usuf Rumjahn, who died in 1947).

25   Confidential Circular, January 11, 1909, CO854/168.
26   David A. Pomfret, "Raising Eurasia: Race, Class, and Age in French and British Colonies," pp. 314–43; see p. 321. See also John G. Butcher, *The British in Malaya 1880–1941: The Social History of a European Community in Colonial South-East Asia*. This recounts the Hansard Debate of March 27, 1912, vol. 36, cc418–22, over abolition of Queen's Scholarships in the Straits Settlements. If all members of civil/police services had to be of pure European descent, how, then, to account for Hong Kong's Ho Kai, the just knighted member of the Royal College of Surgeons? London dodged the questions.
27   CO129/392, no. 31578, October 7, 1912. See also Patricia O'Sullivan, "George Hennessy, an Irishman in the Hong Kong Police," pp. 189–223.
28   CO129/409, no. 983, January 8, 1914. When an extension was sought to the Eurasian cemetery, permission was given without debate. CO129/411, no. 27973, July 31, 1914.
29   JMA, J1/15/2, January 23, 1936; J1/9/4, August 20, 1936.
30   HSBC Archives (London), HQ HSBCK 0003-0001 and 0002, Grayburn Letters, June 20, 1936, January 25, and November 20, 1937, etc.
31   John Darwin in Robert Bickers and Christian Henriot, *New Frontiers: Imperialism's New Communities in East Asia 1842–1953*, pp. 257–58.
32   John Darwin, *After Tamerlane: The Rise and Fall of Global Empires 1400–200*, p. 416.
33   Elizabeth Sinn and Christopher Munn, eds., *Meeting Place: Encounters Across Cultures in Hong Kong, 1841–1984*, p. 172.
34   Ibid., p. 154.
35   Ibid., p. 171.
36   Ibid., p. 172.
37   Ibid., pp. 172–73.
38   CO129/478, letter by Stubbs, September 16, 1922; CO129/462, July 29, 1920.
39   Pomfret, "Raising Eurasia," p. 330.
40   www.youtube.com/watch?v=U_4fQwlcrBQ.

10: THE EURASIANS

1   Samuel's mother, Cheung or Yip, was at some point also the second wife of Sin Tak Fan in a union that produced no children (Carl T. Smith Collection, Index Card 39-783, citing Elizabeth Sinn). His descendant James Lowcock told Anthony Sweeting, October 22, 2007, that "a particular Scottish merchant loved his 'Chinese wife and family' so much that, when he had to leave Hong Kong due to ill-health, he begged his replacement to look after them. The newly arrived merchant did much more than that; he married the woman and gave his name to her children, thereby establishing a rather complex provenance for this particular Eurasian family." Sweeting Papers, p. 102, HKU Archive.

2   As an officer in the Hong Kong Volunteer Defence Corps he was sent to Bangkok and Saigon for rice supplies just ahead of the outbreak of World War Two. Caught in Bangkok as the war began, he went on to Calcutta, where he worked for British military intelligence and was made a major. After the war he was part of rebuilding efforts in Hong Kong and became a regular donor to causes ranging from veterans' funds to lepers, children, family planning, and the Society for the Prevention of Cruelty to Animals. He was such a strong supporter of the Diocesan Girls' School, where most of his progeny were educated, that a plaque in his name graces the campus to this day. His investments focused on the growth of Hong Kong: the pilings to support new and taller buildings offered by Vibro Piling Co.; wharf and warehouse ownership for an expanding port (through China Provident and Trust Co. and its sister company North Point Wharves); bringing of power to fuel another British territory closely linked through the Chinese and Southeast Asian diaspora to Hong Kong, in the Sandakan Light and Power Co. of Borneo; rubber companies; and the Hong Kong Gas Co.

3   Eddie's first wife, Doris Frith, had earlier been married to Oswald Chan of the Tyson-Chan Eurasian clan. Doris had thus been a daughter-in-law of Chan Kai Ming. With Eddie Churn she produced two more daughters; after they divorced, Eddie promptly married his new love, a movie star called Dora/Ting Ho. Carl T. Smith, in correspondence with the family in October 2000: Eddie was thirty-eight by the time he married Doris; they divorced in 1962. The informant says the second wife was Ting Ho. Eddie's sister Mabel married a Belgian financier, Raymond Pierre Mardulyn; he was chairman of five companies, a director of the Hongkong and Shanghai Hotels Co. Ltd. and Peak Tramways Ltd. One of his pallbearers (in 1985) was Michael Kadoorie, standing in for his father, Lord Lawrence.

4   The fourth child, Eva, studied medicine at HKU, and was in Chung-

king, the headquarters of Free China, during World War Two before her asthma sent her to India's mountain air. Top of her class in London, she became a physiotherapist and married Norman Leonard (who had been in the Volunteers and was sent as a prisoner of war to Japan); they produced Joy, Dawn, and Keith. When Eva married Norman, her bridesmaids were her sister Doris and Miss Cicely Kotewall; the ushers were Eva's brother Eddie Churn and H. E. "Bots" de Barros Botelho. Norman Leonard's father, hailing from Liverpool, was in the Hong Kong police in the 1890s. When he died in 1916, he left his widow, Caroline, with twelve children to raise; Norman was the youngest. He described himself as one quarter Chinese and spoke Cantonese with a foreign accent—on purpose! Eva, Norman, and family moved to England in 1963, leaving behind any confusion about being Eurasian, Chinese, or British.

5   Author's interview, Samuel "Charlie" Churn, Hong Kong, March 3, 2018.

6   The leading work is *In the Web* by Peter Hall. Hall illuminates names such as Gittins and Cumine, Ho and Lo, Rothwell and Jex, Fincher, Ahlmann, and more. Despite resistance in some families to discuss their often murky roots, Hall managed to construct interlocking trees for the families of Ablong, Ahwee, Anderson, Baker, Bottomley, Fenton, Belilios, Choa, Broadbridge, Chater, Cheung, Choa, Churn, Cunningham, Ford, Frith, Gittins, Greaves, Grose, Ho Fook, Ho Tung, Bosman, Hopwar, Hung, Lebedev, Kew, Kotwaj, Kotewall, Lowcock, Laing, Lyson, Overbeck, Ray, Randall, Rapp, Ryrie, Shea, Talbot, Tyson, Walkinshaw, Wong Kam Fuk, Wong Sik-to, and Zimmern.

7   Interview, Pat Botelho, January 21, 2019.

8   The elder Adolf also had three other children. The oldest, Mary, was the Protected Woman of Sir Jacob Sassoon in Shanghai, and a brother, Andrew, produced various children, including the well-known Rev. George She. The other daughter, Lucy, married Lo Cheung Shiu, thereby tying the Zimmern line to the Ho Tung.

9   *The Chronicle & Directory for China, Japan & the Philippines, etc.,* 1868–1939; 1871, p. 152.

10 A family story is that George died when he rode a bicycle, then new in town, down steep Garden Road, straight into the harbor. Carl T. Smith Collection, Index Card 51-878, conversation with James S. Lowcock, retired headmaster of DBS, November 1, 1990.

11 Author correspondence, Dr. Ron Zimmern, January 2020.

12 This included Sir Robert Ho Tung and members of the Ruttonjee, d'Almada e Castro, Tso, Mok, Fung, and other families.

13 Hong Kong Stock Market History Project, Interview with Francis

R. Zimmern, Former Chairman of the Hong Kong Stock Exchange 1972–77, November 14, 1996.

14 Carl T. Smith Collection, Index Card 50-117.

15 Interview, Kim Fenton, March 21, 2018.

16 Interview, Patsy Fenton, March 23, 2018, at 114 Waterloo Road.

17 Cicely Kotewall-Zimmern, "Recollections of My Life," p. 62.

18 Ibid., p. 66.

19 John and Doris's father, George Lambert Fenton, traded in Macao, where he took Portuguese nationality. He was a director of the General Improvement Co. Vivienne Baker remembered her grandfather as a very busy man. "He had kerosene concessions, and [owned] the *Fat Shan*, which sank and was lost in the war, also opium and rice—with the Nolasco and Toneco de Silva families—all Macao Mafiosi!" Interview with the author, October 19, 2017.

20 Interview, John Hung, November 17, 2017.

21 Hall, *In the Web*, p. 172.

22 Thanks to Brian Rothwell, correspondence 2019–20.

23 In a letter to express condolences on Lo Cheung Shiu death in 1934, Sir Robert Ho Tung wrote that the loss was of "a dear and trusted colleague who, in his characteristically quiet and unassuming way, bore the responsibilities of Jardine's Compradore Department with singular ability and success. Lo Cheung Shiu and I shared many happy years together." The letter went on to applaud how Lo Cheung Shiu had "brought into the world a circle of extremely capable sons and accomplished daughters." Lo Cheung Shiu, *J.P.: A Memoir by His Sons.*

24 Man Kam Lo had been educated in England from the age of twelve, returning to Hong Kong in 1915 to follow the same path as his father—from the boards of Hongkong Land to the Hongkong and Shanghai Hotels Co. By 1921, he was a justice of the peace; he had joined the Sanitary Board, District Watch, and Tung Wah by 1932 before entering the Urban Council in 1935 and the Legislative Council, 1935–43; he was knighted in 1948.

25 Man Kam Lo stood out in prewar Hong Kong for his activism against discriminatory laws and payment practices; he had represented the seamen's unions in 1922. With José Pedro Braga, the Portuguese manager of various Kadoorie concerns, he had set up the League of Fellowship in 1921, aimed at eliminating racial discrimination and promoting fellowship regardless of race, class, or creed. He argued against the Peak Reservation not, he said, because the Chinese particularly wanted to live there but on the grounds of discrimination. Man Kam's wife became the first female justice of the peace, and a pioneer in education.

26 Stanley Ho, the casino king of Macao, was born in one of these, Stan-

ley Villa, to Ho Kwong, a son of Ho Fook and nephew of Robert Ho Tung. When Stanley's father (who was a comprador with Sassoons) saw his share speculations blow up spectacularly he fled to Saigon. The thirteen-year-old Stanley then discovered the limits of family friendship as no help was forthcoming to his mother's family. Stanley made his own way, claiming to have made a first million out of Macao during World War Two. "I think talent counts. I believe in talent. I don't believe this pedigree business anymore; maybe for a horse, but not for human beings. Although I'm in this business of luck, there is very little luck in success. You must suffer for success. You must be able to fight. I was so fed up when I saw how our rich relatives treated us, how much my mother suffered. Sir Robert invented the name of Ho Tung to distinguish his side of the family from the failures. Sometimes it's very embarrassing—big families, you know, normally they are like that." Interviews, Stanley Ho, April 29, 1984, and May 12, 1985. See Vaudine England, "Hong Kong Taipans—Stanley Ho," *Discovery*, April 1986, pp. 70–71.

27 The Tai Tam home was also a scene of tragedy when one of M.W.'s sons, Norman, showing off his flying license, smashed his plane; the family watched him die.

28 Indeed, exactly this happened when the author walked into his grounds in 1985.

29 Interview, Ian McFadzean, August 15, 2011. Ian is the son of Professor Alec McFadzean, the cantankerous but much respected professor of medicine at the University of Hong Kong.

30 Another family linked to the Ho Tung clan is that of Wong Kam Fuk, product of a Chinese mother and an unknown Scandanavian sea captain. With a wife and two concubines, Wong fathered nine children, the oldest of whom, Wong Sik Lam, married Mary Patricia, a daughter of Robert Ho Tung. Wong and Ho Tung links were thus reinforced in two consecutive generations. Ho Tung had provided the financial guarantee needed for Wong Kam Fuk to become comprador to the Hongkong and Kowloon Wharf and Godown Co. in an earlier era. But tensions also persisted over which family was more "Chinese," with the Wongs usually identifying as such, notes "The Wong Family Chronicle" by Sybil Wong. One daughter of Wong Kam Fuk and her husband had contacts with renowned leftists in China, meeting the New Zealand Communist Rewi Alley in Macao in 1942. Another was proud to consider herself Eurasian, and when at DGS she found eight out of ten of her classmates were Eurasian; her war was spent hobnobbing not with Rewi Alley but with the Soong Sisters and Chiang Kai-shek in Chungking. Another Wong daughter, Jasmine, married Kenneth Chan Tyson, tying

the Wongs to the descendants of Chan Kai Ming, and thus back to the mysterious Mr. Bartou, the Lam sisters et al. (The Chans changed their name back to Tyson in the 1950s.)

31   Herbert Day Lamson (Herbert Day Lamson, "The Eurasian in Shanghai," pp. 642–48; see pp. 642, 647, 648) saw the Eurasians of Shanghai as a "depressed group despised by both the Chinese and the foreigners," but Barbara Merchant, descendant of those very families, has the photos to show a happy time being had by many: "They seemed to live a life quite different from the sorry existence described by Lamson—there absolutely was a 'group spirit' around which the Eurasians rallied, which was composed of all Eurasians, whatever their racial/national origins, and the 'lower paid' Westerners. They didn't mix socially with the upper-class Westerners or Chinese, but many did do well, despite their disadvantaged beginnings." Email correspondence, Barbara Merchant, 2017–19.

32   The four men in receipt of the check were S. M. Churn, John Francis Grose, Hung Hing-kam, and Wong Kam Fuk. They immediately locked into a first-class mortgage at 8 percent for two years. Attendees at their first meeting, on December 23, 1929, were: Lo Cheung Shiu, Hung Tsze-leung, Henry Gittins, Hung Tsze-yee, Ho Leung, S. M. Churn, W. H. Peters, J. L. Litton, J. D. Bush, E. D. Bush. J. Kotwall, A. E. Perry, M. K. Lo, M. W. Lo, Fung Tsok-lam, J. McKenzie, J. F. Grose, Wong Tak-wong, Ed Law, P. Abesser, W. M. Gittins, J. F. Shea, H. K. Hung, Hung Ho-chiu, and C. G. Anderson. This last name refers to Charles Graham "Carl," the son of Hung Hing Kam who had taken the name Henry Graham Anderson. The first president would be Sir Robert Ho Tung, vice president Hon. R. H. Kotewall, honorary treasurer Samuel Macumber Churn, honorary secretary Carl Anderson, and committee members Wong Kam Fuk, Henry Gittins, Ho Wing, M. K. Lo, J. F. Grose, and Wong Tak-kwong. This group largely stayed in charge until World War Two, with the help of P. Abesser and Edward Law—the latter providing free medical treatment to all league beneficiaries. Kotewall was its president from 1937–39, followed by Macumber Churn.

33   Eric Peter Ho, *The Welfare League: The Sixty Years 1930–1990*. Reprinted in Eric Peter Ho, *Tracing My Children's Lineage*.

34   Initially *Eurasian* was defined as the product of a Chinese mother and Occidental father, but cases of care by the league have occurred when the parentage was the other way around. Local Portuguese or Macanese were not considered eligible, as they already had their own comprehensive welfare organizations. The aid often took the form of helping children to an education, almost always at either DBS or DGS. There was debate about whether migration out of Hong Kong should

be paid for, as, in one committee member's view, "Hong Kong after World War II could no longer be regarded as permanent," but this was shot down with the excuse of a lack of funds. Special funds were set up in the names of Samuel Macumber Churn and Carl Anderson. Money left by another past president, Grose, seeded grants to the China Coast Community, a special home for the elderly in Hong Kong. A notable later president was Dr. Douglas Laing. By 1990, the fund was worth about $14 million; it has since grown much larger, but has trouble finding cases or causes to spend money on.

11: DANCING ON THE EDGE

1   JMA L14/9 Wedding Anniversary Booklet—Souvenir of the Golden Wedding of Sir Robert and Lady Ho Tung 1881–1931.

2   *China Review*, London, January–March 1933.

3   Jehangir Hormusjee Ruttonjee had built the distinctive white Homi Villa on a promontory nearby to oversee the brewery's construction. See the Industrial History of Hong Kong Group website, post by Hugh Farmer on November 6, 2016; and May Holdsworth and Christopher Munn, eds., *Dictionary of Hong Kong Biography*, pp. 376–78. Young Jehangir arrived in Hong Kong aged twelve with his mother, Dina, in 1892. After graduating from Queen's College, he joined H. Ruttonjee and Son, taking charge in 1913 when his father retired. He married Banubai Master in India in 1902. A son, Dhun, and two daughters, Tehmi (Vera) and Fremi, were born in Hong Kong. Ruttonjee also adopted his two young nephews and niece—Rusy, Beji, and Minnie Shroff—after they lost their father in a typhoon at sea. Fremi then married Rusy Shroff and Themi married Rustom Desai.

4   The son of the man who founded the brewery, Dhun Ruttonjee, also took a broad view of the world beyond his own communal ties: he married a Chinese woman and served on Hong Kong's Urban and Legislative Councils. His daughter, Parrin, graduated in medicine from the University of Hong Kong and married Nariman Shroff. The Shroff family has since taken on the Ruttonjee mantle in running the continuing legacy of Ruttonjee charities; it also chairs the board of the Zoroastrian Charity Fund of Hong Kong, Canton and Macao. The Ruttonjee Hospital (now called the Tang Shiu Kin Ruttonjee Hospital) began in 1948 as a tuberculosis sanatorium at the former Royal Navy Hospital in Wan Chai in memory of Jehangir's daughter Tehmina, who had died from TB five years earlier.

5   JMA J1/24/52, Paterson/HK to Beith/Shanghai—January 4, 1934.

"When mentioning 'heteros' you may have noticed the benefits Sir Robert himself has received from heterogenesis, that virile Hun and the Canton sing-song girl, the mating of unlikes. But the law is that descendants are no good, you must always return to the original cross. When I think of the elder Hos and then look at their produce I take off my hat to Malthus (was it?). Nature runs these things better than we do, all mules for instance though the blue grey is an exception where the benefit would breed out if one did not arrange otherwise just as is happening to the Hos."

6   JMA, J7/6, May 24, 1929.

7   JMA, J1/24/51, December 28, 1933.

8   JMA, J1/9/1, April 5, 1934.

9   JMA, J1/24/51, December 14, 1933. Five years later, Jardine's J. J. Paterson was telling W. J. Keswick: "You know that Ho Kwong was Ho Leung's evil genius, I have since acquired a few facts necessary to deflate should Ho Kwong act . . ." J4/2/2, April 15, 1937.

10 JMA E3/10 Telegrams, December 22, 1933.

11 JMA J1/2/33, January 5, 1934, D. G. M. Bernard in London spoke to B. D. F. Beith in Shanghai of "being in the clutches of the Hos." J1/24/52, January 11, 1934: "If Sir Robert settles out of Court he may, and probably will, demand as a quid pro quo the right to nominate Ho Leung's successor. If not, however, and we are under no obligation to him I should like to take the opportunity to cut adrift entirely from the Ho/Lo connection . . ."

12 See JMA, J1/24/52, April 13, 1934, when W. J. Keswick wrote, "There is a story here that Sir Robert does know the position, is lying low and doesn't intend to pay up unless he's forced to do so. Meantime, we're going ahead with the preparation of our claim . . ."

13 JMA, J1/24/53, October 25, 1934.

14 See JMA Series E3/10, J1/2/22, J1/2/33, J1/9/1, J1/9/2, J1/24/49, J1/24/51, J1/24/52, J1/24/53, and J7/6. See also Chapter 13 of Eric Peter Ho, *Tracing My Children's Lineage*.

15 Elizabeth Sinn, *Growing with Hong Kong: The Bank of East Asia 1919–1994*, p. 3.

16 Ibid., p. 4.

17 Ibid., p. 13.

18 The sons were Kan Yuet-keung, Yuet-hing, Yuet-loong, and Yuet-fai. The oldest, later Sir Y. K. Kan, succeeded him as chairman of the bank in 1963, was a partner in Lo and Lo, a senior member of the Urban, Legislative, and Executive Councils, and accompanied Governor MacLehose to Beijing in 1979. Holdsworth and Munn, *Dictionary of Hong Kong Biography*, pp. 218–19.

19   Ibid., pp. 154–55. See also Elizabeth Sinn in Veronica Pearson and Ko
     Tim-keung, eds., *A Sense of Place: Hong Kong West of Pottinger Street*,
     pp. 193–94. See also England, "Hong Kong Taipans," pp. 58–59.

20   Frank Ching, *The Li Dynasty, Hong Kong Aristocrats*, p. xi.

21   The event was held at the China Emporium, of which Li and Kan were
     directors. Ivy's brother Y. K. Kan was best man to Kenneth Fung.

22   HSBC Archives (London), HQ HSBCK 0003-0001 and 0002, Gray-
     burn Private Letters, November 13, 1937.

23   Selwyn Selwyn-Clarke, *Footprints: The Memoirs of Sir Selwyn Selwyn-
     Clarke*, pp. 56–57.

24   JMA J4/2/2, August 4, 1937.

25   Interview, Leslie Wright, September 17, 2015.

26   Paul Gillingham, *At the Peak: Hong Kong Between the Wars*, p. 174.

27   Advocates in the Legislative Council were Man Kam Lo and Leo
     d'Almada e Castro. D'Almada's own family, despite his membership of
     the government's Legislative Council, was technically ineligible for this
     costs-covered escape; instead, his brother would command a com-
     pany of volunteers in the fighting to come, and his sister Gloria (later
     Barretto) helped supply internees and send secret messages under oc-
     cupation.

28   *South China Morning Post*, July 3, 1940. See also July 1, 2, and 5, 1940.

29   Joyce Catherine Symons, *Looking at the Stars*, p. 23. See also "Left
     Behind by Racist Policy," *Sunday Morning Post*, August 9, 1998.

30   Vivian Kong, "'Hong Kong Is My Home': The 1940 Evacuation and
     Hong Kong Britons," p. 556.

31   Gwen Priestwood, *Through Japanese Barbed Wire*, pp. 1, 3–4.

32   Gillingham, *At the Peak*, p. 177.

33   Tony Banham, "Hong Kong Volunteer Defence Corps, Number 3
     (Machine Gun) Company," p. 122.

34   These included V. H. White, Norman Broadbridge, George Winch,
     Ernie Zimmern, Harry Gubbay, and George J. White.

35   The journalist was John Prettejohn at the *South China Morning Post*.

36   Whole families joined up—all seven Reed brothers, the Matthewses,
     Broadbridges, Youngs, and all five Zimmern brothers. Often they
     worked together or lived nearby to fellow volunteers, although the class
     spread seen in the location of their homes was vast—from the Peak
     district all the way to dockside housing in Kowloon or small flats in
     Taipingshan.

37   Banham, "Hong Kong Volunteer Defence Corps," p. 129.

12: WARS WITHIN AND WITHOUT

1   Because the girlfriend was called Mimi Lau, the faulty anti-blast concrete blocks became known as "Mimi Laus"; her boyfriend died by suicide.

2   Mrs. Winkler, widow of Ernie whose memory this was, speaking to the researcher Jenny Goshawk in 1994.

3   Such as George Cautherley, who can trace his family roots back to the trading firm of Augustine Heard and Co., and through Bartou and Lobo family lines into the Eurasian clans.

4   Selwyn Selwyn-Clarke, *Footprints: The Memoirs of Sir Selwyn Selwyn-Clarke*, pp. 62, 69.

5   Ibid., pp. 74–75.

6   Henry J. Lethbridge, "Caste, Class and Race in Hong Kong Before the Japanese Occupation," p. 108.

7   Lord Lawrence Kadoorie, Interview with Oxford Colonial Archives Project, Rhodes House Library, South Parks Road, Oxford, UK. With thanks to Amelia Allsop.

8   Barbara Anslow, *Tin Hats & Rice—A Diary of Life as a Hong Kong Prisoner of War 1941–1945*, pp. 27, 31, and 335.

9   G. A. Leiper, *A Yen for My Thoughts: A Memoir of Occupied Hong Kong*, p. 157.

10 Madhavi Thampi, *Indians in China 1800–1949*, p. 216.

11 John R. Hinnells, *The Zoroastrian Diaspora, Religion and Migration*, p. 177.

12 The Star Ferry's future is in doubt, however, due to financial pressures, post-Covid.

13 HSBC Archives (London), HSBC Bankers Opinions, HQ SHG II 688.

14 Their organizing body is the Hoseinee Society and their place of worship is in rooms above the Wyndham Street Post Office, Hong Kong.

15 Interview, Zafir Ebrahim, November 15, 2018. Other leading Bohra families are Barma, Tyeb, and Kayamally.

16 Simon Twiston Davies and David Thurston, "Prophet Motive," *Sunday Morning Post Magazine*, July 1990.

17 *South China Morning Post*, August 24, 1997.

18 Charles was later executed for resistance work.

19 Hong Kong Heritage Project, Oral History Interview, Frank Correa, October 17, 2008.

20 Hong Kong Heritage Project, the Braga Papers, various.

21 Choa Leep-chee. Margaret would later marry Roger Lobo, becoming Lady Lobo; her family tree intertwines with those of Bartou, Belilios, and others.

22   Hong Kong Heritage Project, Oral History Interview, Lady Margaret Lobo, August 25, 2009.

23   Geoffrey C. Gunn, *Encountering Macau—A Portuguese City-State on the Periphery of China, 1557–1999*, p. 124.

24   Geoffrey C. Gunn, ed., *Wartime Macau—Under the Japanese Shadow*, p. 110. Gunn writes that Hyndman was an old Dutch Portuguese family, but Lobo confirmed it was Scots.

25   Simon Holderton, "Ho Surveys Empire That Gambling Built," *Financial Times*, May 20–21, 1995.

26   See also Helena F. S. Lopes, "Inter-imperial Humanitarianism: The Macao Delegation of the Portuguese Red Cross during the Second World War."

27   Interview, Norma d'Almada Remedios, March 16, 2018.

28   *Hongkong News*, March 29, 1942.

29   Communication with Brian Edgar, June 2013.

30   Howard Elias, Jewish Historical Society, October 15, 2018; *China Mail*, July 6, 1938.

31   Carl T. Smith Collection, Index Card 76-1322; *South China Morning Post*, June 14, 1948. Those named are Vivian Benjamin, Leontine Ellis, S. D. Gerzer, Sarah Gubbay, Dr. Rudolf Hoselitz, H. B. Joseph, H. Lipkovsky, A. Samuel, Leo Weill, and Reginald Goldman from the Hong Kong Volunteers, I. L. Goldenberg of the RNVR, and D. Kossick of the Civil Defence.

32   Gunn, ed., *Wartime Macau*, pp. 147, 153.

33   See Gosano's memoir, *Hong Kong Farewell*, for his modest account of his wartime heroism, pp. 25–29, and his bitterness at second-class citizenship under the British. His wife, Hazel Lang, was a niece of the two Kotwall men executed for their resistance work, p. 30. Jimmy Kotwall's widow, Doris, was given neither British passport nor pension, p. 32.

34   Solomon Bard, *Light and Shade: Sketches from an Uncommon Life*, p. 111.

35   Interview, Peter Hall, August 18, 2011.

36   Among those who didn't make it was Donald Anderson, another HKU graduate (in arts, 1932), a brilliant lawyer and cricketer, who died in that desperate battle of Wong Nei Chong Gap. Albert Prew was killed in the massacre at Repulse Bay.

37   This resistance movement had grown out of a Hakka clansmen's group, active in Hong Kong and Southeast Asia before the war. They focused on propaganda, indoctrination, and relief, spreading anti-Japan and save-the-nation messages, and raising significant amounts of money. Students from Hong Kong's top schools and colleges joined the movement in 1937, and the next year a liaison office was opened in Hong Kong under the guise of the Yue Hwa tea trading and import-export

firm. In Hong Kong, the movement had the support of people such as Dr. Selwyn-Clarke's wife, "Red" Hilda, several foreign journalists, and M. K. Lo. Hong Kong's British government had given it erratic support, closing operations down before the war so as not to offend the Japanese, then entering into a deal late in 1941 to give arms for planned sabotage operations, before war stopped play. Instead, the Communist guerrillas provided much of the essential early experience and knowledge for later intelligence successes—as well as the "little devils," or child agents, who carried messages and escorted many Hong Kongers to safety. See Chan Sui-jeung, *East River Column: Hong Kong Guerrillas in the Second World War and After.* Also Chan Lau Kit-ching, *From Nothing to Nothing: The Chinese Communist Movement and Hong Kong 1921–1936.* Also Fanny W. Y. Fung, "Unsung Warriors Set Up in Sai Kung: The Hong Kong Guerrilla Fighters Who Battled the Japanese in WW2," *South China Morning Post*, August 15, 2015.

38   Peter Cunich, *A History of the University of Hong Kong, Volume 1, 1911–1945*, pp. 411–12.

39   "Ozzie" Cheung, another DBS and HKU boy, would become acting headmaster at DBS after the war before qualifying as a barrister and joining the Legislative and Executive Councils, earning a knighthood in 1987. His war service began with an escape to Macao with his family, and on to the French treaty port of Kwang Chow Wan; he was eventually linked up with W. P. Thomson, a former police superintendent of Hong Kong, now head of the British General Liaison Office, part of British intelligence. Young Ozzie's job was to monitor Japanese activity in South China and coastal waters. He recalled problems with secret ink and radio and being often on the run, taking trains with a bag full of coded messages.

40   George Harold Thomas's entire life was spent in Hong Kong. He married Norah Gourdin, daughter of an American trader who had long lived in Hong Kong and had a Eurasian wife. George and Norah produced four children, including three more doctors, and lived in a house called Blarney Stone in western Hong Kong. Osler would marry a Vietnamese-Chinese, Lily Trinh, who had also been brought up in Hong Kong; their children also went through DBS and DGS, and his daughter Audrey returns to Hong Kong annually to lay a wreath in her father's name at the war remembrance ceremony. Carl T. Smith Collection, Index Card 62-665: *Hong Kong Daily Press*, June 3, 1923; *South China Morning Post*, February 25, 1975. Author interview, Audrey Thomas, November 13, 2013.

41   Clifford Matthews and Oswald Cheung, eds., *Dispersal and Renewal:*

Hong Kong University During the War Years. Also Cunich, *A History of the University of Hong Kong*, pp. 401–26.

42 Author interview, Pat Botelho, January 21, 2019.

43 Interview, Charlie Churn, March 3, 2018.

44 John Asome, "Growing Up Eurasian," pp. 7–30; see p. 8.

45 Email correspondence, John Asome, 2017–19.

46 For the only proper study of the Irish of Hong Kong during the war, see Brian Edgar, "Steering Neutral? The Un-interned Irish Community in Occupied Hong Kong," *Journal of the Royal Asiatic Society Hong Kong Branch* 57 (2017): 67–87.

47 International Committee of the Red Cross (ICRC) Archives, BG 017 07-060, Draft Report, February 28, 1943. BG017 07-068, Letter, May 7, 1943.

48 For the full story, see Vaudine England, "Zindel's Rosary Hill—Hong Kong's Forgotten War," pp. 36–66.

49 ICRC Archives BG 017 07-060, Draft Report, February 28, 1943.

50 ICRC Archives BG017 07-067, Letter from Zindel to Geneva, April 30, 1944.

51 ICRC Archives BG017 07-071, Letter from Zindel to Geneva, November 2, 1945.

52 Through the Red Cross cable system Gaddi was able to inform his mother, Constance, back in Switzerland: "Dearest Mother, We are well, still hoping to be very soon with you all. Trust all well at Home. Working for Red Cross. God's blessings. Love, Leopold and Mildred." ICRC Archives BG017 07-065, cable dated March 6, 1944.

53 Bard, *Light and Shade*, p. 118. However, Peter Hall's father told him he had seen only Zimmern men released and assumed it was thanks to Kotewall helping to secure their release.

54 ICRC Archives BG017 07-071; a letter from a Red Cross delegate in Chungking to Geneva recounted Zimmern's inside information, adding: "Mr Zimmern confirms . . . that Mr Zindel has gone grey on account of worries particularly in regard to the Refugee Home which he had started and for which he is continuously in want of funds."

55 ICRC Archives BG017 07-063, Letter from Zindel to Geneva, May 25, 1945.

56 ICRC Archives BG017 07-071, Letter from Zindel to Geneva, December 7, 1945.

13: TOUGH LOVE

1   Gosano got Leo d'Almada to London; he also helped Marcus da Silva, another leading Portuguese lawyer, escape after he had been tortured by the Kempetai in Hong Kong for spying and sending funds into the Stanley camp, although Gosano resented the lack of thanks forthcoming. See Eddie Gosano, *Hong Kong Farewell*, p. 29. For details of Marcus da Silva's war, see Marcus Alberto da Silva, "The Dark World's Fire: Tom and Lena Edgar in War," brianedgar.wordpress.com/2012/07/23/marcus-da-silva/.

2   John Pownall Reeves, *The Lone Flag—Memoir of the British Consul in Macao During World War II*, pp. 38–39.

3   Carl Anderson, who in peacetime had inaugurated the Welfare League in Hong Kong, chaired the association in Macao and gave the speech thanking the British consul Reeves for his departure. He recalled Reeves's "sincerity, friendliness . . . his strong and all-embracing humanitarianism . . . He has looked after our spiritual, educational as well as sporting needs. He has shared with us in our little joys and has felt with us in our hardships. He has even shown to us how to or how not to play hockey . . ." He expressed a wish for more men like Reeves, and Dr. Selwyn-Clarke—"men of sympathetic understanding and of sterling character unknown to snobbery." Ibid., Appendix 4, p. 148.

4   I am indebted to a descendant, Evelyn Fergusson-Laing, for these papers cited.

5   Ride letter, dated February 19, 1943, BAAG Kweilin.

6   Anthony Sweeting, "Hong Kong Eurasians," p. 98, citing BMA Proclamation No. 14, published December 28, 1945, in Hong Kong (BMA) Gazette 1:1, pp. 19–20.

7   Told to me by Anthony Correa.

8   Adam Luck, "Subjects of Rough Justice," *The Standard*, October 28, 2006.

9   CO537/1650, 1–2, TNA, Gimson to Ruston, March 3, 1946, cited in Felicia Yap, "A 'New Angle of Vision': British Imperial Reappraisal of Hong Kong during the Second World War," pp. 86–113.

10   Felicia Yap, "Eurasians in British Asia during the Second World War."

11   Alexander Grantham, *Via Ports: From Hong Kong to Hong Kong.* "The Substitution in the Legislative Council of elected for appointed members . . . which eventually was to lead to internal self-government either within or without the Commonwealth, was the order of the day in British colonial policy. But the problem in Hong Kong is different from that in other colonies, for Hong Kong can never become indepen-

dent. Either it remains a British colony, or it is re-absorbed into China as a part of the province of Kwangtung," p. 111.

12 Interview, Oxford Colonial Archives Project, Rhodes House Library, Oxford. Thanks to Amelia Allsop.

13 Vaudine England, "Hong Kong Taipans—Lord Lawrence Kadoorie," *Discovery*, March 1986.

14 Suzannah Linton, ed., *Hong Kong's War Crimes Trials*. See also John Carney, "Book Sheds Light on Hong Kong's War Tribunals," *South China Morning Post*, April 28, 2013.

15 For much of this subject, the source is CO968/120/1–2, TNA.

16 Philip Snow, *The Fall of Hong Kong—Britain, China and the Japanese Occupation*, pp. 122, 299.

17 Ibid., pp. 120–21.

18 Veronica Needa is unique in having translated her life story into both thesis and theater. Commissioned by the Hong Kong Arts Centre for its FESTIVAL NOW '98: Invisible Cities, her solo show *Face*—directed by Tang Shu-wing—was performed in both Cantonese and English and toured Asia and the UK. The play in both language versions was published by the Hong Kong International Association of Theatre Critics in 1999, in its collection *10 Best Plays* for 1998; it was included in Mike Ingham and Xu Xi's *City Stage: Hong Kong Playwriting in English* (Hong Kong: Hong Kong University Press, 2005). Later performances included audience interaction through the Playback Theatre (see www .playbackschooluk.org for more information), documented in her MA thesis "FACE: Renegotiating Identity through Performance" (trueheart .org.uk/?page_id=654).

19 Snow, *The Fall of Hong Kong*, pp. 121–22.

20 Ibid., p. 221.

21 G. B. Endacott, *Hong Kong Eclipse*, pp. 245–46.

22 Anthony Sweeting, "Hong Kong Eurasians," p. 97.

23 Snow, *The Fall of Hong Kong*, pp. 107–8, 116.

24 John M. Carroll, *Edge of Empires*, p. 185.

25 Peter Cunich, *A History of the University of Hong Kong*, pp. 428–29.

26 Emily Hahn, *China to Me*, pp. 324, 328–29.

27 Interviews by Christopher Cook in 2003, in Cook, *Robert Kotewall: A Man of Hong Kong*, pp. 119–21.

28 Ibid., p. 149.

29 Ibid., p. 152.

30 Hong Kong PRO, HKRS 211, pp. 2–41.

31 The Bank of East Asia's Li Tse-fong was not reappointed to the postwar Legislative Council. "Clearly, however, the British felt there was a differ-

ence between him and Kotewall," noted the Li family biographer Frank Ching, without explaining what the difference was. See Frank Ching, *The Li Dynasty, Hong Kong Aristocrats*, p. 124. The political winner was undoubtedly M. K. Lo. The Bank of East Asia's Y. K. Kan would rise to the Legislative and Executive councils and be knighted, too. He had spent the war playing bridge in the bank's offices with George She, Thomas Tam, and Willy Hung of Deacons. ("Time to Remember," radio interviews, Y. K. Kan interviewed by Wendy Barnes, Radio Hong Kong, February 1973.) Li Tse-fong's son Aubrey joined them at the bank most days.

14: THE HONG KONGERS

1   G. B. Endacott, *A History of Hong Kong* (London/Hong Kong: Oxford University Press, 1964), p. 310.

2   Sarah Karacs, "Born, Raised and Corrupted in Hong Kong: A Chat with Ackbar Abbas," *Zolima City Mag*, September 22, 2018.

3   One of the first Abbas men was called a Serang, a labor supplier, just as Shaik Moosdeen and Mohammed Arab had been. Shaik Abbas (1843–1908) owned land near the mosque on Shelley Street and worked in government service. His wife, Beebun, was described as the oldest member of Hong Kong's Indian community on her death in 1933; she left more than sixty grandchildren. Abbas men had jobs in solidly middle-class professions, at American Express, Dodwell's, the British Council, on local newspapers, as prison wardens, officers in government, navy, air force, and at The Hong Kong Club. Part of the family had intermarried with the similarly prominent Ramjahn and Madar families; one branch was buried in Macao's Muslim cemetery. Others had moved to Shanghai, Texas, or New York or hailed from Sandakan. One, Abdul Rahim Abbass [*sic*] was among the founders of the Islamic Union, Hong Kong's organizing body for Muslims. Others married Catholic Portuguese, and into the old Eurasian clans, too.

4   Ackbar Abbas, *Hong Kong, Culture and the Politics of Disappearance*, p. 3. Anthony King, *Global Cities*, p. 38.

5   Abbas, *Hong Kong, Culture and the Politics of Disappearance*, pp. 72, 73, 76.

6   Ibid., p. 55.

7   Author interview with Leung Ping-kwan, June 5, 2007. Leung Ping-kwan died on January 5, 2013.

8   Han Suyin, *Love Is a Many-Splendoured Thing*, p. 230.

9   Kirsteen Zimmern, *The Eurasian Face*, p. 16.

10 Henry J. Lethbridge, "Hong Kong Under Japanese Occupation: Changes

in Social Structure," Chapter IV in I. C. Jarvie and Joseph Agassi, eds., *Hong Kong: Society in Transition*, pp. 79ff.

11 James Hayes in Jarvie and Agassi, eds., *Hong Kong*, pp. 1 and 5.

12 One of the problems for the Eurasian organization the Welfare League is that it is hard to find people to spend the money on. "The Welfare League has lost its reason for existence because there are no Eurasians anymore. We are descendants, but not a community. We only meet in weddings and funerals; at the latter, sometimes no one turns up. Yes, Eurasians, Armenians, Jews, Parsis were the backbone of Hong Kong's first one hundred years. When it was set up, Eurasian down-and-outs were really outcasts and had no government support. But the community has disappeared." Interview with Michael Tse, April 10, 2018. Another said the problem lay more with certain obstructive personalities. Whatever community feeling there was in the 1930s appears too weak eighty years later to prevent atrophy from setting in.

13 Jürgen Osterhammel, *Colonialism: A Theoretical Overview*, p. 14.

14 Douglas Kerr, "Three Ways of Going Wrong: Kipling, Conrad, Coetzee," p. 24.

15 Lynn Pan, *Sons of the Yellow Emperor: The Story of the Overseas Chinese*, pp. 373–74.

15: EPILOGUE

1 Robert Cottrell, *The End of Hong Kong: The Secret Diplomacy of Imperial Retreat*, pp. 54–55.

2 Ibid., p. 238n26.

3 Ibid., p. 234n6.

4 Their group, Scholarism, and its campaign were helped by the senior government adviser Anna Wu, herself a former member of Hong Kong Observers, founded in 1975, which had announced hopefully their goal to engage in the governance of Hong Kong. Relative to the times, such a step was almost as radical as Scholarism's twenty-first-century agenda.

5 Primrose Riordan and Robert Wright, "UK Says Hong Kong Authorities No Longer Recognise Dual Nationality," *Financial Times*, February 9, 2021.

6 The British government finally opened a route to residence (involving a five-year wait and money to live off) under its British Nationality Overseas passports. The Hong Kong diaspora is alive and growing in all Britain's cities.

7 Jamil Anderlini, "China's 'Recolonisation' of Hong Kong Could Soon Be Complete," *Financial Times*, November 11, 2020.

BIBLIOGRAPHY

Hong Kong Public Records Office—HK PRO
National Archives, UK—TNA
Carl T. Smith Collection
Jamshed Pavri Parsi Papers, privately held
Deacons Archive, Hong Kong University Library Special Collections
University Archives, Hong Kong University—HKU Archives
HSBC Archives, Hong Kong and London
Jardine Matheson Archives, Cambridge University Library Manuscripts
    Room, UK (thanks to the Syndics of Cambridge University Library)
Jewish Community Centre Library
International Committee of the Red Cross (ICRC) Archives, Geneva
Hong Kong Heritage Project
Kotewall Papers, by permission
Oxford Colonial Archives Project, Rhodes House Library, Oxford
London Missionary Society Archive, SOAS, University of London
London Metropolitan Archives

GOVERNMENT PAPERS AND REPORTS

1858—Commission of Enquiry into Charges against D. R. Caldwell, registrar
    general
1860—Caldwell's *A Vindication of the Character of the Undersigned.*
1867–1880—Report of the Commission to Inquire into the Working of the
    Contagious Diseases Ordinance
1881—Correspondence relating to the working of the Contagious Diseases
    Ordinance of the Colony of Hong Kong, London

1882—Further correspondence regarding the Sanitary Condition and alleged restrictions upon the Chinese—London

1882—Alleged Chinese Slavery in Hong Kong

1893—Special Committee on Po Leung Kuk, or Society for Protection of Women and Girls—Hong Kong

1926—Traffic in Women and Children—Annual Report from the Hong Kong Government—Geneva

1929—Correspondence relating to the Mui Tsai Question—Hong Kong

1929—Papers relative to the Mui Tsai Question—London

1930—Sir William Peel. Report by the Governor of Hong Kong on the Mui Tsai Question—London

1937—Report of the Commission on Mui Tsai in Hong Kong and Malaya

1937—Mui Tsai in Hong Kong: evidence heard by the commission (Chairman Sir Wilfred Woods), written answers to questionnaire, and memoranda submitted by witnesses—London

1952—Sir Man Kam Lo's Comments on the Report of the Committee on Chinese Law and Custom in Hong Kong

CO129—Colonial Office papers—indexed by Dr Elizabeth Sinn: obelix.lib.hku.hk/co129/

CO131—Minutes of the Hong Kong Executive and Legislative Councils.

CO133—Hong Kong Blue Books 1844–1940

FO17—Foreign Office General Correspondence—China 1815–1905.

FO233—Foreign Office Miscellanea 1759–1935

Hong Kong Annual Administrative Reports 1841–1941, ed. R. L. Jarman (Oxford, UK: Archive Editions, 1996).

Hong Kong Civil Service List (Hong Kong: Noronha, 1904–1958).

Hong Kong Government Gazette (Hong Kong: Noronha, 1853–1941).

Hong Kong Hansard: Reports of the Meetings of the Legislative Council of Hong Kong (Hong Kong: Noronha, 1890–1941).

Hong Kong Legislative Council Sessional Papers (Hong Kong: Noronha, 1884–1941).

NEWSPAPERS AND PERIODICALS

Canton Press 1838–1844

Canton Register 1841–1843; *Hongkong Register* 1843–1858

The China Directory 1861, 1865, 1874

China Mail 1845–1974

China Mail: Who's Who in the Far East 1906–7

Chinese Repository 1832–1851

The Chronicle & Directory for China, Japan & the Philippines, etc., 1868–1939 (By 1939 it was called *The Directory & Chronicle for China, Japan, Straits Settlements, Malaya, Borneo, Siam, The Philippines, Korea, Indo-China, Netherlands Indies, &c.*)

Eastern Express 1994–1996

Friend of China 1842–1861

Hongkong Almanack and Directory 1846 and 1859, from the *China Mail*

Hongkong Daily Press 1864–1941

Hongkong Telegraph 1881–1924

The Hong Kong Weekly News 1941–45

Hong Kong Weekly Press 1895–1909

Jewish Chronicle

South China Morning Post 1903–

The Standard (launched as the *Hong Kong Tiger Standard* in 1949)

The Star 1965–1984

———

Abbas, Ackbar. *Hong Kong, Culture and the Politics of Disappearance* (Minneapolis: University of Minnesota Press, 1997).

Abend, Hallett. *Treaty Ports* (Garden City, NY: Doubleday, Doran and Co., 1944).

Abu-Lughod, Janet L. *Before European Hegemony: The World System, AD 1250–1350* (New York: Oxford University Press, 1989).

Alabaster, C. G. "Some Observations on Race Mixture in Hong Kong," *Eugenics Review* 11 (1920): 247–48.

Allen, Theodore. *The Invention of the White Race* (London: Verso, 1994–97).

Andaya, Barbara. *The Flaming Womb—Repositioning Women in Early Modern Southeast Asia* (Honolulu: University of Hawaii Press, 2006).

Anderson, Benedict. *Imagined Communities: Reflections on the Origin and Spread of Nationalism* (London: Verso, 1983).

———. *The Spectre of Comparisons: Nationalism, Southeast Asia, and the World* (London and New York: Verso, 1998).

Anslow, Barbara. *Tin Hats & Rice—A Diary of Life as a Hong Kong Prisoner of War 1941–1945* (Hong Kong: Blacksmith Books, 2018).

Aslanian, Sebouh. *From the Indian Ocean to the Mediterranean: The Global Trade Networks of Armenian Merchants from New Julfa* (Berkeley: University of California Press, 2011).

Asome, John. "Growing Up Eurasian," *Journal of the Royal Asiatic Society Hong Kong Branch* 59 (2019): 7–30.

Baghdiantz-McCabe, Ina, Gelina Harlaftis, and Ioanna Pepelasis Minoglou.

Diaspora Entrepreneurial Networks: Four Centuries of History (New York: Berg, 2005).

Ball, Benjamin. *Rambles in Eastern Asia, including China and Manilla, during several years' residence: with notes of the voyage to China, excursions in Manilla, Hong-Kong, Canton, Shanghai, Ningpoo, Amoy, Fouchow, and Macao* (Boston: James French, 1856).

Ballantyne, Tony. *Orientalism and Race: Aryanism in the British Empire*. Cambridge Imperial and Post-Colonial Studies Series (London: Palgrave, 2001).

———. *Between Colonialism and Diaspora: Sikh Cultural Formations in an Imperial World* (Durham, NC: Duke University Press, 2006).

Ballantyne, Tony, and Antoinette Burton, eds. *Bodies in Contact: Rethinking Colonial Encounters in World History* (Durham, NC: Duke University Press, 2005).

Ballhatchet, Kenneth. *Race, Sex and Class Under the Raj: Imperial Attitudes and Policies and Their Critics 1793–1905* (New York: St. Martin's Press, 1980).

Banham, Tony. *Not the Slightest Chance: The Defence of Hong Kong, 1941* (Hong Kong: Hong Kong University Press, 2003).

———. "Hong Kong Volunteer Defence Corps, Number 3 (Machine Gun) Company," *Journal of the Royal Asiatic Society Hong Kong Branch* 45 (2005): 117–42.

Bard, Solomon. *Traders of Hong Kong: Some Foreign Merchant Houses, 1841–1899* (Hong Kong: Urban Council, 1993).

———. *Voices from the Past: Hong Kong 1842–1918* (Hong Kong: Hong Kong University Press, 2002).

———. *Light and Shade: Sketches from an Uncommon Life* (Hong Kong: Hong Kong University Press, 2009).

Barlow, Tani, ed. *Formations of Colonial Modernity in East Asia* (Durham, NC: Duke University Press, 1997).

Bayly, C. A. *The Birth of the Modern World, 1780–1914* (Oxford, UK: Blackwell Publishing, 2004).

Belilios Public School. *120 Years Memoir, 1890–2010* (Hong Kong: Belilios Old Girls Foundation, 2010).

Berney, Jane. "Writing Women's Histories: Women in the Colonial Record of Nineteenth-Century Hong Kong," *Women's History Review* 22, no. 2 (2013).

Betty (pseud.). *Intercepted Letters: A Mild Satire on Hong Kong* (Hong Kong: Kelly and Walsh, 1905).

Bickers, Robert. *Settlers and Expatriates: Britons over the Seas*. Oxford History of the British Empire Companion Series (Oxford, UK: Oxford University Press, 2010).

Bickers, Robert, and Christian Henriot. *New Frontiers: Imperialism's New Communities in East Asia 1842–1953* (Manchester, UK: Manchester University Press, 2000).

Bickers, Robert, and Ray Yep, eds. *May Days in Hong Kong: Riot and Emergency in 1967* (Hong Kong: Hong Kong University Press, 2009).

Bird, Isabella. *The Golden Chersonese* (London: Century Publishing and Gentry Books, 1883; reprinted 1983).

Blake, Myrna L. "Kampong Eurasians in Singapore," Thesis, University of Singapore, 1973.

Blussé, Leonard. *Strange Company: Chinese Settlers, Mestizo Women, and the Dutch in VOC Batavia* (Dordrecht, Netherlands: Krononklijk Instituut Voor Taal Land en Volkenkunde, 1986).

———. *Bitter Bonds: A Colonial Divorce Drama of the 17th Century* (Princeton, NJ: Markus Wiener Publishers, 2002).

———. *Visible Cities: Canton, Nagasaki, and Batavia and the Coming of the Americans* (Cambridge, MA: Harvard University Press, 2008).

Bonacich, Edna. "A Theory of Middleman Minorities," *American Sociological Review* 38 (1973): 583–94.

Bonavia, David. *Hong Kong 1997* (Hong Kong: South China Morning Post, 1985).

Booth, Martin. *Gweilo: A Memoir of a Hong Kong Childhood* (London: Doubleday, 2004).

Braga, J. P. *The Portuguese in Hongkong and China* (1944; reprinted by Fundacao Macau with Introduction by J. C. Reis, 1998).

Braga, Stuart. "Making Impressions: The Adaptation of a Portuguese Family to Hong Kong, 1700–1950," PhD thesis, Australia National University (Canberra), October 2012.

Broeze, Frank, ed. *Brides of the Sea: Port Cities of Asia from the 16th–20th Centuries* (Honolulu: University of Hawaii Press, 1989).

Brown, Judith M., and Rosemary Foot, eds. *Hong Kong's Transitions, 1842–1997* (London: Macmillan, 1997).

Burton, Antoinette. *Burdens of History: British Feminists, Indian Women, and Imperial Culture, 1865–1915* (Chapel Hill: University of North Carolina Press, 1994).

Burton, Antoinette, ed. *Gender, Sexuality and Colonial Modernities* (London: Routledge, 1999).

Butcher, John G. *The British in Malaya 1880–1941: The Social History of a European Community in Colonial South-East Asia* (Kuala Lumpur: Oxford University Press, 1979).

Cannadine, David. *Ornamentalism: How the British Saw Their Empire* (London: Allen Lane, 2001).

Canny, Nicholas, ed. *The Oxford History of the British Empire* (Oxford, UK: Oxford University Press, 1998).

Caplan, Jane, and John Torpey, eds. *Documenting Individual Identity: The Development of State Practices in the Modern World* (Princeton, N.J.: Princeton University Press, 2001).

Carney, John. "Book Sheds Light on Hong Kong's War Tribunals," *South China Morning Post*, April 28, 2013.

Carroll, John M. *Edge of Empires: Chinese Elites and British Colonials in Hong Kong* (Cambridge, MA: Harvard University Press, 2005).

———. *A Concise History of Hong Kong* (Hong Kong: Hong Kong University Press, 2007).

Carroll, John M., and Mark Chi-kwan. *Critical Readings on the Modern History of Hong Kong* (Leiden: Brill, 2015).

Cernea, Ruth Fredman. *Almost Englishmen: Baghdadi Jews in British Burma* (Lanham, MD: Lexington Books, 2006).

Chan Kwok-bun, ed. *Hybrid Hong Kong* (London: Routledge, 2012).

Chan Lau Kit-ching. *From Nothing to Nothing: The Chinese Communist Movement and Hong Kong, 1921–1936* (Hong Kong: Hong Kong University Press, 1999).

Chan, Ming K., ed. *Precarious Balance: Hong Kong Between China and Britain, 1842–1992* (Armonk, NY: Sharpe, 1994).

Chan Sui-jeung. *East River Column: Hong Kong Guerrillas in the Second World War and After* (Hong Kong: Royal Asiatic Society Hong Kong Studies Series, Hong Kong University Press, 2009).

Chan, W. K. *The Making of Hong Kong Society—Three Studies of Class Formation in Early Hong Kong* (Oxford, UK: Clarendon Press, 1991).

Chater, Liz. *Sir Catchick Paul Chater: A Brief Personal Biography* (Calcutta: Armenian Holy Church of Nazareth, 2005).

———. *Marble Hall Hong Kong—A Pictorial Review* (privately published).

Chaudhuri, K. N. *Trade and Civilisation in the Indian Ocean: An Economic History from the Rise of Islam to 1750* (Cambridge, UK: Cambridge University Press, 1985).

Cheng, Irene. *Clara Ho Tung: A Hong Kong Lady, Her Family and Her Times* (Hong Kong: Chinese University of Hong Kong, 1976).

———. *Intercultural Reminiscences* (Hong Kong: David C. Lam Institute for East-West Studies, Hong Kong Baptist University, 1997).

Cheng, Joseph Y. S., ed. *Hong Kong: In Search of a Future* (Hong Kong: Oxford University Press, 1984).

Cheng Po Hung. *Hong Kong Through Postcards, 1940s–1970s*. Hong Kong in Pictorials Series (Hong Kong: Joint Publishing Co., 1997).

———. *A Century of Hong Kong Island Roads and Streets* (Hong Kong: Joint Publishing Co., 2001).

———. *A Century of New Territories Roads and Streets*, trans. Patrick H. Hase (Hong Kong: Joint Publishing Co., 2003).

———. *Early Hong Kong Brothels* (Hong Kong: University Museum and Art Gallery, University of Hong Kong, 2003).

———. *Early Hong Kong's Kowloon Peninsula* (Hong Kong: University Museum and Art Gallery, University of Hong Kong, 2007).

———. *Early Prostitution in Hong Kong* (Hong Kong: University Museum and Art Gallery, University of Hong Kong, 2010).

Cheng Po-hung, and Toong Po-ming. *A Century of Kowloon Roads and Streets*, trans. Irene Cheng, Ko Tim-keung, and Paul Levine (Hong Kong: Joint Publishing Co., 2003).

Cheung, Gary Ka-wai. *Hong Kong's Watershed—The 1967 Riots* (Hong Kong: Hong Kong University Press, 2009).

Ching, Frank. *The Li Dynasty, Hong Kong Aristocrats* (Hong Kong: Oxford University Press, 1999).

Ching, Henry. *Pow Mah: A Historical Sketch of Horse and Pony Racing in Hong Kong and of the Royal Hong Kong Jockey Club* (Hong Kong: Royal Hong Kong Jockey Club, 1965).

Chiu, Patricia Pok-kwan. "'A Position of Usefulness': Gendering History of Girls' Education in Colonial Hong Kong (1850s–1890s)," *History of Education* 37, no. 6 (2008): 789–805.

———. "The Making of Accomplished Women: English Education for Girls in Colonial Hong Kong, 1890s–1940s," in *Meeting Place: Encounters Across Cultures in Hong Kong, 1841–1984*, edited by Elizabeth Sinn and Christopher Munn (Hong Kong: Hong Kong University Press, 2017).

Chiu, Stephen, and Tai-Lok Lui. *Hong Kong: Becoming a Chinese Global City* (London: Routledge, 2009).

Chiu, T. N. *The Port of Hong Kong: A Survey of Its Development* (Hong Kong: Hong Kong University Press, 1973).

Choa, G. H. *The Life and Times of Sir Kai Ho Kai—A Prominent Figure in Nineteenth-Century Hong Kong* (2nd ed.) (Hong Kong: Chinese University Press, 2000).

Choa-Johnston, Simon. *The House of Wives* (New York: Penguin, 2016).

Chu, Cindy Yik-yi. *Chinese Communists and Hong Kong Capitalists, 1937–1997* (New York: Palgrave MacMillan, 2010).

———, ed. *Foreign Communities in Hong Kong, 1840s–1950s* (New York: Palgrave Macmillan, 2005).

Clarke, N. M. *The Governor's Daughter Takes the Veil* (Hong Kong: Canossian Missions Historic Archives, 1980).

Club Lusitano, 150 Years of History, 1866–2016, compiled by Anthony Correa with the assistance of Frederic "Jim" Silva, Joao Bosco Correa, Tony "Toneco" Silva, Henrique d'Assumpcao, and Mark Francis.

Coates, Austin. *Macao and the British* (1966; Hong Kong: Oxford University Press, 1988–89).

———. *City of Broken Promises* (London: Muller, 1967).

———. *A Mountain of Light: The Story of the Hongkong Electric Company* (London: Heinemann Educational Books, 1977).

———. *Whampoa, Ships on the Shore* (Hong Kong: Hongkong and Whampoa Dock Co., 1980).

———. *China Races* (Hong Kong: Oxford in Asia Paperbacks, 1983, 1994).

———. *Myself a Mandarin* (Hong Kong: Heinemann Asia, 1983).

———. *Quick Tidings of Hong Kong* (Hong Kong: Oxford University Press, 1990).

Cohen, Israel. *The Journal of a Jewish Traveller* (London: John Lane the Bodley Head, 1925).

Cohen, Paul. "The New Coastal Reformers," in *Reform in Nineteenth-Century China*, edited by Paul Cohen and John E. Schrecker (New York: East Asia Research Centre, Harvard University, 1976).

Cohen, Robin. *Global Diasporas: An Introduction* (London and New York: Routledge, 2008).

Colley, Linda. *Captives: Britain, Empire and the World, 1600–1859* (London: Pimlico, 2003).

Collis, Maurice. *Foreign Mud (Anglo-Chinese Opium War)* (London: Faber and Faber, 1946; Singapore: Graham Brash, 1980).

Cook, Christopher. *Robert Kotewall, a Man of Hong Kong* (Great Abington, UK: Ronald Zimmern, 2006).

Cottrell, Robert. *The End of Hong Kong: The Secret Diplomacy of Imperial Retreat* (London: John Murray, 1993).

Crabb, C. H. *Malaya's Eurasians: An Opinion* (Singapore: D. Moore, 1960).

Cree, Edward H. *The Cree Journals—The Voyages of Edward H. Cree, Surgeon, R.N., as Related in His Private Journals 1837–1856*, ed. and with Introduction by Michael Levien (Exeter, UK: Webb and Bouwer, 1981).

Crisswell, Colin N. *The Taipans, Hong Kong's Merchant Princes* (Oxford, UK, and New York: Oxford University Press, 1981, 1995).

Cumine, Eric. *Hong Kong Ways & Byways: A Miscellany of Trivia* (Hong Kong: Belongers Publications, 1981).

Cunich, Peter. *A History of the University of Hong Kong* (Hong Kong: Hong Kong University Press, 2012).

Curtin, Philip D. *Cross-Cultural Trade in World History* (Cambridge, UK: Cambridge University Press, 1984).

Cushman, Jennifer, and Wang Gungwu, eds. *The Changing Identities of Chinese in Southeast Asia* (Hong Kong: Hong Kong University Press, 1988).

Darwin, John. *After Tamerlane: The Rise and Fall of Global Empires, 1400–2000* (London: Penguin, 2007).

———. *The Empire Project: The Rise and Fall of the British World System, 1830–1970* (Cambridge, UK: Cambridge University Press, 2009).

———. *Unfinished Empire: The Global Expansion of Britain* (London: Penguin, 2012).

Das Gupta, Ashin. *The World of the Indian Ocean Merchant, 1500–1800: Collected Essays of Ashin Das Gupta* (New Delhi and New York: Oxford University Press, 2001).

Devine, T. M., and Angela McCarthy. *The Scottish Experience in Asia c. 1700 to the Present: Settlers and Sojourners.* Cambridge Imperial and Post-Colonial Studies Series (London: Palgrave Macmillan, 2017).

de Vries, Jan. "The Industrial Revolution and the Industrious Revolution," *Journal of Economic History* 54, no. 2 (June 1994).

Dikotter, Frank. *The Discourse of Race in Modern China* (London: Hurst and Co., 1992).

———. *Sex, Culture and Modernity in China* (Hong Kong: Hong Kong University Press, 1995).

Diocesan Boys' School and Diocesan Girls' School. *Celebrating 150 Years of Educational Excellence* (Hong Kong: Diocesan Girls' School, 2010).

———. *DGS Kowloon: A Brief History 1860–1977.*

———. *Quest*, the DGS magazine.

———. *DBS, 135th Anniversary*, 2004.

———. *The Diocesan Boys School and Orphanage Hongkong: The History and Records 1869 to 1929*, by W. T. Weatherstone, 1930.

———. *A Tribute to Rev Canon George She, Headmaster 1955–1961*, 2004.

———. *Wings, "Sursum corda": a souvenir magazine*, 1937.

———. *To Serve and to Lead, A History of the DBS*, 2009.

———. *Steps*, the DBS magazine.

Drage, Charles. *Two-Gun Cohen* (London: Jonathan Cape, 1954).

Eitel, E. J. *Europe in China: The History of Hongkong from the Beginning to the Year 1882* (Hong Kong: Oxford University Press, 1983; reprint of Kelly and Walsh, 1895).

Emrys Evans, D. M. "Chinatown in Hong Kong: The Beginnings of Taipingshan," *Journal of the Hong Kong Branch of the Royal Asiatic Society* 10 (1970): 69–78.

Endacott, G. B. *A Biographical Sketchbook of Early Hong Kong* (Singapore: Eastern Universities Press, 1962).

———. *Hong Kong Eclipse*, ed. and with new material by Alan Birch (Hong Kong: Oxford University Press, 1978).

England, Vaudine. *The Quest of Noel Croucher, Hong Kong's Quiet Philan-thropist* (Hong Kong: Hong Kong University Press, 1998).

———. *The Chinese International School: The First 25 Years* (Hong Kong: Chinese International School, 2009).

———. *Kindred Spirits—A History of The Hong Kong Club* (Hong Kong: Hong Kong Club, 2016).

———. *Arnholds, China Trader* (Hong Kong: Arnhold and Co., 2017).

———. "Zindel's Rosary Hill—Hong Kong's Forgotten War," *Journal of the Royal Asiatic Society Hong Kong Branch* 57 (2017): 36–66.

———. *Hari Harilela—Made in Hong Kong* (Hong Kong: HK Peridote, 2020).

———. *East of the Levant: The Tapestry of the Bera Family and Omtis* (Hong Kong: Omtis Limited, 2022).

England, Vaudine, with Judy Green. *Empire's Children: A Hong Kong Family* (Hong Kong: Arnhold and Co., 2021).

Epistola, S. V. *Hong Kong Junta* (Quezon City: University of the Philippines Press, 1996).

Evans Thomas, W. H. *Vanished China: Far Eastern Banking Memories* (London: Thorsons, 1952).

Fairbank, John King. *Trade and Diplomacy on the China Coast—The Open-ing of the Treaty Ports: 1842–1854* (Stanford, CA: Stanford University Press, 1953, 1969).

Faure, David. *Colonialism and the Hong Kong Mentality* (Hong Kong: Cen-tre of Asian Studies, University of Hong Kong, 2003).

Faure, David, ed. *A Documentary History of Hong Kong Society* (Hong Kong: Hong Kong University Press, 1997).

Feldwick, W. *Present Day Impressions of the Far East and Prominent Chi-nese at Home and Abroad: The History, People, Commerce, Industries, and Resources of China, Hongkong, Indo-China, Malaya, and Nether-lands India* (London: Globe Encyclopaedia, 1917).

Fernando, Lloyd. "Conrad's Eastern Expatriates: A New Version of His Out-casts," *PMLA Modern Language Association* 91, no. 1 (January 1976): 78–90.

Fisher, Stephen F. "Eurasians in Hong Kong: A Sociological Study of a Mar-ginal Group," PhD thesis, University of Hong Kong, 1975.

Frost, Mark Ravinder, and Yu-Mei Balasingamchow. *Singapore: A Biogra-phy* (Singapore: Editions Didier Millet/National Museum of Singapore, 2009).

Furnivall, J. S. *Colonial Policy and Practice: A Comparative Study of Burma and Netherlands India* (Cambridge, UK: Cambridge University Press, 1948).

Ganachari, Aravind. "'White Man's Embarrassment': European Vagrancy in

19th Century Bombay," *Economic and Political Weekly* 37, no. 25 (June 22–28, 2002): 2477–86.

Garrett, Valery M. *Heaven Is High, the Emperor Is Far Away—Merchants and Mandarins in Old Canton* (Oxford, UK: Oxford University Press, 2002).

Gillingham, Paul. *At the Peak: Hong Kong Between the Wars* (Hong Kong: Macmillan, 1983).

Gittins, Jean. *Eastern Windows—Western Skies* (Hong Kong: South China Morning Post, 1969).

———. *Stanley: Behind Barbed Wire* (Hong Kong: Hong Kong University Press, 1982).

Gluckman, Max. "Gossip and Scandal," *Current Anthropology* 4, no. 3 (1963): 307–16.

Goody, Jack, *The Eurasian Miracle* (London: Polity Press, 2010).

Gosano, Eddie. *Hong Kong Farewell* (Hong Kong: Greg England, 1997).

Grantham, Alexander. *Via Ports: From Hong Kong to Hong Kong* (Hong Kong: Hong Kong University Press, 1965).

Guest, Capt. Freddie. *Escape from the Bloodied Sun* (London: Jarrolds Publishers, 1956).

Gunn, Geoffrey C. *Encountering Macau—A Portuguese City-State on the Periphery of China, 1557–1999* (Macau: Geoffrey Gunn, 2005).

———. *History Without Borders: The Making of an Asian World Region, 1000–1800* (Hong Kong: Hong Kong University Press, 2011).

Gunn, Geoffrey C., ed. *Wartime Macau—Under the Japanese Shadow* (Hong Kong: Hong Kong University Press, 2016).

Guo Deyan. "The Study of Parsee Merchants in Canton, Hong Kong and Macao," Minorias Culturasis de Macau II, in *Revista de Cultura* (Review of Culture), no. 8 (2003): 51–69.

Hacker, Arthur. *Hacker's Hong Kong* (Hong Kong: Gareth Powell and Ted Thomas, 1976).

———. *China Illustrated: Western Views of the Middle Kingdom* (Hong Kong: Tuttle Publishing, 2004).

Hacking, Ian. "Why Race Still Matters," *Daedalus* 134, no. 1, "On Race" (Winter 2005): 102–16.

Haffner, Christopher. *The Craft in the East* (Hong Kong: District Grand Lodge of Hong Kong and the Far East, 1977).

Hahn, Emily. *China to Me* (Philadelphia: Blakiston Co., 1944; Beacon/Virago Press, 1988).

Hall, Catherine, and Sonya Rose. *At Home with Empire: Metropolitan Society and the Imperial World* (Cambridge, UK: Cambridge University Press, 2006).

Hall, Peter. *In the Web* (Birkenhead, UK: Apprin Press, 2012; earlier eds. 1992, 1993).

———. *150 Years of Cricket in Hong Kong* (privately published by the Hong Kong Cricket Club, 1999).

Hamilton, Gary G., ed. *Cosmopolitan Capitalists: Hong Kong and the Chinese Diaspora at the End of the 20th Century* (Seattle and London: University of Washington Press, 1999).

Han Suyin. *Love Is a Many-Splendoured Thing* (London: Jonathan Cape, 1952).

———. *The Comprador in 19th-Century China: Bridge Between East and West* (Cambridge, MA: Harvard University Press, 1970).

Hao Yen-p'ing. *The Commercial Revolution in 19th Century China— the Rise of Sino-Western Mercantile Capitalism* (Berkeley: University of California Press, 1986).

Harper, Tim, and Sunil Amrith, eds. *Sites of Asian Interaction—Ideas, Networks and Mobility* (Cambridge, UK, and Delhi: Cambridge University Press, 2014).

Harris, Frank Reginald. *Jamsetji Nusserwanji Tata*, 2nd ed. (Bombay: Blackie and Son India, 1958).

Harrop, Phyllis. *Hong Kong Incident* (London: Eyre and Spottiswoode, 1943).

Hase, Patrick H. *The Six-Day War of 1899—Hong Kong in the Age of Imperialism*. Royal Asiatic Society Hong Kong Studies Series (Hong Kong: Hong Kong University Press, 2008).

Hayes, James. "Old British Kowloon," *Journal of the Hong Kong Branch of the Royal Asiatic Society* 6 (1966): 120–37.

———. "Hong Kong Island Before 1841," *Journal of the Hong Kong Branch of the Royal Asiatic Society* 24 (1988): 105–42.

Hayes, James, Carl Smith, Helga Werle et al. "Programme Notes for Visits to Older Parts of Hong Kong Island (Urban Areas), and to Kowloon, in 1974," *Journal of the Hong Kong Branch of the Royal Asiatic Society* 14 (1974): 196–234.

Hinnells, John R. *The Zoroastrian Diaspora, Religion and Migration* (Oxford, UK: Oxford University Press, 2005, 2009).

Hirschman, Charles. "The Origins and Demise of the Concept of Race," *Population and Development Review* 30, no. 3 (September 2004): 385–415.

Ho, Eric Peter. *Tracing My Children's Lineage* (Hong Kong: Hong Kong Institute for the Humanities and Social Sciences, Hong Kong University, 2010).

Hoe, Susanna. *The Private Life of Old Hong Kong: Western Women in the British Colony 1841–1941* (Hong Kong: Oxford University Press, 1991).

———. *Chinese Footprints: Exploring Women's History in China, Hong Kong and Macau* (Hong Kong: Roundhouse Publications, 1996).

Hoe, Susanna, and Derek Roebuck. *The Taking of Hong Kong: Charles and Clara Elliot in China Waters* (Richmond, UK: Curzon, 1999).

Holdsworth, May. *Foreign Devils* (Oxford, UK, and New York: Oxford University Press, 2002).

Holdsworth, May, and Christopher Munn, eds. *Dictionary of Hong Kong Biography* (Hong Kong: Hong Kong University Press, 2012).

Hong Kong Centenary Commemorative Talks, Hong Kong University Library Special Collections.

Hong Kong Museum of Art. *Historical Pictures* (Hong Kong: Urban Council, 1991).

———. *Views of the Pearl River Delta: Macau, Canton and Hong Kong* (Hong Kong: Urban Council and Peabody Essex Museum, 1996).

Hong Kong Museum of History, Urban Council. *Historical Photographs of Hong Kong, Part 2* (1991), and *Part 3* (1994).

Hong Kong Tourist Association. *Around and About Hong Kong April 16th 1961* (pamphlet) (Hong Kong: HK Tourist Association, 1961).

Hopkins, A. G., ed. *Globalization in World History* (London: Pimlico, 2002).

Horne, Gerald. *Race War! White Supremacy and the Japanese Attack on the British Empire* (New York: New York University Press, 2004).

Hovannisian, Richard, ed. *Armenian People from Ancient to Modern Times*, 2 vols. (New York: Palgrave MacMillan, 2004).

Howe, Stephen, ed. *The New Imperial Histories Reader* (London: Routledge, 2010).

Hunter, W. C. *The Fan Kwae at Canton Before Treaty Days, 1825–1844* (London: Kegan Paul, Trench and Co., 1882; reprinted Shanghai: Oriental Affairs, 1938).

Hutcheon, Robin. *SCMP: The First Eighty Years* (Hong Kong: South China Morning Post, 1983).

———. *Wharf, the First Hundred Years* (Hong Kong: The Wharf, 1986).

———. *The Merchants of Shameen: The Story of Deacon & Co.* (Hong Kong: Deacon and Co., 1990).

Hyam, Ronald. "Concubinage and the Colonial Service: The Crew Circular (1909)," *Journal of Imperial and Commonwealth History* 14, no. 3 (1986): 170–86.

———. "Empire and Sexual Opportunity," *Journal of Imperial and Commonwealth History* 14, no. 2. (1986): 34–90.

———. *Understanding the British Empire* (Cambridge, UK: Cambridge University Press, 2010).

Hyde, Francis E. *Far Eastern Trade 1860–1914* (London: Adam and Charles Black, 1973).

Jackson, Stanley. *The Sassoons* (New York: E. P. Dutton, 1968).

Jarrett, Vincent H. G. *Old Hong Kong / by Colonial* (Hong Kong: South China Morning Post, 1933–35).

Jarvie, I. C., and Joseph Agassi, eds. *Hong Kong: Society in Transition* (London: Routledge and Kegan Paul, 1969).

Jaschok, Maria. *Concubines and Maidservants: A Social History* (Hong Kong: Oxford University Press, 1988).

Jaschok, Maria, and Suzanne Miers, eds. *Women and Chinese Patriarchy: Submission, Servitude and Escape* (Hong Kong: Hong Kong University Press; London: Zed Books, 1994).

Kerr, Douglas. "Three Ways of Going Wrong: Kipling, Conrad, Coetzee," *Modern Language Review* 95, no. 1 (January 2000): 18–27.

Keswick, Maggie. *The Thistle and the Jade, a Celebration of 175 Years of Jardine Matheson*, revised and updated by Clara Weatherall (London: Jardine Matheson/Frances Lincoln, 1982, 2008).

King, Ambrose Y. C., and Rance P. L. Lee, eds. *Social Life and Development in Hong Kong* (Hong Kong: Chinese University Press, 1981).

King, Anthony. *Global Cities* (London: Routledge, 1990).

King, Frank H. H. *The History of the Hongkong and Shanghai Banking Corporation*, 4 vols. (Cambridge, UK: Cambridge University Press, 1987–90).

Kling, Blair B., and M. B. Pearson. *The Age of Partnership: Europeans in Asia before Dominion* (Honolulu: University Press of Hawaii, 1979).

Kong, Vivian. "'Hong Kong Is My Home': The 1940 Evacuation and Hong Kong Britons," *Journal of Imperial and Commonwealth History* 47, no. 3 (2019).

———. "Exclusivity and Cosmopolitanism: Multiethnic Civil Society in Interwar Hong Kong," *Historical Journal* 63, no. 5 (2020): 1281–1302.

———. "Whiteness, Imperial Anxiety, and the 'Global 1930s': The White British League Debate in Hong Kong," *Journal of British Studies* 59, no. 2 (2020).

Kotewall-Zimmern, Cicely. *Recollections of My Life* (privately published, 2006).

Kulke, Eckehard. *The Parsees in India: A Minority as Agent of Social Change* (New Delhi: Vikas Publishing House, 1974).

Kwong Chi Man, and Tsoi Yiu Lun. *Eastern Fortress: A Military History of Hong Kong, 1840–1970* (Hong Kong: Hong Kong University Press, 2014).

Laird, Egerton K. *The Rambles of a Globe Trotter in Australasia, Japan, China, Java, India, and Cashmere*, 2 vols. (London: Chapman & Hall, 1875).

Lambert, David, and Alan Lester, eds. *Colonial Lives Across the British Empire: Imperial Careering in the Long Nineteenth Century* (Cambridge, UK: Cambridge University Press, 2006).

Lamson, Herbert Day. "The Eurasian in Shanghai," *American Journal of Sociology* 41 (1936): 642–48.

Lane, Frederic. "Family Partnerships and Joint Ventures in the Venetian Republic," *Journal of Economic History* 4, no. 2 (November 1944): 178–96.

Law Wing Sang. *Collaborative Colonial Power: The Making of the Hong Kong Chinese* (Hong Kong: Hong Kong University Press, 2009).

Lee, Vicky. *Being Eurasian: Memories Across Racial Divides* (Hong Kong: Hong Kong University Press, 2004).

Lee Sperry, Ansie. *Running with the Tiger: A Memoir of an Extraordinary Young Woman's Life in Hong Kong, China, the South Pacific and POW Camp* (Portola Valley, CA: Sperry Family Trust, 2009).

Leiper, G. A. *A Yen for My Thoughts: A Memoir of Occupied Hong Kong* (Hong Kong: South China Morning Post, 1982).

Lethbridge, Henry J. Introduction, in Albert Smith, *To China and Back: Being a Diary Kept, Out and Home* (London: Egyptian Hall, 1859).

———. "The Yellow Fever," *Far Eastern Economic Review*, May 2, 1968.

———. "The Best of Both Worlds?" *Far Eastern Economic Review* (October 10, 1968): 128–30.

———. "Caste, Class and Race in Hong Kong Before the Japanese Occupation," in *Hong Kong: The Interaction of Traditions and Life in the Towns*, ed. Marjorie Topley, from a Weekend Symposium, November 25–26, 1972 (Hong Kong: Royal Asiatic Society, Hong Kong Branch, June 1975).

———. *Hong Kong: Stability and Change, a Collection of Essays* (Hong Kong: Oxford University Press, 1978).

———. *Hard Graft in Hong Kong: Scandal, Corruption, the ICAC* (Hong Kong: Oxford University Press, 1985).

Leventhal, Dennis A. *Sino-Judaic Studies: Whence and Whither, an Essay and Bibliography.* Monographs of the Jewish Historical Society of Hong Kong, *Hong Kong Jewish Chronicle*, Vol. I, 1985.

———. *Faces of the Jewish Experience in China.* Monographs of the Jewish Historical Society of Hong Kong, *Hong Kong Jewish Chronicle*, Vol. 3, 1990.

Levine, Philippa. *Prostitution, Race and Politics: Policing Venereal Disease in the British Empire* (New York: Routledge, 2003).

Lewis, Milton, Scott Bamber, and Michael Waugh. *Sex, Disease and Society: A Comparative History of Sexually Transmitted Diseases and HIV/AIDS in Asia and the Pacific* (Westport, CT: Praeger, 1997).

Lewis, Su Lin. "Rotary International's 'Acid Test': Multi-ethnic Associational Life in 1930s Southeast Asia," *Journal of Global History* 7 (2012): 302–24.

Lim, Patricia. *Forgotten Souls—A Social History of the Hong Kong Cemetery* (Hong Kong: Hong Kong University Press, 2011).

Linklater, Andro. *The Code of Love, a True Story* (London: Weidenfeld and Nicolson, 2000).

Linton, Suzannah, ed. *Hong Kong's War Crimes Trials* (Oxford, UK: Oxford University Press, 2013).

Ljungstedt, Anders. *An Historical Sketch of the Portuguese Settlements in China and of the Roman Catholic Church and Mission in China & Description of the City of Canton* (Boston: James Munroe and Co., 1836; Hong Kong: Viking Hong Kong Publications, 1992).

Lo Cheung Shiu. *J.P.: A Memoir by His Sons* (privately published, 1934).

Lo Hsiang-lin. *Hong Kong and Its External Communications Before 1842: The History of Hong Kong Prior to the British Arrival* (Hong Kong: Institute of Chinese Culture, 1963).

———. *The Role of Hong Kong in the Cultural Interchange Between East and West* (Tokyo: Centre for East Asian Studies, 1963).

Lombard, Denys, and Jean Aubin. *Asian Merchants and Businessmen in the Indian Ocean and the China Sea* (New Delhi: Oxford University Press, 2000).

Lopes, Helena F. S. "Inter-imperial Humanitarianism: The Macau Delegation of the Portuguese Red Cross during the Second World War," *Journal of Imperial and Commonwealth History* 46, no. 6 (2018): 1125–47.

Lovell, Julia. *The Opium War* (London: Picador, 2011).

Lowe, K. P. G. "Hong Kong, 26 January 1841: Hoisting the Flag Revisited," *Journal of the Hong Kong Branch of the Royal Asiatic Society* 29 (1989): 8–17.

Lowe, Kate, and Eugene McLaughlin. "Sir John Pope Hennessy and the 'Native Race Craze': Colonial Government in Hong Kong, 1877–1882," *Journal of Imperial and Commonwealth History* 20, no. 2 (May 1992): 223–47.

Luard, Tim. *Escape from Hong Kong: Admiral Chan Chak's Christmas Day Dash 1941.* Royal Asiatic Society Hong Kong Studies Series (Hong Kong: Hong Kong University Press, 2012).

Luff, John. *The Hidden Years: Hong Kong 1941–1945* (Hong Kong: South China Morning Post, 1967).

———. *Hong Kong Cavalcade* (Hong Kong: South China Morning Post, 1968).

Lui Tai-Lok with Stephen Chiu. "Becoming a Chinese Global City: Hong Kong (and Shanghai) Beyond the Global-Local Duality," in Xiangming Chen, ed., *Shanghai Rising: State Power and Local Transformations in a Global Megacity* (Minneapolis: University of Minnesota Press, 2009).

Luk, Bernard Hung-kay. "Chinese Culture in the Hong Kong Curriculum:

Heritage and Colonialism," *Comparative Education Review* 35, no. 4 (November 1991): 650–68.

Mak, Geert. *De levens van Jan Six* (Amsterdam: Atlas Contact, 2016). English translation by Liz Waters, *The Many Lives of Jan Six: A Portrait of an Amsterdam Dynasty* (Amsterdam: Atlas Contact, 2017).

Mansel, Philip. *Levant: Splendour and Catastrophe in the Mediterranean* (London: John Murray, 2010).

Marden, Anne. *Letters to My Grandchildren* (Hong Kong: Anne Marden/ Twin Age, 2006, 2007).

Mark, Chi-kwan. *Hong Kong and the Cold War: Anglo-American Relations, 1949–1957* (Oxford, UK: Clarendon, 2004).

———. "Defence or Decolonization? Britain, the US and the Hong Kong Question in 1957," *Journal of Imperial and Commonwealth History* 33, no. 1 (January 2005): 51–72.

Markovits, Claude. *The Global World of Indian Merchants 1750–1947: Traders of Sind from Bukhara to Panama* (Cambridge, UK: Cambridge University Press, 2000).

Marshall, J. F. *Whereon the Wild Thyme Flows: Some Memories of Service with the Hongkong Bank* (Surrey, UK: Token, 1986).

Mathews, Gordon. *Ghetto at the Center of the World: Chungking Mansions, Hong Kong* (Chicago: University of Chicago Press, 2011).

Matthews, Clifford, and Oswald Cheung, eds. *Dispersal and Renewal: Hong Kong University During the War Years* (Hong Kong: Hong Kong University Press, 1998).

Mattock, Katherine. *Hong Kong Practice—Drs Anderson & Partners, the First Hundred Years* (Hong Kong: Anderson and Partners, 1984).

McClintock, Ann. *Imperial Leather: Race, Gender and Sexuality in the Colonial Context* (New York: Routledge, 1994).

McDonogh, Gary, and Cindy Wong. *Global Hong Kong* (London: Routledge, 2005).

McPherson, Sue (Fulham). "J. L. McPherson: Hong Kong YMCA General Secretary, 1905–1935," *Journal of the Royal Asiatic Society Hong Kong Branch* 46 (2006): 39–60.

Mellor, Bernard. *Lugard in Hong Kong: Empires, Education and a Governor at Work, 1907–1912* (Hong Kong: Hong Kong University Press, 1992).

Meter, David R. *Hong Kong as a Global Metropolis* (Cambridge, UK: Cambridge University Press, 2000).

Mikes, George. *East Is East* (London: Andre Deutsch, 1958).

Miners, Norman. *Hong Kong Under Imperial Rule 1912–1941* (Hong Kong: Oxford University Press, 1987).

Mody, Nawaz. *The Parsis in Western India 1818–1920* (Bombay: Allied Publishers, 1998).

Morris, Esther. *Helena May: The Person, the Place, and 90 Years of History in Hong Kong* (Hong Kong: The Helena May, 2006).

Morris, Jan (formerly James). *Pax Britannica: The Climax of an Empire* (London: Faber and Faber, 1968; Penguin, 1979).

———. *Heaven's Command: An Imperial Progress* (London: Faber and Faber, 1973; Penguin, 1979).

———. *Farewell the Trumpets: An Imperial Retreat* (London: Faber and Faber, 1978; Penguin 1979).

Munn, Christopher. *Anglo-China—Chinese People and British Rule in Hong Kong, 1841–1880* (Hong Kong: Hong Kong University Press, 2009).

Ng, Lun Ngai-ha. *Interactions of East and West: Development of Public Education in Early Hong Kong* (Hong Kong: Chinese University of Hong Kong, 1984).

Ng, Michael H. K., and John D. Wong. *Civil Unrest and Governance in Hong Kong: Law and Order from Historical and Cultural Perspectives* (London: Routledge, 2017).

Ng, Peter Y. L. *New Peace County: A Chinese Gazetteer of the Hong Kong Region.* (Hong Kong: Hong Kong University Press, 1983).

Ngo Tak-wing. *Hong Kong's History, State and Society Under Colonial Rule* (London: Routledge, 1999).

Nocontelli, Carmen. *Empires of Love: Europe, Asia and the Making of Early Modern Identity* (Philadelphia: University of Pennsylvania Press, 2013).

Norton-Kyshe, James William. *The History of the Law and Courts of Hong Kong, Tracing Consular Jurisdiction in China and Japan, and including Parliamentary Debates, and the Rise, Progress, and Successive Changes in the Various Public Institutions of the Colony from the Earliest Period to the Present Time,* 2 vols. (London, 1898; reprinted Hong Kong: Vetch and Lee, 1971).

O'Connor, Paul. *Islam in Hong Kong: Muslims and Everyday Life in China's World City* (Hong Kong: Hong Kong University Press, 2012).

Olson, Sean. "Hong Kong Legacy: A Swedish Connection," *Journal of the Royal Asiatic Society Hong Kong Branch* 46 (2006): 61–74.

Ommanney, F. D. *Fragrant Harbour: A Private View of Hong Kong* (London: Hutchinson, 1962).

———. *Eastern Windows* (London: Longman, 1962).

Osterhammel, Jürgen. *Colonialism: A Theoretical Overview,* trans. Shelley L. Frisch (Princeton, NJ: Markus Wiener, 1997).

O'Sullivan, Patricia. "George Hennessy, an Irishman in the Hong Kong Police," *Journal of the Royal Asiatic Society Hong Kong Branch* 52 (2012): 189–223.

Owen, Roger, and Bob Sutcliffe, eds. *Studies in the Theory of Imperialism* (New York: Longman, 1972).

Palsetia, Jesse S. *The Parsis of India: Preservation of Identity in Bombay City* (Leiden: Brill, 2001).

Pan, Lynn. *Sons of the Yellow Emperor: The Story of the Overseas Chinese* (London: Mandarin, 1991).

Patrikeeff, Felix. *Mouldering Pearl—Hong Kong at the Crossroads* (London: Coronet, 1990).

Patten, Chris. *East and West* (London: MacMillan, 1998).

Payaslian, Simon. *The History of Armenia from the Origins to the Present* (New York: Palgrave Macmillan, 2007).

Pearson, M. N. *Merchants and Rulers in Gujarat: The Response to the Portuguese in the 16th Century* (Berkeley: University of California Press, 1976).

Pearson, Veronica, and Ko Tim-keung, eds. *A Sense of Place: Hong Kong West of Pottinger Street* (Hong Kong: Joint Publishing, Royal Asiatic Society Hong Kong Branch, 2008).

Plüss, Caroline. *The Social History of the Jews of Hong Kong: A Resource Guide*. Occasional Paper Number One (Hong Kong: Jewish Historical Society of Hong Kong, 1999).

———. "Assimilation vs. Idiosyncrasy: Strategic Constructions of Sephardic Identities in Hong Kong," *Jewish Culture and History* 5, no. 2 (May 31, 2012), 48–69.

Pomfret, David A. "Raising Eurasia: Race, Class, and Age in French and British Colonies," *Comparative Studies in Society and History* 51, no. 2 (2009): 314–43.

Pope-Hennessy, James. *Verandah: Some Episodes in the Crown Colonies, 1867–1889* (London: Allen and Unwin, 1964).

———. *Half-Crown Colony: A Hong Kong Notebook* (London: Jonathan Cape, 1969).

Porter, Bernard. *The Absent-Minded Imperialists—Empire, Society and Culture in Britain* (Oxford, UK: Oxford University Press, 2004).

———. "Further Thoughts on Imperial Absent-Mindedness," *Journal of Imperial and Commonwealth History* 36, no. 1 (2008).

Poy, Vivienne. *A River Named Lee* (Scarborough, Ont.: Calyan Publishing, 1995).

Priestwood, Gwen. *Through Japanese Barbed Wire* (New York and London: D. Appleton Century Co., 1943).

Rafferty, Kevin. *City on the Rocks* (London and New York: Viking Penguin, 1989).

Reeves, John Pownall, Colin Day, and Richard Garrett, eds. *The Lone Flag—*

Memoir of the British Consul in Macao During World War II (Hong Kong: Hong Kong University Press, 2014).

Reid, Anthony. *A History of Southeast Asia—Critical Crossroads* (Chichester, UK: John Wiley and Sons/Blackwell, 2015).

Ride, Lindsay, and May Ride, ed. Bernard Mellor. *An East India Company Cemetery: Protestant Burials in Macao* (Hong Kong: Hong Kong University Press, 1996).

Roberts, Denys. *Another Disaster: Hong Kong Sketches* (London: Radcliffe Press, 2006).

Roth, Cecil. *The Sassoon Dynasty* (London: Robert Hale, 1941).

Royal Asiatic Society, Hong Kong Branch. *Hong Kong Going and Gone: Western Victoria, Hong Kong* (Hong Kong: Hong Kong Branch of the Royal Asiatic Society, 1980).

Sayer, G. R. *Hong Kong 1841–1862: Birth, Adolescence and Coming of Age* (1937; reprinted by Hong Kong: Hong Kong University Press, 1980).

———. *Hong Kong 1862–1919* (Hong Kong: Hong Kong University Press, 1975).

Schwarz, Bill. *Memories of Empire, Vol. 1: The White Man's World* (Oxford, UK: Oxford University Press, 2011).

Selle, Earl Albert. *Donald of China* (New York: Harper and Brothers, 1948).

Selwyn-Clarke, Selwyn. *Footprints: The Memoirs of Sir Selwyn Selwyn-Clarke* (Hong Kong: Sino-American Publishing, 1975).

Sergoyan, E. G. *The Gathering Place: Stories from the Armenian Social Club in Old Shanghai* (Seattle: Coffeetown Press, 2012).

Seth, Mesrovb Jacob. *Armenians in India from the Earliest Times to the Present Day, a Work of Original Research* (New Delhi and Madras: Asian Educational Services, 1992).

Shih Shu-ching. *City of the Queen: A Novel of Colonial Hong Kong*, trans. Sylvia Li-chun Lin and Howard Goldblatt (Hong Kong: Hong Kong University Press, 2008).

Silva, Frederic A. "Jim." *Todo o Nosso Passado: All Our Yesterdays—The Sons of Macao, Their History and Heritage* (Macao: Coeccao Extratextos, Livros do Oriente, 1996 [UMA Inc, California, 1979]).

———. *Things I Remember* (San Francisco: privately published, 1999).

Sinn, Elizabeth. *Power and Charity—The Early History of the Tung Wah Hospital, Hong Kong*, East Asian Historical Monographs (Hong Kong: Oxford University Press, 1989).

———. *Growing with Hong Kong: The Bank of East Asia 1919–1994* (Hong Kong: Bank of East Asia, 1994).

———. *Hong Kong: British Crown Colony, Revisited* (Hong Kong: Hong Kong University Press, 2001).

———. "Women at Work: Chinese Brothel Keepers in Nineteenth-Century Hong Kong," *Journal of Women's History* 19, no. 3 (October 2007): 87–111.

———. *Pacific Crossing: California Gold, Chinese Migration, and the Making of Hong Kong* (Hong Kong: Hong Kong University Press, 2013).

Sinn, Elizabeth, ed. *Between East and West: Aspects of Social and Political Development in Hong Kong* (Hong Kong: Hong Kong University Press, 1990).

Sinn, Elizabeth, and Christopher Munn, eds. *Meeting Place: Encounters Across Cultures in Hong Kong, 1841–1984* (Hong Kong: Hong Kong University Press, 2017).

Sinn, Elizabeth, Wong Siu-lun, and Chan Wing-hoi, eds. *Rethinking Hong Kong: New Paradigms, New Perspectives* (Hong Kong: Hong Kong University Press, 2009).

Siu, Helen F. "Cultural Identity and the Politics of Difference in South China," *Daedalus* 122, no. 2 (Spring 1993): 19–43.

Siu, Helen F., ed. *Merchants' Daughters—Women, Commerce, and Regional Culture in South China* (Hong Kong: Hong Kong University Press, 2010).

Smith, Carl T. "English-Educated Chinese Elites in Nineteenth-Century Hong Kong," in *Hong Kong: The Interaction of Traditions and Life in the Towns*, ed. Marjorie Topley, from a Weekend Symposium, November 25–26, 1972 (Hong Kong: Royal Asiatic Society, Hong Kong Branch, June 1975).

———. "Early American Trade in China and Hong Kong: Russell and Company and the Houqua Family," *Hong Kong American Chamber of Commerce* 7, no. 7 (1976): 14–17.

———. "A Glance Backward: Auditoria, Artistes and Amateurs in Hong Kong," *Hong Kong Arts Centre Opening Celebrations* (1977): 29–33.

———. "The Hong Kong and Shanghai Bank Compradors," *HSBC Conference*, Centre of Asia Studies, University of Hong Kong, 1981.

———. "Compradors of Hong Kong Bank," in *Eastern Banking: Essays in the History of the Hongkong and Shanghai Banking Corporation*, ed. Frank H. H. King (London: Athlone Press, 1983), 93–111.

———. "Congregational and Visitors' Registers at Tao Fong Shan," in *Karl Ludvig Reichelt: Missionary, Scholar and Pilgrim*, ed. Eric J. Sharpe (Hong Kong: Tao Fong Shan Ecumenical Centre, 1984), 203.

———. "Shamshuipo: From Proprietary Villages to Industrial Urban Complex," in *From Village to City: Studies in the Traditional Roots of Hong Kong Society*, ed. David Faure (Hong Kong: Centre of Asian Studies, University of Hong Kong, 1984), 73–105.

———. *Chinese Christians, Elites, Middlemen and the Church in Hong Kong*. Reprint in the Echoes: Classics of Hong Kong Culture and History series (Hong Kong: Hong Kong University Press, 1985, 2005).

———. *A Sense of History: Studies in the Social and Urban History of Hong Kong* (Hong Kong: Hong Kong Educational Publishing, 1995).

———. "The Wai Sing Lottery and Its Network of Macau, Canton and Hong Kong Capitalists," in *The Rise of Business Corporations in China from Ming to Present* (paper presented at conference; Hong Kong: Centre of Asian Studies, Hong Kong University, 1996).

———. "Armenian Strands in the Tangled Web of the Opium Trade at Macau and Canton," in *International Symposium on Lin Zexu, the Opium War and Hong Kong* (Hong Kong: Lin Shi Shi Zheng Ju Xianggang Li Shi Bo Wu Guan; Lin Zexu Ji Jin Hui: Zhongguo Shi Xue Hui, 1998).

———. "Sino-Indian Interactions in the 18th and 19th Centuries: Parsees, Armenians and Muslims in Macao, Guangzhou and Hong Kong," in *Distinguished Fellow Award Ceremony for Rev. Carl T. Smith*, University of Hong Kong, Hong Kong Culture and Society Programme and China-India Project, Centre of Asian Studies, 2003.

Smith, Carl T., in *Chung Chi Bulletin* (Chung Chi College, Chinese University of Hong Kong): "Early European Buildings in Hong Kong," 38 (June 1965): 14–20.

———. "Commissioner Lin's Translators," 42 (June 1967): 29–36.

———. "An Early Hong Kong Success Story: Wei Akwong, the Beggar Boy," 45 (December 1968): 9–14.

———. "Ng Akew, One of Hong Kong's 'Protected Women,'" 46 (June 1969): 13–27.

———. "The Gillespie Brothers—Early Links between Hong Kong and California," 47 (December 1969): 23–28.

———. "The Chinese Settlement of Hong Kong," 48 (May 1970): 26–32.

———. "A Register of Baptized Protestant Chinese 1813–1842," 49 (December 1970): 23–26.

———. "Dr Legge's Theological School," 50 (June 1971): 16–22.

———. "The Formative Years of the Tong Brothers: Pioneers in the Modernization of China's Commerce and Industry," 10, no. 1 and 2 (1971): 81–95.

———. "An Historical Survey of an Overseas Chinese Community, Dayton, Ohio, USA," 54 (June 1973): 30–33.

———. "Idols on a School Hill: The American Board School for Chinese Boys in Singapore, 1835–1842," 55 (December 1973): 28–30.

Smith, Carl T., in *Journal of the Hong Kong Branch of the Royal Asiatic Society* (renamed *Journal of the Royal Asiatic Society Hong Kong Branch* in 2004): "Chan Lai-sun and His Family: A 19th Century China Coast Family," 16 (1976): 112–16.

———. "Notes on Friends and Relatives of Taiping Leaders," 16 (1976): 117–34.

———. "Notes on Tung Wah Hospital, Hong Kong," 16 (1976): 263–80.

———. "The Chinese Church, Labour and Elites and the Mui Tsai Question in the 1920s," 21 (1981): 91–113.

———. "The Hong Kong Amateur Dramatic Club and Its Predecessors," 22 (1982): 217–51.

———. "Notes for a Visit to the Government Cemetery at Happy Valley," 25 (1985): 17–26.

———. "Sense of History," Part I, 26 (1986): 213–64. Part II, 27 (1987): 117–253.

———. "The German Speaking Community in Hong Kong 1846–1918," 34 (1994): 1–55.

Smith, Carl T., in *Ching Feng*: "Notes on the Earliest Missionaries in Hong Kong," 19, no. 3 and 4 (1976): 24–28.

———. "The Early Hong Kong Church and Traditional Chinese Family Patterns," 20, no. 1 (1977): 52–60.

———. "The Protestant Church and the Improvement of Women's Status in 19th Century China," 20, no. 2 (1977): 109–15.

———. "Sun Yat-sen as a Middle School Student in Hong Kong," 20, no. 3 (1977): 153–65.

———. "Sun Yat-sen's Middle School Days in Hong Kong: The Establishment of Alice Memorial Hospital," 21, no. 2 (1978): 78–94.

———. "Sun Yat-sen's Baptism and Some Christian Connections," 22, no. 4 (1979): 170–89.

———. "A Look at Ching Feng Over the Past Twenty-five Years," 25, no. 4 (1982): 195–205.

———. "The Adaption of the Protestant Church to a Chinese and Colonial Situation," 26, no. 2 and 3 (1983): 75–98.

Smith, Carl T., and James Hayes. "Hung Hom: An Early Industrial Village in Old British Kowloon," *Journal of the Hong Kong Branch of the Royal Asiatic Society* 15 (1975): 318–24.

———. "Nineteenth Century Yaumatei," in *In the Heart of the Metropolis: Yaumatei and Its People*, ed. P. H. Hase (Hong Kong: Joint Publishing Co., 1999), 96–109.

Smith, Carl T., and Paul A. Van Dyke. "Muslims in the Pearl River Delta 1700–1930," *Review of Culture* 10 (April 2004): 6–15.

Smith, George. *A Narrative of an Exploratory Visit to Each of the Consular Cities of China, and to the Islands of Hong Kong and Chusan, in Behalf of the Church Missionary Society, in the Years 1844, 1845, 1846* (London: Seeley, Burnside & Seeley, 1847; New York: Harper & Brothers, 1857).

Smith, Joyce Stevens, and Joyce Savidge. *Matilda: Her Life and Legacy* (Hong Kong: Matilda and War Memorial Hospital, 1988).

Snow, Philip. *The Fall of Hong Kong—Britain, China and the Japanese Occupation* (New Haven and London: Yale University Press, 2003).

Stokes, Gwyneth G. *Queen's College 1862–1962* (Hong Kong: Queen's College, 1962).

Stoler, Ann Laura. *Race and the Education of Desire: Foucault's History of Sexuality and the Colonial Order of Things* (Durham, NC: Duke University Press, 1995).

———. *Carnal Knowledge and Imperial Power: Race and the Intimate in Colonial Rule* (Berkeley: University of California Press, 2002).

———. *Along the Archival Grain—Epistemic Anxieties and Colonial Common Sense* (Princeton, NJ: Princeton University Press, 2009).

Stone, Lawrence. *The Family, Sex and Marriage in England 1500–1800* (London: Weidenfeld and Nicolson, 1977).

Sutherland, Heather. "Treacherous Translators and Improvident Paupers: Perception and Practice in Dutch Makassar, Eighteenth and Nineteenth Centuries," *Journal of the Economic and Social History of the Orient* 53 (2010): 319–56.

Sweeting, Anthony. *Education in Hong Kong Pre-1841 to 1941: Fact and Opinion, Materials for a History of Education in Hong Kong* (Hong Kong: Hong Kong University Press, 1990).

———. "Hong Kong Eurasians," *Journal of the Royal Asiatic Society Hong Kong Branch* 55 (2015): 83–113.

Symonds, Richard. "Eurasians Under British Rule," in *Oxford University Papers on India, vol. 1, part 2*, ed. N. J. Allen et al. (Delhi: Oxford University Press, 1987).

Symons, Joyce Catherine. *Looking at the Stars* (Hong Kong: Pegasus Books, 1996).

Tarrant, William. *Hongkong* (Canton: *Friend of China*, January 24, 1862).

Taylor, Jean Gelman. *The Social World of Batavia: Europeans and Eurasians in Colonial Indonesia*, 2nd ed. (Madison: University of Wisconsin Press, 2009).

Teng, Emma. *Eurasian: Mixed Identities in the United States, China and Hong Kong, 1842–1943* (Berkeley: University of California Press, 2013).

Thampi, Madhavi. "Parsees in the China Trade," *Review of Culture*, International Edition no. 10 (April 2004).

———. *Indians in China 1800–1949* (New Delhi: Manohar, 2005).

Thapan, Anita Raina. *Sindhi Diaspora in Manila, Hong Kong, and Jakarta* (Honolulu: University of Hawaii Press, 2002).

Thompson, Virginia, and Richard Adloff. *Minority Problems in Southeast Asia* (Stanford, CA: Stanford University Press, 1955).

Thomson, John Stuart. *The Chinese* (London: T. Werner Laurie, Clifford's Inn, 1909).

Tregonning, K. G. *Under Chartered Company Rule, North Borneo 1881–1946* (Singapore: University of Malaya Press, 1858; reprinted by Synergy Media, Malaysia, 2007).

Trench, David. *Hong Kong and Its Position in the Southeast Asia Region* (Honolulu: East-West Center, 1971).

Tripathi, Dwijendra, ed. *Business Communities of India: A Historical Perspective* (Ahmedabad: Business History Archives and Museum, 1984).

Tsai Jung-Fang. "The Predicament of the Comprador Ideologists: He Qi (Ho Kai, 1859–1914) and Hu Liyuan (1847–1916)," *Modern China* 7, no. 2 (April 1981): 191–225. See also "Syncretism in the Reformist Thought of Ho Kai and Hu Liyuan," *Asian Profile* 6, no. 1: 19–33.

———. *Hong Kong in Chinese History—Community and Social Unrest in the British Colony, 1842–1913* (New York: Columbia University Press, 1993).

Tsang, Steve Yui-Sang. *A Modern History of Hong Kong* (Hong Kong: Hong Kong University Press, 2004).

Tse, Liu Frances. *Ho Kom-Tong: A Man for All Seasons* (Hong Kong: Compradore House Limited, 2003).

Vaid, K. N. *The Overseas Indian Community in Hong Kong* (Hong Kong: Centre of Asian Studies, University of Hong Kong, 1972).

Van de Veur, Paul W. *The Eurasians of Indonesia: A Political-Historical Bibliography* (Ithaca, NY: Modern Indonesia Project, Cornell University Press, 1971).

Van Dyke, Paul A. "The Yan Family, Merchants of Canton, 1734–1780," *Review of Culture*, International Edition no. 9 (2004).

———. *The Canton Trade, Life and Enterprise on the China Coast 1700–1845* (Hong Kong: Hong Kong University Press, in conjunction with Instituto Cultural do Governo da RAE da Macau, 2005).

———. *Merchants of Canton and Macao: Politics and Strategies in Eighteenth-Century Chinese Trade* (Hong Kong: Hong Kong University Press, 2011).

van Foreest, H. A., and A. de Booy. *De Vierde Schipvaart der Nederlanders naar Oost-Indië*, 2 vols. (The Hague, 1980–81).

Veronica (pseud.). "Hong Kong" column in the *Hongkong Weekly*, 1907.

Wakeman, Frederic, Jr. *Strangers at the Gate: Social Disorder in South China, 1839–1861* (Berkeley: University of California Press, 1966).

Walker, Kirsty. "Intimate Interactions: Eurasian Family Histories in Colonial Penang," *Modern Asian Studies* 46, no. 2 (2012): 303–29.

Wang Gungwu. *China and the Overseas* (Singapore: Times Academic Press, 1991).

————. *Community and Nation: China, Southeast Asia and Australia* (St. Leonards, NSW, Australia: Allen and Unwin, 1992).

————. *The Nanhai Trade: The Early History of Chinese Trade in the South China Sea* (Singapore: Eastern Universities Press, 2003).

————. *The Eurasian Core and Its Edges: Dialogues with Wang Gungwu on the History of the World* (Singapore: Institute of Southeast Asian Studies, 2014).

Ward, Robert S. *Asia for the Asiatics?* (Chicago: University of Chicago Press, 1945).

Warres-Smith, D. *European Settlements in the Far East* (London: Sampson Low, Marston and Co., 1900).

Waters, Dan. "Hong Kong Hongs with Long Histories and British Connections," *Journal of the Hong Kong Branch of the Royal Asiatic Society* 30 (1990): 219–56.

————. *One Couple, Two Cultures—81 Western-Chinese Couples Talk about Love and Marriage* (Hong Kong: MCCM Creations, 2005).

Wedderburn, Gren. *No Lotus Garden: A Scottish Surgeon in China & Japan* (Edinburgh: Pentland Press, 1987).

Weiss, Anita M. "South Asian Muslims in Hong Kong: Creation of a 'Local Boy' Identity," *Modern Asian Studies* 25 (1991), no. 3: 417–53.

Welsh, Frank. *A History of Hong Kong* (London: HarperCollins, 1994).

Wesley-Smith, Peter. "Kwok A-Sing, Sir John Smale, and the Macao Coolie Trade," in *Law Lectures for Practitioners 1993*, ed. Shane Nozzal (Hong Kong: Hong Kong Law Journal, 1993).

Wesseling, Henk. *A Cape of Asia: Essays on European History* (Leiden: Leiden University Press, 2011).

Westad, Arne. *Restless Empire: China and the World Since 1750* (New York: Vintage, 2014).

White, Barbara-Sue. *Turbans and Traders—Hong Kong's Indian Communities* (Hong Kong: Oxford University Press, 1994).

White, Robin. "Hong Kong, Nationality and the British Empire—Historical Doubts and Confusions," *Hong Kong Law Journal* 19 (1989): 25.

Wing On anniversary book, *A Modest Beginning* (Hong Kong: Wing On Group, 2007).

Wise, Michael, ed. *Travellers' Tales of Old Hong Kong and the South China Coast* (Singapore: Times Books International, 1996).

Wolfendale, Stuart. *Imperial to International: A History of St John's Cathedral, Hong Kong* (Hong Kong: Hong Kong University Press, 2013).

Wong Siu-lin, ed. *Chinese and Indian Diasporas: Comparative Perspectives* (Hong Kong: Centre of Asian Studies, University of Hong Kong, 2004).

Wright, Arnold, and H. A. Cartwright. *Twentieth Century Impressions of*

Hong Kong—History, People, Commerce, Industries and Resources (Singapore: Graham Brash, 1990).

Wright, Nadia H. *Respected Citizens: The History of Armenians in Singapore and Malaysia* (Middle Park, Vic., Australia: Amassia Publishing, 2003).

Wright-Nooth, George, with Mark Adkin. *Prisoner of the Turnip Heads* (London: Leo Cooper, 1994).

Wu, Rose. *A Dissenting Church* (Hong Kong: Hong Kong Christian Institute, Hong Kong Women Christian Council, 2003).

Wu, Rose, Bruce Van Voorhuis et al. *Hong Kong's Social Movements: Forces from the Margins* (Hong Kong: July 1 Link and Hong Kong Women Christian Council, 1997).

Xu Xi. *Dear Hong Kong: An Elegy to a City* (London: Penguin, 2017).

Yahuda, Michael. *Hong Kong, China's Challenge* (London and New York: Routledge, 1996).

Yap, Felicia. "Eurasians in British Asia during the Second World War," *Journal of the Royal Asiatic Society of Great Britain and Ireland* 21, no. 4 (October 2011).

———. "Voices and Silences of Memory: Civilian Internees of the Japanese in British Asia During the Second World War," *Journal of British Studies* 50, no. 4 (October 2011).

———. "Creativity and the Body: Civilian Internees in British Asia during the Second World War," in *Cultural Heritage and Prisoners of War: Creativity Behind Barbed Wire*, ed. G. Carr and H. Mytum (New York: Routledge, 2012).

———. "A 'New Angle of Vision': British Imperial Reappraisal of Hong Kong during the Second World War," *Journal of Imperial and Commonwealth History* 42, no. 1 (2014): 86–113.

Yep, Ray Kin-man. "Cultural Revolution in Hong Kong: Emergency Powers, Administration of Justice and the Turbulent year of 1967," *Modern Asian Studies* 46, part 4 (July 2012): 1007–32.

Zheng, Victor, and Charles W. Chow. *Sir Shouson Chow, Grand Old Man of Hong Kong* (Hong Kong: Hong Kong University Press, 2010).

Zheng, Victor, and Siu-Lun Wong. "The Mystery of Capital: Eurasian Entrepreneurs' Socio-Cultural Strategies for Commercial Success in Early 20th-Century Hong Kong," *Asian Studies Review* 34 (December 2010): 467–87.

Zimmern, Kirsteen. *The Eurasian Face* (Hong Kong: Blacksmith Books, 2010).

AFTERTHOUGHT—HONG KONG FICTION, ALMOST ALL OF WHICH FEATURES CROSS-CULTURAL MIXING OF VARIOUS KINDS

Barnes, Simon. *Hong Kong Belongers* (London: HarperCollins, 1999).

Berg, Cecilie Gamst. *Blonde Lotus* (Hong Kong: Haven Books, 2005).

Booth, Martin. *Music on the Bamboo Radio* (Harmondsworth, UK: Penguin Books, 1997).

Brando, Marlon, and Donald Cammell. *Fan-Tan, a Novel* (London: Arrow Books, 2006).

Chang, Eileen. *Love in a Fallen City*, trans. Karen S. Kingsbury (New York: New York Review Books, 2007).

Cheung, Martha P. Y., ed. *Hong Kong Collage: Contemporary Stories and Writing* (Hong Kong: Oxford University Press, 1998).

Clavell, James. *Noble House* (New York: Delacorte, 1981).

———. *Tai Pan* (London: Michael Joseph, 1966; London: Hodder & Stoughton Paperbacks, 1982).

Coates, Austin. *The Road* (London: Hutchinson and Co., 1959).

Davis, John Gordon. *Typhoon* (London: Michael Joseph, 1978).

Gardam, Jane. *Old Filth* (London: Chatto and Windus, 2004).

Greenway, Alice. *White Ghost Girls* (New York: Black Cat, 2006).

Kent, Simon. *Ferry to Hong Kong* (London: Arrow Books, 1957).

Lanchester, John. *Fragrant Harbour* (London: Faber and Faber, 2002).

Le Carré, John. *The Honourable Schoolboy* (London: Hodder and Stoughton, 1977).

Lee, Janie, Y. K. *The Piano Teacher* (London: Harper Press, 2009).

Leung Ping-kwan. *Travelling with a Bitter Melon* (Hong Kong: Orchid Pavilion Books, 2002).

———. *Islands and Continents* (Hong Kong: Hong Kong University Press, 2007).

Maitland, Derek. *The Firecracker Suite: Comic Tales of a Cultural Collision* (Hong Kong: CFW Publications, 1980).

Mason, Richard. *The Wind Cannot Read* (London: Collins, 1946).

———. *The World of Suzy Wong* (London: Collins, 1957).

Mo, Timothy. *The Monkey King* (London: Vintage, 1978).

———. *Sour Sweet* (London: Vintage, 1982).

———. *An Insular Possession* (London: Chatto and Windus, 1986).

Pierce, Alan B. *Cheung Chau Dog Fanciers' Society* (Hong Kong: Asia 2000, 1996).

Row, Jess. *The Train to Lo Wu: Stories* (New York: Dial Press, 2005).

Wilson, Leslie. *The Mountain of Immoderate Desires* (London: Weidenfeld and Nicolson, 1994).

PHOTOGRAPH CREDITS

1. With thanks to Stephen Davies, maritime historian. Image from the Frank Fischbeck Collection, Special Collections, ASC, The University of Hong Kong Libraries
2. Bath Royal Literary and Scientific Institution Collections
3. Hong Kong Memory Project, www.hkmemory.hk
4. Bath Royal Literary and Scientific Institution Collections
5. The National Archives, UK
6. Image courtesy of Roger Stanton Doo and Special Collections, University of Bristol Library, www.hpcbristol.net
7 and 8. Hong Kong Memory Project, www.hkmemory.hk
9. Special Collections, SOAS Library, University of London
10 and 11. Image courtesy of Lee Edinger and Special Collections, University of Bristol Library, www.hpcbristol.net
12 and 13. With thanks to the Andrew Tse Family Archive
14. Photograph courtesy of the author, with thanks to Eddie Chow
15 and 16. With thanks to the Andrew Tse Family Archive
17. CPAO Photographic Collection, The University Archives, ASC, The University of Hong Kong Libraries
18. With thanks to Liz Chater Genealogy
19. CPAO Photographic Collection, The University Archives, ASC, The University of Hong Kong Libraries
20. Hong Kong Collection, Special Collections, ASC, The University of Hong Kong Libraries
21. Image courtesy of John Young and Special Collections, University of Bristol Library, www.hpcbristol.net
22. Image courtesy of Swires and Special Collections, University of Bristol Library, www.hpcbristol.net

23 and 24. Photograph by Denis H. Hazell. Image courtesy of Special Collections, University of Bristol Library, www.hpcbristol.net

25. Image courtesy of Special Collections, University of Bristol Library, www.hpcbristol.net

26. Photograph by Denis H. Hazell. Image courtesy of Special Collections, University of Bristol Library, www.hpcbristol.net

27. With thanks to Kim Fenton Lamsam

28 and 29. With thanks to Pat Botelho-Smith and Dawn Leonard

30. Image courtesy of Billie Love Historical Collection and Special Collections, University of Bristol Library, www.hpcbristol.net

31 and 32. With thanks to Dr. Ron Zimmern

33. Image courtesy of Special Collections, University of Bristol Library, www.hpcbristol.net

34. With thanks to Dawn Leonard

35. Courtesy of the International Committee of the Red Cross Archives

36. Image courtesy of Billie Love Historical Collection and Special Collections, University of Bristol Library, www.hpcbristol.net

37. Hong Kong Special Administrative Region Government

38. With thanks to Aron Harilela

39. Photograph by Hugh Van Es/Archive Kees Metselaar

40. Photograph by Kees Metselaar

41. Photograph by the author

42. ZUMA Press, Inc./Alamy Stock Photo

INDEX